# O'CASEY THE DRAMATIST

# IRISH LITERARY STUDIES

# O'CASEY
# THE DRAMATIST

Heinz Kosok

Translated by the author and Joseph T. Swann

Irish Literary Studies 19

1985
COLIN SMYTHE
Gerrards Cross, Bucks.

BARNES AND NOBLE BOOKS
Totowa, New Jersey

Copyright © 1985 by Heinz Kosok

First published in Great Britain in 1985
by Colin Smythe Limited
Gerrards Cross, Buckinghamshire

**British Library Cataloguing in Publication Data**

Kosok, Heinz
O'Casey the dramatist.— (Irish literary studies,
ISSN 0140-895X; 19)
1. O'Casey, Sean—Criticism and interpretation
I. Title   II. Swann, Joseph T.   III. Sean O'Casey:
Das dramatische Werk. *English*   IV. Series
882'912   PR6029.C33Z

ISBN 0-86140-168-9

First published in the U.S.A. in 1985 by Barnes & Noble Books
81 Adams Drive, Totowa, N.J. 07512

**Library of Congress Cataloging in Publication Data**

Kosok, Heinz
O'Casey the dramatist.
(Irish Literary Studies; 19)
Includes bibliographical references and index.
1. O'Casey, Sean, 1880-1964—Criticism and
interpretation. I. Title.   II. Series.
PR6029.C33Z674   1985   822'.912   84-24362

ISBN 0-389-20552-4

This work is based on *Sean
O'Casey: Das dramatische Werk*,
published by Erich Schmidt
Verlag, Berlin.

Produced in Great Britain
Set by Crypticks, Leeds, and printed
and bound by Billing & Sons Ltd., Worcester

*For Hans Otto Thieme*

# CONTENTS

# INTRODUCTION

*A good acting play that is not also good enough to be enjoyed in the study is not worth a dying tinker's damn.*
(O'Casey in *The Flying Wasp*)

When Sean O'Casey died in 1964, critics were still busy with the preliminary survey and assessment of his work. From 1960, when the first two important book-length studies of O'Casey's writings appeared, the scene had been set for a large-scale discussion and evaluation. In addition to four plays and a collection of articles published by the octogenarian O'Casey himself, his early writings, including two unpublished plays and an unproduced one, as well as his miscellaneous critical articles were made available, his six-volume autobiography was repeatedly reprinted, and there were various issues of the more popular of his plays. O'Casey's letters appeared in two large volumes edited with the care due to a major writer, and a definitive bibliography emphasized the scope of his writings as well as their far-reaching reverberations throughout the world. On the debit side, there is still no critical edition of his plays that would list textual variants and revisions (in some cases there are three or even four versions) as well as elucidate obscure references and difficult passages. Apart from this deficit, however, O'Casey has been well served by editors and publishers alike, and critics in his case find themselves in a more fortunate position than with many other writers.

At a first glance, it appears that they have well availed themselves of this favourable situation. There is a wealth of published material on O'Casey and his works. More than twenty book-length studies in English, several collections of articles and a number of books in other languages (especially in German) deal with his person and his writings; a journal has, since 1974, been exclusively devoted to O'Casey, and it was joined by an annual in 1982. The wealth of articles is difficult to survey even for the specialist. It might appear, therefore, that little has been left

unsaid concerning his work. This, however, is not so. Part of
what parades as criticism has been marred by a number of
shortcomings. For one thing, some critics developed a certain
degree of possessiveness to O'Casey that led them to react
resentfully when others encroached upon 'their' field. Feuds
developed between individual critics as well as between groups
of them, and these absorbed a great deal of the energy which
otherwise might have gone into an exploration of O'Casey's
works. Reiteration occasioned by unawareness of what others
have written is another of the reasons why not all of O'Casey
criticism is as satisfactory as it might be. Again, critics have
converged on a relatively small number of his plays, especially
the three great 'Dublin' plays, often, and rather senselessly,
called the 'Dublin trilogy'. In addition, they have all-too-willingly
permitted themselves to be drawn into that web of controversies
in which O'Casey himself was caught throughout his life-time.
A great deal of critical energy has been spent on the unceasing
discussion of such subjects as the rejection of *The Silver Tassie*
by the directors of the Abbey Theatre (almost an obsession
among O'Casey critics), the Dublin production of *The Bishop's
Bonfire* or the dubious circumstances surrounding the intended
Dublin première of *The Drums of Father Ned*. Critics have
unceasingly squabbled over the question whether O'Casey's
'exile' was justified and whether it had a liberating or an inhibiting
effect on his writings; they have not ceased to disagree on the
reliability of his vision of Ireland in his later plays, on his
treatment by the intellectuals of his native country, on his private
attitude to churches and political parties and on the biographical
models for his dramatic characters. Moreover, part of O'Casey
criticism is characterized by a tendency towards uncritical eulogy,
combined with a lack of discrimination as far as the use of critical
terms, such as 'naturalism', 'expressionism', 'myth', 'tragedy',
'farce', 'satire', is concerned. Finally, there has been a lamentable
tendency to generalization and consequently to simplification.
One can hardly overstress the importance of the fact that each of
O'Casey's plays is a highly individual work. O'Casey was never
content to apply a successful formula, but searched for a new
approach in almost every one of his plays. Much O'Casey criticism,
however brilliantly it may be formulated and however ingenious
it may sound, misses the specific characteristics of the individual
plays because it generalizes to a degree that is not warranted by
the text. In consequence, despite the wealth of critical insights
that has undoubtedly been amassed during the past twenty

years, there is no entirely satisfactory study that attempts to bring these observations to bear upon a comprehensive analysis of all of O'Casey's plays. Even slightly dated works like *The Star Turns Red* deserve more detailed discussion than the kind of short-circuit evaluation they usually receive from critics bent on extolling the Great Dublin Plays or obsessed with eulogising O'Casey the Humanist.

Here lies the justification for the present study, however defective it may be in many respects. It concentrates on the analysis of the individual play as seen in the context of the whole body of O'Casey's work. Such an analysis is not merely considered as a first step towards a balanced and objective evaluation of his work as a whole, but as a necessary and fruitful task in itself. The examination is based on the assumption that most of O'Casey's plays are unique, complex and effective works of art, and that some of them – especially (as this study will attempt to show) *Juno and the Paycock, The Plough and the Stars, The Silver Tassie, Within the Gates, Purple Dust, Red Roses for Me, Hall of Healing, Cock-a-doodle Dandy* and *The Bishop's Bonfire* – are master-pieces of modern drama. Each of them justifies a patient and dispassionate observation of the interplay of formal and thematic elements. This holds true for the short-plays, too, which have so far received little critical attention. Each individual chapter is intended to be complete in itself and can be used as such.

The interpretative method does not follow a single rigid pattern. It is based on the assumption that the critic has to submit to the writer, that he has no normative prerogative, that his task is elucidation rather than legislation. The starting-point for each individual chapter varies, therefore, according to the individual play's emphasis. It may be found, for instance, in a play's structure, its plot, its setting, in one central character, in the arrangement of the *dramatis personae* as a whole, in a central symbol, in a clearly recognizable theme or in the author's unmistakable purpose. However, each chapter attempts to incorporate, too, all the other aspects that are necessary for an understanding of the work as a whole. Relevant historical, political or topographical details are discussed where they serve to illuminate the meaning of the play; likewise, biographical facts, as well as the publishing and production history of the plays, are considered only where this is essential for an understanding of the play. On the other hand, O'Casey's works are recognized as material for stage production, and his stage-directions are considered as an important part of the play text. Moreover, questions of dramatic genre (tragedy, tragicomedy, farce, short play) have been touched upon where this seemed warranted by the work itself.

The central question which forms the basis for each chapter is that of universality. In what ways, and to what extent do O'Casey's plays transcend their local, regional or national background, how does the writer achieve the dimension of universality that is characteristic of at least part of his work? Critics in Ireland or England have often found themselves prevented from appreciating this universal dimension by O'Casey's superficial reference to specific events and problems in these two countries. It may be easier, therefore, to judge O'Casey's universality from a geographically more distant point of view. This is the decisive criterion for an evaluation of O'Casey's work, as has been demonstrated well enough by the disagreement among critics especially over his later plays.

In the methodological approach sketched above, the evaluation of each play is a result rather than a premise of the analysis. The qualities of a work can be judged only after the interplay of all their individual elements has been taken into account. However, a few of the plays (especially *The Harvest Festival, Oak Leaves and Lavender, Time to Go* and *Behind the Green Curtains*) are so disharmonious in themselves that it has not always been possible to separate analysis from evaluation. In many instances, the findings of the present study deviate from the views of previous O'Casey scholarship. It has been attempted, in the notes, to indicate such differences of opinion. The notes would have become far too numerous, however, if in each and every case the indebtedness of this study to earlier writers on O'Casey had been documented. All those familiar with the history of O'Casey criticism will in any case recognize the influence of its founding fathers, in particular David Krause and Robert Hogan, but also Ronald Ayling, Saros Cowasjee and several others. This is as it should be: criticism can progress only by dialogue, which requires an awareness of what has gone before.

The table of contents will show that certain plays have been grouped together in an attempt to identify, on the basis of chronology, some phases of O'Casey's dramatic career. Although it is generally agreed that the early plays, up to and including *The Plough and the Stars*, form a group of their own, there is no general consent as to the arrangement of the later works. Here it is suggested that five periods can be distinguished in O'Casey's writings. The prefatory note to each group sums up its common features. The different lengths of these introductory passages is a direct measure of the ground that the plays in each group share. It will be seen that the prefatory note to Part IV is much more detailed than the others, because the plays in question permit of a typological approach that establishes them as belonging to a specific dramatic genre. The title of this section, 'Ireland as a Microcosm', explicitly refers back to Part I, 'Dublin as Mirror of the World'. In both cases, an Irish locality is utilized for plays of universal relevance, the difference lying in the dramatist's approach. In the early plays, the Dublin reality is the starting-point, their universality growing out of their depiction of a closely observed reality. In the later plays O'Casey reverses this process: he exemplifies universal themes, motifs and character-types by placing them in an Irish setting that seems almost accidental in nature. As a result, the contrast between these phases is that between realistic and non-realistic works.

It should be stressed that Part VI, 'Continuity and Originality', is *not* to be seen as a summary of the findings of previous chapters. Such a procedure, as far as it would be practicable at all, would be directly opposed to the method employed here and would lead to precisely those simplifications that have been criticized above. Instead, Part VI is designed to stress the general nature of a number of questions that have been touched upon in the individual chapters; it attempts to see them in the light of preceding research and to point out certain profitable avenues for future study.

Page references in the text are to the four-volume *Collected Plays* edition with the exception of those plays that are not contained in it. In such cases, the edition used for the present study has been identified in a note (Volume V of the *Collected Plays* appeared after the present volume had been set up).

An earlier version of this book was first published in German in 1972 under the title *Sean O'Casey: Das dramatische Werk*. For this edition it has been completely revised and re-written, omitting certain sections and adding others.

# ACKNOWLEDGEMENTS

Extracts from *The Complete Plays of Sean O'Casey* are reproduced by permission of Macmillan, London & Basingstoke, and The Macmillan Publishing Company, New York.

# PART I

# Dublin as a Mirror of the World

It is too soon yet to say what will come to us from the melodrama and tragedy of the last four years, but if we can pay our players and keep our theatre open something will come.

(W. B. Yeats in his Swedish Royal Academy Speech – three months before the production of *Juno and the Paycock* – on the situation of the Abbey Theatre at the end of the Irish 'Troubles')

# 1. PREFATORY

Within less than three years, between April 1923 and February 1926, the Abbey Theatre produced five works by O'Casey, three full-length plays and two short-plays. The three full-length plays established his literary reputation and even today are to many critics the single legitimate foundation for his claim to fame. Little is known about his earlier dramatic experiments that preceded *The Shadow of a Gunman* and were rejected by the Abbey Theatre. The absence of anything but a few sketchy remarks in *Inishfallen, Fare Thee Well*[1] and some scanty biographical references make it difficult to reconstruct them.[2] The only earlier play to survive in manuscript, *The Harvest Festival*, remained unproduced and was not published in English until 1980; thus it did not in any way influence the growth of his reputation. O'Casey made his public début, therefore, in *The Shadow of a Gunman*, as an experienced dramatist, and this lack of an ostensible body of experiment, with the unavoidable mistakes of the beginner, has led to a view of O'Casey as a 'natural talent' unable to reflect critically on his medium: one who wrote his plays without any conscious awareness of the possibilities and limitations of the genre. It is one of the objects of the following interpretations to refute this thesis of the eruptive creation of his plays and to show how consciously O'Casey was able to handle the formal techniques of the playwright.

The five produced plays of his initial period show some remarkable similarities, although the two short-plays *Kathleen Listens In* and *Nannie's Night Out* in some respects deviate from the full-length works. One of the reasons for these similarities can be seen in O'Casey's cooperation with the Abbey Theatre (several parts were indeed written for particular actors), and the Abbey also established and transmitted a uniform style of production for these plays, which again stressed their similarities. The predominance of the comic-burlesque peasant-play in the Abbey repertoire, the availability of outstanding comedy-actors and the dominant taste of its audiences led to an undue insistence on the comic traits of O'Casey's plays and to a disregard of their serious elements. This tendency in the early productions became even stronger during the thirties,[3] and in the English-speaking world has its after-effects even today.

The most obvious similarity in the early plays – with the exception of *Kathleen Listens In* – is their setting, the Dublin tenements. These buildings, originally intended for a single family, had in the course of the nineteenth century been turned into dwellings for the city's working classes and for the country population which was at that time thronging into the city. Their spacious rooms, fine windows, magnificent stucco ceilings, marble fireplaces and fanlights form a sharp contrast to their inhabitants' standard of living. At the beginning of the century they were numbered among the worst slums of Europe and have not entirely lost this character even today. Poverty, dirt, disease, unemployment and intolerable restriction of the private sphere belong to the unforgettable experiences of everybody who has grown up in the tenements, and they have impressed their stamp on the plays of O'Casey, who spent most of his first forty-six years in this atmosphere. The attitude of his early plays has in this respect appropriately been termed 'resentful experience'.[4] With a few minor exceptions, all his characters in these plays belong to the tenements and are decisively stamped by this milieu both in their attitude and in their reactions. One aspect of this is the Dublin city dialect, one of the most noticeable characteristics of this phase in O'Casey's career.[5]

It has frequently been noted that O'Casey utilized personal experiences in his plays. Such autobiographical traits, which also recur when he deals with the tenements in his later plays (especially in *Red Roses for Me*), will not be considered in the following interpretations; the interest here centres not on the sources but on the structure and themes of the plays. It is important, however, that O'Casey's roots in the world he presents have contributed decisively to the impact of his plays. As Harold Clurman wrote in 1958:

What most of our playwrights nowadays seem to lack is roots in some reality more fertile and inspiring than their professional world provides. Sprung from a deep soil of reality, the fanatically and explosively honest sensibility of O'Casey was able to produce three or four of the most expressive plays of our time.[6]

These plays have also in common that they are related to a

particular contemporary background which, with the exception of *Nannie's Night Out*, is inseparably bound up with the stage events and contributes decisively to their relevance. O'Casey here deals with the period of the War of Independence and the ensuing Civil War, not however, in a chronological sequence: *The Plough and the Stars*, whose events take place in 1915 and 1916, is the 'earliest' work; it is followed by *The Shadow of a Gunman* (1920), *Juno and the Paycock* (1922), *Kathleen Listens In* (1923) and *Nannie's Night Out* (1923-24). In this respect, the plays may be compared with Lennox Robinson's best work, *The Big House*, which in its individual acts presents the decisive events of those years (1918, 1921, 1923), albeit from a point of view – that of the Protestant Ascendancy – diametrically opposed to O'Casey's, but with the same objectivity and readiness to criticize all sides.

Finally, all these plays, with the exception of *Kathleen Listens In*, belong to the tradition of realistic drama, modified by O'Casey in a characteristic way. It ought to be emphasized here that the term 'realistic drama' does not imply an unmanipulated reflection of reality, the renunciation of artistic form. A. E. Malone's characterization of O'Casey as 'photographic artist', creating 'slices of life in the strictest and most literal sense',[7] has resulted in many false evaluations of O'Casey's work. In the plays of this period, as in any realistic work, the restrictive selection of elements – figures, time scheme, events, language etc. – is subjected to the artistic imagination, and the following interpretations will consider the problem of form at some length. The term 'realism' implies that these plays do not go beyond the limits of what an audience can accept as 'probable', while in *Kathleen Listens In* and most of the later plays, beginning with Act II of *The Silver Tassie* and becoming even more evident in *Within the Gates*, the audience is explicitly made aware that no real-life events are taking place on the stage. Occasionally critics have attempted to see traces of this transition even in the first phase of O'Casey's writing,[8] but their arguments are not entirely convincing. Among the early plays, *Kathleen Listens In* can alone be termed an unrealistic play; even Act II of *The Plough and the Stars* keeps within the boundaries of the possible, which is definitely overstepped in *The Silver Tassie*. Even so, the adherence to reality in the early plays neither precludes the use of symbols nor the presence of a larger theme transcending the uniqueness of the individual case. It is precisely their high degree of universality which gives these plays their importance; but O'Casey here does not exemplify universal problems in particular Dublin situations; the universality (as opposed to that of his later plays) grows rather from the uniqueness of the individual characters and events: it is the final result rather than the starting-point.

These similarities have led to a view of these plays as a single entity, discussing them in comprehensive analyses, using examples from various plays as evidence of their uniformity. Sometimes the plays are even called O'Casey's 'Dublin Trilogy'. In contrast to such a view, the present study will stress the individual character of each play. O'Casey's early works are quite different from such evident trilogies as Arnold Wesker's *Chicken Soup Trilogy* which deals in three stages with a common theme, the role of socialism in present-day England, using the same family as an example. O'Casey's plays differ from one another not only in their characters and their changing historical background, they also deal with different themes. One cannot do justice to them unless one views them as individual works, rather than as parts of a trilogy.

The only play of this period that is generally accepted as unique is *Kathleen Listens In,* a political allegory differing considerably from the other plays. It demands special attention because it is an early document of O'Casey's tendency to unrealistic form and points forward to some of his later plays. *Kathleen Listens In* makes it possible to reject the view, predominant for a long time, that O'Casey was originally a 'spontaneous' realistic dramatist, largely unconscious of what he did, who not until his removal to London was led by literary influences on the path – some critics will say the wrong path – of symbolic-allegoric-'expressionist' techniques. *Kathleen Listens In* will, therefore, be treated here at greater length than its literary qualities alone would justify.

*The Harvest Festival* again stands somewhat apart from the other five plays – not so much because of its dramatic technique and its concept of transforming reality for the stage (in this respect it can be placed somewhere between *Juno and the Paycock* and *Kathleen Listens In*) but because of its quality. It is quite clearly a document of O'Casey's apprenticeship in the drama, an apprenticeship that was remarkably short but, while it lasted, produced in *The Harvest Festival* a play that makes it impossible for the critic to draw a clear line between interpretation and evaluation.

# 2. THE HARVEST FESTIVAL

*The Harvest Festival*, unpublished until 1980[1] and still unproduced, is the only surviving example of O'Casey's period of apprenticeship as a dramatist, and it might be argued that a distinct disservice has been done to his reputation by its publication. On the other hand it might equally be said that his achievement in *The Shadow of a Gunman* and the succeeding plays looks all the more impressive when the unauspicious beginnings of his career become apparent. Whichever the case may be, *The Harvest Festival* is proof of the Abbey directors' artistic as well as psychological judgement, much maligned both by O'Casey and his critics; it is all to their credit that they rejected a play like this and nevertheless went on encouraging the writer until he produced *The Shadow of a Gunman.* Lennox Robinson especially, who wrote to O'Casey to say 'that he liked very much the character of the clergyman in the play',[2] must be credited with remarkable insight, for this figure is indeed one of the few instances of nascent subtlety in the play and points forward, in a shadowy way, to a number of more complex characters in O'Casey's later works.

   *The Harvest Festival* is a play with a purpose or, to use a more pejorative term, a propaganda play, vaguely foreshadowing the concept of the *agitprop*. Plot, setting, structure, characterization and dialogue are subordinated to its overriding purpose. The plot can be summarized in one sentence. While the preparations for the Harvest Festival of the Protestant parish church are going forward, a group of workers, led by Jack Rocliffe, prepare for strike action; in a clash with other workers, Jack is fatally wounded; his body is refused admission to the church where the harvest festival is about to be celebrated. The setting, surprisingly if one considers O'Casey's personal background as well as his future plays, is a predominantly bourgeois milieu, the drawing-room of the Williamsons and their parish church, contrasted in Act II with the tenement background of the working class. The structure in particular demonstrates the writer's lack of experience. The whole of Act I is an extended, rambling exposition, ending only with the arrival of the crowd of strikers outside the house at

7

the conclusion of the Act. Act II then opens with another exposition that repeats much of what has been said before. Act III provides an anti-climax, because the hero, after his highly melodramatic death-scene at the end of the previous Act, is not available on stage. What little action there is occurs in Act II; and it happens off-stage, not, as in later plays, in order to direct the audience's attention to the individual characters' reactions, but quite evidently because O'Casey found it too difficult to handle on stage. The characters are almost exclusively mouthpieces of positions in the basic conflict, and even the dialogue has been made subservient to the overriding purpose. The style, especially where Jack is speaking, is antithetical, with Biblical reminiscences underlining the encounter of irreconcilable values: 'You have taught us to remember others and forget ourselves was the only happiness: We have discovered to remember ourselves and forget others is our only security' (p. 36).

Since O'Casey in this play does not set out to present recognizable segments of reality, he can use the juxtaposition of opposites as the dominant principle of construction. His basic contrasts are those between Protestants and Catholics, Workers and Employers, Strikers and Scabs, Rich and Poor, leading to the basic dichotomy between violent action and submissive acceptance. These dominant opposites are supplemented by a whole range of minor contrasts, for instance those between the harvest festival in the Protestant church and the traditional harvest home in the country (p. 6), the pro-Catholic and militant anti-Catholic leanings within the Protestant Church, the vegetables used to decorate the church and those needed for a navvy's dinner, or between characters within the two camps: Mr. and Mrs. Williamson, Jack and Tom, the Rector and his Curate, Jack and his mother.

It is in the nature of a propaganda play that these contrasts are not allowed to develop naturally from a juxtaposition of balanced values, but are submitted to the author's purpose. In other words, the scales are tipped from the start. Williamson, a worker turned bourgeois after having been made a senior Foreman and Churchwarden, is not only shown as being opposed to the strike action but is also ridiculed in his personal appearance, and so is the stage capitalist Sir Jocelyn Vane. Mrs. Williamson, a pillar of the Protestant Church who sentimentalizes over the Kingdom to Come while ignoring the poverty around her, is not only personally interested in the *status quo* but is also an intolerable nag; she terrorizes her husband no less than the poor workmen who have the misfortune to be employed about her house. Bishopson, the

Curate in support of middle-class prosperity, not only voices violent sentiments against the workers and the poor in general, but also has a figure so round-shouldered '*as almost to amount to a deformity*' (p. 12), and he betrays a grotesque degree of ignorance, in addition to his class bias, whenever he opens his mouth. On the other hand, Jack Rocliffe, the strike leader who is killed in the course of the play, is described as '*a well-developed working man*' with a '*boldly formed*' face, distinguished by '*strength and vigour*' as well as '*gentle and thoughtful eyes*'; he is dressed '*neatly*' and speaks '*earnestly*' (p. 9). Even some of the names suggest the same intentional bias; names like Vane (vain), Williamson (obviously a reference to the Protestant King William who subjugated Ireland and created the conditions under which the Williamsons live), Bishopson, or Nimmo (nemo) have distinctly negative connotations, as Rocliffe has positive ones. The Williamsons' drawing-room is pictured in a stage direction as vulgar and repellent almost beyond belief, while the Rocliffes' home is described without a single qualifying epithet. Further instances of this 'tipping of the scales' in favour of the author's personal views are provided in the plot. When the strikers attack those workers who decide not to walk out (in the play indiscriminately condemned as 'scabs'), Jack is wounded by a 'scab' who defends himself. His death, in the context of the play, is to be seen as the major catastrophe with tragic as well as optimistic connotations. The same workers who are inconsolable over his death repeat with obvious glee: 'We avenged him well, Mrs. Rocliffe; we hit and battered the scab to a pulp an' then threw him into the river' (p. 43, repeated near the end, p. 65). Previously, Bishopson had been presented in a distinctly unfavourable light for his attitude of condescension in intending 'to awake those who are dead in trespasses and sin' (p. 14), but Jack betrays very much the same type of arrogance to his 'comrades' whom he seems to be nearer despising than loving. He tells Tom, whom he addresses as 'you poor unenlightened soul' (p. 11), that the strike 'will kill you or cure you, and either [!] change will mean added strength to the Cause of labour' (p. 10). Similarly, democratic values are supported throughout the play, but when the Rector, favoured with the author's unmistakable sympathy, goes against the unanimous vote of his Vestry and permits Jack's body to be brought into the church, his action is not only condoned but upheld as a model of humanity. In a similar way, Jack (and also the author) rejects all those members of his union who prefer to go on earning their living and oppose the strike.

The juxtaposition of opposites, the development of the plot, the treatment of the characters, their names, external appearance, language and sentiments all point to the superiority of the views held by the author. These can be summarized quite simply as the inherent necessity of strike action, not only to obtain higher wages, but to overthrow the existing social order. Such a goal, it is implied, justifies violence and destruction (the breaking of the windows in the Williamsons' house, the attacks on the carts loaded with food supplies); it demands sacrifice and even death; and it will produce a new order of greater justice and personal nobility (exemplified in Bill Brophy's promise to give up the drink and look after Mrs. Rocliffe). The argument is not, of course, that these views are wrong, but that they are presented in a naively simplified way and that the opposing faction, deprived of any degree of personal attractiveness or integrity, are not permitted to display their position in a way that would have made a true dramatic conflict possible.

If O'Casey's view of society and its conflicts is in this play to be seen for the most part as a crude black-and-white picture, there are at least a few instances where additional shades are introduced. Tom Nimmo, the submissive bricklayer who would prefer to keep things as they are because otherwise they might become even worse, is generally depicted as a despicable product of capitalist society. Occasionally, however, O'Casey permits him to voice arguments that cannot be ignored altogether, when, for instance, he questions the 'glorious Brotherhood' about which Jack is always preaching, after having been himself compared by Jack to slaves and vermin (p. 10), or when he points out that for a man with a wife and eight children it is less easy to fight for 'freedom and a better life' than it is for the independent Jack (p. 8). His position between the demands of the employers and the militant unions, threatened by violence on either side, is depicted with at least a small degree of sympathy. There is also Jack's mother, who is torn between her love for her son, her trust in his integrity, her inability to understand his objectives and her fear of change. And there is the Rev. Jennings, the Protestant Rector, who reflects Mrs. Rocliffe's conflicts on a slightly higher intellectual level. He suffers under the injustices that Jack is out to fight, he admires Jack's character without endorsing his aims, he is deeply hurt by Jack's rejection of the Church and is prepared to stand for a spontaneous humanity against the effects of uncompromising radicalism on both sides of the conflict. It is in the nature of this play that his attitude remains unavailing – he is capable of alleviating suffering but not of preventing or abolishing its causes – but he is also the only character who has to undergo at least a rudimentary conflict: should he oppose the directives of his Vestry, a decision that might result not only in personal difficulties for himself but might disturb the peace and harmony of his congregation and endanger the Church as a whole; or should he sacrifice his spontaneous humanity to an attitude of convenient compliance? His concept of mercy has, of course, no chance, given the premises of this play, but it is significant that it is voiced at all.

The character of the Rev. Jennings, the only figure to transcend in any way the level of near-allegorical simplification, raises the question of the presentation of individual reality in this play. It is, of course, absurd to maintain that *The Harvest Festival* is 'written in the Playwright's naturalistic manner'.[3] If there is any element of naturalism to be found in O'Casey's work at all, it is certainly not in *The Harvest Festival*. The whole play is stylized in accordance with the introductory stage-direction to Act I. Every element is heightened and simplified to support the author's underlying thesis. Nevertheless O'Casey maintains a superficial semblance of reality that, unlike *Kathleen Listens In*, justifies and even demands the application of certain logical and psychological standards. In this respect, especially, the playwright betrays his inexperience. If, for instance, he offers any motivation for the characters' entrances and exits (e.g. the door-bell ringing[4]), he lays himself open to the charge that these motivations are preposterous. If he invents a sequence of events that might have happened in actuality, he provokes the question why these are not more logically connected and why they are kept off-stage. If he bothers to devise a plausible exposition scene he brings upon himself the criticism that the stage characters' behaviour in it is highly improbable. If he attempts to give his *dramatis personae* some individuality by providing them with suggestions of dialect or speech mannerisms, he makes it all the more improbable that some of them should deliver their views in extended soliloquies. It is obvious that O'Casey intended to maintain a certain amount of credibility while at the same time endeavouring to emphasize the general significance of the events. He did so by reducing, without at the same time abolishing, his realistic basis, and the charge of improbability is thus inevitable.

The appropriate dramatic device, as O'Casey himself was to demonstrate so successfully in his later plays, would have been the use of the symbol, which would have permitted a general

significance to emerge from a basis of undiminished reality.
There is only one element in this play that approaches the
complexity of symbolic creation: the harvest festival of the title
tends to acquire, in the course of the play, additional significance.
At the outset it is merely an individual festival of one particular
church for which vegetables and fruit are collected. But in the
course of events, it takes on more general qualities: it becomes
indicative of a deplorable tendency to use the fruits of the earth
for show and decoration while the poor of the parish go hungry;
it illustrates the Church's insistence on empty pomp and cere-
mony; and it demonstrates people's remoteness from the true
demands of Christianity. Moreover, it becomes evident as the
play proceeds that, while the real harvest festival belongs to the
employers, to the rich and the Protestants, there is another
harvest festival, culminating in Jack's sacrifice of his life, whose
fruits others will reap:

If this strike develops much more there will be a Harvest Festival in
Dublin, in which the Labour Leaders will be the clergy, the strikers the
congregation; in which curses will be prayers, hymns will be lamentations,
the choir will be police and soldiers, the seed will be the blood of the
proletariat, and the crop will be the conception of the New Idea of
Labour in Ireland (pp. 9-10).

Moreover the harvest festival in its dual significance is used as an
integrating and unifying factor for the highly heterogeneous
material of the play and thus serves as an important technical
device as well. Apart from this instance of complexity, however,
O'Casey has, in this play, dispensed with the merits of immediate
credibility without achieving a more universal significance in its
place.

The reduction in realistic immediacy is also responsible for the
fact that the background of contemporary Dublin, as well as
O'Casey's personal background at the time, emerges less distinctly than one would have expected. Dublin is mentioned only
once, and quite inadvertently (p. 9), and the reference to Curzon
Street in the stage direction for the Rocliffes' home is the only
other explicit acknowledgement that the play is set in the Irish
capital. There are, of course, a number of indirect indications of
the topography and contemporary situation of Dublin. The play
is set in a large town with an important commercial port, the river
is referred to repeatedly, the social structure and the conflicts
resulting from it are indicated, the religious controversies between

a predominantly Catholic working-class population and a Protestant Church dominated by the employers are displayed quite clearly, with an emerging socialist movement aggravating the conflict. O'Casey's private situation at the time is reflected in the fact that Jack, the hero, is a Protestant and as such an exception among the workers, that until recently he has been very active in the religious community, and also that he lives alone with his aged mother who is seen with great sympathy, although she lacks all understanding for Jack's political aims and arguments. It can be gathered from these personal touches (which are not essential to the theme of the play) that O'Casey saw Jack as a kind of idealized self-portrait, or perhaps rather a wishful image of himself, but in this respect, too, O'Casey stopped half-way between individualized and generalized presentation.

If such criticism of the play sounds harsh, it is to be remembered that O'Casey himself provided the standards for judging it when he wrote the rest of his works. Such comparison is all the more appropriate because there are numerous parallels between *The Harvest Festival* and these later works.[4] The historical as well as the autobiographical background is utilized again in *Red Roses for Me*, where O'Casey, however, goes into much greater detail, providing a realistic basis from which his poetic symbolism can emerge. O'Casey himself, in two letters to George Jean Nathan, explained that he had used his early play as raw material for *Red Roses for Me*, both as to its theme and as to the character of the Reverend Jennings.[5] The basic conflict between workers and employers became a central issue again in *The Star Turns Red*, the play that is also closest to *The Harvest Festival* in its concept of 'tipping the scales' in favour of one side. The festival as a central symbol around which the events are built is taken up in O'Casey's fourth phase, particularly in *The Drums of Father Ned*, which also shares with this play its uneasy wavering between realistic and unrealistic presentation in plot, setting, characterization and dialogue. Individual characters from *The Harvest Festival* frequently appear again, usually, however, in a more individualized form. Mrs. Rocliffe faintly foreshadows Juno, as well as Mrs. Breydon in *Red Roses for Me*; Tom Nimmo is reminiscent of other workmen, especially those in *The Bishop's Bonfire*; the Rev. Jennings points forward to Father Boheroe in the same play, as well as to the Rev. Clinton in *Red Roses for Me*; Sir Jocelyn Vane is not unlike the Lord Mayor in *The Star Turns Red*; while Jack Rocliffe is clearly an early model for O'Casey's semi-autobiographical socialist heroes from the third phase of his writing, Red Jim (*The Star Turns Red*), O'Killigain (*Purple Dust*), Ayamonn (*Red Roses for Me*) and Drishogue (*Oak Leaves and Lavender*); he shares with them their dedication, their readiness for sacrifice and their optimism for the future of the working-class as well as their overriding self-confidence and near-arrogant belief that they alone know all the answers.

O'Casey's manuscript of *The Harvest Festival* contains an incomplete revision of Act I.[6] This is an important document, because it indicates quite clearly the direction in which the author was moving. Some of the more glaring faults of the earlier version are eliminated. For one thing, Jack (here re-named Jim, probably to suggest his proximity to Jim Larkin the Labour Leader), is much more at the centre of the Act. He is on-stage most of the time (in particular at the beginning of the play), and the Curate is well aware of his existence, his political stance, and his previous influence in the Church, instead of being introduced to him officially (and rather improbably) in Act II. Moreover, there is a complete reshuffle of scenes: several irrelevant episodes have been eliminated and in their place O'Casey has introduced a love scene between a highly embarrassed Bishopson and an equally helpless Clarice. In addition to providing some faint traces of humour, it also gives a certain degree of individuality to the persons of the Curate and Clarice who before had been mere mouthpieces of the opposition to Jack in the class war. O'Casey has cut most of the soliloquies and has greatly reduced Jack's tendency to preach, providing him even with some sense of humour when he leads Mrs. Williamson to believe that he is an ignorant and illiterate sinner desperately in need of salvation. On the other hand, he has retained the bickering between Mr. Williamson and his wife, and this may be seen as another attempt to emphasize the immediacy of the stage events and the individuality of the characters. In other words, not only has O'Casey improved the mechanical aspects of the play, speeding up the exposition, smoothing out the sequence of events and concentrating on the central character, but he has also endeavoured to improve the credibility of his *dramatis personae* by increasing their individual features. He is thus moving away from the allegorical tendency that was to emerge once more in *Kathleen Listens In*, and taking instead a first step in the direction of *The Shadow of a Gunman*.[7]

# 3. THE SHADOW OF A GUNMAN

The première of *The Shadow of a Gunman* on 12 April, 1923, represented for its author (who was already forty-three at the time) the decisive breakthrough onto the stage.[1] Since then, the play has become part of the Abbey repertory and has been acted in many countries. Its reputation was, however, soon eclipsed by *Juno and the Paycock*. It appeared in print (in 1925) only when the London production of *Juno and the Paycock* had made O'Casey's name known in England. The text of this early edition was transferred with very few alterations into the *Collected Plays*.

As in many of his following plays, O'Casey in *The Shadow of a Gunman* presents an individual stage action against the broader background of historical events, in this case the fight of Irish insurgents against British dominion in Ireland. By 1920, military power in the country had devolved onto the feared Auxiliaries recruited largely from dismissed officers of the British Army, and the even more brutal Black and Tans who are reported to have had many criminals in their ranks. These semi-military units fought a largely autonomous guerilla war with the IRA, a type of warfare, by no means covered by the Geneva Convention, that was characterized by arbitrary raids, lootings, arrests and the shooting of prisoners 'while trying to escape' which frequently involved innocent people.

O'Casey in *The Shadow of a Gunman* presents a small segment of this fighting, based largely on his personal experiences. Apart from *Red Roses for Me*, *The Shadow of a Gunman* is his most clearly autobiographical play. A comparison with the chapter 'The Raid' in *Inishfallen, Fare Thee Well* and other biographical documents shows that the building in 'Hilljoy Square' is 35 Mountjoy Square, where O'Casey lived for a while with a friend. It is also apparent that many details of the action reflect O'Casey's own experiences and that several figures had models in real life. The central character, the poet Donal Davoren, is probably in many respects a self-portrait.[2] These autobiographical elements (which have already been the subject of several studies[3]) are of minor significance for the interpretation of the play. Much

15

more remarkable is the fact that O'Casey should have shaped these personal experiences in so short a timespan with such a high degree of objectivity that they depict a typical situation of insurrection. His impartiality (by no means caused by lack of emotional involvement) is expressed here in his specific type of dramatic irony. For an ironic attitude, discovering the contrast between pretension and accomplishment, revealing the contradictions between appearance and reality, dominates the play, manifesting itself in several forms from straight-forward comedy to the bitterness of biting satire. It contributes more than any other structural element to the unity of the play and presents a useful approach to an interpretation.

Even the place of the action and the visible scenery reveal this underlying irony. The name 'Hilljoy Square' is not only auto-biographical but also ironic, because, for the persons of the play, the Dublin slums are rather a valley of despair than a hill of joy. A similar effect can be observed in the room where the two central characters, Shields and Davoren, live. The big windows point to the one-time functions of this 'return room', whose past splendours contrast with its present decay. The petty quarrels which Davoren is expected to settle take place between the 'front drawing-room' and the 'back drawing-room', now inhabited by a family each. The discrepancy between the glamorous social events which formerly took place in these rooms and their present status makes the painful conditions of the inmates all the more visible. The scenery also provides a first indication of the tensions dominating the lives of the two central characters: the bunch of flowers, image of Davoren's poetic ambitions, forms a bitter-comic contrast to the chaotic disarray of the room, and the crucifix and religious statues are later set off against Shields' primitive superstitions. As in all O'Casey plays, the stage directions contain important hints for an understanding of the action.[4] O'Casey, who at one time wanted to become a painter, has, in the conception of his plays, always made full use of the visual dimension of drama; a stage designer who disregards the playwright's directions will thus withhold from his audience a key to the understanding of the play.

The dramatist's ironic attitude in *The Shadow of a Gunman* is also evident in his characters. In contrast to later plays where a dramatic idea is frequently the dominating element, *The Shadow of a Gunman* is formed around its characters. They, not a comprehensive theme or a straight-forward plot, determine the structure of the play. The loose construction, for instance, can be explained very simply by the fact that the individual, clearly separated scenes, are divided on the basis of entrances and exits by the various figures (which are not, in fact, always manipulated very plausibly). If the term 'irony' is used in this context, it is not, of course, applied to an ironical attitude in the characters themselves. It is true that Mulligan once turns to Shields *'ironically'* (p. 100) and the Auxiliary later uses a primitive type of irony when he says the opposite of what he means: *'You're a* koind blowke, you are' (p. 147); but none of the characters possesses the intellectual reserve necessary for a consistently ironic attitude; only Davoren, and to an even lesser degree Shields, show an occasional tendency in this direction. The figures are characterized by the discrepancy between their words and their actions, discernible to the audience, but not to themselves. These contradictions, presented in many variations, are responsible for the comic situations as well as for the serious events of *The Shadow of a Gunman*.

The only character exempted from such a view is Maguire. It is true that he, too, is an ambiguous figure, for behind the harmless front of the pedlar trading hair-pins who takes a day off to hunt butterflies, hides the determination of an underground fighter convinced of the necessity of his actions. But in Maguire there is no discrepancy between aims and actions, between pretensions and actual behaviour. He is the only one who is ready to take the consequences for his beliefs. He can, therefore, dispense with verbal justification of his convictions. The brevity of his appearance is no measure of his importance in the context of the play; his death after a raid by British troops, although only reported by others, is the most important event of Act I. Through his behaviour, Maguire becomes a standard by which all the other characters can be measured. This does not imply any support for his political aims: he is not glorified because of his fighting for the independence of Ireland; he stands out because he gives his life for his beliefs. Critics have frequently overlooked the central function of this figure. Indeed one still comes across the simplified thesis that in the early plays of O'Casey the men are merely braggarts and cowards, while the women represent true heroism: 'The women in O'Casey's plays are realists from necessity, the men are dreamers by default. The men are frustrated and gulled by dreams which they are unable and unwilling to convert into realities.'[5] A closer look at O'Casey's plays does not justify such a simple distinction, for only by a careful balancing of each person's behaviour, not by fine-sounding generalizations, can each character be judged.

Maguire's attitude is most closely approached by Minnie Powell. She is a remarkable person in the depressing world of the tenements. Her self-confidence and her lack of inhibitions are combined with charm and good taste. Even more remarkable is the fact that in surroundings pervaded by quarrelling and prejudice, she has a bad word for no one (except for Tommy Owens whom she rightly sums up as a blatherer). Minnie incorporates the small seed of hope that occasionally shows itself in this play. Her person ever so slightly brightens up the depressing image of wasted life in the tenements. Towards the end Minnie proves herself true to her convictions as Maguire before her, and she is indeed closely associated with him by the simple fact that the bag which occasions her death was his. She does not hesitate a moment to take on a task the dangers of which must be clear to her after her previous experiences. This positive appreciation of Minnie is supported by the fact that several of the other characters who are themselves failures speak disparagingly of her.

The death of Minnie is the most moving event of the play, yet such emotions are not so much caused by her death as by the fact that she dies in a tragic error. Here the comedy motif of mistaken identity suddenly loses its comic aspects. Her belief that Davoren is a gunman on the run makes her first approach him, and her admiration for the self-sacrificing patriot, abetted by him, determines the love-scene of Act I. Had Davoren confessed himself to be a harmless individual without political involvement, her affection for him would soon have disappeared. Her last – reported – words add force to such a conjecture: 'She's shoutin' "Up the Republic" at the top of her voice' (p. 153). Maguire's political struggle has become personified for her in Davoren, and she sacrifices herself not simply for her lover but for the patriot who offers his life for Ireland. Although it is too harsh to call Minnie 'the little simpleton who blunders into martyrdom',[6] one cannot overlook the fact that even she shares in the ironic tension that pervades the play inasmuch as she dies for an illusion. Nevertheless there is a considerable difference between her and the other characters. Minnie's integrity is untouched by her illusion since she herself takes the consequences of her error: 'She towers above the others because she at least lives up to her illusions and gives her life for them'.[7] When the other characters' illusions are exposed, this turns against themselves and lays them open to the criticism that finds expression in various forms of comedy.

Three characters are particularly good examples of this discovery of human shortcomings. Tommy Owens is a patriotic braggart who with his blathering rhetoric deceives himself about the fact that he is not willing to make any sacrifice whatsoever. He complains in a whining voice that he has been overlooked: 'I never got a chance – they never gave me a chance – but all the same I'd be there if I was called on – Mr. Shields knows that – ask Mr. Shields, Mr. Davoren' (p. 113). He thus appeals to the person who has already proved himself at some length to be an unreliable coward, at the same time deliberately overlooking the fact that the great struggle has already begun and that he has only to join the insurgents in order to demonstrate his willingness to fight. A minor detail shows the reality of his readiness to sacrifice: when the stop-press announcing Maguire's death is sold in the street, Tommy pretends to have no money for a copy (p. 121). Even more explicit, because presented at greater length, is the contrast between pretension and actual behaviour in the character of Adolphus Grigson. Grigson is stamped as a dubious character when he confesses himself to be an Orangeman and at the same time assures the 'gunman' Davoren of his respect. Although he tries himself to present this as a sign of integrity, it is rather the expression of his attempt to have his cake and eat it. Grigson also insists on his masculine prowess and confirms it for himself by terrorising his frightened wife. Yet during the raid he is ready to do anything to pacify the Auxiliaries. Ironically, he, the Protestant monarchist, is forced to say a prayer for the Irish Republic and, in a humiliating posture, to sing a Catholic hymn. A little later, he sets over against his wife's manifestly truthful report about these events his own more highly coloured version:

Excitin' few moments, Mr. Davoren; Mrs. G. lost her head completely – panic-stricken. But that's only natural, all women is very nervous. The only thing to do is to show them that they can't put the wind up you; show the least sign of fright an' they'd walk on you, simply walk on you. Two of them come down – 'Put them up', revolvers under your nose – you know, the usual way. 'What's all the bother about?' says I, quite calm. 'No bother at all,' says one of them, 'only this gun might go off an' hit somebody – have you me?' says he. 'What if it does,' says I, 'a man can only die once, an' you'll find Grigson won't squeal.' 'God, you're a cool one,' says the other, 'there's no blottin' it out' (p. 154).

Unconsciously he thereby unmasks himself. Not only does he demonstrate for all to see that he is a boaster and a miserable coward, but also that he can neither learn from his experiences nor gain an insight into his own being.

The passage quoted links him directly to Seumas Shields, who for his part attempts to prove his *sang-froid* during the raid, after the audience has just witnessed his trembling submissiveness towards the Auxiliaries. From the start, Shields is accompanied by a chain of ironic contrasts, his behaviour consistently belying his assertions, which deprives him quickly of all credibility. Occasionally, this happens in the form of harmless farcical comedy, as when, with characteristic exaggeration, he praises the quality of his braces: 'I'm wearing a pair of them meself – they'd do Cuchullian, they're so strong' (p. 98), upon which they immediately break. Less harmless is his inability at self-assessment when he projects his own weaknesses into other people and criticizes them. At the beginning, for instance, he complains bitterly of Maguire's unreliability because he has not arrived at the time agreed upon, yet the audience has just witnessed that he himself had to be shaken awake hours after this very same time. His opinion of Minnie is particularly illuminating: '. . . I wouldn't care to have me life dependin' on brave little Minnie Powell – she wouldn't sacrifice a jazz dance to save it' (p. 130). This is a case of double irony; Shields unjustly charges Minnie with his own fearfulness, for it is precisely she who later saves his life; and yet unconsciously he speaks the truth, for she would be highly unlikely to sacrifice her life voluntarily for *him*.

Shields extends to his country as such his tendency to criticize his own failures in others and intersperses his sentences with exclamations like 'Oh, this is a hopeless country!' (p. 99), without realising that the chaotic conditions are due precisely to people like himself. His references to the War of Independence have to be seen as expressions of his cowardice. He praises his own unshakeable equanimity, the fruit of his religious convictions: 'There's a great comfort in religion; it makes a man strong in time of trouble an' brave in time of danger' (p. 133), but when shots are fired, he can only babble incoherent words, and the knocking on the wall which for him ironically is of no danger, engenders more superstitious fear than all the saints of his Church can dispel. One should therefore be sceptical of certain attempts to see in Shields' pacifist attitude the quintessence of the play. When critics maintain that Shields 'voices the playwright's central idea . . .' [8], that he is 'the mouthpiece of the author's spirit of disillusion' [9], 'the ironic Chorus character in the guise of a bumbling clown, a wise-fool who sees the truth' [10], one might suspect this to be a case of preferring the character whose views come closest to one's own. It is not, however, the task of an interpretation to present those utterances as the thematic centre of the play which are most welcome to the interpreter. The importance of a character depends on its rank in the scale of values established within the context of the play. In this respect, Shields, the incorrigible braggart, coward, idler and egotist, holds a low position indeed. However justified a pacifist attitude may certainly be after this century's experiences, in the person of Shields it represents hardly more than the evasion of responsibility, and in the context of *The Shadow of a Gunman* it is, at best, one of several equally tenable attitudes.

The authorial irony here demonstrated in three characters can be observed even in the minor figures. Thus Gallogher, who is something of a weakling, has his children sing patriotic songs and enthuses over 'Faith and Fatherland' (p. 123), but thinks of his protection from noisy neighbours. Mrs. Grigson reduces her anxiety for her husband, staying out late, to the question 'Do the insurance companies pay if a man is shot after curfew?' (p. 137). And even the motherly Mrs. Henderson considers it an important task for the Republican courts to protect Mrs. Gallogher from the insults of her neighbour. All these people, caught in the web of their illusions, have in common that they gain no insight into the discrepancy between their own convictions and reality. This insight is reserved for the audience; in the case of Minnie it arouses compassion, in the other cases mostly laughter. In this respect these other characters differ from Donal Davoren. He without doubt is the central figure of the play, not only because he is the only one continuously on stage, but even more so because towards the end of the play he begins to realize the dubious nature of his own behaviour and is thus provided with at least the opportunity to change.

Davoren moves in a triple set of tensions: between poetry and his slum surroundings, between braveness and cowardice and between egotism and patriotism. He considers himself a poet and lives for his vocation. It is hardly possible to judge, from the few examples of his art, to what degree his claims are justified; there is, however, no reason to denigrate him as a poetaster.[11] O'Casey apparently wants to have him taken seriously as an artist, as may be seen from the many parallels to his own life and still more from the reference to Shaw's Dubedat in *The Doctor's Dilemma* from whose dying speech O'Casey quotes, in a stage direction (p. 93), the decisive sentence.[12] As an artist, Davoren fights a hopeless battle against the manifold intrusions of his surroundings. When, during his midnight attempts at composition, he is disturbed by Shields' incoherent babbling, the situation is predominantly comic, but Davoren's position is more pitiable than ridiculous. On the other hand, he appears in an ironic light when he compares himself not only to his model Shelley, but to Shelley's Prometheus whose lament 'Ah me, alas pain, pain ever, for ever' he has taken as his own leitmotif, or again when he answers Minnie's knocking on the door with the words 'Another Fury come to plague me now!' (p. 105). A greater difference is scarcely imaginable than that between Davoren, living with a pedlar and plagued by irrelevancies, and Prometheus tortured by the Almighty in a cosmic setting. Nor is this simply a difference of degree, for Prometheus defeats his opponent through the principle of endurance and redeems creation with Christian love, while the irritated Davoren is unable to redeem himself.

If Davoren's position is ironically qualified by this contrast, this qualification is intensified by his pretension to fearlessness and his subsequent demasking. He rivals Shields in protesting his courage, believing not in religion but in philosophy: 'You're welcome to your angels; philosophy is mine; philosophy that makes the coward brave; the sufferer defiant; the weak strong; the . . .' (p. 133). When at this precise moment he hears shots, the source of his equanimity dries up, and the first words of this despiser of religion are: 'My God . . .' (p. 133). Later on he gives an even more pronounced example of his cowardice when he allows Minnie in her innocence to take the dangerous bag and to go into her death.

The third illusion is not of Davoren's own making; it is the fruit of his surroundings which see in him a gunman on the run. The poet, however, connives in this, and even enjoys being admired as a patriot, especially when this earns him the admiration of Minnie. Thus in one respect he justifies the title of the play: he is himself the shadow of a gunman. Davoren is here contrasted with the other character to whom the title might also be applied. Maguire, the genuine gunman, appears and disappears like a shadow, leaving, however, a dangerous relic behind, and thereby triggering off the decisive events of Act II. In contrast to him, Davoren is continuously present and offers his opinions on every subject, but he is never more than passive: where Maguire acts he reacts. One is tempted to ask whether something else in his person is of greater substance than his existence as a gunman, whether he is merely the shadow of a gunman or not also the shadow of a man. This is, indeed, supported by the original title of the play, *On the Run*. Maguire and Davoren are both on the run: the gunman tries to escape from the police, the poet from the intrusion of his surroundings, and his behaviour leads one to think that he is on the run from life itself.

Until the concluding raid Davoren always shirks human responsibility. He sees himself as a lone wolf distinguished from other people by virtue of his poetic vocation and fearing their lack of understanding: 'Damn the people! They live in the abyss, the poet lives on the mountain-top . . .' (p. 127). Davoren therefore regards all human contact as a burden. He tries to withdraw from Shields who, after all, has taken him into his room, he curses all visitors and treats their requests with scorn. He accepts Gallogher's letter only because he does not want to have his shadow existence revealed but does not plan to pass it on. The desperate Mrs. Grigson who in her helplessness looks to him, provokes his egotistic reaction: 'Christ! Is she going to stop talking there all the night?' (p. 136). Even Minnie is at first repulsed, and her offer to tidy up his room is rejected for fear the neighbours might talk (p. 110). Only her readiness to take the dangerous bag initiates a change. At this point, without his own doing, Davoren is drawn into a network of mutual responsibility. For the first time somebody does not make demands on him but is willing to sacrifice herself for him. While this event passes Shields without trace, it causes Davoren to put what for him is a most unusual question: 'What way are they using Minnie, Mrs. Grigson; are they rough with her?' (p. 153). While up to now he has only attempted to preserve his own inner sanctuary, he now feels concern for someone else's existence. Minnie has succeeded in opening up the protective but at the same time isolating shell of his egotism. This leads to a further reaction which elevates him above the other characters: he gains an insight into his own inadequacy and thus dissolves for himself the ironic tension that continues to exist for the others: 'We're a pair of pitiable cowards to let poor Minnie suffer when we know that we and not she are to blame' (p. 151). The insight is expressed more forcibly still when Davoren concludes the play with repeated insistence on his own weakness: 'Oh, Donal Davoren, shame is your portion now till the silver cord is loosened and the golden bowl be broken. Oh, Davoren, Donal Davoren, poet and poltroon, poltroon and poet!' (pp. 156-157). Even in such terms as these, his confession does not, of course, mean that Davoren in future will alter his behaviour and conceive of himself as a member of a human community which can only improve its lot together. The quotation from the Book of Ecclesiastes (XII, 6), so artistically introduced, even intimates the danger that Davoren may stylize his newly-won self-understanding into a literary posture and that from now on he may write poems on the vanity of all things and the fallibility of man without changing his own behaviour at all. O'Casey leaves the ending of the play open, stimulating the audience to active participation. Yet even the fact that one character realizes one of his illusions and tries to live without it, provides a ray of hope in the dark world of these self-deceiving people.

One final remark should be added on the author's attitude in this play. *The Shadow of a Gunman* has been called an example of O'Casey's 'anti-heroic vision of life',[13] the words he puts into the mouth of Shields being cited in proof. In contrast to this, the present study has shown that O'Casey observes his characters from an ironic distance and that a careful analysis is required before an order of values can be established for the play. Only three of the characters, Maguire, Minnie, and Davoren, stand out in any way, but even they have an existence of their own and do not represent the author's opinions. Shields' judgements on war reflect a widely held attitude. Similarities, however, between a dramatic character's views and those of the critic are insufficient evidence when it comes to identifying the dramatic idea of a play. Had O'Casey intended to present Shields' views as the concentrated meaning of his play, it would have been imperative for him to minimize Maguire, showing him either as a braggart or as a cynical and brutal fanatic. *The Shadow of a Gunman* is, like *Juno and the Paycock* and *The Plough and the Stars*, an objective work in which the author dramatically juxtaposes various views without identifying with any of them. If these plays are termed 'pacifist plays',[14] the critic incorrectly suggests that the dramatist has anticipated the decision which in reality he leaves to the audience. It is precisely in this respect that these plays differ from O'Casey's later works, where a single character favoured by the author pronounces his opinions, suggesting an affinity with the propaganda play.

There is another decisive difference between *The Shadow of a Gunman* and the later plays. In O'Casey's later works, particularly in *Red Roses for Me*, stage action and background events run parallel (i.e. they begin at the same time, reach their climax simultaneously and finish with the ending of the play). *The Shadow of a Gunman* depicts a section of an historical process that runs independently of the stage action and shows no congruence with it. Thus it is that the characters in this play seem exposed to uncontrollable forces which at any time may interfere with their lives, while in *Red Roses for Me* the power of human beings to influence their own fate is brought out by the dramatic structure itself. This touches on a change in O'Casey's *Weltanschauung* that will demand special attention.

There is, however, another trait which *The Shadow of a Gunman* has in common with the later plays, for even as early as this the specifically Irish setting is of secondary importance. In spite of its autobiographical origin, the play does not so much present events from the Dublin of 1920 as a typical revolutionary situation of the sort that has become more and more familiar to twentieth-century man. It is a play 'about living under conditions of social instability and collapse' in which O'Casey 'goes to considerable pains to present a thoroughgoing picture of breakdown.' [15] Without changing the conditions in any fundamental way, the play might be transferred to a large number of countries which have meanwhile undergone similar experiences. O'Casey is mainly interested in the analysis of the behaviour and misbehaviour of a group of human beings whose everyday life is complicated by the unusual burden of so extreme a situation. In spite of his realistic presentation, O'Casey is not a 'photographic artist' [16], as has frequently been supposed after the appearance of his first work. He does not strive for a reconstruction of the individual case but for the interpretation of a generally valid and feasible situation: '. . . O'Casey . . . like Synge, has the mythmaker's great gift of discerning archetypal characters and situations, of distilling from everyday elements a quintessence of life far superior to the products of any documentary form of realism.' [17] The technique of dramatic irony serves to reveal a contrast between appearance and reality, between illusion and truth. Calmness in danger, faithfulness to one's own ideals and aims and willingness to sacrifice oneself for others as a final consequence of human solidarity are presented here as the criteria of human failure or success.

# 4. KATHLEEN LISTENS IN

*Kathleen Listens In*, produced by Lennox Robinson, was premièred by the Abbey Theatre on 1 October, 1923, either in a double or a triple bill.[1] O'Casey describes the play's reception in *Inishfallen, Fare Thee Well*:

Another experience for Sean! The audience received the little play in dead silence, in a silence that seemed to have a point of shock in its centre. Not even a cold clap of a hand anywhere. They all got up from their seats and silently filed out of the theatre. He was the one and only playwright to have had a play received in silence by an Abbey audience; the only one to be deprived of even a single timid hand-clap. Indeed, it did look as if his talent, too, would have to perish in silence and with malice of afterthought.[2]

Obviously this is one of those typical O'Caseyean simplifications which, in the end, he probably believed himself. Contemporary reviews[3] offer a slightly different picture, confirming, however, that the reception was anything but enthusiastic. There were two reasons for this: the unrealistic concept of the play and its political actuality. The Abbey of the early twenties was dominated by the realistic, preferably comic peasant-play. The reviewer of the *Evening Telegraph* seems therefore to describe the audience's reactions correctly when he says: *Kathleen Listens In* 'was a play to slightly puzzle a first-night audience. To begin with, utter phantasy, however direct of meaning, is not gathered in completely at first to the mind of any audience unless they have been extraordinarily well prepared for it.' [4] The second reason for the audience's lack of enthusiasm is set down as follows by a member of the cast:

Throughout the performance of *Kathleen* there was much sectional laughter. Hardly more than ten percent of the audience laughed together. The effect on the stage was slightly unnerving. In a flash it became clear what was happening. You laughed when my party fell under O'Casey's lash; I laughed when your party caught it. Both of us tried to laugh when the other fellow's party was made to squirm. And then slowly but surely

26

all the laughing died away. When the curtain came down there were a few dispirited hand-claps obviously intended for the players. [5]

In other words, those members of the audience who were not bewildered by the unusual concept of the play found themselves shocked in their political opinions.

This reception determined the future career of the play. It was taken off after seven performances and was only revived once, in March 1925, for a series of six nights (in a new version jointly prepared by O'Casey and Lady Gregory).[6] For three and a half decades the manuscript was supposedly lost, until it was published for the first time in 1961.[7] A slightly different version was published the following year,[8] a third version, apparently the 1925 revision, remains unprinted.[9] Yet even after its publication, critics have shown little interest in the play. If they considered it at all, they have concerned themselves with the reasons for its unfavourable reception in 1923. Such neglect appears unjust: although in the theatre today *Kathleen Listens In* would be no more than a historical curiosity, it deserves critical attention as an important stage in the development of O'Casey's dramatic art.

*Kathleen Listens In*, subtitled *A Political Phantasy in One Act*, is a dramatic allegory set in a definite local and temporal framework and with a strong satirical tendency. Every element in the play – scenery, figures, actions, conflicts – has a concrete equivalent in the Irish reality of 1923;[10] each of these elements is also exaggerated with a satirical intent. The critic, therefore, finds himself confronted with the task of deciphering these allegorical references, some of which may be obscure today even to an Irishman. At the same time, he has to allow O'Casey's dramatic technique to emerge with clarity; and finally the allegorical events will suggest certain conclusions about O'Casey's own opinions at the time of writing.

The simple, uncluttered set, a garden surrounded by house and walls, in itself indicates the allegorical tendency of the play. O'Casey's use of an out-door setting rather than an interior, is appropriate inasmuch as it allows for an easy and spontaneous movement of figures across the stage. House and garden, as is soon apparent, represent Ireland. The Irish flag fixes the date of the events as the period after the foundation of the Free State in December 1921; the clerical past of Ireland is indicated in the church-like windows of the house, the destructive effect of the Civil War in the broken panes.

The owner of the house is Miceawl O Houlihan who has sold

his only cow – representing economic advantage – in order to
buy a house of his own – national independence. Since the price
he got for the cow was not the twenty pounds his friends had
advised him to demand, but only '19, 19 an' 11½ with a postidge
stamp thrun in' (p. 289) – Irish independence was restricted by
an oath to the British Crown, demanded of every Irish government
–, Miceawl is now criticised for having given away the family
cow. Nevertheless he tries to put his house in order; he clears up
his devastated rooms and paints his house-door green, while his
wife is busy all the time with dirty linen, the flood of suspicions
and calumny which was one of the legacies of the Civil War: 'I
don't think there's a house in the whole wide world that there's
so much washin' to be done as there is in this house' (p. 288).
Their daughter Kathleen, personification of the Irish spirit, has
meanwhile withdrawn from all work and is trying to restore her
shaken health.

This initial situation is not, however, immediately apparent,
since O'Casey follows the usual technique of the short play,
dispensing with a separate exposition scene and providing only
a minimum of expository information during the course of the
action. Indeed the play does not contain any action at all, if
'action' is conceived as a logical sequence of events. It consists
instead of a series of short scenes, defined by the entrances and
exits of the numerous figures who involve Miceawl in discussion,
offering him opportunities to present his own views, or harass
Kathleen in the attempt to convince her of the importance of their
various opinions. The scenes fall naturally into three sections of
equal length. Section I (pp. 278-282) is dominated by Miceawl's
confrontation with Joey and Johnny (1st and 2nd Man); in section
II (pp. 283-290) Tomaus Thornton is Miceawl's chief debating
partner; section III (pp. 291-297) is dominated by the conflict
between the various parties trying to win the favour of Kathleen.

It is worth noting that O'Casey makes no attempt to motivate
the entry of his figures. Any such attempt would have obscured
the allegorical reference of the play. He merely prepares for the
appearance of a new figure through having him discussed by the
members of the previous group. O'Casey achieves a certain
liveliness by juxtaposing short and long scenes, small and large
groups of characters, and also by an alternation of discussion and
action which prevents his play from appearing in any way static.
An additional element of visual variety is achieved by the
different attire of the figures, founded in their various opinions
and positions in life; and, as in many later plays, one character

wears a costume that departs entirely from the ordinary (the Man in the Kilts). Finally, the scenes are enlivened by songs. In spite of the lack of a plot, the play, therefore, does not appear simply as a static meeting of mouth-piece characters assembled for theoretical discussion.

Part I is predominantly concerned with fixing the identity of Miceawl O Houlihan. In his discussion with Joey and Johnny it is Miceawl who is under attack, which provides an opportunity for 'characterizing' him: he is asked to throw away the poppies, the English emblem of the trench-war and the 1918 truce, to take down the British coat of arms, to sing the new national anthem before and after meals and to read a chapter from John Mitchel's *Jail Journal* before going to sleep. These references and Miceawl's answer, 'I'm busy now with the plans for th' electhrification of the Shannon an' Suck, th' Lee an' th' Liffey, th' Bann an' th' Boyne an' th' Tolka, so I'll have to say tooraloo' (p. 279), characterize him as a representative of common sense, who after the independence, does not deny the existence of all ties with England and who considers economic measures more important than political ideology. This at the same time identifies his partners as personifications of the radical Republican movement. When they demand 'Yous'll grow shamrocks or yous'll grow nothin'!' (p. 278), they demonstrate their narrow-minded nationalism, setting more store by empty formulas than by the real needs and advantage of their allegedly beloved country: 'We think what we thought, we say what we said, we stand where we stood seven hundhred years ago [before the Anglo-Norman conquest of Ireland]; the world may change but Ireland'll never alther' (p. 279). When Miceawl finally succeeds in throwing them out, they immediately try to get back in, even throwing a stone into the house. O'Casey here criticizes excesses in the nationalists' attitude who, during the Civil War, contributed to the destruction of their country for the sake of an idealized image of it. They justify their demand to see Kathleen with a reference to their participation in the 1916 Rising, a reference that was (and still is) most effective in Ireland: 'The pair of us went to school with Kathleen; we learned our first lesson together in Easther Week' (p. 281). Miceawl's answer reflects O'Casey's view (which at the time was by no means generally accepted) that harking back to the heroism of the past, alluded to in the myth-generating figures of John Mitchel, Patrick Sarsfield, Robert Emmet and Wolf Tone, is much less important than a concern with future developments: 'Yous all went to school with Kathleen; people that don't know how to read an' to

write went to school with Kathleen! You learned your first lesson
in Easther Week! Well, she's learned a lot since then. She's
studyin' mathematics now, she can't be always stuck at her ABC'
(p. 281). The unpopularity of such an attitude was demonstrated
most effectively three years later, in the *Plough* riots. Kathleen
herself shocks her two Republican suitors when she sends them
away because 'I have to practise me Fox Trots and Jazzin' so as to
be ladylike when I make me deboo into the League o' Nations' (p.
282). Internal conflicts indeed prevented the newly independent
Ireland from considering the role that it was to play in international politics.

The satire on reactionary nationalism is here interrupted:
Miceawl's new talking partner is his neighbour Tomaus Thornton.
He is much less obviously a representative of a political group; it
is, rather, O'Casey's sheer delight in creating individual characters that has here broken through. His description of Tomaus
reminds one of many O'Casey characters, above all Seumas
Shields, Jack Boyle and Joxer Daly in the two chronologically
adjacent plays. Tomaus himself confirms this relationship when
he utters his views on subjects he does not understand, when he
demonstrates his cowardice in the face of any authority in spite
of his alleged scorn for authority, and when he reveals his deep-
seated allergy to work. When Miceawl asks him to take over from
him, he at first reacts with characteristic willingness:

Certainly, Mick, certainly. [*He starts to paint.*] Now, I'm goin' to get
nothin' for this. This is a thank you job . . . Oh, I'm not goin' to be a mug
for anybody. [*He leaves off painting, takes a paper from his pocket, and
sings as he goes off.*]

> Let politics go an' be damned,
> It's a thing that destroys an' debases;
> I'll just have a read for to find
> A winner for Fairyhouse Races    (pp. 295-296).

Here it becomes apparent that Tomaus, too, represents a segment
of the Irish population: he stands for those who compensate for
an aversion to work and political abstinence by empty blathering
and a passion for betting, who utter opinions which they are not
prepared to stand by and who, during the country's decisive
years, were active only when their own advantage was at stake.
Tomaus, therefore, is a counter-image to the allegorical representatives of political groups and, like these, is treated satirically.
Without him, the critique of political partisanship would have

remained one-sided and might have been mistaken for support on the part of the author for a straightforwardly unpolitical attitude.

Furthermore Tomaus is the ideal conversation partner for Miceawl, inasmuch as he, like Seumas Shields, voices opinions critical of the situation of Ireland which remain relevant although they come from the mouth of a blatherer. The central topic is the attempt to make Gaelic the official language. Nonsensical exaggerations like the attempt to translate Thornton's name into Gaelic show how questionable this venture really is. The element of ridicule is reinforced by the figure of the Man in the Kilts, the allegorical representative of the Gaelic League, who (like Monsewer in Brendan Behan's *The Hostage*) haunts the play as a ghost of time-worn aspirations. Mrs. O Houlihan admonishes her husband: 'Will the pair o'yous not be talkin' so much Bayurla [English]! If yous don't mind, the Irish speakin' lodger'll hear yous!' (p. 284). The latter is a real burden for all the inhabitants of the house. Miceawl's suspicion that he is slightly mad is set forth in a number of examples: he has filled his room with curious relics of the Irish past, he demands of Kathleen that she read nothing but the *Book of Kells* (a frightening idea for Tomaus: 'God, I'd rather even read The Lives o' th' Saints – an' that's bad enough . . .' [p. 285]), he wants to pull down the house and rebuild it on the legendary Hill of Tara, and he talks continually of the traditional Irish harp, although he himself cannot even play 'Home Sweet Home' on a tin trumpet. The most serious criticism, however, is that 'you could hardly get him to speak before the house was me own, an' now, he'll hardly let anyone else speak!' (p. 284). O'Casey refers here to the Gaelic League's cautiously preserved neutrality during all the conflicts leading up to the establishment of the Free State [11]. Tomaus' uncomprehending reactions show how little response these attempts to revive the Gaelic cultural tradition (what Miceawl calls 'outlandish things'! [p. 285]) could elicit in the ordinary citizen. Nevertheless Miceawl cannot simply ignore the old man, for in spite of his absurdities even the PP (Parish Priest) is afraid of him. When he finally appears in his ridiculous costume, Miceawl and Tomaus immediately put on a *'reverential look'* and willingly recite a Gaelic stanza. Tomaus even resorts to flattery only to return to his critical attitude when the old man disappears. The satire therefore has two aspects, the starry-eyed conservatism of the Gaelic League and its influence on public life to which the average Irishman defers even though its aims remain incomprehensible to him. There is, of course, an additional autobiographical element in this criticism; O'Casey, who himself had taught Gaelic for a considerable length of time, had repeatedly taken the Gaelic League to task in newspaper articles, criticising in particular the inadequacy of its teaching methods.

In comparison to the extended satire on the Gaelic League, other aspects of Irish life are presented more briefly. In section I there is a reference to the Civic Guards' search for poteen (it is no secret that alcohol was the chief object of many military and police raids both during the War of Independence and the Civil War). The unchristian attitude of many Christians during the Troubles is exposed in the image of the children who have broken the window panes: 'Indeed I thought the childer about here were betther reared; servin' at the altar an' a minute after firin' a stone at you . . .' (p. 289). The inside of the house, meanwhile, is destroyed by the nationalist 'Dawn o' Liberty Fife an' Drum Band' which, though it includes many bandmasters, can only play one tune (this may be a reference not only to the one-sidedness of the nationalists but also to the discrepancy between the insistence on a national music tradition and the actual performance of such bands). The *new* band of the young state presents other difficulties: 'T'other band'll only play the one tune, but every member in ours wants to play a defferen' tune . . .' (p. 284).

The final section of the play then serves to demonstrate drastically the political disunity of the times. It begins with Jimmy the Workman, representative of the small but active Labour Party, registering his protest. He has already repeatedly wandered through the scene, uttering vague threats – 'I'll not stick this much longer, so I won't. Th' hardest worked an' th' worst fed in th' house – I'll emigrate to Russia, so I will!' (p. 280). His demands are commented on by Mr. and Mrs. O Houlihan with a lack of understanding typical of the middle classes:

SHEELA. Sure he can't expect to get as good grub as we get.
MICEAWL. If the house wasn't here he wouldn't get any at all.  (p. 289).

Jimmy's insistence on his love for Kathleen is just as incomprehensible to them as is his desire to play the piano; the upshot is that he goes on strike with the radical demand that the house be painted red. O'Casey here puts his finger on one of the most serious problems the new state had to face: the nationalist movement, predominantly middle-class, did not succeed in winning over the workers or in combining national aims with an improvement in the social and cultural conditions of the working classes.[12]

The complexity of the Irish political situation in 1923 is shown in the following scene between the Republican, the Free Stater, the Farmer and the Business Man who, together with Jimmy the Workman, compete for the favour of Kathleen. O'Casey here refers to the parliamentary elections of August 1923, when candidates were proposed by the ruling Free-State Government, the Republicans, the Farmers' Party and the Labour Party, plus several independent groups. The military conflict of the Civil War was thereby transferred to the field of politics, and as a result the enmity of the parties was extremely bitter. O'Casey has every visitor bring a present for Kathleen, the Free Stater most appropriately giving a 'Manual on the Government of a house accordin' to a Constitution' (p. 291). All of them protest their affections for Kathleen in the clichés of a romantic nationalism, yet they reveal the true nature of their alleged selfless love when Kathleen asks for a chair: all five of them rush into the house, break the furniture and fight over the chair. Miceawl's repeated question 'Which o' them, now, would you vote for?' (pp. 292-293) and his heart-felt sigh 'I wish to God they didn't love Kathleen as much as they do!' (p. 293) serve as ironic commentary on this scene. Only the appearance of the Man in the Kilt can halt the visitors for a moment, not however the entrance of a doctor who orders Kathleen to bed. When the Free Stater then asks Kathleen for a kiss, the Republican immediately sees in it the kiss of Judas. Subsequently they all insist: 'That's what we're all looking for – unity an' peace' (p. 295), yet the attempt to form 'a kind o' coalition committee' (p. 295), immediately elicits the Free Stater's suggestion 'Now let us all thake a solemn an' sacred oath', and the Republican's rejoinder 'I won't, I won't, I won't; I'll not take no oath for nobody, so help me God!' (p. 296). The scene at this point thus returns to the situation out of which the Civil War began. The Republican's malapropism when he asks Kathleen to vote for the 'Irish Republic, one an' invisible' has its ironic justification: under such circumstances an indivisible Republic is indeed condemned to remain invisible. The scene ends with an external threat to unity introduced in the person of the Orangeman, beating a big drum and bawling his song in praise of William of Orange. Peace, for which everybody is pretending to fight, remains a long way off.

Kathleen, who has so far hardly been mentioned, speaks only

six sentences in the play and has a smaller share of stage events
than almost any other figure. Nevertheless the play's title is
justified, inasmuch as she is at the centre of almost all the
discussions, and most of the stage figures demand access to her. In
an allegorical sense she is, of course, even more central, for every
word of the play refers to the Ireland that she represents. The
attitude of 'listening in' is less clearly motivated. It may allude to
Kathleen's listening to the wireless (newly introduced at the time),
and this might be taken to represent Ireland's new attitude to the
world: Kathleen can 'listen in' to the world, she can take an interest
in events beyond the sea and thus forget the provincial problems
behind her own garden wall. However, one critic's suggestion
that Kathleen was 'given to ephemeral pleasures' and 'not
conscious of her destiny' [13] cannot be substantiated in the text.

O'Casey's image of Kathleen is radically different from the
conventional, romantic idea of Cathleen ni Houlihan, the personification of Irish beauty and purity conjured up by many
poets. The contrast is especially noticeable when one compares
*Kathleen Listens In* to Yeats's *Cathleen ni Houlihan*, a play that
has contributed like none other to the Irish search for national
identity, so much so that the playwright was forced to ask himself
towards the end of his life:

> Did that play of mine send out
> Certain men the English shot? [14]

When O'Casey wrote a play about Kathleen, the daughter of
Houlihan, he could not ignore Yeats's play; indeed he created a
kind of counter-image, so that a comparison to Yeats's Cathleen
may serve to define his own image of Ireland. Yeats's play has a
historical setting, the landing of French troops at Killala in 1798
(an event that was later used by O'Casey for the play-within-a-
play in *The Drums of Father Ned*). It differs, too, from the
allegorical complexity of O'Casey's play; the Irish family who
prepare for their son's wedding are portrayed realistically. Only
the Poor Old Woman is an exception: she has been expelled from
her house by foreigners and grieves for the loss of her four green
fields, but has also, in all her wanderings, inspired men to make
the ultimate sacrifice to her. Her rejuvenation indicated in the
famous last sentence, is both a natural and a mysterious consequence of this willingness. In Yeats's play, with its impressive
simplicity, the men's patriotism and their readiness to die are
unquestioned premises; there is therefore no conflict, and nobody

doubts that Cathleen is worthy of their devotion. The appropriateness of their sacrifice or even its usefulness in this particular situation are unquestioned, because in *Cathleen ni Houlihan* dying for one's country has an absolute value, unsurpassed by any other experience. The audience cannot but be drawn into this emotion, from which an escape into scepticism is impossible.

O'Casey provides for his audience not a uniformity of emotion but a multiplicity of opinions. His concern is not with the glorification of the individual through his sacrifice for Kathleen, but with the behaviour that can lead most effectively to Kathleen's recovery. Material assistance, rejected by Yeats's Old Woman, would in this case be the appropriate expedient, for O'Casey's Kathleen is not a mythical, awe-inspiring figure, but a natural girl who has to learn her lessons and who would rather play with the ornaments on the mantle-piece than help her mother with the housework. To cure Kathleen's disease, no higher sacrifice is demanded of her lovers than the renunciation of certain personal interests; Kathleen does not need the sacrifice of the dead but the assistance of the living. The play's appeal to the audience is not emotional but rational.

O'Casey's own attitude in this play, therefore, is not one of emotional patriotism but of rational concern for the behaviour that is best for Ireland. It is true that his search for positive alternatives is hidden behind a trenchant critique of the destructive aspects of Irish life, but it is certainly wrong to construe this attitude as pessimistic. Saros Cowasjee commented,

This is the only play in which O'Casey holds forth no vision, no hope. In almost all his other plays there is at least a ray of light, a dream that things could have been different, may one day turn out to be different. But here he sees nothing. The reason may be that he cannot see objectively where Ireland's destiny is concerned. He had been a participant too long in the country's struggle for freedom, and for bettering the lot of the workers; he had spared neither himself nor the little he had, and had at last emerged from the fight disillusioned and disgusted. The theme of the play touched him so closely that he failed to exercise the dispassionate gaze of the artist.[15]

Such a judgement disregards the satirical character of *Kathleen Listens In*, which shows an unsatisfactory situation in distorted exaggeration with the purpose of changing it and with continuous reference to an implied satiric norm. O'Casey himself confirms the didactic intention of his play: 'It was written . . . specifically to show what fools these mortals were in the quarrelling factions soaking Ireland in anxiety and irritations after the Civil War. I imagined that satire might bring some sense to the divided groups practising envy, hatred, malice, and all uncharitableness.' [16] It is surprising that O'Casey, after his experience, and disillusionment, with various political and cultural organisations, as can be deduced from his autobiography, decided to write such a play at all. His hopes and expectations for Ireland are clearly discernible. He demands social equality for the workers, the reorientation of the Gaelic League and a constructive attitude to the Gaelic national heritage, a rejection of those ties to the past that cannot be made fertile for the future, and greater attention to the technical and economic problems of the present; most of all, however, he calls for national unity, pleading at one moment of the play in quite explicit terms: 'Can't yous be united if it was only for five minutes an' give little Kathleen a chance' (p. 295).

A survey of O'Casey's early writings from the period 1905 to 1925 [17] shows to what extent these themes always occupied him. Indeed *Kathleen Listens In* expresses in summary form the views he formulated in numerous stories, articles and letters to newspapers. One even finds an allegorical story, 'The Seamless Coat of Kathleen: A Parable of the Ard Fheis' (1922) [18] that reads like a preliminary, if unsuccessful, draft of *Kathleen Listens In*. This story apparently closely resembled O'Casey's lost play *The Seamless Coat of Cathleen* which was rejected in 1922 by Yeats, Robinson and Lady Gregory because of its propaganda-like character and its topical allusions. [19]

If one adds to these works his other lost play, *The Robe of Rosheen*, which seems also to have been to some extent allegorical, [20] one is obliged to revise the view that O'Casey's early writings were uniformly realistic. O'Casey himself has rejected this view – frequently used to disparage his later works – in articles, letters and interviews, but only the publication of *Kathleen Listens In* and 'The Seamless Coat of Kathleen' provided factual support for his claim. *Kathleen Listens In* as a consistently unrealistic play already points forward to the works of the second and third periods, especially *Within the Gates* and *The Star Turns Red*, where O'Casey, rejecting mimesis, undertakes a direct presentation of ideas in dramatic form; and indeed the later 'Irish' plays from *Cock-a-doodle-Dandy* contain many of the same themes. Like *Kathleen Listens In*, these later plays criticize aspects of political, social and cultural life in Ireland, and they use unrealistic techniques with semi-allegorical figures. [21] Yet these plays are much more complex, they go beyond any mere criticism of Ireland and present problems of universal significance. In contrast to *Kathleen Listens In*, they do not lose their relevance through change in the conditions criticized. Finally, the allegorical technique of *Kathleen Listens In* fore-shadows the six volumes of the autobiography, where a tendency to allegory can be observed throughout.

In spite of these traits, *Kathleen Listens In* does not stand in isolation from the other early plays. Tomaus Thornton, the wise good-for-nothing, shares with other early characters their comic behaviour, their unreliability and their insights into the political situation of Ireland. Another similarity is in the links, apparent in all the early plays, to a specific historical situation. *Kathleen Listens In* therefore takes up an intermediate position between O'Casey's early works and the later plays; it contains in seminal form techniques and themes which the playwright was later to develop with far greater success.

Since O'Casey has written a considerable number of short plays, it is also important to note to what extent the dramatist already recognized here the special requirements of this particular dramatic form. Although the short play has since the end of the nineteenth century developed in various directions, it is possible to define some common traits in the genre and, thus defined, to apply them to *Kathleen Listens In*. The dominant characteristic of a good short play is its tendency to extreme concentration. This makes itself felt in the unity of setting and time, the limited number of figures, whose characterization is also reduced to a few significant traits, and particularly in the development of the action which, instead of a static exposition, begins with immediate energy and leads directly, without slackening tension, to a single climax, a decisive crisis in the life of one or a few persons. Such a crisis or turning point reveals in a flash, without explicit presentation, a whole life; the one moment represents the whole, it becomes symbolic.

Although *Kathleen Listens In* reveals some of these traits of the short play, it does not achieve its effects in terms of a real human situation but through transposition and allegory, the audience's emotional engagement being replaced by the rational process of constructing and following analogies. This technique does not allow for an intensification towards a single climax; it makes for an irregular variation of tension which at the end is no greater than at the beginning – if indeed one may in any sense use the term 'tension' here, with its connotation of the audience's expectation being manipulated by the author towards a particular end.

One of the reasons why *Kathleen Listens In* does not convey a unified impression is the fact that O'Casey merely develops an allegory of figures, not an allegory of action; he presents an allegorical equivalent for the various political groupings in Ireland, but only in section III does he attempt to show their conduct towards each other. This third section might, with its greater emphasis on plot, have offered a more effective frame for the whole play. In all his later plays with a similar allegorical tendency, O'Casey attempts to ensure the unity of the work through a logical sequence of events which are either part of the allegory themselves (*The Star Turns Red*) or which serve as a definite frame-work for the allegorical elements (e.g. *Within the Gates*). In his later short plays, O'Casey also observes more exactly the special requirements and possibilities of the genre. Yet in spite of these shortcomings, and in spite of its depressing reception on stage, *Kathleen Listens In* was an important step towards some of O'Casey's best plays.

# 5. JUNO AND THE PAYCOCK

The historical events which form the background to *Juno and the Paycock* fill the time-span between the events of *The Shadow of a Gunman* and those of *Kathleen Listens In*. The play is set in September (Acts I and II) and November (Act III) of the year 1922, at a time when the first climax of the Civil War was over. The Republican troops, beaten in several battles, had returned to the type of guerilla-warfare that had proved successful in the War of Independence. Their conflict with the Free Staters over the 1921 Treaty with England is the darkest chapter in recent Irish history. The decision for or against the Treaty, the question whether an oath to the British crown was acceptable to Irish politicians or not, led to bitterness and hatred among the Irish troops who only recently had fought together against British dominion, and it has continued to influence political life in Ireland to the present day. Above all, however, the Civil War inflicted new suffering on the majority of the people, who had taken no part in the fighting and who found themselves at the mercy of fanatics on both extremes. This aspect of the conflict is the subject of O'Casey's play.

*Juno and the Paycock* was produced by the Abbey on March 3, 1924.[1] Again only a short time had elapsed between the historical events treated in the play and the première. As in *The Shadow of a Gunman*, O'Casey makes use of a number of personal experiences; indeed he especially included several of his acquaintances with their peculiar idiosyncrasies of gesture, speech and habit, sometimes not even changing their names. A great deal of painstaking labour has been spent on the reconstruction of the identity of these models for Jack Boyle, Joxer Daly and others.[2] More important, however, than such biographical spade-work is the fact that Dublin audiences seem to have recognized immediately the traits that make these figures into typical representatives of the world of the Dublin slums.[3] It was its twofold actuality, its temporal closeness to the historical events and its topographical immediacy to the slums of the Dublin city centre, which made for the play's spontaneous acceptance by the Abbey audience. Yet the favourable reception it found in London the following year, resulting in its publication and in the award to its unknown author of the Hawthornden Prize, cannot be explained merely by its immediate actuality. The London production made it clear that *Juno and the Paycock*, in spite of its Dublin roots, takes up a basic human situation in a way that affects audiences (and readers) from quite a different national and social background. This effect has not been lost over the years: *Juno and the Paycock* is the O'Casey play most frequently acted outside Ireland and has been accepted into the theatrical repertoire of many different countries.

Its appeal is partly due to the fact that from the point of view of technique *Juno and the Paycock* is O'Casey's most conventional play. Audiences and critics are not impeded in their understanding by those barriers of experiment in technique which O'Casey introduced in his later plays. The author here shows that he can handle traditional techniques to perfection; when he deviated from these in his later works (beginning with *The Plough and the Stars*), this cannot therefore be ascribed to lack of skill, but has to be seen as a consequence of his dissatisfaction with conventional forms. O'Casey's own derogatory remarks about *Juno and the Paycock*, with which he began to shock his most ardent admirers a few years after the first production,[4] are probably due to this dissatisfaction with the play's lack of formal originality.

*

If in *The Shadow of a Gunman* the dominant structural element was the dramatic figures themselves, in *Juno and the Paycock* it is a logically developed plot, rich in events, which progresses from the expository opening scene through first hints of imminent danger to the false climax of Act II with the subsequent unmasking of illusion, the possibility of a happy outcome and its frustration to the final catastrophe. In accordance with conventional techniques, three lines of action are interwoven, each of them triggered off and propelled by a motif familiar from the history of drama. There are, however, three deviations from a well-made play in the nineteenth-century tradition: (1) as in *The Shadow of a Gunman*, the action is not autonomous but takes place against an historical background by which it is influenced at decisive moments; (2) while two of the three lines of action are conceived progressively, the third is constructed analytically, i.e. it does not show a complete sequence of events but only their final outcome, reconstructing what has gone before in an exposition that extends across the whole play; (3) a series of static scenes, showing no development but contributing significantly to the meaning of the play, is intercalated between the three lines of the action.

It will be advisable to deal with these three lines of action and the sequence of static scenes separately, although they are so closely interwoven that the attempt to isolate individual threads constantly endangers the whole texture of the play. This becomes apparent right at the start. The first two sentences of dialogue introduce all four areas of the action: the first sentence, spoken by the central character of that part of the action concerned with Mary, introduces the action around Johnny, the second sentence, spoken by Juno, the central character of the third line of action, prepares for the scenes around 'Captain' Boyle and Joxer Daly. The whole exposition scene (pp. 4-8), which extends to the first moment of dramatic impact, the entry of Jerry Devine, is a masterpiece of realistic theatre. In a few sentences, without violating the limits of probability, a wealth of important information is introduced. The situation of the family as a whole and of its individual members is presented; in alternately direct and indirect characterization the personality of all the central characters is sketched in and their relationship towards each other is introduced; the report of the shooting arouses the audience's expectations and turns them in the intended direction. From now on the lines of action can progress simultaneously rather than consecutively.

The action concerned with Johnny is the easiest to isolate from the context of the play, although it shows a misunderstanding of the play as a whole when a critic declares that it is unrelated to the other parts of the plot.[5] Among the few documents which bear on the genesis of O'Casey's plays, none is as important as the following by Gabriel Fallon:

He had been telling me for some time about a play he had mapped out, a play which would deal with the tragedy of a crippled IRA man, one Johnny Boyle. He mentioned this play many times and always it was the tragedy of Johnny. I cannot recall that he once spoke about Juno or Joxer or the Captain; always Johnny.[6]

At the outset, therefore, it was not the figure of Juno or of the Paycock with which O'Casey was mainly concerned, but the fate of Johnny. The same critic explains that *Juno and the Paycock* initially contained an additional scene, 'the shooting of Johnny Boyle which took place in darkness in a roadside setting'.[7] This scene was cut by the Abbey directors, because it would have weakened the peculiarly oppressive finality of this part of the action, achieved precisely by the technique of suggestion. After some hesitation, O'Casey accepted this cut for the printed version. It is also reported that O'Casey wrote down the opening lines of his new work, one of the most effective openings of any play in English literature, on the very evening he had been so deeply disappointed by the unfavourable reception of *Kathleen Listens In*.[8]

All the important events of this line of the action, with the one exception of Johnny's arrest and death, lie before the beginning of the play. The disclosure of these events, which runs parallel to the two other, progressive plot lines, is brought on by the motif of guilt pursuing a murderer, torturing him with apparitions of his victim and driving him to the verge of betraying his crime itself – a motif frequently used, from *Macbeth* to nineteenth-century melodrama, in order to render a murderer's pangs of conscience dramatically effective and visible. In *Juno and the Paycock* it also serves to generate suspense; at first it is not clear why Johnny should react so hysterically to any question concerning death in general and the death of Robbie Tancred in particular. Only gradually is it revealed that he has betrayed his former IRA comrade to the Free Staters and thereby caused his death. It is even more difficult to understand his reason for the betrayal. The only hint of an explanation is contained in his words: 'It's not because he was a Commandant of the Battalion that I was Quarther-Masther of, that we were friends' (p. 55). But it is left open whether military ambition, jealousy of his successful comrade or the hope of being promoted more quickly after Robbie's death, could really be the motives for his deed.

Johnny's fate is connected with a stage property that gradually takes on the function of a symbol: the votive-light in front of the picture of the Virgin that Johnny continually fears to see extinguished, becomes a symbol of his life. O'Casey's progress in dramatic technique after *The Shadow of a Gunman* can be observed in detail, when one compares the function of this symbol with the role of the omen in the earlier play. In *The Shadow of a Gunman*, the knocking on the wall remained a blind motif, misleading the audience without dramatic justification. In *Juno and the Paycock* the votive-light is closely associated with Johnny's life, and, consistently with this, it goes out the moment his executioners enter the house. The improbability of the oil being exhausted at this precise moment can easily be overcome by the producer if he arranges for the votive-light to be upset during the symbolic removal of the furniture. In this way, Johnny's fate would be associated even more closely with that of his family, and the demands of realism would be maintained.

The figure of Johnny is a successful psychological study of fear grown out of guilt. The qualification is necessary, for Johnny has previously shown that he is by no means simply a coward. He has therefore more reason than, for instance, Tommy Owens in *The Shadow of a Gunman* to speak of his principles and to insist somewhat pompously: 'Ireland only half free'll never be at peace while she has a son left to pull a trigger' (p. 31). It is, of course, possible to condemn such a ruthless attitude, but Johnny has at least proved that he is prepared to risk his health and his life for his convictions. O'Casey gives him more credit, potentially, than some critics are prepared to recognise, and it would be erroneous to take Juno's words, 'Ah, you lost your best principle, me boy, when you lost your arm . . .' (p. 31) as the author's own opinion.[9] Whatever his personal preferences may be, the critic is confronted here with two radically opposing attitudes: that of the mother who cares for her family but does not look beyond it, and that of the patriot who is inclined to undervalue the existence of the individual. If Johnny is liable to censure, it is because of his betrayal of Robbie Tancred; his insistence on principles and patriotism, which Juno does not understand, is criticized only when he no longer behaves according to them. Johnny's later behaviour cannot be measured by ordinary standards. When he reproaches his mother, of all people, with 'Not one o' yous, not one o' yous, have any thought for me!' (p. 78), or when he wants to cast Mary out, he must be understood as acting in a state of hysteria, arising from the consciousness of his guilt as well as from the fact that his betrayal has been discovered; he flees both from his conscience and from his pursuers. In the person of Johnny, O'Casey has depicted the fate of someone who through a single rash deed has jeopardized all the principles of his life, who has made his past worthless and his future hopeless, a Lord-Jim situation without a second chance. Even if the family had in fact inherited the money, Johnny would not have been saved, because the apparition of his dead comrade would have followed him beyond any possible escape from his real pursuers.

The 'Johnny' action has three main functions for the play. First, Johnny's injury, his persecution mania and his final kidnapping are part of the catastrophe that besets the Boyles, particularly affecting his mother; his death contributes to the ruin of the family. Secondly, it is in this line of action that the historical background events enter the play. Like other boys, Johnny (perhaps as a member of Fianna Eireann) has taken part in the Easter Rising, where he was wounded. After the Free State Treaty

he has fought on the side of the Republicans and has lost an arm
during the battle in O'Connell Street (1-5 July, 1922). Robbie
Tancred was an officer of the Republican troops who after their
defeat continued fighting as guerillas and who were known as
die-hards. The effect of these conflicts on the life of the ordinary
individual can be deduced from Juno's words:

. . . look at the way they're afther leavin' the people in this very house.
Hasn't the whole house, nearly, been massacreed? There's young
Dougherty's husband with his leg off; Mrs. Travers that had her son blew
up be a mine in Inchegeela, in Co. Cork; Mrs. Mannin' that lost wan of
her sons in ambush a few weeks ago, an' now, poor Mrs. Tancred's only
child gone west with his body made a collandher of (p. 56).

Here it becomes apparent that the background events do not
concern Johnny alone. If they are less decisive in their impact
than in *The Shadow of a Gunman* and *The Plough and the Stars*,
yet they still overshadow the stage actions, dominating the
characters' imagination and even entering their way of expression.
Boyle asserts: 'If th' worst comes . . . to th' worse . . . I can join a . . .
flyin' . . . column' (p. 88) and explains his newly-won self-
confidence with the (characteristically incorrect) image: 'Today,
Joxer, there's goin' to be issued a proclamation be me, establishin'
an independent Republic, an' Juno'll have to take an oath of
allegiance' (p. 27).

    The third function of this line of action is closely related to the
historical events. It serves to elevate the play beyond the limits of
a mere family drama and to underline its representative character.
Johnny is shot because he has betrayed the son of a neighbour,
who again was responsible for another's death: '. . . I'm told he
was the leadher of the ambush where me nex' door neighbour,
Mrs. Mannin', lost her Free State soldier son' (p. 54). While the
Boyles' suffering is presented in detail, the suffering of the
Tancred family appears in one scene only, and that of the
Mannings is only alluded to a few times. Thus in precise gradations
from the extended stage events to the merest hint, a chain of
suffering is revealed, reaching far beyond the family and the
community of neighbours. Suffering, personified in Mrs. Tancred's
stage appearance in Act II, is not limited to the Boyles, it concerns
the whole country and points even beyond those national limits.
Mrs. Tancred's and Juno's sufferings for the death of their sons is
simply a mother's suffering for a loss which in her eyes must
always appear meaningless.
    In this respect, the 'Johnny' action goes beyond the function

of the action concerned with Mary. In other respects, however, there are close analogies between the two. They correspond with each other in four points: they both depend on a single traditional motif, they provide the audience with the same opportunities to judge the central characters, they show how an individual life can be determined through a single irreversible decision, and they contribute in a similar way to the fate of the family. The action around Mary is governed by the motif of seduction, the girl being deserted by her faithless lover. This is certainly one of the most traditional of all literary motifs; in twentieth-century English drama, from Houghton's *Hindle Wakes* to Wesker's *Roots*, it has been employed repeatedly. O'Casey's specific contribution to the literary tradition may be seen in the unobtrusiveness with which he has depicted Mary's seduction. He is less interested in her relationship to Bentham and her specific disaster than in its effect on the whole family, especially on Juno. The central function of this line of action, in analogy to that concerned with Johnny, is its contribution to the final catastrophe.

If Johnny is best judged by his attitude to the patriotic movement, Mary can be judged through her attitude to the strike in which she participates. Again, one should not see her only with her mother's eyes: Juno in her maternal egotism rejects any responsibility for others, but this is neither the author's opinion nor the quintessence of the play. Even though Mary transfers part of the sacrifice demanded of her to her mother, one should not undervalue her willingness to come out on strike for a colleague who was not even well liked. Mary is neither entirely egotistical, nor is her insistence on principles and human solidarity so much windy rhetoric. Her behaviour towards Bentham and Jerry Devine is equally ambivalent. Her superficial vanity and her disdain for the milieu in which she has been brought up certainly contribute to her decision for Bentham and against Devine, but this is not the only reason. Even when she knows that Bentham has left her, she still insists on her love for him and refrains from condemning him (p. 62). If she had merely considered him as a means of social advancement, her reaction at this stage would have been different. Mary's character shows the tension between the repressive conditions of her surroundings and her own weak attempts at intellectual and social emancipation. She tries to keep all traces of dialect out of her pronunciation and vocabulary, she reads Ibsen and learns Gaelic, but she does not succeed in liberating herself from the world of the slums. Her weaknesses, her delusion by Bentham and her continuous irritation in her relationship with her family, can be explained as arising from this conflict.[10] Ironically it is Bentham, to whom she looks for release from her surroundings, who is responsible for her irrevocable commitment to them. As with Johnny, a single false step leads inescapably to her downfall, and it would be hard to decide whether Johnny's death or Mary's future life might be reckoned the graver fate.

Closely associated with the 'Mary' action is the figure of Jerry Devine. Dramaturgically, his entrance in Act II opens up the possibility of a brief counter-movement when he declares his continued love for Mary, permitting, it seems, a half-way 'happy' solution. Over and above this, Devine (who in ironic contrast to his name poses as an atheist) is also interesting as a character; indeed he has certain traits in common with Mary. Like her, he endeavours to achieve emancipation from his social surroundings and is foiled in the attempt. In his failure he almost reaches tragic stature. He is convinced that he has freed himself from petty bourgeois and religious prejudices, and therefore promises Mary: 'No matther what happens, you'll always be the same to me' (p. 19). This promise is repeated after her affair with Bentham: 'What does it matter what has happened? . . . With Labour, Mary, humanity is above everying; we are the Leaders in the fight for a new life' (p. 80). But when he realizes that she is pregnant, he finds himself caught precisely in those moral conventions which he has struggled to transcend, and he reacts – to his own dismay – with the cliché that perfectly expresses them: 'My God, Mary, have you fallen as low as that?' (p. 81). A 'fallen woman' is for him as shocking an idea as it is for his less intellectual neighbours whom, as a socialist, he wants to lead to a new humanity based on mutual tolerance. If one considers Jerry's origins and his social background, it is hardly possible lightly to condemn such a reaction. Regret rather than criticism is called for, inasmuch as Jerry is intellectually capable of recognizing his own situation without having the strength to free himself from it.

A third line of action that might be called the 'family' action, is based like the others on a traditional motif, an inheritance that, depending on the type of play in question, can either lead through a sudden turn to a happy conclusion or through its non-arrival to a final catastrophe. In *Juno and the Paycock* the motif is used for both purposes. At first the unexpected news of the death of a distant relative and his surprising legacy promises to bring a turning point in the fate of this family that is already on the way to disintegration. Not only would the inherited money have improved their hopeless financial situation, it would also, through

the family's removal to another town, have mitigated the subsequent blows of fate: Johnny could have escaped from the revenge
of his former comrades, Mary from the neighbours' hostile talk.
The news that there has been a mistake in the drawing-up of the
will hits the Boyles all the harder. This counter-turn is the end of
the mock-release in tension, and it precludes any prospect of
help from outside. From now on, it is left solely to the family-
members to cope with the multiple catastrophe and to rescue
from the wreckage what they can. Only Juno succeeds, and she,
therefore, deserves special attention. Before turning to her,
however, a few remarks on the figure of Bentham and on the
sequence of static scenes around Boyle and Joxer are in order.

Bentham, bourgeois and intellectual, who triggers off both
turning-points in the family-action, is cast more obviously as a
type than any other character in the play. If in earlier plays the
villain was frequently the nobleman bent on seducing the
innocent, unprotected girl, here a representative of the middle-
class forcibly enters the world of ordinary people and destroys it.
One reason for O'Casey's characterization of Bentham as a stage
bourgeois may be that he wanted to illustrate the impression
made by such a figure on the tenement people. He had in that
case to remain shadow-like, for they have no access to his mental
world. They are, then, unable to realise that he follows aims as
egotistical as most of theirs (whereas Juno, for instance, can
always see through Joxer). There is no way of knowing whether
Bentham is at first seriously interested in Mary and is repelled,
as she thinks, only by the stupidity and tastelessness of her
surroundings (p. 62), or whether his intentions are from the start
directed towards the inheritance of which he has heard by
accident and which he tries to secure for himself through his
marriage to Mary. Ironically he is foiled in his attempt to secure
the money not, as would have been the case in nineteenth-century
melodrama, through the virtuous girl's resistance but through
his own trivial error in the drawing up of the will: his idea of his
own infallibility is thus reduced to absurdity.

If Bentham is capable of recognizing the reprehensibility of his
actions, such moral standards can hardly be applied to 'Captain'
Boyle, the 'Paycock' of the title. He is the most remarkable
representative of a long series of characterless good-for-nothings
in O'Casey's plays who nevertheless appear attractive in a
strange way and who can certainly number Falstaff among their
ancestors.[11] Boyle, in his companionship with Joxer Daly, is also
related to Sir Toby Belch and Sir Andrew Aguecheek. Yet such

models should not be valued too highly; literary influences are less important than O'Casey's personal acquaintance with the people of the Dublin tenements. There he found sufficient examples of the type of the stupid and arrogant blatherer who is allergic to work, boasts of imagined heroic deeds and acts purposefully only when his way leads to the pub. It is one of O'Casey's remarkable achievements that he establishes a certain amount of sympathy for such a character although, in reality, repugnance would be more probable; and he does so despite the fact that Boyle neglects his family in a most irresponsible way, leaves the burden of care solely to his wife and at a decisive moment rejects his daughter in an outburst of moral indignation that in him is entirely unjustified.

The reason for Boyle's attraction lies mainly in the irresistible comedy of his appearances, this being based on the continuous confrontation of talking and doing, of pretension and fulfilment, of appearance and reality. While the audience quickly recognizes this discrepancy, Boyle is incapable of such an insight. It is with full conviction that he can boast of his experiences sailing the world although he has only travelled once, and that only to Liverpool; he can brag of his willingness to accept any work and nevertheless feel pains in his leg whenever a job is offered to him; he can order a coat on credit and announce in the same breath that he has known for some time of the will's invalidity. He does not, however, lie on purpose, but permits himself to be drawn again and again into the web of his fantasy, deceiving himself with his image of an industrious, patriotic, calamity-stricken father and husband. Unlike O'Casey's later plays, these scenes are dominated by character-comedy rather than situation-comedy.

Their impact is intensified by the introduction of Joxer who supplements Boyle (in spite of their character differences) in an ideal way. Both of them contradict themselves continually, but if with Boyle this is due to lack of judgement, with Joxer it is due to calculation. Joxer is more than a match for Boyle because he knows the effects of his words and actions. He is by no means only a submissive hanger-on who turns his admiration for his master into the occasional triumph of a petty revenge. He is much more closely related to the type of the parasite, personified in Ben Jonson's Mosca, who is intellectually superior to his opposite number, can manipulate him at will, and betrays his contempt for him only when there is nothing to be gained. Actors have varied in their portrayal of Joxer between a fearful, harmless, comic and a sinister, threatening, demonic figure; O'Casey's intention seems to lie somewhere *between* these extremes.

The characters of Boyle and Joxer, who are unable to take decisions and incapable of development, render the sequence of their scenes static rather than dynamic. It is impressive evidence of O'Casey's dramatic power that he is able to incorporate two central characters into his play who contribute nothing to the progress of the action. Even more remarkable is it that their roles are not limited to comic relief, but that they contribute significantly to the meaning of the play. Several times Boyle, without stepping outside his role, provides the audience with important insights which one would hardly expect in burlesque drunkard scenes. Occasionally this happens in a purely comic manner, when Boyle, for instance, without realizing the ambiguity of his words, assures his partner: 'The two of us was ofen in a tight corner' (p. 49). The most complex example of such an unconscious contribution to the meaning of the play, exceeding by far the intellectual horizon of the characters themselves, is the final scene. If one considers Boyle's and Joxer's last appearance after the triple catastrophe to be no more than the senseless babbling of two drunkards in whose dimmed consciousness a few memories rise up like bubbles of marsh gas and burst without effect, it is possible to argue that this scene is superfluous.[12] Yet its relevance for the meaning of the play as a whole makes it, in fact, indispensable.

The setting of the final scene, the room emptied by the removal men, is, it has been suggested, itself 'a physical symbol of a disintegrating family and a disintegrating country'.[13] This sense of calamity is underlined in Boyle's first words, 'I'm able to go no farther', for this expresses not only his drunken exhaustion, but the end of his existence as 'Paycock' after Juno has finally turned away from him. When he continues to brag that 'Captain Boyle's Captain Boyle', he epitomizes his chronic incapacity for self-knowledge and the blind inadaptability which, contrary to his heroic understanding of himself, has contributed to the disintegration of his family. His slogan 'Irelan' sober . . . is Irelan' . . . free', coming from the mouth of a drunkard, is, then, another instance of O'Casey's irony: already passing beyond Boyle's unconscious self-interpretation, it contributes to the meaning of the play as a whole. This movement is continued in a sequence of sentences in which Boyle in three stages, albeit unconsciously, sums up the play. Entering his flat, he shouts 'The blinds is down, Joxer, the blinds is down!', then 'The counthry'll have to steady itself . . . it's goin' . . . to hell', and finally 'I'm telling you . . . Joxer . . . th' whole worl's . . . in a terr . . . ible state o' . . . chassis!' The blinds have really been pulled down since the furniture has been taken away, but the lights over this family have gone out in a much more comprehensive sense. The whole country will approach destruction if the mutual extermination of its people, as the play has shown it, is continued, and the whole world is destined for chaos if people do not begin at last to turn it into a better place. The final sentence of the play thus directs the audience's attention once more to the only attempt that has been made at warding off chaos: Juno's acceptance of her own suffering and her sacrifice for Mary and her child.

Juno in several ways is the central character of the play. Dramaturgically she is the most important link between the different lines of action, participating equally in all of them. Moreover, she has to bear the weight of all three catastrophes, the effects of which are made manifest in her person. Formally, therefore, she is the dramatist's most important device in preserving the unity of his play. As a character, Juno from the start demands more attention than the others. She also stands out because she is the only one to undergo a development; and towards the end she takes on symbolic significance. If one wants to do justice to this play one should note that Juno is not portrayed from the start as the author's ideal. It is true that, from the beginning, she is superior to others. This becomes evident when she is the only one to accept human weaknesses in others and to understand them without merely criticizing them: she gets her husband's breakfast in spite of his parasitical life-style, she reassures Johnny, accepts the company of Mrs. Madigan and Joxer and looks after her sickly daughter. Yet Juno, like all the other characters, is not without weaknesses herself.[14] She, too, is egoistic, but with the difference that her egotism is not limited to her own person but includes her family. Whatever exceeds the bounds of her family finds her uncomprehending and even offensive. She sees no point in Mary's strike and shows no compassion for the girl who has been unjustly dismissed. Similarly, she has no understanding for the Republican aims and criticizes Johnny's participation in the War of Independence: this for reasons of family egotism rather than political conviction. One may be inclined momentarily to compare her attitude to that of Countess Rosmarin in Fry's *The Dark Is Light Enough*:

Only
Tell me what is in this war you fight
Worth all your dead and suffering men.[15]

Yet Rosmarin is quite willing to weigh the arguments for and against war, and she retains her humanitarian convictions in spite of her understanding for the fighters' justification, while Juno remains inaccessible to any such understanding and does not even make an effort in this direction. Later her egotism becomes even plainer when she forgets the funeral of Robbie Tancred, holds her family celebration precisely at the time of the funeral procession and even remarks rather nastily: 'In wan way, she [Mrs. Madigan] deserves all she got; for lately, she let th' Die-hards make an open house of th' place . . .' (p. 56). Mary is not entirely unjustified when she explains to her mother why she could not have discussed with her the reasons for Bentham's disappearance: 'It would have been useless to tell you – you wouldn't understand' (p. 63). Even after Johnny's abduction, Juno's concern contains a certain degree of egotism: 'if anything ud happen to poor Johnny, I think I'd lose me mind' (p. 84).

Juno's triumph in this crucial test lies precisely in the fact that her own prediction does not come true. The news of Johnny's death call for her ability to offer – at the moment of most intense grief – the kind of consolation to others which she so badly needs herself. The loss of her own son enables her to answer to Mary's lament for the child that will grow up without a father: 'It'll have what's far betther – it'll have two mothers' (p. 86). And even more decisive is Juno's spontaneous willingness to go on her own to identify her dead son: 'I forgot, Mary, I forgot; your poor oul' selfish mother was only thinkin' of herself. No, no, you mustn't come – it wouldn't be good for you. You go on to me sisther's an' I'll face th' ordeal meself' (p. 87). Then she speaks those decisive words which show that she has overcome her family egotism and has won a new insight into the equality of all human beings in the face of death: 'Maybe I didn't feel sorry enough for Mrs. Tancred when her poor son was found as Johnny's been found now – because he was a Die-hard! Ah, why didn't I remember that then he wasn't a Diehard or a Stater, but only a poor dead son!' (p. 87).

If Juno at this moment takes up the prayer spoken before by Mrs. Tancred, it becomes obvious that she has taken on symbolic traits: Juno 'becomes by extension Mrs. Tancred and all bereaved mothers, including the Blessed Mother.'[16] Such a repetition would not have been justified if the prayer had merely contained a humanitarian message,[17] repeated by the dramatist so that the audience would take more notice of it. It is inaccurate to think of Juno, although this frequently happens, as a personification of O'Casey's philosophy of life, simply because humanly speaking she is so appealing, and thus to designate O'Casey as a pacifist and fatalist.[18] Taken to an extreme, this would mean that human beings ought patiently to suffer poverty, misery, disease and death without striving for an improvement in their lot. In reality each of the characters in this play incorporates an element of what then constitutes a whole. O'Casey 's'interdit scrupuleusement de prêter à ses personnages ses propres idées. Il ne permet pas à ses préférences individuelles d'obscurcir sa vue claire et courageuse des données de l'expérience. Ami des déshérités, il ne les a point idéalisés.'[19] Juno, too, is an autonomous character: O'Casey does not isolate her from his other figures by turning her into an ideal that everybody ought to follow but by conferring on her the symbolic features of the suffering mother who, in spite of all her limitations, with an optimism bordering on obstinacy and against all hope, again and again takes up the battle for the people entrusted to her care.

In such a symbolic context Juno's name takes on new meaning. Her husband's explanation is striking for its banality: 'You see, Juno was born an' christened in June; I met her in June; we were married in June, an' Johnny was born in June, so wan day I says to her, "You should ha' been called Juno," an' the name stuck to her ever since' (pp. 31-32). Yet this serves mainly to typify his superficiality and lack of understanding, for Juno – even if the Boyles do not realize this – bears the name of that Roman goddess who, with her train of peacocks, functioned as the guardian of the hearth and the protectress of matrimony. The mythological context has an entirely different function here from that which it performs in *The Shadow of a Gunman*, where Davoren's comparison of himself to Prometheus leads to an ironic reduction of unjustified pretensions, while here the authorial comparison, of which Juno is not at all aware, discovers a hidden but universal analogy.

A further level of meaning in the character of Juno is more specifically national in import. The small world of the tenement house incorporates – as it does in *Kathleen Listens In* – all the basic attitudes relevant to the Ireland of the twenties: socialism and ultra-patriotism, sympathy for Republicans and for Free Staters, grandiloquent passivity and silent activity, criticism of the clergy and justification of their conduct, betrayal and human solidarity, and finally oppression arising from the miserable conditions of daily life. The house becomes in this way symbolic of the Ireland of those years,[20] and Juno becomes a Cathleen ni Houlihan of the slums for whom, in the circumstances of her life, the liberation from poverty, dirt and disease ranks above all political independence.

Juno's prayer, combining echoes of Shelley's *Adonais*[21] with reminiscences of the prophet Ezekiel (XI, 19), requires a brief discussion of the element of religion in *Juno and the Paycock*. Critics have usually taken up Juno's sentence 'Ah, what can God do agen the stupidity o' men!' (p. 86), as a confirmation of her religiosity and sometimes even as an instance of the whole play's Christian tendency.[22] Yet this sentence suggests, in fact, the opposite interpretation inasmuch as it refers to the impotence of a God who can do nothing against human stupidity – and this, surely, implies that prayers to such a God must remain without effect. The scepticism of this view can be observed in various ways throughout the play. It lies behind Boyle's changing attitude to the clergy, whom he condemns at one moment (p. 25), but whom in the next, when he has been treated respectfully by a priest, he admires. Boyle, in his description of Devine, also provides the comic definition of a Christian: 'I never heard him usin' a curse; I don't believe he was ever dhrunk in his life – sure he's not like a Christian at all!' (p. 24). Devine is the atheist of the play, and his opinions rub off on Mary: 'Oh, it's thrue, it's thrue what Jerry Devine says – there isn't a God, there isn't a God; if there was He wouldn't let these things happen!' (p. 86). Even if this attitude is not implemented by the context, for Devine does not live up to his views and even thoughtlessly calls upon God when he rejects Mary (p. 81), it is not, however, opposed by any effective and convincing belief. At the opposite extreme to Devine is Bentham: 'One that says all is God an' no man; an' th' other that says all is man an' no God!' (p. 39); but Bentham's confused theosophic ideas are not an acceptable alternative to atheism and do not find expression in human actions either.

It is, of course, possible to see these various attitudes to religion simply as part of the dramatist's technique of characterization. But even Juno's attitude to Christianity which is usually accepted as the play's central standard (and not only as an individual character trait), is not consistent at all. Not only does she refer to the impotence of God, she also insists: 'With all our churches an' religions, the worl's not a bit the bether' (p. 42). Most of all, however, there are several moments when the dramatist calls the

validity of Christian standards into doubt, using other means
than the words of a particular character. The hymn, resounding
from the funeral procession, is contrasted, for instance, with the
superficial curiosity of the viewers. The text of the hymn contains
the words:

> . . . Blest be with loudest song
> The Sacred Heart of Jesus
> By every heart and tongue.

The Boyles (including Juno) and their guests react to this call to
religious worship with banal commentaries on the funeral as a
spectacle, culminating in Joxer's 'Oh, it's a darlin' funeral, a
daarlin' funeral!' (p. 59). The prayer that concludes Act II has a
similar effect:

> Hail, Mary, full of grace, the Lord is with Thee;
> Blessed art Thou amongst women, and blessed, etc. (p. 60)

In the context of the play these words function as a bitter
commentary on the fate of the living Mary who likewise expects a
child but has to live without grace and does not feel the presence
of God. Mary also quotes that poem which depicts most plainly
of all a world abandoned by God, 'Like the story of a demon, That
an angel had to tell' (p. 82).[23]

Juno's prayer therefore is not the highest expression of an all-
pervading trust in God that might counterbalance the miserable
situation of mankind. Even in itself it contains a reproach: 'Blessed
Virgin, where were you when me darlin' son was riddled with
bullets . . .?' (p. 87). The whole 'prayer' is largely secularized, and
its central sentence, 'Sacred Heart o' Jesus, take away our hearts
o' stone, and give us hearts o' flesh!' (p. 87) pleads for an attitude
that could equally well be taken by the atheist Devine: the
predominant role of active, understanding and forgiving love. It
is Juno alone, however, who puts this principle into practice and
thereby arouses the element of hope that, in spite of all reasons
for pessimism, pervades the play.[24] In this respect more than in
anything else Juno's prayer can be distinguished from the other
great prayer of Anglo-Irish literature, Maurya's last sentence
from Riders to the Sea. When Maurya says 'They're all gone now,
and there isn't anything more the sea can do to me',[25] this is the
expression of a final resignation. At the end of a long heroic
battle, Maurya succumbs to an inexorable fate and accepts defeat
without murmur. For Juno, her prayer is not an ending but the

beginning of a new development: her (possibly irrational, but nevertheless admirable) optimism leads her into a new battle against fate for the existence of the people entrusted to her.[26]

If in *Juno and the Paycock* transcendental references are limited to a few relics of traditional religion, all the more emphasis is placed on man's proving himself in this world. This, in fact, is the central theme of the play: human integrity is put to the test in numerous different situations where several characters, confronted with the same task, succeed or fail, and where success or failure, determining moral rank, provides the co-ordinates for the evaluatory system of the play. It is possible for the reader or spectator to verify his own spontaneous evaluations of individual characters by referring to these test-situations. It soon becomes clear that Juno succeeds in most of them, while Joxer and Boyle fail in all the tasks put to them and the other characters range somewhere between these two extremes. A few examples may illustrate this.

At the beginning of the play, the irritable Johnny asks for a glass of water. Mary's and Juno's different reactions enable the audience to recognize an initial difference between the two women:

MARY. Isn't he big an' able enough to come out an' get it himself?
MRS. BOYLE. If you weren't well yourself you'd like somebody to bring
   you in a dhrink o'wather.
   [*She brings in drink and returns*]  (p. 5)

The offer of a job for Boyle has a similar effect. While Juno has taken on an additional job without hesitation in order to keep her family, Boyle reacts indignantly to the chance of giving up his existence as a loafer. He characteristically takes refuge in his world of fantasy from which he suddenly produces the vision of a job at the other end of the town and soon believes in it himself. Joxer characteristically follows him in every detail. The family celebrations in Act II provide two particularly revealing test-situations. All the participants are asked to sing a song. Juno and Mary succeed honourably if not brilliantly. The naive but kind Mrs. Madigan sings '*in a quavering voice*' (p. 51), but at least she manages to finish her song, while Joxer on his own is not able to accomplish anything. Bentham who moves outside the circle of these people is not even confronted with such a task. The 'Captain' takes up a special position, because he does not content himself by singing a song like the others, but recites a poem of his own, i.e. a product of his fantasy.[27] If one recognizes the function of this scene as a test-situation, it is not possible to say that it 'n'ajoute rien à la signification de l'oeuvre . . .'[28] This scene is preceded by a more serious test. When Johnny believes himself to have seen the apparition of the dead Tancred, somebody has to go into the bedroom to make sure that in reality the votive-light is still burning. Everybody under some pretext or other passes on the request to his neighbour. Not only do the terrified Johnny and the fearful Boyle refuse to enter the room, but also Mary, and even Juno hesitates, until Bentham voluntarily offers to go. This is one of the occasions that prevent Juno from being stylized into an implausible, ideal figure, while at the same time Bentham is given some positive traits. Another instance when Juno, like all the others, fails, is her attempt to cope with the unexpected prosperity. The room filled with useless junk 'of a vulgar nature' (p. 36) and the gramophone that she carries in, show that she has not succeeded in handling the borrowed money in a useful way. On the other hand, she succeeds entirely in misfortune. When Mary's pregnancy becomes known, Johnny insists 'She should be dhriven out o' th' house she's brought disgrace on!' (p. 75), and Boyle (as the frequency of the personal pronoun shows) thinks only of himself: 'Oh, isn't this a nice thing to come on top o' me, an' the state I'm in! A pretty show I'll be to Joxer an' to that oul' wan, Madigan! Amn't I afther goin' through enough without havin' to go through this!' (p. 74), while Juno is able to forget her own person and to appreciate Mary's situation:

What you an' I'll have to go through'll be nothin' to what poor Mary'll have to go through; for you an' me is middlin' old, an' most of our years is spent; but Mary'll have maybe forty years to face an' handle, an' every wan of them'll be tainted with a bitther memory (p. 74).

In a similar way she triumphantly passes all serious tests and thus attains the moral rank that she occupies towards the end of the play.

*

Finally, the question of literary genre must be raised. O'Casey himself subtitled Juno and the Paycock, A Tragedy in Three Acts, but critics who usually consider such authorial designations with some scepticism, should be sceptical in this case, too. The play can be considered as a tragedy only if one applies the term in a very general sense to terrible, passion-evoking events which

raise the spectator to a 'higher' level beyond the limits of his own
personal problems.[29] If, however, one expects a tragedy, more
specifically, to show the downfall of a human being of some
intrinsic greatness, someone who has consciously experienced
the conflict between two near-equal values, *Juno and the Paycock*
remains outside the definition. Juno, who alone could qualify for
a tragic role, is never in a situation where every decision must
lead to failure. This would, perhaps, be the case if Boyle were an
honourable husband with rigid principles whom Juno loved;
this might force upon her the (conceivably tragic) option for
either her rejected daughter or her husband. As the play stands,
however, no hesitation is called for. It is Juno's specific quality
that she takes up every challenge of fate and proves herself equal
to it. It is true that there is a rudimentary tragic conflict in Devine,
who fails in the decision between his love for Mary and his
inherited moral conventions, but this remains an isolated
episode and does not influence the play as a whole. If *Juno and
the Paycock* is to be placed in any category at all, it belongs
to tragicomedy, but only if tragicomedy is considered as an
autonomous genre and not simply as a combination of comic and
tragic scenes.

Juno and the Paycock can be seen in a twofold literary tradition.
On the one hand it belongs to those literary works which, in
realistic or symbolic form, centre on a dominant mother figure.
Such works seem to have become more frequent in recent years;
at a time when religious, ethical and moral standards have become
ever more doubtful, a mother's care and willingness to sacrifice
herself for her family has remained as one of the few unquestioned
values. These works, of course, are not limited to drama; they
have appeared both before and after *Juno and the Paycock*
without immediately suggesting an influence on or by O'Casey.
One might think of Steinbeck's Ma Joad (*The Grapes of Wrath*),
Hauptmann's Mutter Wolffen (*Der Biberpelz*), Odets's Bessie
Berger (*Awake and Sing!*), Wesker's Sarah Kahn (*Chicken Soup
with Barley* and *I'm talking About Jerusalem*), Gorki's Wassa
Schelesnowa in the play of the same title and – in an entirely
different social sphere – Waugh's Lady Marchmain (*Brideshead
Revisited*). Even Wilder's Mrs. Antrobus (*The Skin of Our Teeth*)
possesses, in allegorical foreshortening, the essential traits of the
character in question, inimical to progress and without any
understanding for political ideas, but indomitable and invaluable
as a refuge for the people entrusted to her.

Other, slightly different works also have a central mother figure.

The comparison with three of them may help to pin-point Juno's peculiar position. One of them is *Riders to the Sea*, where Maurya's lifelong battle with fate ends in resignation because her struggle to preserve her family remains futile. Entirely different to this is another play, strongly influenced by Synge and using the same basic situation, but drawing from it opposite conclusions: Brecht's *Die Gewehre der Frau Carrar*. Here the miseries of the family have political causes; it is, therefore, possible to combat them through political or military action, as the mother figure realizes towards the end of the play, after prior insistence on a Juno-like attitude. The third variation is represented in Brecht's *Mutter Courage* where the title character is an example of obstinacy, uncritical adaptability to existing conditions and the refusal to listen to reason.[30] These three plays form a system of co-ordinates in which Juno assumes the central position. With the obstinacy of Mother Courage she struggles not only for herself, but for her family, and, under similar circumstances to those of the other figures, she neither succumbs to Maurya's resignation, nor does she turn to Teresa Carrar's political activity.

A second literary tradition that is of importance for *Juno and the Paycock* is that of bourgeois tragedy. This statement demands two qualifications. On the one hand, the term 'tragedy', as has been shown above, cannot properly be applied to O'Casey's play. On the other hand, the bourgeois milieu has here been exchanged for the proletarian, just as in the eighteenth century the bourgeois tragedy introduced a new social class to a form that up to then had been dominated by the nobility. Notwithstanding these changes, however, the basic pattern, transmitted from Lillo through Lessing, Schiller and Hebbel to the twentieth century, has remained largely unchanged. This becomes evident if one compares *Juno and the Paycock* to two typical plays of this tradition, Hebbel's *Maria Magdalena* (1846) and Hauptmann's *Vor Sonnenaufgang* (1889).

Considering O'Casey's reading, it is hardly possible that he was directly influenced by these two plays, which makes it all the more remarkable that *Juno* should exhibit the common features of a comprehensive literary tradition. In *Maria Magdalena*, Clara is caught, like O'Casey's Mary, in a network of lower middle-class prejudices and inhuman moral standards. Like Devine, the Secretary does not succeed in overcoming these; his sentence: 'Darüber kann kein Mann weg!'[31] corresponds exactly to Devine's 'My God, Mary, have you fallen as low as that?' (p. 81). One should add that Meister Anton, if with greater justification, insists on similarly narrow-minded ideas of virtue and morality as the 'Captain'. Also, the motif of the loss of a large sum of money as well as the sub-plot concerning the arrest of Clara's brother both contribute to the final catastrophe, which enhances the similarity to *Juno and the Paycock*. The most decisive difference is in the character of Juno, who protects Mary from the hopelessness of Clara's situation and from her tragic death. Such a redeeming character is lacking, too, in *Vor Sonnenaufgang*. In all other respects, however, there are remarkable similarities between Hauptmann's and O'Casey's plays, and, from a historical perspective, they can be seen in the context of the literary tradition which, at the time of their first productions, was obscured by the novelty of the plays' subject matter. The most remarkable parallel is in the characters of Loth and Devine. Both are idealists and want to better the situation of mankind, but fail when put to the test in a concrete situation, because they cannot overcome their prejudices. They withdraw their help precisely from that person who needs it most and who could be 'redeemed' most easily. Hauptmann's Helene is, like Mary, half-educated, and therefore open to Loth's ideas. In both cases, moreover, the father is a drunkard and good-for-nothing who affords no refuge to his daughter. The motif of sudden wealth erupting into a milieu of poverty, bringing results with which the characters cannot cope intellectually, underlines this relationship. It is a striking fact that O'Casey and Hauptmann in their different personal spheres should have taken up such similar human problems and should have given them so similar a dramatic form.

Emphasizing O'Casey's adherence to a literary tradition, however, in no way diminishes the originality of *Juno and the Paycock*. This originality is most obvious in three respects: O'Casey opened up the social sphere of the slums for modern drama, he projected his play onto the background of historical events, and he created the redeeming character of Juno. These elements ensure a high degree of individuality even in this, his most traditional play. To what extent O'Casey himself initiated a new literary tradition with this play is a question which will be discussed below.[32]

# 6. NANNIE'S NIGHT OUT

Looked at as a stage in O'Casey's development towards his masterpiece *The Plough and the Stars, Nannie's Night Out* is in no way comparable in importance to *Juno and the Paycock*. O'Casey's own deprecatory remarks show that it was merely a stop-gap between the two great plays. In a characteristic way, O'Casey projected his own attitude onto the audience of the first production; in the important chapter 'The Temple Entered' from *Inishfallen, Fare Thee Well* he devoted no more than half a sentence to it: 'Passing by his third play [actually it was his fourth produced play], a one-act work called *Nannie's Night Out*, a play no-one liked, except A.E., otherwise known as George Russell, who thought it O'Casey's best work; an opinion that didn't bother Sean, for he knew A.E. knew nothing about the drama, and felt it a little less . . .'[1] In reality the reception of the play, produced by the Abbey on September 29, 1924 (in a double bill with *Arms and the Man*) was less negative, yet it did not find sufficient interest to justify a revival.[2] Only in 1961 did O'Casey's growing reputation as a dramatist lead to another production and, two years later, to publication.[3] Like the three full-length plays of his first period *Nannie's Night Out* is set in the world of the Dublin tenements and contains figures and episodes from the author's own range of experience. In particular O'Casey made use of an event which later, in *Drums under the Windows*, is reworked much more impressively as the narrator's confrontation with 'Mild Millie'.[4]

The events in *Nannie's Night Out* belong to approximately the same period, too, as those in the other early Dublin plays. *Nannie's Night Out* is set at a time when the transition from the chaos of the 'Troubles' to a precarious normality has just taken place, i.e. a little later than *Kathleen Listens In*. In the 'Doyle' (Dáil Éireann, the Irish Parliament) the members quarrel over irrelevancies, the police can again occupy themselves with arresting drunkards, and when a gunman appears, he is not a rebel patriot but an ordinary robber. On the other hand the Gaelicization of Irish life has not yet been generally accepted, and the decisive problems of the country, external security, the North, and social grievances, are unsolved, as is shown in Joe's ironic remark: '. . . we have to put the army on a solid basis, an' then, th' Boundhary Question has to be settled too – in comparisement with things like them, a few cripples o' chiselurs [children] is neither here nor there' (p. 321). This context illuminates the provocative quality of Nannie's exclamation: 'Republicans an' Free Staters – a lot of rubbidge, th' whole o' yous! Th' poor Tommies was men!' (p. 314). In spite of such topical references, there is a decisive difference between *Nannie's Night Out* and the other early plays, inasmuch as the historical background here has no function for the stage action. *Nannie's Night Out* lacks the continuous interaction of background events and stage action which, in the full-length plays of this phase, results in numerous ironic contrasts and thus contributes to their complexity. The difference from *Kathleen Listens In* is even more decisive: in *Kathleen Listens In* the background events of the other plays, shorn of their individuality, have petrified into political allegory, while in *Nannie's Night Out* the individual events, detached from their political background appear – with the exception of a few moments – trite and superficial. Yet O'Casey's versatility as a dramatist is illustrated by the fact that even at such an early stage of his career he could employ such divergent dramatic forms.

Another difference from the rest of the O'Casey canon should be noted. Frequently the structure of his plays is dominated by an alternation of serious with comic or farcical scenes, a number of static farcical scenes being interpolated into a serious plot on which they then serve as an ironic commentary. In *Nannie's Night Out* this structure – for which *Juno and the Paycock* may be taken as an example – is reversed: a comic plot which occasionally turns into farce is interrupted by occasional serious scenes, without, however, there being anything more than a superficial connection between the two. This structure can probably be explained in the genesis of *Nannie's Night Out*. One of O'Casey's acquaintances from those years states: 'Dans la première ébauche, la pièce devait s'appeler *Les Amoureux de Pénélope*, et Nannie n'était qu'un personnage secondaire, fournissant un épisode comique.'[5] The earliest version of *Nannie's Night Out* was evidently therefore, a comic-farcical short play, not dissimilar from *A Pound on Demand* or *The End of the Beginning*. Its pseudo-mythological title shows the attempt to rouse interest in the new play from the success of *Juno and the Paycock*. The author must then, however, have found himself fascinated by the character who had burst into his play just as recklessly as she forces her way into the lower middle-class world in which the play is set. One can only suppose that eventually O'Casey realized that he could not do justice to this Irish Nannie in so short a scope, and that he hastily finished his play with the intention of returning to her more fully in a larger work. O'Casey's dissatisfaction with *Nannie's Night Out* is reflected in the fact that, at the instigation of the Abbey directors, he was prepared to write three different conclusions for the play. An interpretation of *Nannie's Night Out* will thus take account of four different factors: the basic comic-farcical structure, the serious interpolations, the divergent final scenes, and the future development of the character of Nannie.

The plot is based on a conventional comedy motif: three men, courting a lady, have to undergo various tests in which they fail and are consequently rejected. The comic element is strengthened, but also coarsened, by the fact that the three suitors, Oul Johnny, Oul Jimmy and Oul Joe, are over sixty and that their sweetheart, the widow Mrs. Pender who owns a small grocer's shop, is fifty years of age. Obviously the three men are looking for a refuge for the final years of their lives, yet they act the role of youthful lovers, dress up to a ridiculous degree, present bunches of flowers with roguish compliments, boast about their iron constitution, their courage and their undiminished agility. Put to the test, such pretensions are quickly reduced to a pitiful reality; these comic moments of disillusion are almost the only source of laughter aroused by the play. Johnny does not succeed in ejecting the beggar, Jimmy is so short-sighted that he does not discover his rival, and Joe has fallen while trying to jump off a tram. Mrs. Pender enjoys inventing further tests and has the three line up for gymnastic exercises. This suddenly turns into a serious trial, for, after the three of them have assured her of their courage and strength in the face of any burglar, even if he was armed, the surprising entrance of the gunman demands a sudden proof of their claims. All three of them fail miserably; only Mrs. Pender 'bars the way to the till' (p. 326). Nannie, who is drunk, then puts the gunman to flight without even realizing it, which renders the three protectors' failure even more ridiculous. Understandably Mrs. Pender then dismisses them. The farcical character of this scene is underlined by the trebling of the suitor figure, by O'Casey's choice of names, the black-and-white characterization, the dominance of physical over semantic comedy and by the static make-up of the scenes, none of which admits of any character development.[6] O'Casey does not demonstrate his comic inventiveness except for a few rare moments, for instance in Mrs. Pender's malapropism: 'A big fellow like you to be afraid of a poor oul' scrawl that was thin to th' point of emancipation' (p. 313).

Irish Nannie's explosive entrance into this conventional series of harmless scenes could be compared to the sudden emergence of the early O'Casey plays into the conventionalized world of the Abbey Theatre. In both cases, the existing scenario was simply thrust aside in the confrontation with so unusual, original and vital a phenomenon. Irish Nannie is able to impress her name on a play in which she makes very few appearances, just as the Abbey of the twenties became in literary history, through no more than three full-length plays, the theatre of Sean O'Casey.

When she first appears, Nannie has just been released from the 'Joy' (Mountjoy Prison) where she has done two months for assault on a policeman. According to conventional moral standards she is an outcast: when she is not in prison she drifts about without a regular abode, beats her crippled child, steals, breaks windows and gets drunk on 'spunk', cheap spirit which has ruined her health. Nevertheless O'Casey succeeds in awakening the audience's sympathies on her side. The question why this should be so is one of the most interesting points the play raises.

First, O'Casey makes it clear that Nannie is not free to control her own life. She is a victim of the circumstances into which she has been born. Hardly any other O'Casey character is determined to such an extent by social factors, although no more than a few details of her previous life are reported. She has spent her life in bitter poverty and has never known a home: 'When Nannie was a chiselur any oul' hall she could find was Nannie's home – afther gettin', maybe, a morguein' from her oul' wan' (p. 309). Later she spent years in caring for her crippled father, '. . . good money she earned for him, when it was to be got; an' bad money when there was nothin' else knockin' about' (p. 321). When she began to drink she was encouraged by others who found her wildness a source of amusement; finally society could defend itself against her only by sending her to prison. Nannie is completely uneducated; she has the instinctive feeling that there must be someone guilty for her situation, but she can identify him only in the visible manifestations of power and therefore attacks every policeman she meets. She is thus a personified accusation of the society that has driven her to her present state of degradation; she is an outcast not because she has chosen to leave human society but because she has been rejected by it. The second reason for the sympathies that Nannie arouses is her courage to live. In spite of her degradation, she is the personification of that unreserved acceptance of life which O'Casey ranks highest among the values by which his characters are to be judged and which he has frequently expressed in dance and song. Throughout the play Nannie's irrational joy in life is contrasted with the petty worries of the other characters: 'It's merriment Nannie wants ... singin' an' dancin' an' enjoyin' life ... What's the use o' bein' alive if you're not merry?' (p. 309). This unreflected affirmation, occasionally heightened into hysterical outbursts, is Nannie's only defence against impending death: 'I'll die game. [*Screaming*] I'll die game, I'll die game!' (p. 309). The two decisive lines from the song with which she accompanies all her entrances can therefore be referred back to her:

> Tho' she wears no fine clothes, nor no rich silken hose,
> Still there's something that makes her divine ... (p. 307).

Her whole behaviour and in particular the many implicit prophecies of her death make it dramatically necessary for Nannie to die at the end of the play. Only the moment of death can be an adequate test for the durability of her attitude to life. Again, only her death at the end of the play can turn her one and only night out, her night of freedom from prison, into a simile for her whole life.

O'Casey has taken up this very logical conclusion in one of the three endings he wrote for the play. Critics have differed on which was the original conclusion and which was the one demanded, and used, by the Abbey directors. Yet a glance at O'Casey's other plays shows that it would have been consistent for him to decide on the death of Nannie as the right ending for the play. O'Casey never evaded death on stage for fear of producing sentimental or melodramatic effects. It was difficult to convince him that in *Juno and the Paycock* the scene of Johnny's death should be eliminated, and in *The Plough and the Stars* (to take up only those plays next in time to *Nannie's Night Out*) he used the death of Bessie as the climax to the final act. In the second version[7] Nannie is overwhelmed off-stage by three policemen and taken back to prison; this conclusion places more weight on the comic action around Mrs. Pender, and hardly justifies the title. A third version which is supposed to have omitted the gunman episode and to have presented Nannie's fight with the policemen on stage,[8] has not been published. Although there is no conclusive evidence, it is probable that O'Casey's version ended with the

death of Nannie and that he altered this when asked by the
Abbey directors to do so after he had lost his real interest in this
play.[9] While the death-scene is more appropriate to the play and
agrees with O'Casey's preference for strong effects, the harmless
conclusion with Nannie's arrest is more in keeping with the type
of comic-farcical peasant-play written by George Shiels and
others which had become the standard fare at the Abbey after the
death of Synge.

The moment of Nannie's death is the most crucial test for her
attitude to life. She does not fail in this test; her final words betray
no deviation from the obstinate courage she has shown before:
'God'll not be too hard on poor Irish Nannie ... poor Irish Nannie
... Say a prayer, will you ... some o' yous ... Nannie's goin' ...
she's goin' ... She'll die game, she'll ... die ... game' (p. 328). Like
a child she speaks of herself in the third person and in this process
of distancing approves of her own life. On the one hand she is
certainly 'une incarnation vivante de la misère': 'objet de risée
dont nul ne se soucie, elle passe un instant sous nos yeux, atome
imperceptible de l'immense douleur humaine, déja marquée par
cette mort qu'elle craint et qui sera sa seule délivrance.'[10] But she
is also an embodiment of that invincible vitality which gives the
best among O'Casey's characters their resilience and which is the
basis for that mature optimism which in most of his plays shines
through the poverty and degradation of outer circumstances.

Another aspect of Nannie should be noted: she continually
speaks of herself as *Irish* Nannie. Like Kathleen in O'Casey's
preceding short-play, but with stronger roots in the reality of an
individual character, she takes on the features of a personification
of Ireland, a Cathleen ni Houlihan of the slums, dirty, ragged and
drunk, as a counter-image to that unreal vision who dominated
the romantic imaginings of the nationalists, but with the unbroken
courage which O'Casey always recognized and admired in his
country.[11] Nannie's frequent song of the 'oul fashion'd mother o'
mine' is certainly a reference to Ireland, and the Ballad Singer
makes this context even more explicit when he sings repeatedly:

> For Ireland is Ireland thro' joy an' thro' tears.
> Hope never dies thro' they long weary years.
> Each age has seen countless, brave hearts pass away,
> But their spirit still lives on in they men of to-day! (p. 305).

The last line is an example of O'Casey's double irony: on the one
hand there is the obvious contrast with the wretched cowardice
of the three suitors; on the other hand this 'spirit' really lives on

in Nannie, but it is the methylated spirit on which she has got drunk. Nevertheless this does not simply negate the affirmative content of the song. With characteristic ambivalence, O'Casey in the context of his play confirms the song's optimism even while treating it with irony.

The Ballad Singer who at the beginning is simply a half-comical, half pitiable figure from the slums, undergoes towards the end an alteration that is not entirely justified by the context but which points forward to later developments in O'Casey's plays. He takes on the function of a mouth-piece in a way characteristic of such figures as the Dreamer in *Within the Gates*, the Messenger in *Cock-a-doodle Dandy* and Father Boheroe in *The Bishop's Bonfire*. In the moving prayer, reminiscent of *Juno and the Paycock*, that he speaks at Nannie's death, he transcends for the first time the limitations of his own language, as these have become apparent in previous scenes:

May God look down on th' spirit of our poor sisther, that, feelin' th' wind, maybe got no message from it; that, lookin' up at th' sky, maybe seen no stars; that, lookin' down at th' earth, maybe, seen no flowers. Rememberin' th' bittherness of th' shocks her poor body got, may God give th' soul of our sisther th' sweetness of eternal rest! (p. 329)

In the sentences which follow, the author's indignation usurps the Ballad Singer's character altogether:

Yous gang o' hypocrites! What was it made Nannie what she was? Was it havin' too much money? Who gave a damn about her? It was only when she was dhrunk an' mad that anywan took any notice of her! What can th' like o' them do, only live any way they can? Th' Poorhouse, th' Prison an' th' morgue – them is our palaces! I suppose yous want us to sing 'Home Sweet Home,' about our tenements? D'ye think th' blasted kips o' tenement houses we live in'll breed Saints an' Scholars? . . . It's a long time, but th' day's comin' . . . th' day's comin' . . . Oh, it's cruel, it's cruel! (pp. 329-330).

This open expression of social criticism, unprepared for in the previous scenes, can only be directed at the audience, not at the other stage characters, among whom there is no one whose behaviour might justify such a reproach (up to this moment, the question of responsibility for Nannie's fate has not been raised at all). The explicit nature of this criticism points forward to the plays of O'Casey's third phase, especially *The Star Turns Red* and *Hall of Healing*, and the vague reference to 'th' day's comin' . . .' is a first allusion to the radical change of society which O'Casey projects in *Purple Dust*, *Red Roses for Me* and *The Star Turns Red*.

The Ballad Singer seems in this way to embody one general tendency of modern drama which O'Casey did *not* follow in his later plays. He stands on the verge of that chorus-cum-stage-manager figure who does not simply pronounce the author's opinion as a character within the dramatic context, but steps outside the stage events with the explicit task of reducing the distance between audience and play. It is easy to imagine a new version of *Nannie's Night Out* where the Ballad Singer would from the start take on such a chorus function, providing the audience with an inescapable perspective of social criticism. It is doubtful whether O'Casey in 1924 was aware of the full possibilities of this technique; but it is interesting to note that in his later plays he never again employs such a figure. Although richly inventive himself and keenly aware of dramatic innovations introduced by others, O'Casey has always insisted on a clear separation between stage and audience, considering the use of a chorus character through whom the author could supply his own interpretations as too easy a solution for the playwright's task.

In other respects, however, *Nannie's Night Out* does foreshadow later developments. Nannie shows a certain similarity to Bessie Burgess, who is equally vulgar and quarrelsome, but also just as admirable as Nannie and whose death is presented in a similar way. In several later plays, especially in *Red Roses for Me* and *Cock-a-doodle-Dandy*, the dance is used again as a symbol of the affirmation of life, and frequently O'Casey reverses the conventional order of values, insisting on the superiority of a character who seems to occupy the lowest rank in society. It is, however, in *Within the Gates* that these various elements coincide. When O'Casey declared in 1925: 'The Abbey Directors finally allowed the author to withdraw the work because he felt the character of Nannie deserved the richer picture of a three-act play',[12] there can be no doubt that this plan of a full-length play with the character of Nannie at its centre – modified in many ways – was finally to be realized in *Within the Gates*. Jannice, the Young Whore (in later versions Young Woman) in this play has had a similar fate to Nannie's. She too has grown up without parents, and circumstances – whose depressing influence is revealed just as graphically in the Down-and-Out as in the slum figures from *Nannie's Night Out* – have forced her into prostitution. Jannice is shown, like Nannie, as a young woman driven prematurely to the verge of death; both of them are threatened by a heart-attack to which both of them finally succumb. Both are explicitly cleared of any responsibility for their own fate. In spite of occasional hysterical fits of fear, both show a courage to live that in their situation is entirely admirable. Their affirmation of life in the face of death is expressed in almost identical words: Nannie's frequent exclamation 'I'll die game, I'll die game!' (p. 328) is echoed in Jannice's words 'I'll go, go game, and I'll die dancing!' Dance and song which in *Within the Gates* appear as ingredients of a developed O'Caseyan liturgy, are the vital elements of Nannie's night out with which she fills the few scenes of her life. Both of them are finally judged in the words of the Dreamer: 'You fought the good fight, Jannice; and you kept the faith . . .'

These similarities, however, do not conceal the considerable differences between the two plays which are not simply a matter of quality and length. The decade between the two plays saw the decisive change in O'Casey's career as a dramatist. The individual character of Nannie, full of vitality, who at most shows a few additional symbolic traits, turns into the every-woman Jannice; the specific atmosphere of the Dublin tenements is replaced by the everywhere-scape of a symbolic park; the intellectually complex, precisely manipulated search of modern man for God and the right life is substituted for Nannie's impulsive immediacy. It is this opportunity to observe the change in O'Casey's style from a presentation of immediate reality to an interpretation of life which above all justifies a continued interest in *Nannie's Night Out.*

# 7. THE PLOUGH AND THE STARS

When *The Plough and the Stars* was first produced by the Abbey Theatre on 8 February, 1926, the Easter Rising, and with it the spectacular beginning of the Irish struggle for independence in the twentieth century, was not more than ten years past. The War of Independence, the Treaty and the ensuing bitter Civil War were vivid in the memory of every Irishman. At this time a play dealing with the Easter Rising and using the flag of the Irish Citizen Army in its title could be expected to have the qualities of a national drama, glorifying the insurgents, and especially those who died, without attention to psychological detail and celebrating in their sacrifice the rebirth of a nation oppressed for almost eight centuries. It is, therefore, not surprising that the first performance stirred up one of the greatest theatrical riots in Ireland's history, comparable only to those which followed the production of *The Playboy of the Western World*,[1] for *The Plough and the Stars* is a national drama with reversed premises, a national drama from the perspective of the slums. Even before the première, the play had caused conflicts in the Abbey company, themselves intensified through personal disagreements with O'Casey.[2] The protests against the production, led by participants in the Easter Rising and by relatives of its victims, but also by vociferous neo-patriots and advocates of cultural isolation in Ireland, had far-reaching consequences. For a while, they threatened the very existence of the Abbey Theatre, as well as initiating an extensive press-campaign against O'Casey which was the main reason for his eventually moving to England, this being, perhaps, the most important event in the history of Anglo-Irish drama since Synge's return from Paris.

Over the years, the general attitude towards *The Plough and the Stars* has changed. Even in Ireland, it has been accepted that few other works can compete with this play for the status of the most important twentieth-century drama in English. It became one of the most frequently performed plays in the country, and in 1966, at the time of the celebrations for the fiftieth anniversary of the Easter Rising, the new Abbey was opened with a production of *The Plough and the Stars*. The play's popularity in all English-speaking countries is confirmed by the numerous editions that followed the first publication, until it was republished with minor revisions[3] in the *Collected Plays*. It has also found a firm position in the theatrical repertoire of many countries. Dramatic critics have documented their interest in the play in a number of extensive interpretations. An unusual indication of the play's popularity is the fact that Denis Johnston could call his own, quite different play on the Easter Rising *The Scythe and the Sunset*, knowing full well that everybody would understand the satiric reference to O'Casey.

As in his previous plays, O'Casey in *The Plough and the Stars* makes use of numerous personal experiences. Early reviews of the play have admired 'the astonishing accuracy of his photographic detail'.[4] The play is set in the world of the tenements; all the characters (with the exception of the Woman who appears in one episode) belong to this milieu, and many of them apparently had definite models in O'Casey's surroundings.[5] O'Casey was also emotionally involved in the Easter Rising and the preceding events.[6] He was secretary of the Irish Citizen Army, founded in 1913 during the great Dublin strike and lockout, and wrote its history, published in 1919, in a version considerably cut by the British censor. In *Drums under the Windows* he gives a moving account of the moment when the flag of this organisation was unfurled for the first time.[7] It is true that, in 1916, following disagreements with the leaders of the Citizen Army, he was no longer a member and therefore did not take part in the insurrection, but he was an eye witness of the fighting and of the widespread looting, he was (by his own account) several times in acute danger of his life and, like the survivors in his play, he was imprisoned in a church. The historical and autobiographical references must have appeared to his contemporaries as the centre of the play, and any impression of factual misrepresentation they conveyed was taken as a ground for justifiable protest. Today, however, they appear more and more marginal. At a greater remove from the actual events it is easier to see that O'Casey provides a valid, realistic and objective representation of a revolutionary situation which, after changing a few details, might be transferred to other countries and periods. The historical events themselves diminish in importance compared to the behaviour of the people who are confronted with them, and they will for this reason be left aside in the following discussion.

★

The unusual structure of the play has contributed considerably to its impact. It has been compared to the plays of Chekhov as well as to individual plays by Gorki, Shaw, Odets, Rice and others.[8] The dominant feature of this Chekhovian structure is the fact that the action does not, as in traditional drama, progress as a conflict between protagonist and antagonist through protasis, epitasis and catastasis to the final catastrophe. Instead of one hero there is a group of central characters who initiate a number of equally important actions. These present divergent aspects of the same theme and at the end converge in a synthesis from which the play's central theme emerges. The play's impact is thus intensified, with several characters arriving by different ways at the same goal; the defeat of a whole group of people underlines its universality, whereas the defeat of an individual can easily turn him into an outsider. In this type of play, the attention of the audience must be directed equally to all the characters – an important prerequisite for a production, where the usual distinction between character actors and supporting parts has to be avoided. The various lines of action are skilfully interwoven, intensifying each other and serving as ironic commentary on each other. In addition, they are projected on to a line of background events running parallel to the stage action, thus producing an extremely complex structure which becomes even more involved through the alternation of ensemble-scenes and 'duets'.

It is doubtful whether this structural scheme can be applied in the same way to O'Casey's other plays, the more so when its application results in his being criticized for not having used it to equal effect in all his works.[9] It can, however, contribute considerably to a better understanding of *The Plough and the Stars*. It is difficult to say to what degree O'Casey was influenced in this structure by other dramatists. In an article published in 1943, he called Chekhov 'One of the World's Dramatists' and affirmed that he had been acquainted with his works for thirty years.[10] It is not impossible, therefore, that O'Casey, consciously or subconsciously, used Chekhov's works, especially *The Three Sisters*, as models for the structure of *The Plough and the Stars*.

Whatever the case may be, O'Casey's mastery of complex techniques in this play remains undisputed. Critics have sometimes been unable to follow him in the peculiar intricacy of his structure. They have, for instance, presented Fluther, Nora, Rosie and the Covey by turns as the central character or even as the author's mouthpiece.[11] In reality, *The Plough and the Stars* contains nine central characters of equal importance (Jack, Nora,

Peter, the Covey, Bessie, Mrs. Gogan, Mollser, Fluther and Brennan), all of whom demand equal attention and none of whom, on his own, presents the author's opinions.[12] Each of them undergoes a certain development in a separate line of action which in each case ends in Act IV when Jack, Bessie and Mollser are dead, Nora has fallen victim to insanity, Brennan, Fluther, Peter and the Covey are led away into imprisonment and Mrs. Gogan is overcome by the death of her daughter. These lines of action are held together by the background events, which reflect the progression of the uprising: in Act I, preparations for the rebellion are hinted at, the mass-meeting of Act II openly propagates an insurrection, Act III takes place at the height of the fighting, defeat emerging as imminent, and Act IV shows the suppression of the rebellion. All the stage characters are decisively affected by these events. Additionally, there is a direct connexion between the stage characters as a group and the political-military happenings. The insurgents' temporary control of parts of the city has its parallel in the stage action: By analogy to the British control of the city before the rebellion, the characters in Act I are confined to the narrow sphere of their tenements; in the pub-scene and mass-meeting of Act II they push beyond this sphere, in Act III they find themselves driven back to the street in the slums which they can only leave in danger of their lives, and in Act IV they have been expelled from their flats, huddle together in the narrowest room of the house and eventually are turned out even from there, while British soldiers re-enact the occupation of the city in the requisitioning of the room. This 'suggestive use of dramatic space . . . is one of the central symbols in the play.'[13] The stage accordingly becomes a mirror of the background events, but these are frequently seen as in a tarnished and distorting glass.

The interaction between the events of the rebellion and the fate of the stage characters induces a scepticism in the spectator towards any pretension that cannot be verified precisely. He becomes particularly suspicious of the alleged heroism and unselfishness of the insurgents. When the stage actions are dominated by envy, hatred, mockery, folly, egotism and cowardice, the rebellion mirrored in them is put in a dubious light. In many cases, stage actions serve as ironic commentary on the larger battle in the background. When in Act I the ridiculous Peter runs around in his shirt, cannot fasten his collar, and eventually appears in his dress-uniform with his over-long sword with which he cannot even ward off the Covey, then the attitude of the

patriots who gather in uniform to take an oath for the liberation
of Ireland is made to look distinctly questionable. Similarly, the
fighting itself is qualified ironically. While in the background the
rebellion is being prepared and is taking place, fighting breaks
out on the stage, too, but this takes the form of vulgar, unmotivated
and senseless brawls. Again, the insurgents' intentions are made
to appear doubtful. Yet this is not the only effect of the analogy
between background events and stage action; for at the moment
when it becomes clear that the insurgents, despite previous
qualifications, are ready to make genuine sacrifices, this is seen
to reflect back on the stage characters who in their turn now
begin appear doubtful. If the insurgents' alleged idealism is
questioned in the course of the play, the stage characters' alleged
realism is questioned none the less. It is not true that O'Casey, as
has sometimes been suggested, intends to portray the superiority
of a realistic, materialistic attitude.[14] He presents the tension
between idealism and realism, expressed even in the title of the
play: the flag of the Irish Citizen Army, which depicts the
constellation of the plough projected onto an actual, if stylized
plough, incorporates the dominating contrast of the play.[15]
O'Casey forces his audiences into renewed reflection on the
relation between these two basic attitudes, and he makes it
evident that neither, in its pure form, is possible nor even
desirable. The complete interpenetration of ideal and material
motives in human action is thus one of the important insights
attained to in *The Plough and the Stars*. The relationship between
these elements will be discussed here in three stages: at first
according to the progression of the acts, then by observing a key-
scene, finally in a survey of the characters and their scale of values.
The formal approach – the reciprocal relationship between stage
actions and background events – may thus be seen to lead directly
into the thematic centre of the play.

*

In Act I the political events are at first kept in the background,
and the stage action can therefore begin relatively peacefully.
The play starts with two people (Fluther and Mrs. Gogan)
understanding each other – a rare situation in the world of this
drama. It is true that there is an initial quarrel between Peter and
the Covey, but neither of them takes this quite seriously; it is
essentially a comedy-scene, permitting the audience to laugh
freely. The preparations for the insurrection are intimated in the

workers' departure for the patriotic demonstration, observed by Mrs. Gogan, but with the exception of the Covey, who significantly comes off work before his time, none of the characters is concerned with this. The first part of Act I thus portrays the deceptive leisure-time atmosphere in a worker's home, beset with lower middle-class ambitions and disturbed occasionally by petty quarrels. The relationship between Jack and Nora even shows signs of becoming idyllic. The incursion of the military happens then quite suddenly, with the entrance of Brennan in uniform. Here the destructive effect of the rebellion is anticipated in the private sphere: not only does Jack leave his wife to take up his new post, but suspicion has been roused between them when it turns out that Nora has burnt the letter in which Jack's promotion had been announced. Nora's sentence 'I don't care if you never come back!' (p. 190) hints at future events, but at the same time characteristically misrepresents her own attitude ('I don't care . . .'). At this point, the proceedings at the beginnings of the Act take on a new meaning. There, Mrs. Gogan had talked about Jack's military ambitions, saying of his new belt: 'God, I think he used to bring it to bed with him!' (p. 166). This ostensibly funny remark can now be seen as revealing the compensational function of Jack's role as an officer, thus pointing forward to the destruction of his marriage. An ironic light is cast on him, too, by the foregoing entrances of Peter, whose ridiculous, bombastic uniform reflects his ridiculous political views. Jack in this Act is not given a chance to prove in what way he differs from Peter, whose firmly established comic character is thus in part transferred to him. The imminent uprising is thus shown in an almost exclusively negative light. It arouses peoples' vanity, creates selfishness and suspicion, destroys human relations and, in the loneliness of Mollser whose mother takes part in the demonstration, leads to the isolation of those who most need companionship.

In the light of the parallelism between individual actions and background events, the community of the tenements can be seen, even in the first Act, to take on symbolic traits. Against an acoustic background of anti-British demonstrations and of Irish troops marching off to battle in Flanders, the tenements appear as a microcosm of Ireland in 1915. The braggart patriot Peter, the hot-tempered, thoughtless and conceited revolutionary Jack, the Covey who, as a socialist, rejects any national conflict, Fluther who is interested in politics and religion only as the subject of occasional quarrels, the Protestant unionist Bessie, Nora striving for social advancement, the naive Mrs. Gogan who is untroubled by all problems, and Mollser as the passive victim of social injustices, represent as a group the manifold and involved attitudes immediately before the Rising, and one should add that O'Casey not only reflects the situation in Ireland but gives a typical impression of human attitudes, weaknesses and merits immediately before an event that will later on be presented by the opposing factions as unmistakeably 'good' or unmistakeably 'evil'.

The second Act originally formed an independent short play with the ironic title *The Cooing of the Doves* which was rejected by the Abbey Theatre and was then integrated by O'Casey, with some minor alterations,[16] into his new play. In this Act, O'Casey takes the daring step of incorporating passages from the speeches of Pádraic Pearse into his text[17] and confronting them with the attitudes of everyday people. Pearse is the type of fanatic idealist, ready to sacrifice himself and entirely untouched by everyday reality; these typical traits are underlined by the fact that his name is not mentioned and his features are not seen. The Speaker represents one extreme of current attitudes to the Rising, the other is embodied in the inhabitants of the tenements, each of whom is in this Act directly concerned by the political events, but in a different way than the Speaker supposes. Rosie the prostitute complains of business being slack because of the demonstration ('They're all thinkin' of higher things than a girl's garthers' [p. 193]), and the Barman, too, suffers financial loss. Peter and Fluther are not entirely unimpressed by the meeting, but their patriotism finds expression in empty words and gestures ('I was burnin' to dhraw me sword, an' wave an' wave it over me—', as Peter explains [p. 195]), and the only marked effect of the political agitation is their thirst that several times during the meeting drives them into the pub. The Speaker prepares his audience for battle as a religious experience with clear parallels to the Passion, when he transfers the situation of the World War to Ireland:

The old heart of the earth needed to be warmed with the red wine of the battlefields . . . Such august homage was never offered to God as this: the homage of millions of lives given gladly for love of country. And we must be ready to pour out the same red wine in the same glorious sacrifice, for without shedding of blood there is no redemption! (p. 196)

In analogy to these preparations for battle, the stage becomes a battlefield, too, but for reasons entirely trite and egotistical,

when Mrs. Gogan finds her matrimonial virtue doubted, or Rosie
is offended because she has been addressed by her professional
title.

The behaviour of the stage characters thus offers a graphic
commentary on the words of the Speaker, showing how everyday
people react to his idealistic visions. The Speaker manifestly
misjudges or ignores human nature. The tenement people prefer
to drink their beer, to help Rosie to some income or to carry on
their daily quarrels, instead of fighting for the abstract idea of
national liberation. The Speaker's ideals are neither criticized
nor ridiculed by this contrast,[18] but the chances of their realization
become ever more doubtful. The insurgents, who have taken an
oath to fight, are at the centre of this conflict between ideal and
reality. At the end of the Act, the three officers Jack, Brennan and
Langon swear a triple oath which serves as a premonition of
future events:

CAPT. BRENNAN [*catching up The Plough and the Stars*]. Imprisonment
   for th' Independence of Ireland!
LIEUT. LANGON [*catching up the Tri-colour*]. Wounds for th' Indepen-
   dence of Ireland!
CLITHEROE. Death for th' Independence of Ireland!
THE THREE [*together*]. So help us God (pp. 213-214).

Their behaviour illustrates the confusion of their intentions: the
ensuing stage direction says: '*They drink*' (p. 214). The pub
setting ironically qualifies their idealism which, according to the
Speaker, should be free of all material and personal interest.

The stage actions of Act II have already intimated what the
reality of the allegedly holy and purifying war will be like: dirty,
painful and cruel with an admixture of the comic. The realities of
the fighting form the background events of Act III. Just as in
battle petty differences are forgotten in view of a common
enemy, so here there is an unusual degree of solidarity among
the stage characters. Mrs. Gogan looks after Mollser, Bessie
brings her some milk, Fluther finds Nora after her senseless
search for her husband, Peter and the Covey manage a better sort
of understanding than before, and even Bessie and Mrs. Gogan
set their differences aside in view of a common task, but this task
is not national liberation but the looting of shops. The episode of
the frightened Woman shows how far the fighting has spread
and that its effects are no longer limited to the slum people.[19]
With the appearance of the three officers, the background events
are projected onto the stage, and Langon's wound is a visible

expression of the reality of war in contrast to the religious passion proclaimed by the Speaker. This contrast is underlined by the fact that the officers have to fight off not English soldiers but Irish looters and that Jack even has to liberate himself from the embraces of his own wife. After Brennan, Nora then becomes the second visible victim of the fighting; towards the end of the Act, as at its beginning, her egotistical attitude makes demands on the helpfulness of her neighbours and is criticized through this as endangering others.

Act IV takes place at a time when the insurgents have been crowded together in a few buildings and their capitulation is imminent. In analogy to this, the stage characters have left their flats, seeking refuge in Bessie's shabby room. Meanwhile the fighting has demanded further victims: Mollser has died, Nora helplessly screams for her dead child and can prepare for the idyll of domestic happiness only in a state of insanity, while Brennan has already brought back the news of Jack's death. Nora's confusion mirrors the situation outside: the world is in a stage of chaos. Finally the men, like the insurgents, are led away into imprisonment, while the British soldiers occupy the house as well as the city. Their conquest, however, is less than impressive: a pot of tea is all they have captured, and during their search for the last snipers they mistakenly shoot Bessie, who is on their own side. This, again, is a symbolic action, suggesting the grave errors of the British leaders during and after the Rising. The ending of the play is marked once more by that type of authorial irony which appears at various places in the play and, being applied equally to all sides, makes for the play's objectivity: with the sky reddened by burning houses, the British troops sing the sentimental soldiers' song 'Keep the home fires burning' (p. 261).

*

This survey of the relationship between stage actions and background events can be complemented by an interpretation of an individual scene. Particularly suitable for such a purpose is the scene where military events overflow onto the stage itself. In Act II Jack and Brennan appear with the wounded Langon whom they are carrying away from the battle-zone. Nora rushes from the house, clings to her husband and tries to keep him back. He has to use violence to separate himself from her, and she falls down unconscious as the officers drag themselves on.

This scene is significant in four respects: (1) It elucidates the actual battle situation, operating much more effectively than the reports previously given by other characters. Where the Speaker in Act II had called for a sacred willingness in the face of death, here we are shown the other side of the coin: death for one's country loses much of its romantic aura when it is preceded by a wound such as Langon has received.

(2) The scene serves as a contrast to the preceding and the ensuing episodes. Immediately prior to the scene in question, Bessie and Mrs. Gogan have demonstrated *their* version of the war when they appear with looted plunder that will in future uselessly encumber their cramped dwellings. Immediately afterwards, Fluther enters in a state of complete intoxication, having broken into a pub. O'Casey thus dares to present in close juxtaposition the contrasting extremes of his drama, inevitably running the risk that one side or the other will be depreciated, but doing so with triumphant skill. It is one of the most impressive documents of the maturity of his art that he can preserve his objectivity even in a situation which would have led almost any other dramatist into an accusation either of the soldiers or of the looters. O'Casey's sequence illustrates the various aspects of war without condemning any of them.

(3) The scene is to be seen in connection with a number of others to which it either refers back or points forward. It repeats the situation in Act I where the appearance of Brennan (placed in a similar position towards the end of the Act) had led to an earlier separation of Jack and Nora – in neither case, it may be noted, is Brennan reproached for it. This repetition enhances one's impression of Nora's egotism. If the burning of the letter can be excused as an understandable endeavour to keep her husband for herself, in Act III Jack's most pressing task is immediately and concretely visible in the person of his wounded comrade. If Jack had given in to Nora's demand, he would have betrayed not only his political aims, and his fellow officers into the bargain, but he would have evaded his basic human responsibility to help those who most need assistance. Shortly before the ending of Act II the three officers had also appeared. There they had shown that they had overcome their hostility to each other (as members of two rival organisations, and, in Jack and Brennan's case, as rivals both for the favour of Nora and for the rank of captain), and they had promised in surprising unanimity to accept imprisonment, wounds and death for the liberation of Ireland. Their scene in Act III makes clear for the first time that they have not tried to evade the consequences of their vow. The dramatic prophecy of Act II is

thus confirmed, and after Langon's prophetic oath has been fulfilled, the audience will expect imprisonment for Brennan and death for Jack. The line of development ends in Act IV, where Brennan brings the news of Jack's death and is himself led into captivity.

(4) The scene under discussion contributes considerably to the characterization of the figures involved in it, at the same time clarifying O'Casey's own attitude. It is remarkable that the officers are not shown in a more questionable light. Langon understandably insists on being taken to a doctor. Brennan in this situation proves remarkably understanding of the situation of Jack and Nora; when he finally insists on going on, it is merely to find help for Langon. Jack's attitude is less clear-cut. He is more considerate than Brennan, who asks him to shoot at the looters while Jack fires over their heads. His happiness at meeting Nora is as genuine as his desire to stay with her, while at the same time he sees the necessity of leaving her again for the sake of Langon. Such a potentially 'heroic' attitude is, however, undermined by his fear of losing prestige. His exclamation, 'Now, for God's sake, Nora, don't make a scene' (p. 232), tarnishes the image of a soldier who, in the conflict between love and duty, decides for duty, but by the same token it makes Jack more credible as a human being. Nora on her part is unable even to realize the existence of such a conflict. She is dominated by a single thought, her desire to recreate the past idyll, to ignore the world, to render the events of the past few days undone. Whatever one's personal reaction to such an attitude may be, it does not enable Nora to continue existing in this world; she evades the world by going mad, this being the only way in which she can reconstruct the past from its fragments. Bessie, too, has a share in this scene. If the officers were never in any doubt about the reasons for their fighting, Bessie had never understood them. She can therefore rejoice at their retreat. That even she is not exclusively right, becomes apparent, however, in her triumphant exclamation 'Runnin' from th' Tommies . . .' (p. 235), for, as is shown later on, Jack and Brennan do not hide but return to their posts. Her repeated phrase 'Choke th' chicken . . .' (a reference, literally, to Brennan's job as a chicken butcher) turns her into a weird figure, predicting with demonic intensity the disaster in which she will herself be implicated.

This scene shows more clearly than any other that the Rising is not a farce, that the insurgents are suffering, that they have to undergo conflicts and that they emerge from them neither as

mere braggarts, nor as cowards, nor as fanatics inspired only by
blind hatred. It becomes explicit here that O'Casey does not see
his work as a one-sided criticism of the Easter Rising. Critics'
comments like 'In "The Plough and the Stars" he implies that the
men of 1916 were cowardly . . .',[20] or that the insurgents were
'sunshine soldiers who lack the stamina and courage to carry the
colors to the front'[21] miss the complexity of characterization in
this play. O'Casey himself several times rejected such remarks
and even insisted that 'There isn't a coward in the play.' Addres-
sing Mrs. Sheehy-Skeffington, the leader of the demonstrations
against the play, he gave examples for this assertion:

Clitheroe falls in the fight. Does Mrs. Skeffington want him to do any
more? Brennan leaves the burning building when he can do nothing
else: is she going to persist in her declaration that no man will try to leap
away from a falling building? . . . Langon, wounded in the belly, moans
for surgical aid. Does she want me to make him gather a handful of his
blood and murmur, 'Thank God that this has been shed for Ireland'? I'm
sorry, but I can't do this sort of thing.[22]

O'Casey was even prepared to excuse the insurgents' vanity:
'There was a dire sparkle of vanity lighting this little group
of armed men . . . But it was a vanity that none could challenge,
for it came from a group that was willing to sprinkle itself into
oblivion that a change might be born in the long-settled thought
of the people.'[23] It is, therefore, a simplification to say that in *The
Plough and the Stars* O'Casey takes the side of the ordinary
people against those responsible for the Rising. The dramatist
does, as we have seen, reveal personal ambitions and pretensions
in the insurgents, he shows that their patriotic aims are inextricably interwoven with private motives, but he does not reject their
aims *in toto*. He does not pass any judgement, but shows a group
of people exposed to an extreme crisis who – as in *Juno and the
Paycock* but now under even harder conditions – have to prove
themselves. Their behaviour makes it possible to judge their
human qualities and renders explicit the scale of human values
in *The Plough and the Stars*.

*

All the characters have in common certain illusions, self-
deceptions and unrealizable hopes with the help of which they
try to cope with life: 'Each of the characters is lost in a private
dream of self-importance, but each lacks a definite, effective,

relationship with his world.'[24] These illusions are shown to dissolve in the course of the play, just as the illusion of a successful rebellion against British dominion in Ireland is shown to dissolve – and in this two-fold dissolution lies the final and most important function of the parallel between stage action and background events. The comic effects, pervading the play, reflect the same dichotomy. Desmond MacCarthy wrote in the *New Statesman* that

. . . his effects are chiefly based upon the contrast between the shining qualities which the characters attribute to themselves and their actual behaviour, between the romantic world within them and the grimy world without. The exhilaration and the sardonic fun springs from the indomitable, heroic obstinacy with which they insist that the inner dream is true, in spite of their pretensions and idealism collapsing every moment at the prick of fact. While relishing enormously such humiliations in the case of others, they one and all ignore them in their own.[25]

Each of the figures in the play is characterized by some specific behaviour. Nora, at the beginning of the play, has Fluther fix a new lock on her door, symbolizing the exclusiveness of the relationship with Jack that she has been trying to achieve. She believes in a life of artificial isolation, unsoiled by reality. The fragility of this illusion is demonstrated before she has even appeared on the stage: Mrs. Gogan and Bessie enter her little world without difficulty, Peter and the Covey quarrel in it, Mrs. Gogan is informed exactly about the problems of her marriage, and, later on, Brennan's knocking on the door suffices to destroy her refuge for ever. Nora, her painfully helpless actions regularly resulting in the opposite, tries again and again to preserve her idyll: when she burns the letter, when she searches for Jack behind the barricades, when she desperately tries to restrain him by force, she becomes always more estranged from her husband than before. Nora has something of Juno's egotism without sharing her newly-won insight into the necessity of human solidarity. During the whole play, she does not make a single gesture for anyone else except for Jack: 'What do I care for th' others? I can think only of me own self' (p. 220). The moment Jack is no longer there, her world breaks up, she goes mad. When towards the end she is for once urgently asked to help another person, she uncomprehendingly shouts for Jack and shrinks back from the dying Bessie. It is hardly possible, therefore, to conceive of Nora's fate as a 'tragedy', as some critics have called it.

Jack's characteristic quality is his vanity. In Act I (after references have already been made to his fetishism concerning his uniform) he decides to take part in the demonstration only after news has come of his promotion. Yet, in contrast to Nora, he accepts the consequences of his belief in himself as a heroic leader, although he is offered a plausible excuse for desertion. Nora is certainly right when she sees that he, like all the soldiers, is afraid, but this in no way reduces his moral stature – O'Casey is even on record as saying that the insurgents' resistance in a hopeless situation would have been unremarkable if they had not been afraid.[26] Nora's report of the rebels' fear (pp. 221-222), often taken as proof of O'Casey's criticism of them,[27] is nothing more than a description, slightly distorted by Nora's hysteria, of the real situation, without inherent authorial comment. The rebels' worth is reinstated precisely in the fact that they are shown not to have been supermen. If Jack goes into battle for largely egotistical motives, he acts consistently and has the courage not to give in to his fear. Brennan is a similar case. He leaves the Imperial Hotel only when it cannot be defended any longer. It is hardly just to criticize him for not being able to carry the dying Jack out of the collapsing building, especially after he has previously saved Langon, and it would be equally unjust to condemn him for his attempt to escape imprisonment in civilian clothes. His position is weakened when he clings to clichés even after the general collapse and after he has experienced the reality of war: 'Mrs. Clitheroe's grief will be a joy when she realizes that she has had a hero for a husband' (p. 244). Such a notion is reduced to absurdity by the appearance of the demented Nora.

Peter, who looks like 'somethin' you'd pick off a Christmas Tree' (p. 166), is a counter-image to Jack and Brennan. In him, the officers' vanity is exaggerated without being supplemented by their willingness to earn their reputation in action. When, at the very beginning of the play, he sets about with fanatical intensity to dress himself in his gala uniform, he is immediately identifiable as a farcical character. He is the person who attracts least sympathy in this play; whenever he arouses laughter, it springs from criticism rather than from identification or understanding, as is the case with Fluther. His illusion of exemplary patriotism is transparent right from the start. Only occasionally does he show some timid human traits, when, for instance, he clumsily tries to console Nora (pp. 221, 245). But it is much more in character that he is repeatedly compared to a child. In Act I, Nora sends him off to the demonstration like a little boy: 'S-s-sh. Now, your hat's on, your house is thatched; off you pop!' (p. 183); in Act III Mrs.

Gogan offers him to 'Get up in th' prambulator an' we'll wheel you down' (p. 228). With childish stubbornness he clings to his illusion and cannot prove himself in any real situation because he is incapable of discerning any situation as real.

The Covey is his partner in numerous quarrels. His cherished illusion is his belief in his role as a preacher of world-improving theories, drawn from a single tract that he constantly quotes. Although he wants to change the world, there is a great gap between his self-appraisal and his behaviour. He wants to create new human relationships and addresses others as 'comrade', but he is unable to establish ordinary human contacts: he does not know how to behave in Nora's flat, with Peter he lives in a state of permanent civil war, and he can keep off Rosie only by being rude to her. The essence of his character is revealed in two places. When Bessie brings the news of the lootings, his reproach, in spite of his proclaimed ideals of working-class solidarity, is merely private: 'Th' selfishness of that one – she waited till she got all she could carry before she'd come to tell anyone!' (p. 225). Then he himself sets off to take part in the looting. Even more explicit is his reaction to Brennan when the officer wants to hide in Bessie's room: 'There's no place here to lie low. Th' Tommies'll be hoppin' in here, any minute!' (p. 247). Significantly, he here drops the term 'comrade'; in contrast to Jack and Brennan, personal security ranks for the Covey above the human solidarity he so often propagates. He is distinguished from Peter by the comparative reasonableness of his views, but like Peter he is not prepared to live by his own ideals and reduces them thereby to the status of illusions.

A special position is taken by Mrs. Gogan who is something of an exception to the thematic patterns discussed above. It is true that she, the gossip-monger *par excellence*, holds a particularly glaring illusion about herself: 'Cissie Gogan's a woman livin' for nigh on twenty-five years in her own room, an' beyond biddin' th' time o' day to her neighbours, never yet as much as nodded her head in th' direction of other people's business . . .' (p. 202). But this illusion does not serve as a test for her character; it is employed by the dramatist to establish contact between the stage action and the audience. Through her curiosity and her inability to keep anything to herself she becomes the ideal intermediary, supplying a wealth of information to the audience without disturbing the credibility of the play's structure. At the beginning of Act I and again at the beginning of Act III (which takes place a few months later) it is she who is mainly employed for expositional purposes, vitally important in a play with nine lines of action as well as an additional sequence of background events. As the most neutral character, she is at the end the only figure to remain unscathed, although ironically she has talked more than any of the others about death. She takes care of Nora and thus ensures the continuity of a human solidarity that has in this play proved at the most critical moments to be of decisive importance. It is Mrs. Gogan, too, who helps Mollser to cling for a short while to the life-preserving illusion that she will recover from her illness. This, however, is the most hopeless of all hopes, and Mollser, accordingly, dies early in the play. O'Casey, who was to return to the figure of Mollser in another context,[28] saw in her the victim of social conditions which in his eyes demanded just as much resistance as did the political dominion by a foreign nation.

Two characters, Bessie and Fluther, stand out from the others in their relative lack of illusion about themselves and their consequent ability to master life better than their fellows. Bessie's illusion is her belief that she is superior to others because she leads a virtuous life. The audience quickly realises that this pretension, considered by conventional moral standards, is false. Not only is she forever getting drunk; she forcibly enters Nora's flat, provokes others to the point of violence, takes part in the looting and can still talk pompously about justice and her Christian conscience (p. 229). She is, however, always ready when people need her assistance, and she never puts her readiness to help on show: '*When they have gone in, she gives a mug of milk to Mollser silently*' (p. 222). It is from others that the audience hears that this was no exception (p. 215). Thus it is understandable that the dying Mollser does not call for her mother but for Bessie (p. 224). It is she, too, who helps Nora (whom she despises) into the house when Jack has left her (p. 237), who fetches a doctor for her in spite of the street-fighting (p. 238), who looks after her for three nights (p. 241) and whose death is the direct result of trying to keep Nora back from the window. The death of Bessie is not a conscious gesture of heroic sacrifice; she instinctively does what is necessary at the right moment, and O'Casey avoids any false heroism when he has her abuse Nora with her dying breath. This is one of those small indications of O'Casey's maturity as an artist. Many another dramatist would have turned the scene into a sentimental display of harmony, supplying the dying Bessie with words of understanding and forgiveness for Nora, perhaps even with the wish that she might become happy again in spite of everything. O'Casey's Bessie, with words like 'you bitch', 'blast you', 'you jade' (p. 258), remains instead true to the form she has had since the beginning of the play. This, of course, implies that even at the beginning she would have been ready for this kind of sacrifice without regard to her personal feelings. Her behaviour in this ultimate crisis is an expression of an attitude to life which under the existing conditions deserves admiration.

Fluther (whose family name is 'Good'), is told by Nora: 'You're a whole man' (p. 177). Such a 'whole man' is here distinguished in three respects: whatever he does, he does thoroughly; at the decisive moment he chooses instinctively the right action; and in spite of all personal weaknesses he shows courage and willingness to help when it is most essential. Fluther is the only one among the characters whom one can observe at work, when he fixes a new lock to the door, and his delight in this task (confirmed in a characteristic comparison: 'Openin' an' shuttin' now with a well-mannered motion, like a door of a select bar in a high-class pub' [p. 177]), distinguishes him from the start. Fluther repeatedly demonstrates his fitness for life: in Act I he tames the quarrelsome Bessie; in Act II he intimidates the Covey and knows how to cope with Rosie; and even when he gets drunk, he does so thoroughly: '. . . *down the street is heard a wild, drunken yell; it comes nearer, and Fluther enters, frenzied, wild-eyed, mad, roaring drunk*' (p. 237). His (relatively harmless) illusion is the hope of eventually giving up the drink. The audience can directly watch the futility of this hope, for after every promise of this kind he can be seen drinking. Yet, in contrast to Peter, the Covey and Nora, his illusion does not reduce his courage and willingness to help, nor does it undermine his instinctively appropriate behaviour in critical situations. When the British soldiers enter, it is he who interrupts the futile quarrel over Brennan's presence, takes up the cards, includes the officer on the run in the game and thus prevents his being discovered. Immediately afterwards he proves his courage when he comes to the rebels' defence without regard to his own security. Next to Bessie, it is Fluther who provides most assistance to others: he courageously fetches Nora from the futile search for her husband, and later he organizes the funeral for Mollser when her own relatives are too timid to do so. It would, of course, be a mistake to see in Fluther a hero-figure in the conventional sense. He is a braggart like the Covey who frequently does not quite realize the motives for his actions and who cannot endure being put in the wrong. Yet under the given circumstances, as a realistic character, he belongs to those who prove themselves in this world.

None of the characters in this play resembles in the slightest the idealistic image outlined by the Speaker, yet Jack and Brennan among the insurgents, and even more so Bessie and Fluther on the other side approach a compromise between the force of circumstances and the Speaker's unrealistic ideals, while Nora, Peter and the Covey fail in all decisive respects.

*

There are several reasons why *The Plough and the Stars* can today be considered the best work of O'Casey and one of the most important plays of the twentieth century. First, it came at the end of the 'early' phase in O'Casey's dramatic career, combining in a single play the technical achievements gathered from the experience of his previous works. As has been shown, these plays have many traits in common, leading in *The Plough and the Stars* to a perfection of technique. In his later career, O'Casey gave up this process of cumulative perfection and consciously attempted formal experiments, thus enhancing the danger of failure. Secondly, O'Casey achieves in *The Plough and the Stars* a very high degree of universality uncommon in a realistic play. This can easily be seen from a comparison with his previous plays. *The Shadow of a Gunman* predominantly shows the fate of an individual, even if the fate of his country is hinted at in the background events. *Juno and the Paycock* centres on the fate of a family, while references pointing to a larger context are more frequent than in *The Shadow of a Gunman*, and the climax of the play not only shows an individual mother's suffering, but the suffering of all mothers in an archetypal situation. *The Plough and the Stars* reveals several concentric circles ranging beyond the case of the individual. The smallest circle is the family who, as in *Juno and the Paycock*, are surrounded by the other tenement dwellers, who are again representative of all the slum-dwellers of Dublin; their situation in turn mirrors the fate of the whole city, this is representative of Ireland, and the typical traits of a situation of insurgence point even beyond the confines of the country itself. None of the previous plays incorporated to such a degree the fate of larger groups of people; and it has been shown that the situation of the stage characters parallels in detail the course of the Rising.

The third reason for such an exceptional evaluation of *The Plough and the Stars* lies in its objectivity. This is a particularly marked difference from O'Casey's later works, where in most cases the author's judgements and prejudices influenced his dramatic technique and where the audience is frequently forced to accept opinions instead of observing them in a conflict unmanipulated by the author. In *The Plough and the Stars* O'Casey created a large number of credible characters who are left to decide their own fate, being exposed to an extreme crisis. O'Casey does not intend here to show that one of his characters is right but to analyze how different people behave in such a situation. He therefore does justice both to the insurgents and to the tenement people and even to the British soldiers who suppress the Rising. During the first performances, every member of the audience felt himself to be treated unjustly, because every one thought only himself to be criticized. When one critic observed, 'To this day I do not know just where the author's sympathies lie . . .',[29] this remark, meant derogatorily, in reality contains a high degree of praise. In addition to O'Casey's objectivity, his specific form of authorial irony is most effective. As has been shown above, this irony is not so much put into the mouth of individual characters (as in *The Shadow of a Gunman*) but has been integrated into the action itself. If the Speaker fanatically appeals to people's patriotism and this merely makes the stage characters thirsty, if he enthuses about the idea of a holy war and on the stage two women have a fist-fight, all ideals are challenged. The existence or the value of ideals is not generally denied, but they are called into question and thereby endangered in a high degree. This in particular shows the modernity of O'Casey's attitude. His irony is not founded on hopeless pessimism, it does transcend the borderline of cynicism, yet it makes all human values uncertain indeed and leaves no traditional code of values untouched.

Finally, the quality of *The Plough and the Stars* is determined by the large number of themes it touches on despite its formal concentration. In addition to the overriding theme of people's ability to face up to life and all its crises, as well as the contrast of idealism and realism, such heterogeneous problems are touched upon as the relation of husband and wife and their claim to absolute loyalty from their partner, the question of the possibility of a just war and the meaning of sacrifice for justified aims, the conflict of genuine and false patriotism, the introduction of socialist ideas to an uncomprehending group of people, the dangers to human privacy in crowded tenements, the moral assessment of prostitution, the situation of a Protestant in Catholic surroundings and the relationship of private interests to the demands of society. Only if one considers this multiplicity of themes, in addition to the fact that O'Casey in this play mastered extremely complicated formal problems, can the importance of *The Plough and the Stars* be fully appreciated.

# PART II

# Experiments

O'Casey's exile caused him to write like a European rather than an Irishman. Opinions will clearly differ as to how 'local' we like our plays to be: but I think it is most important that future judgements of O'Casey's work should be based upon the understanding that his later writing was continuously experimental in form, theme, and vocabulary.

(John Arden)

# 8. PREFATORY

O'Casey's biographers and critics usually see the refusal of the Abbey directors in May 1928 to accept *The Silver Tassie* as the decisive event in O'Casey's life and in his dramatic career. This is only partly correct. The first phase of his career came to an end on the day in March 1926 when O'Casey left Dublin for London where the production of *Juno and the Paycock* in the Fortune Theatre was at the time making his name known beyond the narrow confines of Dublin. His visit drew on, evidently, as he began to look back and to see the limitations of his Dublin life and of his previous ideas, and a number of factors from his private life contributed to the fact that his planned stay of a few days became a life-long, self-chosen 'exile', the experience of separation from his native country which, in the second half of his life, overshadowed all other impressions, even that of the Second World War.

If one follows the sparse biographical documents of this period, especially the letters, there seems to be no doubt that *The Silver Tassie* was conceived only *after* O'Casey's removal to London. Not until several months after his departure from Dublin did O'Casey for the first time mention the idea of a new drama. Towards the end of September 1926 he had sketched the beginning and planned the outline of the other acts; in January, 1927, the play was progressing, four months later Act I had been finished, another four months later Act II, following a new idea, had been considerably altered, and in December 1927 O'Casey finished the first version preparatory to selecting and re-modelling the whole.[1] On 28 February 1928, the manuscript was ready to be submitted to the Abbey directors.[2] Contrary to the occasionally held opinion that O'Casey had planned *The Silver Tassie* in Dublin,[3] these letters show that both the theme and the dramatic form of *The Silver Tassie* was conceived only after his removal to London. Both mark a decisive turn from the previous plays. Even if the Abbey Theatre had produced *The Silver Tassie*, this would hardly have led O'Casey back to the lines of his earlier work. One

91

cannot, of course, come to any conclusion – and indeed even to speculate in this matter is idle – as to what his subsequent plays would have been like if he had remained in his familiar Dublin surroundings. The question of cause and effect has to be left unanswered: it cannot be decided whether O'Casey's dissatisfaction with his previous work triggered off his decision to stay in London or whether it was only in London that he became fully conscious of the great variety of dramatic forms and modes of expression open to him. However, if one remembers the *Kathleen Listens In* of his early phase, one is inclined to say that O'Casey did not, in England, break radically and completely with his previous ideas on the drama.

The dates of origin, production and publication of his next works are sufficient to indicate the influence that the separation from Dublin had on his future career. His five produced works of the first period were written and staged within four years; they were all published *after* their performance. His two full-length plays of the second period are six years apart; they were published in book-form before they reached the stage. After the première O'Casey introduced considerable revisions which cannot be neglected in any interpretation. Between *The Silver Tassie* and *Within the Gates*, there are only two short plays which O'Casey himself evidently did not take very seriously.

The differences between the first and second periods of his writing are even greater when one considers the themes and dramatic forms he chose. Once in London, he turned away from Dublin as the scene of his plays (with the exception of *A Pound on Demand*) and exchanged the background of Irish contemporary events for the wider sphere of world problems: The World War and the world-wide economic crisis were substituted for the Irish War of Independence and the Civil War. At the same time, O'Casey exchanged his predominantly reality-centred presentation for a technique of formal experiment consciously employing unrealistic features. This experimental character is the only trait that his otherwise very divergent plays of this phase have in common. It may be observed most clearly in *The Silver Tassie* where (not without internal tensions) O'Casey, within the scope of a single play, turns from Dublin to a locally independent scenery, from Irish people to representative stage characters, from the illusion of a specific slice of reality to the theatrical presentation of universal events. Apart from *The End of the Beginning* and *A Pound on Demand*, which belong to the same formal type of play and therefore can be considered in the same chapter, the divergences in this phase are greater than in any other period of O'Casey's dramatic career. Here he shows that from now on he will not accept any thematic or formal limitations. His separation from Dublin, and the additional separation from the Abbey Theatre which this brought with it, meant a kind of liberation for him; but the gain in intellectual scope was paid for by the loss of social and moral ties that had been important both for his life and his work. From now on, O'Casey saw himself again and again confronted with the task of defining the very norms of his work. During the next two decades each of his plays was to be a new beginning and to serve as a document of the dramatist's wrestling with the basic forms and ideas of the drama.

# 9. THE SILVER TASSIE

On 20 April 1928, Yeats wrote his famous (or infamous) letter to O'Casey indicating to all practical purposes the Abbey's refusal to produce *The Silver Tassie* and finalizing the decisive reversal in the dramatist's career that had begun with his removal to London. The ensuing controversy, carried on in several newspapers, led to the continuing estrangement between the Abbey directors and O'Casey and confirmed him in his decision not to return to Ireland. His description of these events in *Rose and Crown*,[1] written more than two decades after the event, still shows how deeply hurt O'Casey was and how passionately he reacted. The question of the degree to which Yeats was justified and of the consequences of his refusal both for O'Casey and for the Abbey have become an obsession of literary critics, occupying them to such an extent that they have frequently, for sheer controversy, been unable to see the play itself. Yet they have usually overlooked the fact that, because of the Abbey decision, *The Silver Tassie* was the first play by O'Casey to appear in print before it had been tried out on the stage. The differences between the 1928 version and the 'Stage Version' of the *Collected Plays* show to what extent O'Casey was attentive to the requirements of the stage and to what degree he was prepared to change his own text if such alterations proved advisable in performance.[2]

*

The most remarkable feature of *The Silver Tassie* is its second act. The question whether its inclusion was necessary, justified or superfluous, has frequently occupied O'Casey critics and has decisively influenced the evaluation of the play. In this debate, summary judgements have usually prevailed over a patient attentiveness to the relevant details. The following interpretation will also concern itself with this question, dealing separately with Acts I, III and IV on the one hand and Act II on the other; this may help to underline the differences. Subsequently, it will be possible to discuss the connections between the two sides of the play and to develop its common theme from them.

If for the moment one ignores Act II, there are gradual, but no fundamental deviations from the previous plays, *Juno and the Paycock* in particular proving to have many parallels to *The Silver Tassie*. Accordingly, *The Silver Tassie* shows a predominantly realistic sequence of events interspersed with certain symbols. It presents the fate of several individual characters, projected onto a general background of historical events, without there being such a close congruence between stage action and background events as in *The Plough and the Stars*. The language the characters use is determined by the limits of their personalities, i.e. it also appears 'realistic'; only at a few, albeit decisive points in the text does the audience notice the consciously shaping hand of the author. As in *Juno and the Paycock*, the serious action is shot through with comic interludes which not only serve as comic relief but also contribute to the meaning of the play.

The central character is Harry Heegan, a young Dublin worker who during the First World War serves as a volunteer in the British Army. While on leave, he scores the decisive goal in a cup match and helps his football team to win for the third time the silver tassie which from now on will remain in their possession. After his return to the front, Harry is seriously injured, and although his friend Barney Bagnal drags him out behind the lines, he remains paralyzed from the hips down. In the Dublin hospital where he now lands up, all attempts at an operation are unsuccessful.[3] Finally he returns to the place of his greatest triumph; as a cripple he attends the celebrations of his football club and in his despair destroys the valuable cup.

In Harry's attitude to life there is no element of intellectual reflection. His self-confidence is based exclusively on physical superiority. Consequently, the remarkable exposition scene between the two comic figures Simon and Sylvester stresses solely his physical achievements, his successes in sport and his defeat of a policeman in a boxing match. His triumphant entry shows him as entirely unconcerned with the future. Although the troop transporter is about to leave and he could be sentenced as a deserter if he misses it, he waves aside all warnings and even tries to persuade his comrades to stay another night. His recklessness is also underlined by the fact that he has joined the army as a volunteer (military service was not compulsory in Ireland). He scarcely thinks about what is awaiting him at the front, and treats friends and relatives in an equally thoughtless way. Harry is an ordinary person who, temporarily, has attracted everybody's attention through his youth and physical abilities. His injury is bound to hit him hard because it leaves him with no purpose in life. From now on, he cannot find his way. He is resigned and optimistic, irritated and passive in turn; he violently tries to cling to something he has lost irrevocably. He looks for some responsibility for his fate and, since he lacks all ability for abstraction, he can find it only in the people surrounding him. It is easily possible to imagine his future life: his hysterical outbursts will become less frequent, but he will develop an increasing bitterness based on a deep perplexity, thus losing the friendship even of those who are most willing to understand him. If one talks of tragedy in this play,[4] it is exclusively of a physical order. The 'tragic' fall of Harry and the inevitability of his fate are measured in the contrast between his physical prowess and its loss.

Harry's personal fate is turned into something much more universal by the fact that the Harry action is mirrored as a whole as well as in many details in the events concerning Teddy Foran. Teddy is like an older Harry who has lost his youthful attractiveness. He is *'big and powerful, rough and hardy. A man who would be dominant in a public-house, and whose opinions would be listened to with great respect'* (p. 22). When he first enters, he appears, like Harry, as an awe-inspiring victor; however, in place of the opposing football team, he has beaten only his own wife. He carries his wife's wedding-bowl as Harry does the silver tassie; when he breaks it, this points forward to Harry's future destruction of the cup and again symbolizes the dissolution of human relationships through the war. Just as Harry's mother is anxious to see him reach the troop transporter in time, Mrs. Foran does everything to move her husband to return to the front. In both cases, the war experience has the same result: while Harry is paralyzed, Teddy becomes blind. Both are taken to the same hospital and finally meet during the club celebrations, both tormented by the aimlessness of an existence emptied of all meaning. The parallels between their fates are underlined in a few stylized sentences which stress O'Casey's purpose: to present an image of the effects of war extending beyond the private fate of Harry Heegan:

HARRY. I can see, but I cannot dance.
TEDDY. I can dance, but I cannot see.
HARRY. Would that I had the strength to do the things I see.
TEDDY. Would that I could see the things I've strength to do   (p. 94).

The series of people maimed by the war is continued in the figure of a nameless patient, called simply 'Twenty-three', who continually shouts for the nurse and about whom the callous doctor says: 'Uh, hopeless case. Half his head in Flanders. May go on like that for another month' (p. 66). The very number serves to create the image of an endless chain of victims, of whom Harry, Teddy and 'Twenty-three' are merely examples.

A further line of action, that which concerns Barney Bagnal, differs from the Teddy-action in forming a direct contrast to the fate of Harry. If the line of Harry's action declines from the moment of his first appearance, Barney's line rises in the same degree. The two lines reach their point of intersection at the moment when Barney carries the wounded Harry out of reach of the enemy's fire. At the beginning, Barney is totally overshadowed by his friend, he is allowed to carry his coat and feeds him the admiring cues for his description of the football match, but commands little respect himself (for instance, he cannot be as free with the girls as Harry [p. 30]). Acts III and IV show the reversal of this situation when the uninjured Barney, who has been awarded the Victoria Cross, is superior to the paralyzed Harry. In Act III he is still ashamed of the fact that Harry's girl now visits him, but in Act IV he dances openly with her and even tries to seduce her in Harry's presence. The contrast to Act I becomes even clearer when Barney, irritated by Harry's constant back-biting, attempts to strangle him and Harry, who was once so strong himself, has to call pitifully for help. If Barney thus steps into his former friend's place, the author does not want to see him condemned for it. None of his actions show him as having an 'inferior character'; for instance he bears Harry's taunts at first with a considerable amount of patience. He is simply one of the lucky ones who have survived the war in full health; Harry, in his situation, would not act differently. Condemning Barney would be detrimental to the author's intention, because it would solve the question of responsibility in an all too simple way. O'Casey is not out to show that the uninjured have not done their duty by the wounded and the dead: he condemns war as such, showing how blindly it selects its victims.

Barney's and Harry's fate are connected by the figure of Jessie, Harry's former sweetheart, who, as a worker in an ammunition factory, serves the war just as thoughtlessly as the two men. Without reflection, she simply and instinctively admires the strongest and most impressive of them. In Act I she jealously watches over Harry's affections; but when he is wounded, she just as naturally turns to Barney who is now superior to him. The moment when Harry is wounded is again shown to be the point of intersection for all the developments in the play: Barney can save Harry only by reminding him of Jessie's tears (p. 99). But in Act III Jessie refuses even to see Harry, who is left waiting desperately for her, and visits the healthy Barney instead. The radical change can be explained only by the fact that Harry's and Barney's relationships with Jessie are exclusively based on physical attraction. Harry's desire for Jessie is less directed at her person than at the personification of his youth and strength the loss of which finds its most radical expression in his impotence. The sexual metaphors of Act I, where Harry fills the cup for Jessie and himself, are a preparation of this reduction of 'love' to sexual attraction:

HARRY. . . . Out with one of them wine-virgins we got in 'The Mill in the
   Field', Barney, and we'll rape her in a last hot moment before we set
   out to kiss the guns! . . .
BARNEY [*taking a bottle of wine from his pocket*]. Empty her of her
   virtues, eh?
HARRY. Spill it out, Barney, spill it out . . .
BARNEY [*who has removed the cap and taken out the cork*]. Here she is
   now . . . Ready for anything, stripp'd to the skin! (p. 29).

Acts III and IV are similarly shot through with sexual imagery. The atmosphere in the hospital is crystallized in Surgeon Maxwell's hardly ambiguous song, the situation during the club celebrations in the seduction scene between Barney and Jessie. This emphasis on sexuality increases Harry's isolation, for in future he will be excluded precisely from this aspect of life. It also serves to de-heroize the wounded ex-soldiers. In contrast to many other attempts to harmonize their situation, *The Silver Tassie* shows drastically the real extent of their loss and makes it clear that nobody can compensate them for it.

The character of Susie, too, and her change from Act I to Act III, so frequently discussed by critics, can only be explained in terms of this same sphere of sexuality. When someone had complained that no 'gradual transformation' was evident in her development,[5] O'Casey declared bluntly 'no gradual change is shown because no change takes place.'[6] This reply is justified, because although Susie changes in her behaviour (and even in her language[7]) between Acts I and III, such a change is not based on any fundamental alteration in her character. Her religious fanaticism in Act I does not spring from a deep-seated religiosity, but is a sublimation of her unrequited affection for Harry. This can be

easily deduced from her behaviour towards Harry (p. 30), her
jealousy towards Jessie (pp. 18-19) and also from certain remarks
which in their shrill exaggeration lead one to suspect the opposite:
'What's the honey-pot kiss of a lover to the kiss of righteousness
and peace?' (p. 11). In Act III, Harry is no longer an object for her
desires. This readily liberates her from her repression and leaves
her free to indulge her inclinations with Maxwell.[8]

Again it should be stressed that O'Casey does not imply any
criticism of her behaviour.[9] In the second version of the play it is
precisely Susie who justifies the attitude of those not hit by the
war:

Teddy Foran and Harry Heegan have gone to live their own way in
another world. Neither I nor you can lift them out of it. No longer can
they do the things we do. We can't give sight to the blind or make the
lame walk. We would if we could. It is the misfortune of war. As long as
wars are waged, we shall be vexed by woe; strong legs shall be made
useless and bright eyes made dark. But we, who have come through the
fire unharmed, must go on living. [*Pulling Jessie from the chair*] Come
along, and take your part in life! [*To Barney*] Come along, Barney, and
take your partner into the dance!  (p. 103)

It is true that those who have stayed at home have their
weaknesses, their uncomprehensions, perhaps, and their
egotism, but not to a more than usual degree. Mrs. Foran looks
forward to Teddy's return to the front because she will not have
to suffer his violence. Mrs. Heegan prevents Harry's and Jessie's
marriage because this would deprive her of financial support: for
the same reason she presses her son not to miss the boat. Jessie's
final words betray her lack of insight into the situation of the
soldiers at the front: 'You'll not forget to send me the German
helmet home from France, Harry?' (p. 30). The same lack of
understanding is shown by the visitors in the hospital who, for
all their pity, are unable to bridge the gap between their everyday
world and the soldiers' experiences. Yet when Jessie, towards the
end, can still commiserate with 'poor Harry' after he has
thoroughly spoiled the celebrations for her, it becomes apparent
that those who have stayed at home cannot be lightly condemned,
and even Barney's exclamation, 'You half-baked Lazarus, I've
put up with you all the evening, so don't force me now to rough-
handle the bit of life the Jerries left you as a souvenir!' (p. 99) is,
despite its cruelty, explicable in terms of Harry's previous
behaviour. The decisive point of the play is not that those who
have been untouched by the war react wrongly or maliciously to

the victims. If this were so, the remedy would be easy: a simple alteration in people's behaviour would right the balance. The point is that no behaviour whatsoever could improve the victims' situation, because they now live in that other world that Susie described; and the healthy have no access to this world. The most moving testimony of this fact is in the final sentence of the play, when Mrs. Foran so pathetically remarks: 'It's a terrible pity Harry was too weak to stay an' sing his song, for there's nothing I love more than the ukulele's tinkle, tinkle in the night-time' (p. 104). She, and the others with her, will never be able to penetrate beyond the surface of their lives into that 'other world' of suffering.

So far, the author's neutrality towards his characters has been emphasized. There is, however, one exception. Dr. Maxwell, the president of the Avondales (p. 27) and the hospital surgeon of Act III, is laid bare to the spectators' criticism when his lack of interest in his patients' suffering is drastically demonstrated. He puts off Harry with the cliché 'While there's life there's hope [*with a grin and a wink at Susie*]' (p. 68), flirts with Susie during his examination of Sylvester and, in the third act, after Harry's outbreak of despair, turns away with the words 'Come on, all, we've wasted too much time already' (p. 102), revealing in these asides an attitude that is entirely foreign to the others. This is all the more noticeable because his profession and his intellectual superiority should provide him with deeper insights into the problems of the wounded than, say, Mrs. Foran. This form of authorial criticism of an individual character is detrimental to O'Casey's manifest intention, the accusation of war as such. It is, however, the only occasion in this play where O'Casey constructs such a form of individual responsibility. In accordance with Susie's speech quoted above, the other characters remain free of direct authorial evaluation.

Susie has another function, too. She introduces the theme of religion that plays an important part in the play. While her religious fanaticism, as has been mentioned above, is due, psychologically, to sexual repression, yet this does not reduce the relevance of her thoughts and exhortations. In part they are used to show the religious indifference of the other characters, as, for instance, when Simon rejects Susie's appeal with the words 'Heaven is all the better, Susie, for being a long way off' (p. 14). Yet her words also reveal the contrast between the demands of Christianity and the preparations for war, uncritically accepted by all, when, for instance, Susie, while polishing Harry's steel

helmet, holds forth on 'the miserableness of them that don't
know the things that belong unto their peace' (p. 10), or when she
maintains that 'the men that go with the guns are going with
God' (p. 29). This ironic contrast pervades the whole play. It can
be observed in the confrontation between Harry's nihilistic
outburst and the ringing of the convent bells:

[*The bell of a Convent in grounds begins to ring for Compline.*]
HARRY [*with intense bitterness*]. I'll say to the pine, 'Give me the grace
and beauty of the beech'; I'll say to the beech, 'Give me the strength
and stature of the pine'. In a net I'll catch butterflies in bunches; twist
and mangle them between my fingers and fix them wriggling on to
mercy's banner. I'll make my chair a Juggernaut, and wheel it over the
neck and spine of every daffodil that looks at me, and strew them
dead to manifest the mercy of God and the justice of man! (p. 77).

Here, as in his drawing of characters, O'Casey (in contrast to his
later plays) preserves his objectivity. Harry, who has lost all belief
in a divine miracle, is juxtaposed to the nun who admonishes
him: 'And Twenty-eight, pray to God, for wonderful He is in His
doing toward the children of men'; her attitude, however, not
being denigrated in any way, for the stage direction explicitly
says: '*Calm and dignified she goes out into the grounds*' (p. 78).
   The religious context of the play is directly visible for the audience in the scenery.[10] In each act the cross is present: in Act I in
the form of the troop ship's mast, in III in the wooden devices
that enable the wounded to pull themselves up, in IV in the
lamps described in a stage direction as showing '*an illuminated
black cross with an inner one of gleaming red*' (p. 80). In Act I, the
religious associations are even plainer in the altar-like table,
placed directly under the 'cross', which is used to exhibit Harry's
sports decorations.[11] Later Harry appears '*with his arm around
Jessie, who is carrying a silver cup joyously, rather than reveren-
tially, elevated, as a priest would elevate a chalice*' (p. 25). The
cup is thus associated with a chalice from which Harry drinks the
wine that will soon be turned into his own blood. One wonders,
however, whether the religious implications are so pervasive
that Susie can be considered as 'the priestess serving the altar',
Simon and Sylvester as 'the chorus celebrating the divine
superiority of the chosen youth'[12] and Harry himself as the dying
and reborn God. Too many aspects of the play have to be overlooked and other details to be overstressed, if one wants to see
*The Silver Tassie* as a 'Passion Play' with an admixture of pre-
Christian rites.[13]

Such a ritualistic interpretation (for which O'Casey himself apparently had little use[14]) can be refuted not only in terms of the scarcity of evidence supporting it, but also because it can be shown that the religious aspects of the play serve another purpose altogether. They are employed for contrast, contributing to the overall principle of juxtaposition that (as will be shown below) dominates the play. If in Act I there appear to be certain parallels between Harry's fate and the sacrifice of Jesus Christ, all further developments deviate harshly from this. After Harry has gone through the Golgotha situation of Act II, there is no glorious resurrection for him, but a monotonous continuation of everyday life. The redemption of man, present in the figure of the cross, contrasts with the unredeemable Harry who not only succumbs to his suffering in this world but loses all hope of a future resurrection when he loses his faith.

This thesis – that the religious associations in *The Silver Tassie* serve an overall structure of contrast – is confirmed by those passages where feelings of despair are expressed in Biblical diction and frequently even in Biblical terms. Teddy's lament on the loss of his eyes (p. 89) is an obvious example. Another is Harry's reply when he is asked to choose red or white wine: 'No, red wine; red like the blood that was shed for you and for many for the commission of sin!' (p. 92). O'Casey commented on this sentence in an article written probably in 1935: '. . . the last sentence is taken – with an alteration of one word – from the Anglican Rubric of the Service of Holy Communion . . .'[15] His alteration, of course, was his substitution of *commission* for *remission*, thus reversing the meaning of the words. In this context, O'Casey rejected all accusations of blasphemy: 'The sentence was introduced in an effort to convey a suitable symbol of the anguished bitterness that the unhappy Harry might conceivably feel for what he thought to be the fell waste of the war.'[16] It is indeed Harry, not the author, who can be blamed for his criticism of Christianity. O'Casey places Haery in an objectively depicted Christian framework and leaves it to the audience to conclude that there are no relations whatsoever between the situation of his protagonist and the maxims of religion.

O'Casey's contrastive technique is not limited to the religious context. If no play can be written without the use of contrast, *The Silver Tassie* certainly makes abundant use of this principle, and does so with the obvious purpose 'to enlarge the audience's vision by effects of calculated irony'.[17] Not only does O'Casey contrast certain characters (for instance Harry and Maxwell, Susie and

Jessie, Teddy and Mrs. Foran), he also contrasts the healthy and the victims of war, the soldiers and those who have stayed at home, the understanding and the uncomprehending. The parallels between Acts I and IV, both governed by the football celebrations, underline the contrast between Harry's triumph and his despair. In many places this contrast-technique takes on the form of an authorial irony that influences the very speech of the characters. After Teddy's outbreak of violence in Act I, Mrs. Heegan says: '. . . you'd imagine now, the trenches would have given him some idea of the sacredness of life!' (p. 20). Later Mrs. Foran introduces Harry's blind friend with the words: 'I brought Teddy, your brother in arms, up to see you, Harry' (p. 72). The nurse greets Barney with the words 'Standing guard over your comrade, Twenty-two, eh' (p. 78), after Barney has just hurt Harry immeasurably by estranging Jessie from him. Here and in many other places the spoken word, without the speaker being conscious of it, contrasts with the situation as the audience knows it. This results in the audience's increasing awareness of the victims' hopeless situation.

The comic interlude scenes usually dominated by Simon and Sylvester, offer another form of contrast. Three examples will illustrate this. In Act I, they conduct an extended dispute as to whether Harry once knocked down a policeman with a left hook or a right hook. Their opinions differ only in such details, for Harry's general superiority in any kind of conflict is indisputable to them. Later on, this is contrasted most painfully with that larger battle in which Harry's strength and agility are useless, because an unseen hand knocks him down and turns him into a cripple for life. In Act III, Simon and Sylvester are directly contrasted with Harry. They have, due to some harmless illness, become room-mates, but exaggerate their situation most drastically, while the paralyzed soldier suffers mutely. In Act IV, the telephone scene, one of the most brilliant pieces of farcical comedy in O'Casey's work and in modern drama in general, is juxtaposed with Harry's deeply moving attempts to keep intact some of the connecting links with his previous life. Harry's despair is pin-pointed by the others' excitement over irrelevancies. But, as in the final scene of *Juno and the Paycock*, this scene is not only employed for contrast purposes but also serves to underline the meaning of the play. It is significant that Simon, Sylvester and Mrs. Foran are incapable of working the telephone as a means of communication. When Mrs. Foran concludes, 'Curious those at the other end of the telephone couldn't make themselves understood' (p. 88), she unconsciously expresses a world – her world – in which there is no chance of communication beyond the exchange of incomprehensible sounds.

The final example for the employment of contrastive techniques in *The Silver Tassie* is also the most weighty: the juxtaposition between three dominantly realistic acts and a fourth that deviates from these decisively in structure, characterization, language and meaning. Here O'Casey has advanced to that point beyond which it becomes impossible to contrast opposites in any meaningful way.

*

Act II, called by Shaw, to Denis Johnston's displeasure, 'the finest thing ever written for the stage',[18] presents as a whole a complex symbol of war. In a letter, O'Casey explained his intention of refraining from any realistic depiction of the battle situation:

I had seen war plays where attempts at 'realism' would consist of explosions that would near lift one out of one's seat. I determined to do a play in which a shot wouldn't be heard. And, to depict the war it would have been useless to try to make it real (I've heard of a production of *Journey's End* in which real grass grew on the sandbags); so I set out to show the spirit of war, and, to judge by the howling, it seems to be a success.[19]

Accordingly, in *The Silver Tassie* it is unimportant to which unit the soldiers belong, and even to which of the fighting parties; it is equally unimportant on what battle-field they fight and what war they are fighting. The contacts with reality are limited to those elements that are common to any war: hunger, fatigue, dampness, dirt, coldness, pain, homesickness, criticism of the superior officers and envy of those who have stayed at home. These, and the unanswered question as to a meaning for the whole, the undefined longing for a religious interpretation and the very real fear of the enemy's attack, are the constituent elements of this act.

The scenery as suggested by O'Casey has an important function for the play. '*Every feature of the scene*', it is proposed, should seem '*a little distorted from its original appearance*' (p. 36), a directive that applies to all the other aspects of the act as well. The stage shows the ruins of a partly destroyed monastery immediately behind the main line of battle, where a front-line hospital as well as a big howitzer have been installed. The scenery is dominated by the contrast between the principles of war and peace, the silhouette of the howitzer on the one hand, and a picture of the Virgin in a church window lighted from inside together with a crucifix on the other hand. The crucifix has already been hit by the war: '*A shell has released an arm from the cross, which has caused the upper part of the figure to lean forward with the released arm outstretched towards the figure of the Virgin*' (p. 35). The sky is occasionally lit up by Very lights.

The impact of *The Silver Tassie* was decisively influenced by the scenery designed for the first performance by Augustus John, O'Casey's painter friend.[20] John apparently succeeded in visualizing the uncanniness of the scene, contrasting it with the everyday reality of the other acts by stressing its dominant elements. He refused to include all the details that O'Casey had suggested in his stage directions, for instance the macabre view of the trenches: '*Here and there heaps of rubbish mark where houses once stood. From some of these lean, dead hands are protruding*' (p. 35). Apparently he also omitted the placards that O'Casey wanted to employ for ironic contrast: 'PRINCEPS PACIS' at the foot of the cross, 'HYDE PARK CORNER' in front of the howitzer, 'NO HAWKERS OR STREET CRIES PERMITTED HERE' at the hospital entrance. These last two signs are almost indispensable, for in their black humour they point forward to the bitter comedy played out in the scenes of the Visitor and the Staff-Wallah. John's scenery also neglected O'Casey's suggestion that Barney who, according to war regulations, has been tied as a punishment to the big wheel of a gun, is to be positioned opposite the crucifix, thus stressing both contrast and similarity between the crucified Christ and the crucified soldier.

In spite of such reservations, John's scenery is inseparably bound up with the play. Some critics have questioned whether it is legitimate to have the visual aspects take over part of the function of the spoken word.[21] Although this conflict between the philologist who considers only the written dialogue, and the theatrical practitioner who sees the written text as a mere score to be realized on stage, cannot be resolved here, it has to be stressed that in O'Casey's works the visual means are inseparably integrated into the whole. Without them, the text in many places would not be meaningful or even comprehensible. As his extensive stage directions show, O'Casey placed almost as much emphasis on the description of the scenery as on the dialogue text. Act II of

*The Silver Tassie* and Act III of *Red Roses for Me* are only the most
obvious examples of the dramatist's pervasive intention to render
the visual scenery as part of the total impact of his play. If one
criticizes the visual elements in *The Silver Tassie*, one would also
have to reject the role of the decaying mansion in *Purple Dust*, the
disjointed house in *Cock-a-doodle Dandy*, the distant fire in *The
Bishop's Bonfire*. Such a view would make extraneous demands
on a work of art instead of understanding it in terms of its own
individual existence. O'Casey's plays, which have been designed
for realization in the theatre, cannot be understood with reference
to the spoken text alone. It in no sense detracts from their value
that they owe part of their effect to their visual impression.

Similar reservations have been voiced concerning the language
of Act II of *The Silver Tassie*. It has been objected that the meaning
of the language has yielded to the simple acoustic function of
rhythm.[22] It has to be conceded that the verses, presented in plain
song (*cantus planus*), vary considerably and are not always
convincing. Some passages impressively suggest the situation of
the front-line troops, for instance when the 1st Soldier dreams of
home, or of those associations that for him constitute 'home':

I sees the missus paryding along Walham Green,
Through the jewels an' silks on the costers' carts,
Emmie a-pulling her skirt an' muttering,
'A balloon, a balloon, I wants a balloon',
The missus a-tugging 'er on, an' sying,
'A balloon, for shime, an' your father fighting:
You'll wait till 'e's 'ome, an' the bands a-plying!' (p. 38).

Here the very simplicity of expression has become a convincing
equivalent for the ordinary soldier's unspeculating home-sickness.
In other passages, O'Casey departs from the immediate experiences of ordinary soldiers, but captures the situation on the front
in frightening, unforgettable images:

Squeals of hidden laughter run through
the screaming medley of the wounded
Christ, who bore the cross, still weary,
Now trails a rope tied to a field gun (p. 53).

There are, on the other hand, certain passages which are neither
appropriate to the speaker nor completely clear to the listener,
where the syntax becomes confused and no clear concept is visible
behind the muddled images:

To hang here even a little longer,
lounging through fear-swell'd, anxious moments;
The hinderparts of the god of battles
Shading our war-tir'd eyes from his flaming face (p. 45).

Criticism is unjustified, however, when it is not directed against the images and ideas of the stanzas, but against the mode of presentation itself, prescribed in detail by O'Casey (pp. 3, 105-110). O'Casey in this act did not so much aim at precise statements as at the emotional evocation of a situation. One can hardly imagine a better mode of achieving this than the monotonous litany-like chants of the soldiers, acoustically suggesting the monotony of life at the front. If the meaning of the words can be perceived only as through a veil, this corresponds to the situation presented, in which the soldiers have lost all direct contact with a comprehensible reality and are confronted in utter confusion with a bizarre world. There is little point in criticizing a dramatist for employing the full range of theatrical expression, including music, to bring about an effective realization of his vision.

It has been said that the main function of this act is to evoke a situation. Nevertheless it shows considerable structural variety. One can distinguish twelve sections, separated by a variation in the grouping of the figures and by changing moods. Section one (p. 36-37), dominated by the Croucher, sets the tone for all subsequent passages. The Croucher on the one hand is a soldier suspended from service because of his injuries; on the other hand he is the personification of death, this being suggested by his mask and his position *above* the other soldiers (p. 3). He intones an impressive, abbreviated version of the prophecies of Ezekiel (Ch. 37), inverting the Biblical prediction into its opposite. Although the vision of the valley of bones has been repeatedly used in modern literature,[23] no other presentation has been so unremitting in reversing the Biblical context. The contrast between the Croucher's hopelessness and the ideas of Christianity is intensified by his prophecy of death being juxtaposed with the sound of the organ and the voices from the monastery: 'Gloria in excelsis Deo et in terra pax hominibus bonae voluntatis' (p. 36).

The representatives of that 'exceeding great army' that according to the Croucher will decay to a 'valley of dry bones' (p. 37) appear in the subsequent scene: a group of soldiers who after twelve hours of labour behind the front group themselves around a brazier in utter fatigue. In sections two (pp. 37-39), five (pp. 43-46)

and ten (pp. 52-53), which are reserved for them, their desires
and fears become clear, the hopelessness of an endless trench
warfare, their hatred of the officers, their longing for home leave,
their awareness of the continuous presence of death. Finally one
of them expresses the question that moves them all: 'But wy'r we
'ere, wy'r we 'ere, – that's wot I wants to know!' The only reply he
receives is in the words of a World War I song: 'We're here
because we're here, because we're here, because we're here!' (p.
39). The irony of this answer is increased by its being sung to the
sentimental tune of 'Auld Lang Syne'. The soldiers' lethargy is
repeatedly interrupted by the Corporal. In section eight (pp. 50-
51) he brings the longed-for post from home, but this last means
of contact serves only to underline the lack of understanding on
the part of those who have stayed at home, for while the soldiers
hope for cigarettes or playing cards, they receive a prayer-book
and a ball with the sarcastic remark 'To play your way to the
enemies' trenches when you all go over the top. Mollie' (p. 51). In
section eleven (pp. 53-55) the Corporal announces the enemies'
imminent attack and under his guidance the soldiers, *'their
forms crouched in a huddled act of obeisance'* (p. 54), assemble
for the prayer to the big gun. The canon of war has thus finally
usurped the place of the peace-giving deity or has at least taken
on equal rank so that the same 'service' is due to it. The chorus
repeatedly says 'We believe in God and we believe in thee', thus
underlining the reversal of all traditional standards: God and war
(as is evident in the scenery) have taken on equal rank.

The future fate of the soldiers is projected in the central episode
of this act. In section seven (pp. 47-50) two Stretcher-Bearers
bring in two seriously injured soldiers. They are spoken of in the
neuter mode implying that from now on they will be mere objects
(of surgery, of charity and of compassion). Real life is from now
on closed to them:

The power, the joy, the pull of life,
The laugh, the blow, and the dear kiss,
The pride and hope, the gain and loss,
Have been temper'd down to this, this, this,
The pride and hope, the gain and loss,
Have been temper'd down to this (p. 48).

In contrast to these passages which depict the ordinary soldier's
plight in great concentration, but without distortion, five other
passages contain traces of satire. The Staff-Wallah and the Visitor
are not shown as they are but as they appear in the eyes of the

soldiers, their negative traits being overstressed as in caricature.
The soldiers' hatred of the officers, especially of the staff-officers,
had been emphasized repeatedly in the previous sections,
especially in section seven:

1ST STRETCHER-BEARER. The red-tabb'd squit!
2ND STRETCHER-BEARER. The lousy map-scanner!
3RD STRETCHER-BEARER. We must keep up, we must keep up the
    morale of the awmy.
2ND STRETCHER-BEARER [*loudly*]. Does 'e eat well?
THE REST [*in chorus*]. Yes, 'e eats well!
2ND STRETCHER-BEARER. Does 'e sleep well?
THE REST [*in chorus*]. Yes, 'e sleeps well!
2ND STRETCHER-BEARER. Does 'e whore well?
THE REST [*in chorus*]. Yes, 'e whores well!
2ND STRETCHER-BEARER. Does 'e fight well?
THE REST [*in chorus*]. Napoo; 'e 'as to do the thinking for the Tommies!
    (p. 49).

The Staff-Wallah in sections four (pp. 42-43), nine (pp. 51-52)
and twelve (pp. 55-56) thus appears as a fop, moving like an
automaton, reading senseless orders and disappearing without
the slightest contact with the soldiers. The gap between the soldiers
and the Visitor (sections three [pp. 40-42] and six [pp. 46-47]), is
even greater; he regards his short stay in the fighting zone as a
dangerous adventure and conceals his fear behind the orders of
the authorities. He does not have the slightest understanding for
the soldiers' fatigue or for the situation of the wounded. In one
episode he thoughtlessly strikes a match on the crucifix. When
the soldiers knock it out of his hand, it is for two reasons: on the
one hand they fear very realistically that the glow of light will
attract the enemy's shells, on the other hand they fear his sacrilege,
for 'There's a Gawd knocking abaht somewhere' (p. 46). Both
ideas are equally remote to the Visitor. If the soldiers are not
devoted Christians, God nevertheless has a stronger reality for
them than for those who have stayed at home. God and war, as
is shown again in this episode, have taken on for them very
much the same position.

Several critics have suggested that O'Casey was under the
influence of international expressionism as a literary movement
when he wrote his unrealistic second act for *The Silver Tassie*. It is
possible to see such influences in the dialogue, largely independent of the individual characters, in the reduction of psychological

treatment and in the preference for the general over the individual. The models suggested for these experiments range from Strindberg and O'Neill to Kaiser and especially Toller who, alone among German expressionists, enjoyed a certain reputation in the England of the twenties. It is impossible to say to what extent O'Casey was really influenced by these authors. In 1951 he declared: 'I don't know what Expressionism means. I never did anything to perpetrate it in any play of mine.'[24] On the other hand it is known that in his Dublin years he made extensive use of the opportunity provided by the Dublin Drama League to see the plays of foreign playwrights, among them Claudel, Pirandello, Toller, Kaiser and Strindberg.[25] His interests at this time are said to have foreshadowed his change of direction in *The Silver Tassie*: 'He was particularly attracted by Strindberg and the work of the German expressionists', *The Dream Play* and Toller's *Masse-Mensch* being among his favourites.[26] It is therefore more than doubtful whether '. . . it was O'Casey's chance acquaintance with Eugene O'Neill's *The Hairy Ape* that strongly impelled the Irish dramatist to discard his previous dramatic manner.'[27]

Among the dramatists mentioned above it is Ernst Toller whose approach most resembles that of *The Silver Tassie*. At this time, three of his plays, *Die Maschinenstürmer, Masse-Mensch* and *Hinkemann*, were available in English translation.[28] The fate of Eugen Hinkemann, emasculated in the war, may have provided certain suggestions for the subject matter of *The Silver Tassie*.[29] More important, however, are the formal innovations which O'Casey may have found in *Masse-Mensch*. There he saw a situation reduced to its basic features without any individualistic trimmings. He found a language severed from the person of the speaker, discovering new effects of rhythm, pathos, abstraction and choral recital. All this took place against a background that, as in a dream, retained merely a few relics of reality, and among nameless figures conceived as types of larger groups or even as embodiments of ideas. It cannot be doubted that such a dramatic form must have deeply impressed the self-taught O'Casey, opening his eyes to new possibilities for the drama. On the other hand it should not be overlooked that O'Casey in *Kathleen Listens In* had already experimented with unrealistic forms, nor should one ignore the considerable differences between *The Silver Tassie* and the plays of Toller. In contrast to expressionist drama, O'Casey does not present a radical tension between individual and society, his plays are without the pathos of brotherhood and friendship and the endeavour radically to change humanity; and above all he lacks the intellectual discussion of problems on an abstract level which turns Toller's plays, and expressionist drama in general, into plays of ideas in disguise. The distance to practical reality, too, is greater in Toller than in Act II of *The Silver Tassie* where in many places the concrete situation on the front is still visible. It seems, therefore, more appropriate to see O'Casey, 'poussé par une nécessité intérieure', as one among many dramatists who were turning away from realism and not as in any special dependence on one particular style.[30]

★

So far, only the *differences* between Act II and the other acts have been stressed, giving perhaps the erroneous impression that the two parts are incompatible. There are, however, several traits which both parts of the play have in common. In addition to the logic of the sequence of events (Act I shows the soldiers' departure for the front, Act II the situation at the front and the last two acts the soldiers' native country after their return), the most obvious link is the fact that in Act II two characters from the 'realistic' section reappear. The 4th Soldier is said to be '*very like Teddy*' (p. 37). Barney is even mentioned by name, and his presence is justified in his punishment for theft. This is the most dubious of all parallels between the two sections of the play. If Barney is present in Act II, the audience will immediately look for Harry, and this would detract their attention from the real problems of the act. There is little in the other acts to justify the surmise that Barney is 'the one character who has not fused into this mass subconsciousness, the only character thus likely to escape uninjured and mould the destiny of the play',[31] and it is patently absurd to suggest that 'Barney's stealing of the cock, belonging to a citizen of a friendly state, is symbolic of his stealing his friend's girl.'[32]

It is much easier to answer the question why Harry is not present in Act II. If this act is a symbol of war, dealing with the situation of all soldiers, Harry's individual fate would be out of place here. O'Casey's play is effective precisely because the soldiers have individual traits only at home, while the war turns them into indistinguishable ciphers, a situation from which many of them will not escape in future. It would be quite inappropriate to introduce a soldier 'very like Harry' into Act II or to turn him, complete with his ukulele, into the character of the Croucher.[33] Critics who do not want to forgo Harry's individuality, would have to insist that the decisive moment in his life, the moment when he is hit by the shell, should be presented as well. This would turn *The Silver Tassie* into a second *Journey's End*, which O'Casey specifically wanted to avoid. It is, therefore, much more appropriate for the critic to recognize, and for the producer to preserve, a consistent anonymity in Act II.

This would by no means sever all continuity between the two sections of the play. There are a number of details in Act II that refer to the 'realistic' section without being bound up with one particular character. Reference to the 'seperytion moneys' (p. 39) reminds one of the women of Act I, and the football match around the gun (p. 51) in its pitifulness and its abrupt ending contrasts with Harry's glorious first appearance. The class-conflict suggested in the character of Dr. Maxwell and the social criticism associated with it, reappears in an intensified form in the figure of the Staff-Wallah. The picture of the Virgin of Act II reappears in the statue of the Virgin in Act III. The religious theme is present equally in both parts of the play and is employed for the same ironic contrast. Formally, the technique of contrast dominates all the acts. And finally, Acts I, III and IV are by no means so unequivocally realistic as they may appear at a first glance. They, too, show remarkable dissociations of character from speech,[34] underlining the parallels to Act II. Certain figures tend to break out into a metaphorical language inappropriate to their characters, certain stylized sentences are set off from the rest of the dialogue by rhythmical repetition (pp. 31, 33, 94-95); various songs suggest the chants of Act II.[35]

These correspondences are sufficient to integrate Act II into the context of the play, but they are not strong enough to disguise its special position. This act is the most effective means conceivable to ensure the play's universality. It has a similar function to a framework action: what is said here about war in general, is exemplified in the experience of Harry and his friends. War in its blind indifference hits its victims; human beings are at its mercy, and there is no hope for the victims. Significantly, *napoo*, a term from soldiers' slang, is used repeatedly and takes on central importance, from Harry's frivolous reference to Jessie's legs, 'Napoo, Barney, to everyone but me!' (p. 29) to his bitter 'Napoo Barney Bagnal and Napoo Jessie Taite' (p. 101), suggesting his loss of all human ties. The play's universality is already hinted at in the title which refers not to Harry's name but to the silver cup that in the text is interpreted as a 'Sign of youth, sign of strength, sign of victory' (p. 26). The destruction of the cup thus directly presents the destruction of youth, strength and victorious power through war. There are few examples in modern drama where a symbol is so convincingly deduced from a concrete situation that nevertheless powerfully incorporates a universal meaning.[36] The song by Burns which originally suggested the play's title[37] is, it may be appropriate to mention, relevant only to Act I, for 'My Bonnie Mary' that, with certain textual variants, is sung by Harry and Barney (pp. 32-33), presents only the departure of the soldier, where 'The shouts o' war are heard afar . . .'[38] Both the terrors of war and the sufferings of the returning soldiers are ignored by Burns.

Paradoxically, *The Silver Tassie* could be termed an 'objective propaganda play'. Certain minor exceptions apart, O'Casey does not express any straightforward criticism. He presents the three-fold situation of the soldier – departing, fighting and returning – objectively. It is precisely this technique, however, that makes it less easy for the audience to escape the impact of his play. In his later works, it is relatively easy to evade the full weight of his criticism by blaming O'Casey for being biased. His criticism of Catholicism can be rejected, for instance, by suggesting that his priest figures are distorted and his polemics unjustified. In *The Silver Tassie*, on the other hand, it is almost impossible to deny the relevance of what O'Casey says. In addition, O'Casey does not in any way distribute personal responsibility among his characters. Barney and Jessie are just as innocent of Harry's situation as he himself. The audience's indignation is thus directed at war itself, for which no justification (e.g. patriotism, defence of one's country or one's honour) are offered. It is this unmitigated directness that justifies one critic's reference to *The Silver Tassie* as 'war without any anaesthetic'.[39] It was not only because he had to engage in the greatest controversy of his life for this play that O'Casey to the end of his days considered *The Silver Tassie* his favourite work;[40] it was also because he felt that here, as later on only in *Hall of Healing*, he had succeeded in combining an uncompromising accusation with an equally uncompromising objectivity of presentation.

# 10. THE END OF THE BEGINNING and A POUND ON DEMAND

According to O'Casey's own report, his two short plays *The End of the Beginning* and *A Pound on Demand* were written between *The Silver Tassie* and *Within the Gates*.[1] They were not published, however, until 1934, when they appeared in his miscellaneous volume *Windfalls*.[2] *The End of the Beginning* was the only play after *The Plough and the Stars* that was premièred by the Abbey (on 8 February, 1937). With this exception, they have usually been ignored by the professional stage but found considerable interest among amateurs and have been republished in a number of anthologies for the amateur theatre.

The discrepancy in subject matter between the two plays would suggest that they differ considerably in type. *The End of the Beginning* is, according to O'Casey, 'almost all founded on a folk-tale well known over a great part of Europe',[3] while *A Pound on Demand* is based on an actual occurrence in a Dublin post office of which O'Casey had been told.[4] The subtitles, too, suggest different types of plays: *The End of the Beginning* is termed a comedy, *A Pound on Demand* a sketch. Nevertheless they are more similar than any other two O'Casey plays and therefore can be dealt with in the same chapter.

The common denominator of the two plays is the farce. The origins of the farce can be traced back to popular entertainments, and in England it retained its popular character in the drolls of the nineteenth-century fairs and later on in the sketches of the music-hall. However, it also found its place in the professional theatre, the eighteenth and nineteenth century curtain-raisers and after-pieces being predominantly farces. Most farces are of their very nature short plays; for, while the comedy (even the comedy of character) is based on a complex plot, the farce is based on an individual situation. Although it is not uncommon to find a sequence of several situations, in most cases the farce remains limited to the length of a single act. When, owing to social changes in the theatre-going public, the curtain-raiser and the after-piece disappeared from the programme of professional

114

theatres, the farce was reduced in importance until it almost
vanished from most theatres. As a consequence of this development and in contrast to the situation in previous centuries,
serious dramatists very rarely turned in the 20th century to the
farce. It is true that some authors, especially Shaw, employed the
traditional form to expose conventional ideas and moral values,
but the continuation of a genuine tradition of farce was almost
exclusively left to authors writing for the amateur theatre, who
were content to provide an extensive if largely unrecognized
market with conventional fare. O'Casey is one of the few
respected dramatists of the modern stage who have not been
ashamed to write farces, and among them he is certainly the most
skilful. Not only has he introduced many farcical scenes into his
full-length plays, but with *The End of the Beginning* and *A
Pound on Demand* he has also written two plays that correspond
to the type in all its virtues and limitations. If more recent English
dramatists seem to show a renewed interest in the genre, O'Casey
has to be cited as one of the most important intermediaries
between the nineteenth century tradition and the present day.

The End of the Beginning* and *A Pound on Demand* are both
based on a simple but effective situation. In *The End of the
Beginning*, Darry Berrill exchanges roles with his wife Lizzie
to prove that housework is an easy matter for a man; in *A
Pound on Demand*, Jerry and Sammy, two drunken labourers,
try to withdraw a pound from Sammy's postal savings account.
According to the conventions of the farce, the various possibilities
resulting from these situations are played out. There is no logical
development of plot, nor is there any definite result. The end can
be foreseen right from the beginning; the audience's interest is
not so much in the ending as in the process by which it is
reached. Darry Berrill, with the help of his friend Barry Derrill,
succeeds in a short time in bringing about 'a panorama of ruin'
(p. 290), Sammy and Jerry cause similar havoc in the peaceful
post-office. The dramatist consciously leaves aside all rational
considerations, for it is precisely in the grotesque traits of a
cumulation of events that the play's effectiveness lies.

In the course of these plays, the importance of the word is
reduced in comparison to the function of gesture and mime and
of the comedy of objects which take on an independent existence.
Thus the stage-directions are of equal importance to the dialogue,
and even the spoken text is largely composed of disguised stage-
directions, triggering off and commenting upon the characters'
actions. Only in the field of invective does the dialogue spread

out; O'Casey is justly considered an unequalled master in the invention and continuous variation of comic sequences of abuse, swearing and nagging. Darry, for instance, calls out to his friend: 'You snaky-arm'd candle-power-ey'd elephant, look at what you're after doing!' (p. 279).

The malice of inanimate objects and the characters' struggle with them takes up a large amount of space in these plays, the objects repeatedly defying the characters' alleged superiority or giving in to them only after considerable resistance. At the beginning of *A Pound on Demand* the two drunkards need three attempts to get through an obstinate swing-door, and later it inadvertently pushes Sammy out into the street again. The writing implements, too, resist Sammy's attempts to sign his name, so that he cannot obtain his money. To make such conflicts with ordinary objects more credible, the characters of farce are often physically disabled. Thus Sammy is on the verge of complete intoxication, and Barry in *The End of the Beginning* is short-sighted. In this second play, the objects take on an even higher degree of independence and play an insolent game with their helpless human adversaries. The spring of the alarm clock breaks when Darry winds it up, the gramophone plays the gymnastics course either too slowly or too quickly, Lizzie's apron resists Barry's attempts to put it on, crockery crashes, Darry's confrontation with the door-frame results in a bleeding nose, a razor cuts Barry's finger, the broom handle, apparently without Barry's interference, breaks a window-pane, the light suddenly turns itself off, the oilcan empties itself, a shelf collapses, Barry's spectacles get lost. The cumulative effect of these events prepares the audience for the ending when both men attempt to prevent their cow from falling off a bank. A rope is tied to the cow's neck and pulled through the chimney, where it is fastened to a chair. This soon begins to move across the room; both men together hardly succeed in holding it down; finally Darry is pulled up through the chimney only to drop down again when Lizzie cuts the cow loose. It is entirely just to call *The End of the Beginning* "one of the most brilliant sequences of comic *peripeteia* to be found in any farce written in English."[5]

The characters who are exposed to such conflicts are types, i.e. they have no individual existence but are reduced to a single isolated feature. Sammy is the drunkard (and nothing else), Barry is short-sighted, Darry is a know-all. They are incapable of development, because they are incapable of realizing the consequences of their actions. At the end, Sammy is just as drunk as he was at the beginning, and Darry in the play's last sentence shouts at his wife: '. . . my God, woman, can you do nothin' right!' (p. 291). It is impossible to identify with such types, therefore an audience can experience no compassion with their 'fate'; on the contrary, one's enjoyment rises with the amount of pain the stage figures experience. Malevolent glee is the appropriate emotion for the audience of a farce. The comic effect is multiplied by the fact that, as frequently in farce, the central figures appear in pairs. Darry and Barry as well as Sammy and Jerry with their near-identical names differ only in minor details. Their actions and reactions dominate the stage, while the other figures, like the straight-man of music-hall, merely provide the cues. In his other plays, O'Casey has frequently repeated the doubling of central actors in farcical scenes after having found it difficult in *The Shadow of a Gunman* to rely on one actor alone. Captain Boyle and Joxer Daly in *Juno and the Paycock*, Peter Flynn and the Covey in *The Plough and the Stars*, Simon and Sylvester in *The Silver Tassie*, Poges and Stoke in *Purple Dust*, Michael Marthraun and Mahan in *Cock-a-doodle Dandy* and Rankin and the Prodical in *The Bishop's Bonfire* are the most successful in a long series of comic pairs whose origin can be traced back, at least in part, to the farce.

It hardly need be mentioned that O'Casey's farces do not have any serious intent. In *A Pound on Demand* he does not intend to portray the ordinary man's conflicts with the repressive forces of bureaucracy, nor does he present in *The End of the Beginning* the problems of the impoverished Irish small farmer, although the starting-point of both plays might have suggested such a treatment. If a critic describes *A Pound on Demand* as 'eine kleine Clownerie vom Menschen, der sich nicht ausweisen und nicht korrekt seinen Namen schreiben kann und hilflos vor der Übermacht des bürokratischen Ritus steht",[6] this implies a critical potential which is simply not present in a farce which intends neither to intensify man's understanding of life, nor to discuss ideas nor to contribute to an improvement of the world.

It would, therefore, be easy to by-pass these two plays with the remark that O'Casey mastered this form of drama among many others, if they did not show many parallels to his other works. In his full-length plays, he incorporated the farce, whose possibilities he here tries out in its pure form, into the assembly of manifold and frequently heterogeneous elements which constitute his major works. Almost all his full-length plays have farcical scenes which neither exist for their own sake nor as mere comic relief.

They contribute rather to the general impact of the play in question, promoting the characterization of individual figures, deepening by contrast the insight into the bitterness of individual experience or intensifying by comic parallels the meaning of the other parts. Wherever these functions are most clearly present (for instance in *Juno and the Paycock, The Silver Tassie, Purple Dust, Cock-a-doodle Dandy* and *The Bishop's Bonfire*), they will be discussed in the context of that particular play. Here it remains to be stated that O'Casey (in contrast to the opinion of several critics who have seen his works as the unreflected eruptions of a natural talent) consciously and purposefully acquired the various forms of the drama which, just as purposefully, he juxtaposed in his plays. The farce, as that type of play that perhaps can be most easily identified, serves as an instructive example of this process.

# 11. WITHIN THE GATES

*Within the Gates* was the first full-length play that O'Casey wrote without a definite theatre in mind, and in which he therefore could not rely on actors, stage conditions and audiences familiar to him. It was published in 1933 after he had attempted in vain to interest Alfred Hitchcock in a film with the same theme (under the title *The Green Gates*).[1] The first production (Royalty Theatre, 1934) was not only a financial, but apparently also an artistic failure; O'Casey himself referred to 'a paltry production which brought to light all the darkness his poor heart had feared',[2] and this is confirmed by the reviews.[3] A New York production in the autumn of the same year succeeded better in transferring the play's ideas into the realities of the stage.[4] Yet even this production left a bitter after-taste, for a tour to several American towns had to be cancelled after the mayor of Boston had given in to the pressure of Catholic and Methodist opinion and prohibited the performance of the play because of its alleged anti-religious and immoral tendencies.[5] O'Casey had been invited to the New York rehearsals and experienced in all its detail the transformation of his text into an actual performance, realizing in the process some of its weaknesses. It is not surprising that he frequently discussed *Within the Gates*, both intellectually and technically his most complex play, in his theoretical writings.

It is also understandable why in the edition of the *Collected Plays* he presented an entirely new text – the 'Stage Version' – based on his experiences with the London and New York productions. His revisions are more decisive than in any other play. If critics have frequently differed in their opinions concerning this play, their disagreement may well be due to the fact that they have used different texts. It is therefore necessary to preface the interpretation with a short comparison of the two versions.[6]

The alterations from the first to the second version have two effects: on the one hand the play's suitability for the stage is improved, on the other hand the central themes are accentuated and are freed from an overgrowth of irrelevancies. Even the external differences between the two texts are considerable. The stage version is shorter by about one tenth; eight of the twenty

seven stage figures of the first version are omitted, only one
(The Man in the Straw Hat) has been added. Several scenes have
been cut completely, others have been redistributed among the
remaining characters, placing more emphasis on several of these.
A number of the incidental songs have been omitted, others have
been shortened or rephrased. The introduction of the characters
has been handled more skilfully; in the first version, for instance,
Jannice, the central character, does not appear in the first thirty
printed pages; in the stage version, however, she is introduced
after four pages, and the succeeding scene clarifies her unusual
fate. The audience's attention is thus directed towards her much
earlier and more effectively. The names of several of the characters
have also changed; the Young Whore of the first version becomes
the Young Woman. This alteration suggests that O'Casey has
tried to avoid any unnecessary provocation of the audience, a
tendency that can be observed in several of the textual alterations,
too. At the same time the status of Jannice in the thematic context
of the play is altered, the general problems of a young woman
being substituted for the more exceptional fate of a prostitute.
This is reflected in the omission of the Scarlet Woman and the
adventure-seeking Young Man in Plus-Fours who in the first
version had reflected Jannice's way of life.

These revisions already go beyond the alterations required by
stage practice. The extent of O'Casey's alterations can be gauged
from the fact that only about half the scenes are retained even
in their general outline. Yet even they have been revised
considerably; it is true to say that hardly a line of the text remains
entirely unchanged. There are a few scenes where the revisions
are relatively small: in Act I[7] the scenes between Jannice and the
Atheist and her ensuing encounter with the Salvation Army
Officer and the Gardener (pp. 140-147), in Act II the scene between
Jannice and the Bishop, which is interrupted by the Old Woman
(pp. 158-168), in Act III part of the scene between Jannice and the
Bishop (pp. 189-195), and the final section of Act IV (pp. 224-231);
O'Casey also retained several comic discussion scenes between
minor figures, but redistributed the dialogue among the characters.
Beyond these sections, only small passages have been retained
unaltered, and large parts of the stage version seem in fact to be a
new play.

The differences between the two texts can perhaps be demonstrated from a passage that stands between the two extremes
of unchanged repetition and complete re-writing. The scene
where the Atheist informs the Dreamer of Jannice's past may

serve as an example. It will be noticed immediately that in the earlier version the two characters appear without motivation, while in the stage version the Atheist hurries in when the Dreamer attacks the Chair Attendants because Jannice has rejected him – the discussion is thus skilfully connected with the preceding scene. It is also immediately obvious that the scene has been shortened considerably, due to the fact that irrelevant details have been omitted. A representative passage from the earlier version reads:

Then, when the kid was six or seven, crowned with paper orange blossoms over a white veil, the mother marries a heavy dragoon home from the front on leave; 'as a star-lit time with the warrior for a week; 'ad an allowance flung at 'er from the Government, which grew into a pension when 'er dragoon disappeared in one of those hail 'en farewell advances from the front line.[8]

This is changed to:

Then the mother married an Irish dragoon, a brave, decent man, Dreamer, home from the front on leave; had a star-lit time with the warrior for a week; then the dragoon disappeared in one of those vanishing advances from the front line an' the widow settles dahn on 'er pension. (pp. 123-124)

The second passage omits facts which are not essential for the audience, and it is also easier to speak. In spite of such reductions, the second scene contains an important addition:

DREAMER. And did you bring her into touch with song?
ATHEIST. Song? Oh, I had no time for song!
DREAMER. You led her from one darkness into another, man. [*He rises and walks about – angrily*] Will none of you ever guess that man can study man, or worship God, in dance and song and story! (p. 124).

While in the earlier version the Dreamer simply provides the cues for the Atheist's report, here he characterizes his own position as well. At the same time, a central theme of the play, the religious implications of the imagination as opposed to the a-religious rationalism of the Atheist, is introduced. Finally, the new text shows the Old Woman in a less unfavourable light; this tendency to retain some kind of respect for her, noticeable throughout the second version, avoids a serious break between Acts III and IV and makes her final, pitiful appearance more understandable.

Finally, another alteration which may appear unimportant in comparison with the more decisive revisions, nevertheless deserves some attention, because it can influence the interpretation of the whole play. At the end, O'Casey succeeds in eliminating an ambiguity inherent in the first version by simply revising the sequence of sentences, and adding a sentence and a stage direction. The original text reads:

DREAMER [*looking towards the* BISHOP *and the figure of the* YOUNG WHORE]. Hail and farewell, sweetheart; forever and forever, hail and farewell!

BISHOP [*in low and grief-stricken tones*]. She died making the sign of the cross, she died making the sign of the cross!
[*The* DREAMER *gazes for a moment at the* YOUNG WHORE, *then turns and begins to go slowly out. The music, sounding slow and soft, of the song he sang to her is heard; in the middle of the melody the gates begin to close slowly, coming together on the last few notes of the tune.*][9]

The stage version reverses the order of the last two speeches, and the Dreamer, who now gives the final interpretation, adds the decisive words: 'You fought the good fight, Jannice; and you kept the faith . . .' (p. 231). This indicates that the sign of the cross may be important to the Bishop, but not to the dramatist. When O'Casey's additional stage direction is considered, it becomes clear that Jannice does not die a death of contrition and repentance, but of optimistic affirmation of those values incorporated in the Dreamer; for he writes: '*The sky's purple and black changes to a bright grey, pierced with golden segments, as if the sun was rising, and a new day about to begin*' (p. 231).

The essential characteristics of the revision may be summarized as follows: (1) Several characters are revaluated; (2) the structure of the play is brought out more clearly; (3) the central theme is accentuated; (4) the style appears less stilted and farfetched, confused images are often omitted (the clarity of the style is also improved by reducing the Cockney dialect of the first version). It becomes apparent that O'Casey took considerable pains to follow up the two productions of his play. He conscientiously and skilfully created a new version that far exceeds the earlier text both in its intellectual clarity and its stage effectiveness. The following interpretation will therefore be based entirely on the stage version.

★

It is important for an understanding of *Within the Gates* to distinguish between three aspects of the play. O'Casey first of all provides an image of the world in its multiple appearances. Secondly he criticizes certain aspects of this world by satirizing them. Thirdly (and this became the most important aspect of the stage version) he emphasizes a particular, decisive problem of human existence, the search for the 'right' way to live and the quest for a new belief, i.e. the religious theme. Although O'Casey succeeded in skilfully interweaving these three elements, it is advisable to consider them separately.

O'Casey's starting point in writing *Within the Gates* was the desire to create a mirror-like image of the modern world without employing realistic details. He sketches a scenic panorama which, in the literal sense of the term, becomes a *Welt-Bild*, an image of life. The scenery of a park is admirably suited to such a purpose. It might be objected that O'Casey drew on his own memories of Hyde Park and that, therefore, the play was representative only of London or at best of England. Yet it should be noted that O'Casey apparently strove to avoid all specific references to the London scene. Occasional place names ('Kensington', p. 203), and allusions to the situation of England in the thirties (sterling crisis, unemployment) are so few and far between that they do not detract from the play's universality. Even the Cockney dialect used for a number of characters is not employed to create a specific London atmosphere but to provide a certain credibility for those characters for whom any kind of standard language would be inappropriate. Like no other drama of O'Casey's, *Within the Gates* could be transferred to any other city simply by changing the dialect. It is therefore not enough to consider the play as 'O'Casey's indictment of what is wrong with England of the Depression and post World War I years and what, if anything can be done.'[10]

The play's universality could be achieved only by abandoning any semblance of reality and by using a high degree of allegory. This is very clearly expressed in the scenery. O'Casey chose the setting of a park, an everyman-scenery, where the most diverse people can be brought together. Lawns, shrubs and pathways permit easy and vivid movement, counter-acting the danger of petrification that is always inherent in allegory. At the same time, the stylization of the scenery makes it clear that no realistic events are to be expected. A dominant feature of the setting is the war-memorial, its 'skeleton-like hands' (p. 117) suggesting a continuous threat to this park-world and the omnipresence of

death. This scenery is shown in four different stages: a spring
morning, a summer noon, an autumn evening, and a winter
night. The combination of the progress of days and seasons points
to the progress of human life in general; the cyclic character is
underlined by the dawning of a new day at the end of the play.
The beginning and the end of each act are accentuated by the
symbolic opening and closing of the park-gates in the form of a
stylized curtain, suggested by O'Neill's *Mourning Becomes
Electra*, but certainly more effective than O'Neill's idea in being
part of a more generally stylized approach.

The park-world is inhabited by numerous different people.
O'Casey's scale ranges from a baby to an old man, it includes
different occupations (from prostitute to bishop) as well as the
various social levels and classes (from the unemployed to an
aristocratic infant). Characters have very little existence of their
own, they are less interesting as individuals than as representatives of certain groups, views of life or modes of thought. This is
suggested even by their 'names': jobs (A Gardener), family
relations (The Bishop's Sister), confessions (The Atheist) or even
garments (A Man Wearing a Bowler Hat) are employed to
distinguish between the various stage figures. Only a few of
them, and only occasionally, address each other by Christian
names (the Young Woman is called Jannice and the Bishop
Gilbert).

The events that occur in this world are just as heterogeneous. A
mother beats her daughter, lovers exchange caresses, a wreath is
laid at the memorial, a prostitute is arrested, the Salvation Army
conducts a meeting, a poet obtains an advance against his new
book, unemployed persons importune the Bishop, etc. O'Casey
deploys the whole vividness of his imagination in inventing
numerous such scenes which reflect the diversity and variety of
life. It is, then, the purpose of this aspect of the play to give a
comprehensive as well as an objective vision of the world.[11]

★

O'Casey does not confine himself, however, to such an objective
presentation. Certain facets of life are distorted by exaggeration,
thus rendering them ridiculous and an object of the audience's
criticism. The most obvious example is the scene with the
newspaper readers (pp. 181-187). Four minor figures open their
newspapers, that have only one word on the title-page: 'Murder',
'Rape', 'Suicide' and 'Divorce'. Each of them then reads out a

concentrated passage of the type that a public, hankering after sensations, expects from the yellow press:

MAN WEARING BOWLER [*reading from behind the paper marked Divorce*]. The housemaid said she climbed the ivy, got to the verandah, looked in through the window, saw the co-respondent in bed, the respondent in her camisole trotting towards the bed; then came darkness, and she would leave the judge and jury to guess the rest (p. 184).

They then intone the song 'London Bridge is falling down', probably a reference to Eliot's *Waste Land*, because their interests are the perfect expression of a modern world of civilization deserted by God. In addition to his satirical presentation, O'Casey also gives a more direct expression to his indignation when the Young Woman parodies a prayer:

Let every sound be hushed, for the oblate fathers are busy reading the gospel for the day. Furnishing their minds with holy thoughts, and storing wisdom there. Let us pray! Oh, Lucifer, Lucifer, who has caused all newspapers to be written for our learning – stars of the morning and stars of the evening – grant we may so read them that we may always find a punch in them, hot stuff in them, and sound tips in them; so that, outwardly in our bodies and inwardly in our souls, we may get closer and closer to thee! [*Indignantly*] Why the hell don't you all say Amen! (p. 182)

In other passages, his criticism is implied in the simple comic effect created by the isolation and exaggeration of certain aspects of modern city life. Among these is the respect induced by the pram that contains the baby of a duchess (pp. 126-127), or the city dwellers' impoverished attitude to nature, expressed in clichés like 'The busy birds warbling a sylvan sonata' (p. 130). The superficial patriotism of the Chair Attendants is ridiculed, too, when they find themselves persuaded into chauvinistic emotions by a radio programme called 'Pageant of England' (p. 134), as is the sentimental soul-massage provided by newspaper columnists (p. 131). At times, unveiled social criticism takes the place of this kind of satire, for instance in the song that condemns the unnatural life style of a business-man, of a church-goer and of a politician (pp. 149-150), in other places the satire turns into some kind of harmless comedy. The scenes concerned with the four men obsessed by a desire for discussion are a border-line case between satire and farcical comedy. Without any factual basis they turn to any topic, from the theory of relativity to proofs of divine existence. It is not clear whether O'Casey means to criticize the modern tendency to discuss any and every subject without knowing enough about it, as it is encouraged by the media and by institutes for further education, or whether he simply intended to introduce the otherwise absent dimension of the comic into his work. In any case these scenes remain, in spite of their effectiveness, an alien element in the complex structure of the play.

*

The two aspects of *Within the Gates* discussed above, world-image and social criticism, characterize the play as a panorama or pageant but say little as to its dramatic value. Its specific dramatic qualities are inherent in the theme that is interwoven in this pageant: the quest for the right way of life and the question about a possible after-life. The questing and questioning is embodied in Jannice, the Young Woman. In the figures she encounters, the dramatist offers her a number of exemplary patterns of behaviour and belief. Jannice is the daughter of the Old Woman, seduced by the Bishop during his time as a student. He had the child brought up in a home run by nuns, where Jannice as 'a child of sin' was made familiar with all the terrors of hell. During the war the Old Woman married a soldier who was killed soon afterwards; and from then on she lived with the Atheist. He freed Jannice from the hands of the nuns and tried to re-educate her according to his lights. When her mother became both alcoholic and religious she fled from home, but had to change her job several times to escape her employers' approaches, and, at the time of the play, she now earns her living as a prostitute. This life history appears melodramatic if *Within the Gates* is considered as an individual drama, and it has indeed been criticized as 'sentimental melodrama'.[12] If, however, Jannice is seen as an allegorical 'everywoman',[13] oscillating between various forces struggling for her allegiance, the events of her youth become an important prerequisite for her constantly changing preferences. It is less fortunate that occasionally O'Casey tends to provide psychological motivations for his figures' behaviour. The Bishop's attitude, for instance, is largely dominated by his fear of being recognized as Jannice's father, and the audience's attention is drawn to the largely irrelevant question whether Jannice and the Old Woman will eventually discover the identity of the Bishop and his sister. Such suspense in the usual sense of the term is inappropriate to

*Within the Gates*; the audience's expectation ought to be directed exclusively to the question which of the various forces is to be victorious in their struggle for the possession of Jannice.

The figures who compete for her or with whom she hopes to find some security, can be subdivided into three groups, an a-religious, a Christian and an anti-Christian group. Since her quest is deeply religious, those figures who are beyond religion cannot offer her any assistance. The Police Woman, as the embodiment of law and order (O'Casey ironically calls her a 'symbol of woman dressed in a little brief authority' [14]), thinks to solve the problem inherent in Jannice by arresting her. The Bishop's Sister, representative of bourgeois morality, assumes the same attitude: 'Be off out of the Park, and hide yourself, you shameless thing, or I'll send the police to take you out!' (pp. 224-225). This lack of compassion turns her, the companion of a high church dignitary who in her social position could afford to show some *caritas* and even would have the duty to do so, into an especially unpleasant person and into the only completely negative figure of the play. The Gardener sees Jannice as a means of enjoying himself and can enthuse about her beauty as long as she does not make any demands on him. But when she wants to marry him, for fear of being alone with her visions of hell, he retreats. He represents those people who attempt carefully to separate work and pleasure and who are not willing to undergo any emotional engagement, giving free rein to their egotism unhampered by transcendental ties and any feeling of responsibility.

The two Nurse-Maids stand between these a-religious and the Christian figures in the play. Thoughtlessly, they confess to be Christians when they are asked, but lead their lives of small joys and sorrows unencumbered by metaphysical problems. Jannice cannot therefore enter into any relationship with them. The two opportunistic Chair Attendants appear in a less favourable light, because they simulate humility and faithfulness to their Church as long as there is some promise of material advantage. When the Bishop, however, does not provide them with money they break out into a flood of abuse against the clergy. Another perversion of Christian behaviour, as a comic variation, is shown by the Man Wearing a Trilby Hat who naïvely and intolerantly takes the Bible literally and would still believe it if it claimed that Jonah had swallowed the whale (p. 152). The Old Woman's attitude, alternating between fits of drunkenness and of religiosity, offers similar problems. When she attempts to beat her daughter as soon as she sees her, she is obviously trying to chastise the sins of her own youth. These various kinds of perverted Christianity do not provide any serious patterns of behaviour and belief for Jannice.

Yet in the figure of the Bishop, the Evangelist, the Salvation Army Officer and the Down-and-Outs she is offered four forms of Christianity that she finds less easy to reject. O'Casey has carefully differentiated here and has not attempted to present 'the' Christian as a type. The two Evangelists represent humility and a turning away from reality. They carry the single maxim of their lives, *'Once to Die . . . After that Judgement'* (p. 129) about them in the form of placards. What happens before their death is immaterial to them as long as they believe their souls saved. They are, therefore, indifferent to their half-repulsive, half-comic appearance as *'sullen, long-forgotten clowns'* (p. 129). In O'Casey's scale of values, however, this disqualifies them from any serious consideration, for beauty, strength, colour – as signs of life-affirmation – here rank highest, while ugliness, weakness and colourlessness are at the bottom of the scale. For Jannice, the Evangelists' attitude is for a time a genuine temptation because, in the passivity of their negation of life, they seem to offer her a way out of the despair of her quest. It is significant that the Evangelists without resistance join the group of the Down-and-Outs, while the Chair Attendants, who have the same fate, show their fear in some slight if unavailing resistance.

The Down-and-Outs are one of the most impressive and at the same time one of the most sinister and haunting inventions of O'Casey's. Undoubtedly they were suggested by the hopeless demonstrations of the unemployed in the England of the Great Depression, but this is not the only meaning inherent in them. They stand for all those who do not have enough courage to face up to the problems of existence and who wait for their end in despair and submission. They are a continuous threat for Jannice, i.e. for humanity. While in Act I their muffled song, a distant warning, is only heard by the Chair Attendants, who are most exposed to danger, in Act II they have come nearer and are heard by Jannice, too. In Act III they become visible for the first time, a grey procession of people defeated by life, and not only the Chair Attendants, but Jannice too is petrified with fear, while even the Bishop trembles. Their hollow song, with the impressive image 'We carry furl'd the fainting flag of a dead hope and a dead faith' (p. 196) even seems to darken the sky and to exclude the warmth of the sun. In Act IV, they advance to the centre of the scene, enclose the Chair Attendants and the Old Woman and threaten Jannice. She is able to escape from this extreme danger of despairing shortly before her death only through her dance, the symbol of life-affirmation, and with the help of the Dreamer she finally defeats the forces inimical to life.

In contrast to the Down-and-Outs and the Evangelists, the Salvation Army turns purely to people's emotions. With uniforms, flags, music and song, with the irrationality of a pompous procession (pp. 197-202) they woo Jannice. Impressive images, especially the idea of the lost sheep, are substituted for logical arguments and create a feeling where the individual is ready to succumb to the sheer ecstasy of being saved. It is shown quite early in the play that this conscious appeal to the emotions can easily take the wrong course when, in Act I, the Young Salvation Army Officer who has tried to convince Jannice of God's forgiveness, inadvertently begins to pat her knee and thus leads her back to the healthy sobriety of normal life: 'Oh, God, don't do that, please! You'll make a ladder, and silk stockings aren't easy to get' (p. 144). O'Casey called the Young 'Officer' a 'symbol of the coloured sob-stuff in organized religion that reflects no gleam from the mind of God, and brings no gleam to the mind of man'.[15] The Bishop seems to be of a similar opinion; he rebukes the Salvation Army Officer when he describes the path to God as a simple step 'Out of self, into Christ, into glory!': 'The saints didn't find it quite so simple, my young friend' (p. 174). From then on the Salvation Army Officer rejects the Bishop as a 'ritualist' (p. 198). On the other hand, the Man Wearing a Trilby Hat rejects him because he does not follow the Bible literally (p. 153). Jannice's quest is all the more arduous for the fact that the very Christians who pray to the same God disagree about the correct path to Him, but all claim the monopoly of rightness in their guidance and endeavour to estrange her from the others.

While Jannice early on succeeds in liberating herself from the sense-oriented, anti-rational appeals of the Salvation Army (in Act IV the Salvation Army no longer appears), the Bishop remains her companion to the end, sometimes rejected, then again desired. The situation of humanity between belief and unbelief could not be symbolized better than by the fact that Jannice is the illegitimate daughter of the Bishop and the legitimate step-daughter of the Atheist. The Bishop at first appears merely as a representative of institutionalized Christianity; the question raised by several critics whether he is a Roman Catholic or an Anglican seems to have been left open on purpose in order

to preserve the universality of the play. In the course of the
action, however, he begins to claim the audience's sympathy as
a person who is driven by his own doubts. He then loses the
comic traits which in Acts I and II result from his forced joviality
in his relationship with the 'ordinary people'. Paradoxically, he
is guilty of the sin of pride precisely because, conscious of his
own superiority, he condescends to speak with the visitors to the
park on their own level, while his sister represents the opposite
form of pride: 'A bishop should be in the midst of the incense, in
the sanctuary safe away from the sour touch of common humanity'
(p. 133). She also addresses the warning to him that is supposed
to remind him of his own sin, but rather serves as a reminder of
his humanity: 'Remember what happened to you in your student
days!' (p. 133). At first, however, he remains untouched by this
appeal, delivers pseudo-poetic speeches on the birds, interferes
with pompous advice in the affairs of the Guardsman and the
Nursemaid and enjoys being celebrated as a 'man of the people'
by the Chair Attendants. He is deceived by any pretence of
religiosity, and it is due to his own naïveté that he immediately
becomes the object of their angry scorn when he fails to honour
their 'friendship' with a few pound notes. Up to this point his
behaviour corresponds to the role played, in O'Casey's view, by
the Church in the twentieth century.

His confrontation with Jannice, however, makes his situation
much more complicated. At first he still behaves 'typically', i.e.
when a human being really needs him, he refuses to help because
he is not supposed to interfere in private affairs. He can offer her
nothing but some clichés, including the highly ironical sentence:
'Go and talk these things with your father and mother' (p. 160).
Jannice's slightly hysterical outbursts are here entirely justified
by his behaviour: 'A tired Christ would be afraid to lean on your
arm. Your Christ wears a bowler hat, carries a cane, twiddles his
lavender gloves, an' sends out gilt-edged cards of thanks to
callers. Out with you, you old shivering sham, an' go away into
the sun to pick the yellow primroses!' (pp. 163-164). Yet he
himself is not unmoved by this confrontation. Even if he disowns
his own name (pp. 166, 217), adding another sin to the sin of his
youth, he gives the Dreamer the money for Jannice that he had
refused the Chair Attendants, and thus shows a first indication
of responsibility. In Act III he already calls her 'my little Jannice'
and 'my child' (p. 187). He cannot understand that it would be no
help to put her under the care of an order of pious sisters, and
even recommends the Down-and-Outs as a model for her:

There go God's own aristocracy, the poor in spirit! Their slogan, Welcome be the Will of God; their life of meek obedience and resignation in that state of poverty unto which it has pleased God to call them, a testimony that God's in His heaven, all's well with the world . . . Join them, my daughter, in the spirit of penitence and prayer! (p. 196)

For himself, he ignores the advice, for immediately prior to this he had told Jannice 'When trying to help you, I must be careful of what others may think' (p. 191), and even to be seen in her company is embarrassing for him (p. 193). In Act IV, at least in theory, he has rejected this attitude: 'That has been my besetting sin all along – fear of the respectable opinion of others. I renounce it now!' (p. 205). It is true that in practice he cannot overcome his weakness so quickly and once more disavows his interest in Jannice (p. 217). Yet the decisive point is that he is trying to change, accusing himself to his sister: 'Being too sensible has been my curse all along. By trying to save my honoured soul, I am losing it. Go home, woman, and let me find a way to my girl and my God!' (p. 206). Towards the end he thus appears as a *'sad and dignified figure'* (p. 226), who still tries to associate Jannice with the Down-and-Outs but does not reject her when she prefers her dance of affirmation to submission and even fulfils her final demand, making the sign of the cross over her. His concluding words to his sister, 'Go home, go home, for Christ's sake, woman, and ask God's mercy on us all!' (p. 231), are a moving document of his newly-won insight into the complexity of the human attitude to God. This humility, quite different from the self-abasement of the Down-and-Outs, will, in an O'Caseyan world, bring him nearer to God than all the knowledge that he had previously held to be so unshakeable.

The Bishop is, then, at least at the end of the play, more than the simple representative of organized religion. It would be more correct to speak of him as the positively utopian image – for O'Casey – of a Church so converted that it no longer believes itself to know the only way to God, but in all humility, without rash judgements, offers its assistance to those who need it most.

O'Casey uses three other figures each of whom has dissociated himself from the Church and its representatives, to show that this is not the only way to master life. One of them, the Man with the Stick (in the last Act Man with Umbrella), shows the comic distortion of an anti-religious attitude (just as the Man wearing a Trilby Hat is the comic distortion of a believing Christian). His object in life is 'to bounce the idea of a Gord from men's minds . . .'

(p. 125). He is a fanatical disputant, omitting no occasion to prove
the possibility of understanding the world rationally; to him, the
songs praising the mysteries and miracles of life must therefore
appear as 'Nonsense' (p. 137). He also presents a picturesque
interpretation of the physical relationship between space and
time:

Now, suppose that one night, when we all slept, th' universe we knows
sank down to the size of a football, en' all the clocks began to move a
thousand times quicker, – no, slower – it wouldn't mike the slightest
difference to us, for we wouldn't realize that any difference 'ad tyken
plice, though each of us would live a thousand times longer, en' man
couldn't be seen, even under a microscope (p. 209).

Under these circumstances, the Guardsman's question seems to
be entirely justified: '. . . if a man couldn't be seen under a
microscope, wot abaht 'is kids?' (p. 209).

Whilst the Man with the Stick has no relationship with Jannice,
the Atheist, his more serious parallel figure, is one of the people
who have shaped her life. He represents a sober rationalism
without the comic-fanatical excesses of the other character. He is
the moving force among the group of disputants, who do not
know how to begin without him, but he also offers an alternative
to the beliefs of the Bishop. That his attitude has to be taken
entirely seriously, becomes clear when everybody except him
trembles before the invading Down-and-Outs: '*The scene grows
dark and chilly, and even the Bishop shivers, though the Atheist
seems not to notice the change . . . the Down-and-Out . . . go
behind the Atheist, but he stands there, indifferent to march or
chant*' (p. 195). His attitude excludes any complete self-negation
and self-degradation, such as the Bishop recommends to Jannice.
But he also lacks the capacity for enthusiasm and the sense of all
those values of the imagination embodied in song and dance
which are not open to rational understanding. For Jannice his
existence means the chance of a refuge; he finally rejects her not
because he is hard-hearted but because she has twice left him
after a short time. Her liberation from the hands of the nuns ('. . .
you saved me from their crosses, their crowns, and their canes . . .'
p. 141) was a more unselfish act than anything the other figures,
including the Dreamer, are willing to do, and Jannice herself
acknowledges his friendliness (p. 188). If he cannot finally offer
her a way out of despair, it is because he cannot substitute
anything more pleasant for the visions of hell that still occupy her
imagination.

The Dreamer achieves precisely this, and he therefore remains victorious in the struggle for the soul of Jannice. All the same he is not an ideal person. His very first words, spoken to the Chair Attendants, show his intolerance towards everybody who does not accept life as he does: 'Here, you two derelict worshippers of fine raiment – when are you going to die?' (p. 120). And towards the end he expresses the same attitude when the Bishop prays for the souls of the dying Chair Attendants, and the Dreamer replies full of contempt: 'Let them sink into the grave, O Lord, and never let their like appear on the face of the earth again' (p. 227). He likewise feels no pangs of conscience in looking after his own interests; when the Bishop gives him three pound notes for Jannice, he pockets one of them and later offers it to her as payment for the pleasures of a night. Even Jannice realizes his egotism: 'Your way, young singer, though bright with song, is dim with danger. At the end of the way, I might find myself even lower than I am. There is no peace with you' (p. 173).

The Dreamer, however, has realized a secret that makes him superior to all the others. He knows that Jannice, other than the life-negating Salvation Army Officer, cannot find her peace without the joy of life: 'To him, peace may bring joy; to such as you, only joy can give you peace' (p. 178). Thus he is the only one who at least for a time can mitigate her fear, and when he appears, '. . . the look of fright fades from her face' (p. 200). The Dreamer, therefore, is an influential rival to all those who struggle for the possession of Jannice's soul, and the Bishop explicitly warns her to keep away from him as a danger to morals and tradition (p. 188). The source of joy he offers her is love. As always in O'Casey, sexual love is explicitly presented as a positive value, but only when it is not isolated (as in the Gardener's case) but is part of an affection that includes the willingness to master life's difficulties. Jannice finally follows his summons: 'Come, sweet lass, and let's transmute vague years of life into a glowing hour of love!' (p. 170), and spends a few happy months with him. Yet the decisive test for the attitude he represents is Jannice's approaching death. She can now find no satisfaction in her affirmation of this world and sends him out to search for the Bishop. The final scene of *Within the Gates* thus becomes a dramatic conflict, unusual in its intensity in an allegorical play. The Dreamer confronts the Bishop's demand that Jannice should join the Down-and-Outs with his repeated request: 'Sing them silent, dance them still, and laugh them into an open shame!'

(p. 228). When she collapses in her dance and dies, it is he who sums up her life: 'You fought the good fight, Jannice; and you kept the faith . . .' (p. 231).

This faith that he has passed on to her is faith in the beauty of existence. The Dreamer does not struggle for a life without religion, but he fights for a life without anxiety. His God (whom he repeatedly mentions) is best honoured by affirming life and not by negating it for fear of some later punishment. The elements of his religious worship are song, dance and laughter; the Dreamer, as the poet who himself composes several songs in the play (pp. 133, 136, 171), thus becomes a mediator between God and man in the park-world of this play. It is hardly surprising that O'Casey should here refer to the dramatist whom he admired most: to Shaw. The words of the Dreamer, quoted above, are those of the dying Louis Dubedat in *The Doctor's Dilemma*: '. . . I have never denied my faith . . . I've fought the good fight.' [16] Like the Dreamer, Dubedat who, to the abhorrence of his partners, calls himself 'a disciple of Bernard Shaw',[17] despises all moral conventions. Both of them ignore, with a considerable degree of recklessness, the interests of their fellow human beings, to whom they are superior by reason of their artistic potential and their endeavour for self-fulfilment. Both of them finally succeed in transferring their quest for a full life to the women who love them, thus making the latter happy in a Shavian sense.

If Jannice in the course of the play moves closer and closer to the Dreamer, and finally even defends him to the Bishop, this is intended by the dramatist as an important value judgement. Jannice herself would not be capable of such a step because she is not the driving force but rather the personification of driven impotence, attracted by the magnet that is strongest at the moment. This does not imply any criticism of the play: her status as every-woman would be reduced if she had clearly defined individual characteristics.[18] She has only *one* characteristic, the weakness of her heart, and this is not a private disease but symbolizes the mortality of human beings exposed to death. Jannice has to develop a positive attitude to life in view of this constant threat of death. She wavers between various extremes. One of them, a slightly hysterical contempt of death expressed in her repeated phrase 'I'll go, go game, and I'll die dancing!' (p. 228), had been presented before by O'Casey in his Irish Nannie (*Nannie's Night Out*). *Within the Gates*, however, is remarkable for the comprehensiveness of its views, the manifold attitudes to life it offers and which Jannice duly tries out. It is therefore entirely justifiable to see *Within the Gates* as 'O'Casey's most comprehensive achievement' [19] and 'the most comprehensive and the greatest of O'Casey's plays – both in theme and form'.[20]

★

His achievement is the more remarkable when one considers that several autobiographical experiences have been incorporated into the play. The Dreamer has without doubt certain features of the playwright, as, for instance, can be shown by a comparison with O'Casey's own poems (e.g. 'The Dreamer Dreams of God') from the volume *Windfalls*, published a year after *Within the Gates*. Several hints in *Rose and Crown* also suggest that O'Casey saw in Jannice certain similarities with his wife Eileen who had been educated in an Ursuline convent and who at first found it difficult to adapt to O'Casey's liberal, life- and art-affirming attitude.[21] Such biographical details, however, are much less important for an evaluation of the play than the fact that they were incorporated smoothly into the dramatic context and do not in any way impair the artistic unity of the play.

Nevertheless *Within the Gates* is not without weaknesses, though to say so is not to endorse such self-disqualifying judgements as James Agate's description of *Within the Gates* as 'pretentious rubbish'.[22] There are two major targets for any well-considered criticism of the play. On the one hand, the figure of the Dreamer has repeatedly been censured: '. . . the Dreamer, who to judge by his songs is not much of a poet, is also shaky in his philosophy.' [23] The values which he embodies remain too un-defined to be convincing: '. . . the good life insofar as it is embodied in the Dreamer lacks force, depth, and complexity';[24] the Dreamer 'does not symbolize all that the dramatist demands of him.' [25] If *Within the Gates* can, with full justification, be called 'a play about O'Casey's humanistic vision of salvation',[26] it should be added that this vision would be even more impressive if one saw more clearly the values *for* which Jannice finally decides, after having been given such an impressive account of the values she rejects. On the other hand, O'Casey's language, especially the lyrical passages, has been criticized: 'The verse is turgid and repetitious; and its eloquence is often bombast. Instead of giving intensity to the emotional moments of the play, it relaxes tension.'[27] Although the stage version has gained considerably in precision and intensity, it still contains passages that justify such a judgement. The Dreamer's song for Jannice is an obvious example. Its initial stanza reads:

Her legs are as pliant and slim
As fresh, golden branches of willow;
I see lustre of love on each limb,
Looking down from the heights of a pillow!
Looking down from the heights of a pillow! (p. 171).

This song has an important structural function in that it influences Jannice's first conversion to the Dreamer's attitude, and its tune recurs whenever he is victorious in the struggle for her soul. In a stage performance, the music may perhaps hide the embarrassing clichés of the lines, but they remain indefensible all the same. Perhaps one can find an explanation for them in the dramatist's autodidactic education, which prevented him from identifying with any poetic tradition, forcing him to search for his place and occasionally to employ hackneyed expressions. Yet it is understandable that a play as comprehensive in form and scale as *Within the Gates*, 'one of the few plays in modern drama that has taken all of life for its theme',[28] should have its weaknesses; it is remarkable that O'Casey with so few exceptions mastered the manifold problems of this experiment.

Finally, the play's relationship to the tradition of expressionist drama ought to be considered. It should be stressed that *Within the Gates*, even less than *The Silver Tassie*, shows no influence at all of the drama of German expressionism, with which it has very little in common except the fact that it is clearly unrealistic. One should remember, however, that almost simultaneously with *Within the Gates* such variously unrealistic plays as Eliot's *The Rock*, García Lorca's *Bodas de Sangre*, some of Brecht's *Lehrstücke*, Auden-Isherwood's *The Dog Beneath the Skin*, Bridie's *Jonah and the Whale*, Shaw's *Too True to be Good*, Maugham's *Sheppey* and Cocteau's *La Machine Infernale* appeared, none of which could be called 'Expressionist' except by generalizing the term beyond recognition: *Within the Gates* is thus part of a general movement against realism on the stage, but it is not 'Expressionist' in any precise sense of the term, nor does it show any marked influence by other individual plays (such as O'Neill's *The Hairy Ape*[29]). It is a remarkably original work written by an author who would have agreed with O'Neill's definition of the dramatist's task in the modern world:

The playwright today must dig at the roots of the sickness of today as he feels it – the death of the Old God and the failure of science and materialism to give any satisfying new One for the surviving primitive religious instinct to find a meaning for life in, and to comfort its fears of death with. It seems to me that anyone trying to do big work nowadays must have this big subject behind all the little subjects of his plays or novels, or he is simply scribbling around on the surface of things and has no more real status than a parlor entertainer.[30]

# PART III

# Ideology and the Drama

What's the use of writing a play that's just as like a camel as a whale?
(Sean O'Casey)

# 12. PREFATORY

The first publication of *Within the Gates* and O'Casey's next play, *The Star Turns Red*, are no less than seven years apart, an indication of the crisis into which O'Casey was led after his separation from the Abbey Theatre. The dates of his following plays show how he overcame this crisis. While in the thirties only one full-length play was published, the following decade saw no less than five, and *The Star Turns Red* (1940), *Purple Dust* (1940) and *Red Roses for Me* (1942) are again as close together as the great Dublin plays. A re-orientation in O'Casey's writing had been evident in the publication of his polemical and critical articles in *The Flying Wasp* (1937), with which he intended to attack the established theatre critics, but which also indicated a certain degree of reflexion on the drama and its function in the modern world. The plays of his third phase mirror the results of these considerations.

Again, as in his previous phases, his short plays would have to be excepted from such a statement because again they deviate from the full-length plays, *Hall of Healing* being reminiscent of his early work just as *Kathleen Listens In* had pointed forward to later plays. *The Star Turns Red*, *Purple Dust*, *Red Roses for Me* and *Oak Leaves and Lavender*, however, in spite of their diversity, are distinguished from his preceding plays in the clarity with which they reveal the author's own opinions. Critics might disagree on O'Casey's attitude to the War of Independence in *The Shadow of a Gunman*, to Mary's strike in *Juno and the Paycock* or to the Easter Rising in *The Plough and the Stars*; the plays of the third phase leave very little scope for such speculation. In many places, the ideal of dramatic objectivity has been discarded; the scale of values established in these plays is no longer determined by human attitudes only, by failure or success in concrete situations, but also by opinions, theses and ideologies. These are predetermined as destructive or useful, their value does not have to be tested but only to be demonstrated. It is the task of the individual chapters to note in what way and to what degree the plays and their quality were affected by this new approach.

141

O'Casey's sympathies were now with socialism. In spite of his repeated assertion that he had been a communist from birth,[1] this attitude (foreshadowed by *The Harvest Festival*) does not become fully clear in his plays until *The Star Turns Red*. The following chapters will discuss to what degree these plays are influenced by socialist ideas and how these ideas can be defined more precisely.[2] Yet it should be noted even here that the four full-length plays of the period show an, albeit varying, tendency to social utopia. O'Casey prefigures changes in the social situation, or at least suggests their possibility, as he himself desired them. His turning to socialist ideas led to a further estrangement from his audiences, which is itself mirrored in the stage history of his plays. Earlier friends now turned away from him,[3] maintaining frequently that the degree of socialist ideology was equalled by a lack of artistic quality, while O'Casey himself always insisted on the dramatist's right to proclaim his opinions from the stage. O'Casey's most prominent critic was O'Neill, who after the New York production of *Within the Gates* had become O'Casey's friend, but who wrote after the publication of *The Star Turns Red*:

I suppose . . . these lousy times make it inevitable that many authors get caught in the sociological propaganda mill . . . But O'Casey is an artist and the soap box is no place for his great talent. The hell of it seems to be, when an artist starts saving the world, he starts losing himself.[4]

Even if *The Star Turns Red* might justify such a view, it would be rash to condemn the other plays of this period as propagandist. Indeed the degree of artistic integration of ideological elements varies considerably.

The inclusion of socialist ideas has consequences for the dramatic form. If the individual case is employed as an example of what is desirable in terms of changes in society, it is bound to deviate from a direct representation of reality. Thus the following chapters will have to discuss the question of new allegorical or symbolical techniques in these plays. In this respect in particular these plays differ considerably among themselves (compare, for instance, the allegorical *The Star Turns Red* with *Red Roses for Me* which consists of a network of symbolic references); in fact they share only one feature which might be called a departure from O'Casey's earlier work: in each play the figure of the socialist-minded, youthful hero whose opinions, slightly veiled, are manifestly those of the author, plays an important role. Red

Jim, O'Killigain, Ayamonn and Drishogue cannot hide their kinship to the heroes of popular entertainment drama; they are distinguished from them chiefly by their political convictions. In moral stance as in external appearance they are immaculate, they are irrefutable in discussion, and they sacrifice private ambitions to their ideas without hesitation. Such idealist characters have, however, two momentous drawbacks for the drama: firstly, they are not capable of any development or alteration, because any change would mean betrayal of their ideals, and secondly they do not admit of any dramatic conflict with an uncertain ending. In these characters, O'Casey's idealized memories of the Dublin trade union organiser Jim Larkin were combined with his equally idealizing projection of a 'new', socialist human being. It is possible to gauge O'Casey's dramatic power when one realizes how little the dramatic effectiveness of his plays has suffered through the inclusion of such figures.[5]

*Red Roses for Me* deserves special attention in this period, not only because it takes up a central position in O'Casey's dramatic career (it was the twelfth of twenty-three preserved plays, and chronologically it appeared exactly in the middle, 1942, between the first work, 1923, and the last, 1961), but also because its themes look back to his earlier plays as well as pointing forward to the later works. As one critic puts it: '*Roses rouges* est la pièce la plus représentative d' O'Casey; elle offre comme une synthèse de son idéologie et de sa dramaturgie.'[6] In its reflection of events from O'Casey's Dublin period, it can easily be identified with the first period of his work; its unrealistic third act with its predominance of visual techniques looks back to *The Silver Tassie* and *Within the Gates*; the socialist ideas of its hero Ayamonn and his insistence on better conditions for the workers link *Red Roses for Me* to the other 'red' plays of this period; the vision of an Ireland liberated from external coercion and dominated by beauty and joy as an example of a 'new' world points forward to the fourth period, especially to *The Drums of Father Ned*. *Red Roses for Me* therefore presents the critic with special difficulties when he tries to associate it with one particular aspect of O'Casey's career. No inclusion in a particular category is, indeed, possible in this case, but much more important is the question what techniques the dramatist employed to give unity to the diverging aspects of the play. The problem of internal unity, therefore, is both the starting point and the central question of the interpretation of *Red Roses for Me*; the findings of this chapter can, *mutatis mutandis*, be transferred to the other plays of this and also of the following phase.

# 13. THE STAR TURNS RED

*The Star Turns Red* was first produced in March 1940 by the London Unity Theatre, a fact which may in itself serve to characterize the play, for at the time, Unity was the leading amateur workers' theatre in Britain, propagating the ideas of the trade union movement while at the same time bringing many international plays with leftwing tendencies to Britain. O'Casey's play cannot be entirely separated from this context.[1] This implies some degree of criticism, for a play that can only be understood against the background of a particular theatre has little claim to any kind of universality. On the other hand, it is important to note the connection with the Unity, inasmuch as critics who ignore this background have often accused O'Casey of failing to achieve objectives to which he simply did not aspire. As a play written for (although not commissioned by) Unity Theatre, *The Star Turns Red* was bound to have a very definite purpose, even if it were not a propaganda play.

*

The chief object of such a play is to influence the audience, to 'convert' them to a certain attitude. Any interpretation will have to take special note of two questions: how can this attitude be defined, and what techniques does the author use to achieve it? The second question is basic for any evaluation of the play. Terms like 'genuine characters' and 'credible situations' or 'objectivity of presentation' are not in such a case appropriate criteria. It is, of course, possible to denigrate the propaganda play as a type, and, judging from his later plays, O'Casey even shared this view to a certain extent,[2] but it is inadequate to make demands on a play which it does not intend to fulfil. In most cases, therefore, previous critical reactions to this work aim wide of the target.

Formally, *The Star Turns Red* is the most unified and, in this particular respect, one of the most successful plays in the whole O'Casey canon. Its homogeneity is partly due to the fact that O'Casey succeeded in keeping autobiographical elements out of the play. This is not to say that *The Star Turns Red* is not in part

144

based on the author's personal experiences. Its dedication, 'To
the men and women who fought through the great Dublin lockout
in nineteen hundred and thirteen' (p. 239), is reminiscent of one
of O'Casey's most vivid experiences, a strike and lockout fought
with great bitterness. The figure of Red Jim is without doubt
based on Jim Larkin, the great Dublin trade union leader who
was one of O'Casey's ideals; as early as 1922 O'Casey had planned
'a play around Jim Larkin – *The Red Star* – in which he would
never appear though be responsible for all the action.' [3] Larkin's
famous motto, 'An Injury to One is the Concern of All', decorates
the union office in Act II of the play. The collector of biographical
curiosa would probably succeed in pointing out further connections between O'Casey's life, and figures or plot elements in *The
Star Turns Red*.[4] In this case, however, it is superfluous to note
such elements, because here, in contrast, for instance, to *Oak
Leaves and Lavender*, they have been completely integrated into
the context of the play. Thus it is irrelevant for an interpretation
to know whether O'Casey had particular models for his figures
as long as they obtain their function from the play itself and are,
within the play, autonomous.

His disregard of the personal element made it possible for
O'Casey to create *The Star Turns Red* as a consistent allegory; no
direct delineation of reality can therefore be expected from it. If
an influential critic believes that 'In this play O'Casey returns to
the shell of the naturalistic form, but he creates inside it not
characters, but caricatures . . .', such an ignoring of the overall
dramatic structure must lead to misrepresentation and even to
obvious contradiction: 'On the naturalist level the story concerns
a symbolic household.' [5] In *The Star Turns Red* all the figures
carry certain meanings, all specific events represent a general
process. The relations between stage events and the intended
level of meaning are unmistakable; any symbolic ambiguity is
precluded. The play's loss in complexity is at the same time its
gain in clarity of structure.

O'Casey avoids the danger of over-simplification by constructing two parallel lines of action. One of them concerns the
confrontation of rival organisations, while the other joins together
a number of private events in the sphere of family and everyday
life. The general action shows the conflict of the trade unions
with a Fascist organisation, the Church and the power of the
state. After a labour conflict the unions plan a demonstration,
while the Saffron Shirts, supported by the Christian Front, the
bishops and the army, prepare the downfall of the Communist

movement. Some corrupt union officials have come to a secret agreement with the Church in order to displace Red Jim, the militant workers' leader, from his position on the central union council. He, however, prevails over his adversaries, which in turn anticipates the final outcome of the conflict. The mass-demonstration leads to a battle which almost ends in defeat for the workers until, at the crucial moment, the soldiers take up their part, thus deciding the issue. These events, which in part cannot be presented on stage, are visualized in a confrontation between the leaders of the various groups. The final street-battle is enacted in a kind of modern *teichoskopia*, the reports from the various scenes being transmitted by wireless to the workers' headquarters which is shown on stage.

The events of the 'private' sphere of action are representative, too, and should not be mistaken for the presentation of a real family situation. Jack and Kian, the sons of the Old Man and the Old Woman, belong to the opposing parties. When Jack's sweetheart Julia confronts the Fascist leader, he has her whipped; her father (Michael), who tries to protect her, is shot down in cold blood by Kian. His death is the final motive, if by no means the general cause, for the battle of Act IV. Before this, there is a verbal battle between the representatives of various attitudes around Michael's coffin. The death of Jack in the concluding street-battle finally leads to Kian's desertion of his Fascist friends. When Julia mourns for Jack, she is encouraged by Red Jim with words that would be entirely out of place in any realistic context: 'Up, young woman, and join in the glowing hour your lover died to fashion. He fought for life, for life is all; and death is nothing!' (p. 353). This private action is interspersed with a number of scenes that serve to outline in greater detail the various attitudes of the disputing parties. It should be stressed that each of the figures embodies an attitude to the central conflict different from that of all others. O'Casey certainly did not take the line of least resistance, as is indicated by the large number of persons (over thirty), of whom only two (the two priests) appear in all acts and five others in three acts. The division of the figures into 'Fascists', 'workers' and 'neutrals' can only be provisional and has to be further differentiated.

Among the 'neutrals' the Old Man is the type of the conformist and opportunist who prides himself on having always done his duty. He has never taken part in a strike and has been praised by his employers for his 'reliability'. He dissociates himself from any responsibility for his sons' political attitudes, and while the decisive conflict is under way, he fills in his football pools. Order, according to him, has to be preserved by the police. He does not or will not realize that with his alleged neutrality he is in reality supporting the *status quo*. The Old Woman, equally unable to understand the political conflict and to take sides in it, has an intuitive feeling for the growing insecurity, and endeavours in her own helpless way to preserve at least domestic peace. She still looks for a compromise when the time for it has long gone by. When Kian has shot Michael, she is the only one to recognize that at this moment Kian needs her compassion most, but her understanding of private affairs is not sufficient to prevent the larger conflicts in society nor to solve them, and in *this* play (as opposed, for instance, to *Juno and the Paycock*) her attitude is therefore criticized. Joybell is the typical product of a clerical education. His naïve optimism, his subservience to the Purple Priest and his sexual abstinence (which, once broken, leads to uncontrollable reactions) render him incapable of taking part in the conflict. He is not only a-political, but he also represents an attitude to life opposite to Red Jim's enlightened and liberal ideals. The Brown Priest suffers most from his position between the fronts. As a representative of a humble, non-repressive Christianity he is respected by the workers, while he finds himself corrected by the representatives of his Church. He is repeatedly forced into political decisions and turns more and more away from the Fascists; he warns Red Jim of the treacherous pact made by his own Church and at the end openly takes the workers' part:

The star turned red is still the star
Of him who came as man's pure prince of peace;
And so I serve him here (p. 351).

He proves not only that his initial position between the fronts is untenable, but also that the workers' victory, as seen in the context of this play, will lead to a new synthesis of Christianity and Socialism.

Among the Fascists, the Leader of the Saffron Shirts and his troopers are embodiments of a cold, cynical inhumanity, liquidating their opponents without any qualms. Kian (= Cain) who in the person of Michael kills his 'brother' in the family of man, originally belongs to them, too, until he finally turns away from them and in his ensuing isolation experiences the despair of the misled. The Purple Priest uses his alliance with the Fascists to enforce narrow-minded morals and to remove any dissenters

from his creed. It is characteristic of him to associate Red Jim with
the devil in order to be able to outlaw him in the name of God.
The Lord Mayor as a representative of the Law is a ridiculous
figure throughout: the state has already lost all influence on the
course of events. The state's inability to solve social problems is
shown in a crassly ironical scene when, at the height of the battle
for power, the 'deserving poor' receive gifts from a Father
Christmas figure; this scene underlines the necessity of those
changes for which Red Jim is striving. The Lady Mayoress is a
variant of this type; for a while she courts the workers in order to
obtain their support, and even tries to appear resolute, but she
does not understand the signs of the times and therefore at the
end is simply pushed aside. The poor, too, paradoxically take the
side of the Fascists when in Act III (as in *Hall of Healing*) they
exhibit their wretchedness. This scene even more than the street-
battle outlines the immensity of Red Jim's task. If even those for
whose well-being he fights denounce him as an enemy of the
people, who wants to rob them of their last hope, religion, it
remains doubtful whether he will ever succeed. It is significant
that the outcome of *this* conflict, in contrast to the physical
confrontation, is not shown in the play.

More so than in the other groups, O'Casey has differentiated
between various types among the workers. Here the scale reaches
from his ideal character Red Jim to the traitor Sheasker. This
definitely serves to render the play more convincing. Red Jim is
the type of fearless, self-confident, unselfish and at the same time
sensitive leader who instinctively understands every situation,
who always and immediately takes the right decision and who
is a master of psychology in the treatment of his subordinates.
It is true that he also reveals certain traits of a dubious and
undemocratic authoritarianism (he disposes of the union funds
in a high-handed fashion and ignores the committee's decisions),
but he is not, apparently, to be criticized for such actions, for his
opponents in these quarrels are always shown as despicable and
egotistic weaklings, which serves to increase Red Jim's status in
the play's scale of values. The self-sacrificing Jack is a younger
foil to Red Jim, adhering to the tactics agreed upon and taking the
consequences. All the other workers show varying degrees of
egotism interwoven with their devotion to the common cause. It
takes Julia considerable time before she decides to take part in
the demonstration rather than going to the fancy-dress ball.
Michael proves his lack of self-control even before the attack on
the Leader of the Saffron Shirts that leads to his death, and is

reproached for it by Jack (p. 243). It is true that his impulsiveness
is understandable under the circumstances, but Michael places
personal feelings above the common cause. Brannigan goes a
step further when he endangers the movement's reputation
through his drunkenness and in his fits of violence thinks only of
himself. Even more so the Union Secretary considers only his
private profits when he, with certain reservations, comes to terms
with the treacherous union leaders. The latter are the real enemies
inside the movement. Their pact with the Purple Priest and their
willingness to surrender Red Jim are the greatest danger to the
workers' victory. Their pitiful failure to face up to Brannigan
characterizes them as cowards. But even they are not completely
alike, and Sheasker who has been blackmailed by the employers
to end the strike and has then accepted presents from the 'grateful'
workers holds the lowest position in this scale of values. O'Casey
has been successful in avoiding over-simplification by idealizing
only a few representatives of the workers' movement.

This survey of the dramatic figures answers, at least in part,
the question how O'Casey attempted to achieve the audience's
'conversion'. Firstly, he characterizes the representatives of
Fascism as cruel and brutal, thus evoking the audience's abhorrence. Secondly, he degrades those figures who take up the
'wrong' political attitude by pillorying their personal behaviour:
when the union leaders turn away from Red Jim, they are at
the same time characterized as deceitful and cowardly in their
private lives, and the audience's condemnation of their personal
behaviour is transferred to their political allegiance. Thirdly,
certain comic traits are employed to influence the audience. A
series of comic situations serves to ridicule the representatives of
the attitude that is rejected throughout the play: Sheasker sees
the image of Julius Caesar in his own repulsive portrait, the Lord
Mayor is offered two chairs and tries to sit on both, the trade
union leaders have to kneel in front of the drunken Brannigan
and accept the 'honour' of proletarian knighthood. There is only
one comic scene without such a function (Joybell and the Old
Man hanging up the garlands, pp. 340-344), which, therefore, in
spite of its inherent effectiveness, appears out of place in the
play. Fourthly, O'Casey creates parallel situations, illustrating
the different behaviour of the Fascists and the workers: in Act I,
Julia hits the Fascist leader and is whipped as a punishment. In
Act II, Brannigan spits at the trade union leader Brallain from a
similar feeling of contempt, but Red Jim who undertakes to
'punish' him merely puts him to shame by conferring some

responsibility on him. Julia is confirmed in her hatred of the
Fascists, Brannigan on the other hand becomes an even keener
supporter of Red Jim. Fifthly, in the course of the play several
figures change sides. While the despicable trade union leaders
side with the Fascists, the peace-loving Brown Priest, after
hesitating for a long time, takes up the cause of the workers, and
at the end even Kian, moved by his brother's death, leaves the
Fascist camp.

In order to differentiate between the three 'parties' and to
direct the audience's sympathies to one of them, O'Casey has
employed visual scenery to a degree that is unusual even for him.
The allegory of colours, used to distinguish between the figures
(Purple Priest, Brown Priest, Red Guards, Saffron Shirts), has an
even more important function in the scenery, where it serves to
differentiate between the various factions. The walls in the house
of the indifferent old people are painted in black, the colour of
death, in the Lord Mayor's residence they are purple and gold, in
the union office green, *'a bright green, the colour of new grass or
the opening of fresh leaves on the trees in advancing spring'* (p.
277). The old people's house also has a tablecloth in the papal
colours and a black cupboard with a white tea-pot, *'symbol of
life's necessities'*; a few white chairs *'give an indication of
occasional rest'* (p. 241). The world of the undecided, dominated
by the Catholic Church, does not offer more than the mere
necessities of life, but they are overshadowed by death and
permit no hope. The alternatives to this attitude are also reflected
in the stage settings. In each act, one can see a church spire
through one window, two foundry chimneys through the other,
to which are added the portaits of a Bishop and of Lenin in Act I
and *'a white cross on which a red hammer and sickle are imposed'*
in Act II (p. 277). The development from Fascist domination to
the workers' victory is paralleled by the development of the visual
imagery: from act to act, the foundry chimneys appear nearer,
while the church spire is further removed; the star, initially to be
seen near the church, moves towards the foundry, and finally
undergoes the change predicted in the title of the play. The
allegorical scenery thus corresponds to an allegorical action
between allegorical figures; *The Star Turns Red* in a single unified
movement progresses to a clearly defined conclusion.

★

There has, however, been considerable controversy about the

terms in which the philosophy of the victorious workers' movement might best be defined. It would be easy to speak of the
author's Socialist or Communist attitude if the play did not
contain an exceptionally large body of Christian ideals and
Christian symbolism.[6] It is true that the power-oriented Church
sides with the Fascists and in the end is rejected together with
these, but one can observe another, different Christian attitude,
respected by the workers, whose parallels with Red Jim's aims
are underlined by the dramatist in various ways. *The Star Turns
Red* takes place on Christmas Eve, and the star of the title is the
star of Bethlehem. Even when it changes its colour, it remains the
star of the divine incarnation, as the Brown Priest declares in his
central speech of Act IV, the importance of which is emphasized
by its unusual rhythms (p. 351). It is under this star that the
workers fight; Jack and Red Jim wear a red star in their lapels (pp.
242, 294). The language of the play is shot through with Biblical
references and religious terms and it continually employs stylistic
devices from the Bible. An example may illustrate this. Julia says
of Michael: 'He hath walked in the vigour of life; he hath
disquieted himself for the people; he hath heaped up the riches
of comradeship, and his children shall gather them, and live
greatly' (p. 317). O'Casey himself confessed: '. . . the language
and ideals of the play is not taken from Marx or Lenin, but from
the Authorized version of the Bible . . .'[7] Christmas carols are
used repeatedly, creating impressive contrasts. Especially effective
is the ending of Act II where Brannigan has the arrested union
leaders sing 'God Rest You Merry, Gentlemen' (p. 306). If, on such
occasions, the union movement appears to become dissociated
from Christianity, it is always a debased pseudo-religion supported by a corrupt, power-obsessed Church that is rejected.
It is only from this that the workers turn away, as Red Jim's
programmatic speech shows: 'If the heritage of heaven be the
heritage here of shame and rags and the dead puzzle of poverty,
then we turn our backs on it! If your God stands for one child to
be born in a hovel and another in a palace, then we declare
against him' (p. 324-325). Julia, glancing at the crucifix, declares:
'Against you, dear one, we have no grudge; but those of your
ministers who sit like gobbling cormorants in the market-place
shall fall and shall be dust, and shall be priests no longer' (p. 315).

One of the key terms of this play, filled as it is with controversies
of various kinds, is *peace*. In Act I it occurs no less than sixteen
times, almost as frequently in Act III where the religious controversy is predominant, and again repeatedly in the final Act.

Initially, it refers to the kind of false peace which, in other key words, is identified with *order* by the undecided, with *power* by the Fascists and with *obedience* by the Church. It is one of the theses of this play that the 'true' peace associated with Christmas can be achieved only through the victory of the workers and has to be paid for by sacrifice. It would, of course, be most inappropriate to categorize *The Star Turns Red* as a Christian play. Yet it is equally faulty to insist on O'Casey's 'Communist' attitude and, as the majority of critics have done, to regret it. It is important to underline his unusual attempt at harmonizing Socialist and Christian attitudes. Only one critic has attempted to describe this attitude more precisely: O'Casey's 'Communism reduced to its barest is nothing more than a deep concern for the poor and the neglected. Intrinsically he is a Christian at heart who has turned Communist because Christianity has sat heedless in the midst of injustice and oppression while Communism, without acknowledging God, has moved forward to fulfil God's plan on earth.' [8] It is, perhaps, doubtful whether O'Casey really could be termed 'a Christian at heart'. *The Star Turns Red*, however, supports the view that '. . . as O'Casey saw it Communism is Christ's kingdom on earth. Communism is not replacing Christ, it is replacing a Church that has failed Christ.' [9] This is entirely compatible with O'Casey's own view: 'There is no Communist *Dogma* in *The Star Turns Red*. It is, as Shaw saw – the spirit and prophecy of the Authorized Version of the English Bible.' [10]

It is important for the future reception of *The Star Turns Red* that O'Casey, in addition to his own memories of 1913 Dublin, referred to the political tendencies and events of his own time. The references to National Socialism are obvious and can be identified immediately in sentences like 'Our Leader's new order will overwhelm the living world!' (p. 251). The repeated references to the Spanish Civil War are even clearer; there O'Casey found the alliance of Fascism with the Catholic Church which, from his own personal experiences, could not but meet with his particular scorn. Certain suggestions were also taken (as he himself confirmed[11]) from the short-lived Fascist movement in the Ireland of the thirties, the Blue Shirts, and from the Mosleyite British Union of Fascists founded in 1932, whose symbol, the flash of lightning in a circle, serves as the Fascists' emblem in this play. In spite of its allegorical structure and the indefinite, hopeful description of its time of occurrence as 'To-morrow, or the next day' (p. 240) *The Star Turns Red* is thus bound to the period of its origin and cannot be transferred without modification to different social conflicts and new political constellations. This, even more than its links to the conventions of the early Unity Theatre, makes the play a historical if impressive document of the late thirties rather than a living drama.

# 14. PURPLE DUST

*Purple Dust* had an exceptionally unhappy stage history. The play was finished and published in 1940, at a time when England, threatened in its very existence, had begun to recall its traditional virtues, when even satirists like Evelyn Waugh (at the end of *Put Out More Flags*) had turned to the delineation of positive values. The production of a play caricaturing English character-traits would have been out of the question at that time in London. In New York, too, political consequences, in particular a strengthening of isolationist attitudes, were feared, and the play was not performed during the war.[1] The later popularity of *Purple Dust* suffered from these initial setbacks, for the commercial London and New York theatre, obsessed by the demand for novelty, finds it difficult to accept a play that is less than an immediate commercial success. The play's popularity was not helped by the fact that it was finally produced outside London (1945 by the Old Vic Company at the Liverpool Playhouse). Even the Mermaid production during the 1962 O'Casey Festival did little to secure it a firm position on the English stage, although outside England and America it has been accepted as one of the finest examples of modern stage comedy.

A critic finds himself in this case confronted with additional problems, because the play's textual history is more complicated than that of any of the preceding works. O'Casey's newly-won insights into problems of dramatic theory and his resulting critical attitude towards his own writings is reflected in the fact that *Purple Dust* exists in four considerably differing versions. Critics have usually ignored these various versions and their relationship to each other. It is therefore necessary to preface the interpretation with a short textual comparison.

The original version (published in 1940) differs in about fifty instances from the *Collected Plays* text. Some of the corrections are negligible, as, for instance, when the chorus of the pseudo-pastoral song is altered [2] or when O'Casey, in one of his rare concessions to popular taste, leaves out '. . . and, on his mother's side, Churchill' from the enumeration of Stoke's comic-bombastic names.[3] Such details merely illuminate O'Casey's thoroughness of revision. Leaving these aside, the majority of the corrections belong to one of three categories. Firstly, a number of verbal arguments and debates are eliminated, especially the pseudo-profound debate on a philosophical definition of the primrose, Stoke's reflections on the possibility of intellectual insights in one's bath and a few other passages where the verbal comedy had become divided from any direct links with the action.[4] O'Casey, however, added to the farcical passages of the play, where the comedy is based on physical action. The futile attempts to cut a hole into the ceiling for Poges' lamp, the defence against the alleged *bull* (in the second version, the stage directions always refer to a *cow*), Poges' struggle with the lawn roller, the Yellow-bearded Man's lament for the loss of his cow and the transport of the quattrocento-desk have been effectively enlarged.[5] Thirdly, O'Casey completely rewrote a scene that he apparently considered particularly inadequate: O'Killigain's and O'Dempsey's courting of Avril and Souhaun.[6] In the first version, this scene contains little more than the unfounded suggestion that the girls should leave the atmosphere of ignorance and sterile riches in which they live; the girls' decision therefore is a surprise not only for their lovers but also for the audience. In the more explicit second version, however, the two lovers offer a poetical description of that free and natural life which would be open to Avril and Souhaun in their company, and their vacillation is indicated in their contradictory reactions, even if they do not take their final decision just here. Finally, the insecurity is extended to Poges and Stoke who at first consider the courting as a purely comic spectacle, but are made aware of the uncertainty of their own future. Not only does this scene increase the psychological credibility of the figures and of their actions, but it also makes the life-affirming attitude of the conclusion more convincing. This is underlined in an addition to the second version that, in its programmatic brevity, could serve as a motto for this play:

We are no' saints, and so can abide by things that wither, without shudder or sigh, let the night be dark or dusky. It is for us to make dying things live once more, and things that wither, leaf and bloom again. Fix your arm in mine, young and fair one, and face for life (p. 16).

A third version of the play was performed by the Cherry Lane Theatre in New York in 1956 and was published in 1957.[7] It differs in about 130 places from the *Collected Plays* text. It is especially

noteworthy that this version lacks most of the corrections of the
Collected Plays text – and thus corresponds to the first version –
while at the same time numerous new alterations have been
introduced. At a first glance it might be supposed, therefore, that
the third version is a second revision of the original text, prepared
without reference to the Collected Plays, yet this is refuted by the
fact that the courtship scene mentioned above corresponds
almost entirely with the Collected Plays text. It is not the purpose
of this study to reconstruct the biographical background for the
relationship between the three versions. It is, however, necessary
to give a short survey of the most decisive differences between
the second and the third version and to draw some conclusions
from it concerning the most unified and effective text.

The majority of revisions concern isolated sentences; it is not
possible to trace a common purpose behind these changes, nor
does their necessity always become apparent. The following
more extended alterations should be mentioned: The shepherds'
song of Act I contains two additional stanzas.[8] O'Killigain's
entrance song is omitted,[9] while later he sings an additional
song, 'The Ruin'd Rowan Tree', which becomes possible because
the dried-up rowan-tree is throughout substituted for the withered
thorn-tree, symbol of Avril's buried capacity for love.[10] Half of
O'Killigain's hysterical outbursts against Wordsworth have
been omitted (surely an improvement for the play).[11] The phrasing
of the second version is frequently funnier; while Barney there
complains of the 'bitther breeze whirlin' through the passages
that ud make the very legs of a nun numb!', in the third version
he says: '. . . that ud numb the legs of a Mother Superior.'[12] On
the other hand it is certainly advantageous to have excluded the
destruction of the allegedly valuable vases, one of the least
original inventions of the second version.[13] It is worthy of special
notice that in the third version, the Act II love-scene between
Souhaun and O'Killigain, with minor modifications, has been
transferred to Souhaun and O'Dempsey.[14] This makes Souhaun's
concluding flight with O'Dempsey more credible, saving her
from the suspicion that she joined O'Dempsey only after her
attentions for O'Killigain had proved ineffective. The love action
apparently continued to trouble O'Casey, as can be seen from the
courting scene of Act III.[15] Although in general O'Casey decided
in favour of the Collected Plays version, he again introduced
more than thirty corrections, eliminations and additions, thus
rendering this scene the most thoroughly revised of the whole
play. Finally, in the third version the conclusion of the play has

been significantly altered.[16] Poges here does not, as in the other versions, climb up on the roof of the house with the other persons, but hides himself in his quattrocento-desk that is then closed like a coffin while the floods engulf the room. This ending confers a special position to Poges which is not justified by the rest of the play, while the grotesque and obtrusive symbolism of his hopeless commitment to the past endangers the precarious balance between realistic and unrealistic traits that makes the conclusion so effective.

The fourth version, first published in 1965 in *Three More Plays*, is supposed to have been approved by O'Casey shortly before his death [17] and could thus be considered the author's final edition. It does not, however, differ considerably from the *Collected Plays* text; only the love-scene between Souhaun and O'Killigain in Act II is, as in the third version (with some further corrections) transferred to Souhaun and O'Dempsey.[18] This alteration, although appropriate, is not important enough to justify a separate consideration of version four, when the question of the most convincing text of *Purple Dust* is discussed. The real decision lies between the *Collected Plays* text and the third version. It would be ideal to have the two combined, but as long as no critical edition of O'Casey's plays is available, the second version, for the reasons mentioned above is in general to be preferred. It contains a number of improvements over the first edition which are not contained in the third. The following interpretation is therefore based on the *Collected Plays* text. *Purple Dust* shows particularly clearly how important a new, complete and critical edition of all O'Casey's plays would be for a proper appreciation of his work.

★

Among O'Casey's full-length plays, *Purple Dust*, next to *The Drums of Father Ned*, is the most light-hearted. That O'Casey himself shared this impression, may be gathered from the fact that he dedicated it to his daughter Shivaun in 1939; it can also be deduced from the subtitle, *A Wayward Comedy in Three Acts*. This subtitle, however, also shows that *Purple Dust* cannot be considered a comedy without certain reservations. It is a whimsical, unpredictable and wilful, indeed an entirely untypical comedy. This is especially obvious in the conclusion, where fantastic, irrational and symbolic traits predominate, throwing new light on the realistic events of the preceding acts. It will be advisable for an interpretation initially to ignore this conclusion and to discuss it (and its meaning for the whole play) in a separate section.

Leaving aside the conclusion, then, *Purple Dust* can be considered as a successful combination of three different comic levels: it unites elements of comedy in a narrower sense, of farce and of satire.[19] Critics have frequently failed to do justice to the play by recognizing only one of these levels; otherwise it would not have been possible to call *Purple Dust* a 'purely satirical comedy', a 'farcical fantasy', 'a slight, farcical work' or 'a lampoon of the British character'.[20] These terms contradict one another, because they touch only one aspect of the play respectively, and when critics say: 'Not all O'Casey's later plays are so embarrassingly bad as that class-conscious, rural musical . . .' or that *Purple Dust* 'ist grundverschieden zu O'Caseys vorausgegangener literarischer Arbeit und ist seiner völlig unwürdig',[21] they base their judgement on a narrow self-created norm that is inadequate to the whole conception of the play.

The actual *comedy* action of *Purple Dust* is based on a traditional motif common to comedies over the centuries: the old, rich, repulsive lover loses his sweetheart to a young, vital, attractive rival. O'Casey has doubled this motif, carefully differentiating between the respective characters. Cyril Poges and Basil Stoke are duped by O'Killigain and O'Dempsey and lose their mistresses Avril and Souhaun. These six characters dominate the action. In spite of occasional over-characterization, this is confined to a realistic and individual sphere: it depicts individual fates, life being mastered or wasted, without reference to the conflict between social groups. According to the principles of comedy, this is achieved without involving the audience in a high degree of emotional commitment. The stage conflicts do not trigger off conflicts in the observer, because positive and negative values are clearly apportioned and the 'victory' of the one side can only result in satisfaction, not in contradiction.

Poges and Stoke have so few loveable traits that their defeat cannot arouse any compassion. It is true that at the beginning all advantages seem to be on their side. As well-to-do businessmen and stock-exchange speculators they have brought their mistresses from London to Ireland to lead the proud lives of feudal lords in a restored Tudor mansion. Thus they voluntarily set themselves up within reach of their adversaries; their ignorance and their arrogant belief in the impregnability of their own position prefigures the height of what is to be their imminent fall. This fall is referred to even in the exposition scene: 'Th' two poor English omadhauns won't have much when th' lasses decide it's time for partin' ' (p. 5). Their dominant character trait is their lack of insight into their own situation. Both believe themselves to be superior to their surroundings to such an extent that the very possibility of a threat to it is unthinkable. Stoke relies on his Oxford education, useless in reality, and on his relationship with one of the oldest families in the country, including a 'K.G.' (Knight of the Garter); his Christian names 'Basil Horatio Nelson Kaiser' (p. 103) show how ridiculous are his demands for respect. Poges, on the other hand, prides himself on his lack of education as a self-made man; his self-confidence is founded on his stocks and shares and on his natural superiority as an Englishman. The comedy scenes are largely based on the same motif: Stoke's and Poges' high pretensions are reduced *ad absurdum* without their gaining any better insight into their situation. Stoke quite literally begins the series of comic situations with the fall that proverbially follows pride, when he thinks he can master an Irish horse with the technique learned in a London riding-school. Poges demonstrates his ignorance when he tries to impress others with quotations from Wordsworth and with his knowledge of history. Both quickly prove that they are incapable of keeping up their self-elected position as feudal lords. Not for a moment do they win the respect of those whom they consider their inferiors, nor can they even enforce obedience.

Their relationship with their mistresses serves to pinpoint their human shortcomings. Even at the beginning of the action, they have lost the girls' respect and trust, if, that is, they have ever possessed it. Both appear sexually impotent, Avril describing Stokes as:

That thing! [*With bitter contempt*] A toddler thricking with a woman's legs; a thief without the power to thieve the thing he covets; a louse burrowing in a young lioness's belly; a perjurer in passion; a gutted soldier bee whose job is done, and still hangs on to life! (pp. 15-16).

And Poges, who is twice as old, is entirely occupied by his interests in his dubious art treasures, status symbols of the *nouveaux riches*. They were improvident enough to sever the last ties with their mistresses when they made them financially independent. From that moment onwards they are unable to prevent Avril and Souhaun from flirting with other men.

O'Killigain and O'Dempsey are in every respect counter-images to Stoke and Poges. The young, vital, good-looking O'Killigain who, as an ordinary worker, has acquired an astonishing range of knowledge is equally superior to the wooden Stoke as the more fanatic O'Dempsey whom one might take for a 'wandherin' king holdin' th' ages be th' hand' (p. 18) is to the conceited Poges. As frequently in comedy, the youthful hero is the least interesting character. He appears as an ideal figure without weaknesses who never hesitates before a decision, leaving Avril no other choice the moment he begins to court her. O'Dempsey is a less unequivocal character who finds it more difficult to gain the audience's sympathy (necessary for his role) as well as Souhaun's affections. At the beginning, he seems to be quite close to the type of useless blatherer whom O'Casey had presented in earlier plays, and only gradually is it shown that the legendary world of his fantastic digressions really exists for him.

O'Dempsey's courtship of Souhaun, therefore, takes up more time and more interest than the relationship between Avril and O'Killigain. Avril is won in the first courting scene, resisting only for a short moment because she believes herself to have been treated too coarsely, but O'Dempsey is probably right when he observes: 'If I was asked anything, I'd say I saw a spark of pleasure in the flame of pain that came into her eyes when she was hot [hit]!' (p. 14). O'Killigain demonstrates his power over Avril's apparent self-confidence when he insists on the blasted thorn-tree as the place of their first rendez-vous and convinces her that love is stronger than the demonic powers that haunt that place. From now on Avril's attitude to the foreman is unchanged; even her short hesitation before she finally departs with him (p. 107) can hardly be taken seriously. She is kind to Stoke only when this will gain her another cheque. Yet she has to fear for O'Killigain's faithfulness, because Souhaun and even Cloyne, her maid, are striving for his attentions, and even when the big floods arrive she is not sure whether he will be true to his promise until he finally removes her doubts.

Souhaun has to take a much more difficult decision. She has not simply to choose between vitality and paralysis. At thirty-three, the material security offered by Poges is a much greater temptation when compared to an insecure future at O'Dempsey's side. Although she realizes quite clearly what sort of person Poges is and has no illusions about her life with him, for a long time her decision to stay with him seems irrevocable. She is confirmed in this when she has to realize that she cannot win

O'Killigain from her younger rivals and even has to accept a rebuke from Cloyne: 'There's a withering old woman, not a hundred miles from where I am, who ought to take her own advice, an' keep from thryin' her well-faded thricks of charm on poor Mr. O'Killigain herself!' (p. 31). It is characteristic of Souhaun that she is continually occupied with decorating the house, choosing materials, hanging up pictures, carrying pieces of furniture, while Avril uses any opportunity to escape from such tasks. Souhaun accepts her position as the mistress of Ormond Manor. O'Dempsey's first advances therefore must appear to her entirely unrealistic. While her relationship with Poges is characterized by her sarcasm, abandoned only occasionally for tactical reasons, she meets O'Dempsey with a kind of good-natured irony. Even after the floods have begun, when she has already admitted that 'The house'll be lonesome without you' (p. 105), she can still ridicule his eloquent courting: 'Where is the lady who would be slow to give a man with such a coaxing way an invitation to her pillow?' (p. 106). But while her reason still excludes any such possibility, emotionally she has already been won over, as her quip (spoken *'half joking, all in earnest'*) shows: 'If you only had a horse handy, I'd ride away with you!' (p. 108). When Avril finally reports that Souhaun has been true to her word, a decision has been taken that to the end had remained doubtful.

The comedy action, then, is propelled by the motif of courting, leading Avril in Act I, Souhaun in Act III to the side of their 'proper' lovers and leaving Stoke and Poges in loneliness. Its comic effects are predominantly based on the characters of the two Englishmen. From the middle of Act I, the audience has gained sufficient insight into the disproportion between their pretensions and reality to express their own feeling of superiority by laughing at them. Only as far as Souhaun is concerned, does this action gain a certain amount of complexity. In general, its simplicity reminds one of the small degree of variation within the stereotyped figures of the *commedia dell'arte*.

This analogy (not to be mistaken for any kind of literary influence) is even more obvious when one considers the numerous *farcical* scenes which serve to support the uncomplicated comedy action. The comedy of character is here superseded by the comedy of situation typical of farce. O'Casey's mastery of this literary form can be demonstrated from a short scene. In Act I, a lively discussion concerning Avril's and O'Killigain's riding adventure is interrupted by an unexpected event:

[*Plaster falls and a hole appears in the ceiling, almost directly over the fireplace; then a thin rope, with a bulb attached to its end, comes dangling down, followed by the face of a heavily Yellow-bearded Man, who thrusts his head as far as it can go through the hole.*]

YELLOW-BEARDED MAN [*to those below*]. Hay, hay there; is this where yous want the light to go?

POGES [*with a vexatious yell when he sees where the rope hangs*]. No it isn't, no it isn't, you fool! [*Indicating a place near the centre and towards the back*]. There, there's where it's wanted! Where my desk will be! Oh, they're knocking down more than they're building up!

YELLOW-BEARDED MAN [*soothingly*]. Don't worry; just a little mistake in measurement, sir. Never fear, we'll hit th' right spot one o' these days! The one thing to do, sir, is to keep cool. [*He takes his head out of the hole and disappears, leaving Poges furious*] (p. 43)

Here, the predominance of the spoken word, characteristic of comedy, gives way to a dominance of visual impressions, indicated on the printed page by the extent of the stage-directions. The farcical effect results from the discrepancy between what is intended and what is achieved: instead of making the house more habitable, it is recklessly destroyed. The surprising descent of the wire with a naked bulb attached to it in the Tudor surroundings arouses laughter, as does the unexpected appearance of the head with the yellow beard. It is irrelevant what kind of person the Yellow-bearded Man is; his function is limited to his struggle with obstinate and intractable objects. He can withdraw as soon as his function is fulfilled, to reappear, however, at various critical moments in the action – this kind of repetition being another traditional effect of farce.

The whole play is interspersed with similar scenes, most of them more extended. Again and again, objects defeat the endeavours of men. Such scenes predominate in Act II where the comedy action makes little progress. Even the beginning of this act, with Poges' and Stoke's grotesque camping out in their own house and Barney's vain attempts to light a fire, is pure farce. The frightening appearance of the harmless cow, the breaking of Poges' allegedly valuable vases and his 'battle' with the outsize lawn-roller are the farcical climaxes of this act. Even more effective is the scene in Act III where the workers attempt by sheer force to press Poges' valuable quattrocento-desk through a narrow doorway. If one adds to these the picture-hanging scene and the sale of hens in Act I, Poges' repeated struggle with the telephone and a few reported scenes (Poges' fall from the horse, his attempt on the life of the cow) it becomes

clear to what extent O'Casey's inventiveness has served to make
his play effective on the stage.

It should be added, however, that these scenes have been
integrated most skilfully into the context of the play. The scene
with the Yellow-bearded Man, for instance, serves to demonstrate
the workers' preference for fantastic exaggeration: once he has
been introduced, every event that has been observed by the
audience can be retailed to him with considerable distortion.
Other farcical scenes are interrupted by parts of the comedy action:
Poges' struggle with the lawn-roller, for instance, is at first
interrupted by the thematically important discussion with
O'Dempsey and again by the equally significant courting-scene
between Souhaun and O'Killigain, the transitions from comedy
to farcical action having been skilfully disguised. All the farcical
scenes, moreover, provide additional instances of Poges' and
Stoke's doubtful human attitude and serve both to upgrade their
adversaries and to justify Souhaun's and Avril's final decision. In
each of these situations, the Englishmen's pretensions are revealed
as unjustified; each of them highlights, in accordance with the
simplifying tendency of farce, one of their character-traits:
intolerance, cowardice, avarice, inconsiderateness, conceit etc.,
thus creating an image directly opposite to the one they have of
themselves. The farcical scenes, therefore, are not mere additions
to a rather weak comedy action, but support it most effectively.[22]

They gain additional significance when one considers the
*satirical* aspect of the play, because this integrates the farcical
conflicts into a unified concept. If the action of *Purple Dust* took
place in England among Englishmen or in Ireland among Irishmen,
it could remain confined to a comic-realistic conflict between
individuals. But as soon as Englishmen, in Ireland, are confronted
with Irishmen, the politico-historical aspect of 800 years of occupation history is present, and the stage-figures as representatives
of their nations fight out the pent-up emotions. O'Casey has
consciously enlarged his play so as to include the national conflict
(Poges and Stoke attempt to re-establish the English feudal
system of Tudor Ireland) and he employs it for the purpose of
national satire, i.e. characteristic English and Irish traits are
exposed in comic exaggeration. The satirical traits are so clear
that some critics have taken them for the only aspect of the play.

In addition to linguistic differences,[23] Irishmen and Englishmen in *Purple Dust* differ in two major respects: in their attitude
to the past and in their relationship to nature. In both cases, the
natives prove the more successful. As workers and craftsmen,

they have strong roots in their present-day existence which provides them with a firm point of reference for their attitude to the past. The past is relevant to them as far as it is effective in the present. For O'Dempsey, the figures of Irish myth are just as much alive as those men who, like Wolfe Tone and Parnell, have shaped the history of Ireland. The central conflict between O'Dempsey and Poges shows that the Irishman sees the best of his nation's past as continuing in the present, while the Englishman, for all his interest, is without bonds and supports a petrified traditionalism. A reference to Finn Mac Coole provokes them into characteristic reactions:

POGES [*solemnly*]. A great man, a great man, surely; a great man gone for ever.
2ND WORKMAN [*sharply*]. He's here for ever! His halloo can be heard on the hills outside; his spear can be seen with its point in the stars; but not with an eye that can see no further than the well-fashioned edge of a golden coin (p. 69).

For the Englishmen, their interest in the Tudor period is not more than a fashionable craze. They know hardly more about this period than that it existed long ago, and therefore decorate their house with museum pieces of various times. They are not even consistent in their folly: although the house is to be lit with candles, Poges has an electric lamp installed over his desk, and the telephone, as an indispensable tool of civilization, is connected immediately. One gets the impression that Poges and Stoke would, with equal enthusiasm, live in a lake-dwelling, a Norman castle or an Egyptian pyramid.

Their relation to nature is satirized in their very first scene, when they, in the garb of pastoral poetry, demonstrate their lack of any real feeling for their surroundings. Later, a cow frightens them to death, they cannot control a horse, and bird calls appear to them as 'Jungle noises' (p. 48), while to the Irishmen animals are part of everyday life.

An occasional digression into literary satire also serves the purpose of criticizing the Englishmen. The line 'God's green thought in a little green shade' from the pastoral song (p. 7) goes back to Marvell's 'The Garden',[24] for O'Casey the embodiment of an artificial attitude to nature which he rejects. The names of the two Englishmen, of course, refer to the village of Stoke Poges that suggested Gray's 'Elegy Written in a Country Churchyard'. This, again, was to O'Casey an unacceptable harmonizing of village-life as seen by a city writer.[25] O'Casey's criticism becomes more

straightforward when Poges attempts to demonstrate his education by (incorrectly) quoting from Wordsworth's well-known
sonnet: 'Life is too much with us, O'Killigain; late and soon,
getting and spending, we lay waste our powers' (p. 21). O'Killigain
reacts to it with an unusually sharp attack:

A tired-out oul' blatherer; a tumble-down thinker; a man who made a
hiding-place of his own life; a shadow parading about as the sun; a poet,
sensitive to everything but man; a bladder blown that sometimes gave a
note of music; a fool who thought the womb of the world was
Wordsworth; a poet who jailed the striving of man in a moral lullaby; a
snail to whom God gave the gleam of the glowworm; a poet singing the
song of safety first! (pp. 21-22).

O'Casey obviously approves of this attack, because he has Poges
defend Wordsworth with entirely inadequate arguments. And
even the play's last sentence contains a literary reference when
Poges, who has failed in every sense of the word, misappropriates
the sentiments of Browning's 'Home-Thoughts, from Abroad':
'Would to God I were in England, now that winter's here!' [26]
In these quotations, O'Casey not only criticizes the literary
ignorance of allegedly educated Englishmen that he deplores in
his autobiography; he also exposes the lack of original feeling,
compensated for by the clichés of prefabricated literary formulae.
    And finally, O'Casey criticizes the Englishmen's lack of any
understanding for the national character, the history, the countryside and the special problems of the Irish. Again it is Poges who
expresses this attitude: 'All the Irish are the same. Bit backward
perhaps, like all primitive peoples, especially now, for they're
missing the example and influence of the gentry; but delightful
people all the same. They need control, though; oh yes, they need
it badly' (p. 23). This is reminiscent of a discussion with the British
Prime Minister Baldwin that O'Casey humorously describes in
*Rose and Crown*.[27] Baldwin's lack of appreciation rivals that of
Poges to such a degree that one is inclined to see in the latter a
caricature of the politician. Complementary to this attitude is the
Englishmen's consciousness of their allegedly God-given
superiority, repeatedly reduced to absurdity in *Purple Dust*:

POGES [*stormily*]. . . . every right-minded man the world over knows, or
    ought to know, that wherever we have gone, progress, civilisation,
    truth, justice, honour, humanity, righteousness, and peace have
    followed at our heels. In the Press, in the Parliament, in the pulpit, or
    on the battlefield, no lie has ever been uttered by us, no false claim

made, no right of man infringed, no law of God ignored, no human law, national or international, broken . . . I say, sir, that Justice is England's old nurse; Righteousness and Peace sit together in her common-room, and the porter at her gate is Truth!

O'KILLIGAIN [*quietly, but sarcastically*]. An' God Himself is England's butler! (pp. 73-74).

This exposure of the English character has led to the general impression that the satire in *Purple Dust* is directed against the English alone.[28] In reality, it is double-edged, because in certain ways the Irish are satirized too. The workers' neglect borders on sabotage, their complete carelessness not only provokes the Englishmen, but serves to destroy things of real value. Their delight in rumour and their inclination to fantastic exaggeration is documented when they take Stoke's metaphorical exclamation 'Naked and unashamed, the vixen [Avril] went away with O'Killigain!' (p. 43) literally, discuss the effects of such an escapade and soon believe themselves to have seen the undressed girl. Even O'Dempsey's poetical outbursts do not lack in satirical exaggeration, when, for instance, he remembers:

When less than a score of the Fianna brought back the King of England prisoner, invaded Hindostan, an' fixed as subjects the men of all the counthries between our Bay o' Dublin and the holy river that gave to holy John the holy wather to baptize our Lord (p. 68).

Another object of criticism is, as frequently in O'Casey, the influence of the priest, who tries to stop harmless amusements but overlooks the Englishmen's far more 'immoral' behaviour because they pay for his goodwill with their cheques. Except for this last point, however, the weaknesses of the Irish are lovable and are mildly ridiculed, while those of the English are detestable and are severely condemned. For long passages of the play one has the impression that, in a strange metamorphosis, the much-criticized stage-Irishman of 18th-century drama has come to life again in two stage-Englishmen.

*

In the field of satire, therefore, O'Casey does not remain completely objective. This is the major difference between *Purple Dust* and another play with which it has much in common and by which it was decisively influenced: *John Bull's Other Island*. In *Drums under the Windows*, O'Casey describes the impression his first reading of Shaw's play made on him:

> At tea he began to read the green-covered book, the play first, then the preface; the clock ticked, the time passed; the Gaelic League forgotten, he read on till dawn was near, and but a chance for a few hours' sleep before he rose to begin another day's work. From that day, for quite a while, Sean seemed to see Shaw everywhere; his tall figure, in his Irish homespun, marched in front, and whenever he looked behind him, there was Shaw following quick to overtake him.[29]

O'Casey always retained his admiration for 'the second Saint Bernard' and even in *Under a Colored Cap* stressed the influence of Shaw's Irish play: '. . . I abandoned the romantic cult of Nationalism sixty years ago, and saw the real Ireland when I read the cheap edition of Shaw's *John Bull's Other Island*; hating only poverty, hunger, and disease.'[30] It is hardly surprising that this admiration should have resulted in concrete influences on his plays. *Purple Dust* is the best example.

It employs the same initial situation as *John Bull's Other Island*: a wealthy Englishman with his friend comes to a remote Irish village to establish there his own mode of life. The juxtaposition of Irish and English character-traits results in a series of conflicts that dominate the action and contribute to a satirical analysis of the contrasts between the two nations, this being the basic theme of the two plays. Among the characters, Broadbent and Poges are especially closely related. Both are characterized by their national pride, their sentimentalism, their superficial optimism, their belief in efficiency, their pragmatic-cum-materialist attitude, their lack of comprehension for all forms of irony, and their inability to distinguish between their romantic ideas of Ireland and its reality. Other O'Casey figures have models in Shaw, too, especially Canon Chreehewel in Shaw's Father Dempsey; and O'Casey embodied a chief result of Shaw's analysis, the role of the imagination as the dominant trait of the Irish, in the figure of O'Dempsey.[31]

If an influence is so obvious (the similarities can be traced even in insignificant details[32]) it is more important to discuss the differences, because otherwise the individuality of the second work may be obscured. The differences between the two plays can be summarized as follows: Shaw attempts a rational analysis; he does not evade complexities; his wit and his irony serve to make the audience thoughtful; as a final result he provides a logically justified inventory of conditions and of their resultant problems. O'Casey, on the other hand, employs criticism based

on emotion, greatly simplifying the problems; by farcical means
he arouses the audience's laughter; his final result is a vision that
cannot be rationally substantiated. O'Casey was not capable of any
such detailed analysis as Shaw, whose 'Preface for Politicians'
underpins the tenor of his play. Instead, he exaggerates the
contrasts between British and Irish, employing a series of effective
farcical scenes, while the only corresponding situation in Shaw's
play (the transport of Haffigan's pig with its ensuing comic
catastrophe) is merely reported. Shaw provides a more careful
balance than O'Casey; he even makes Broadbent succeed,
thereby implying his criticism, while Stoke and Poges are exposed
to the full blow of their final defeat. The most significant difference
lies in the conclusion of the two plays. While *John Bull's Other
Island* preserves its realistic-satirical tone to the end, in *Purple
Dust* a new, fantastic-cum-symbolic dimension is introduced
that differs considerably from what has gone before. It raises
O'Casey's play above the specific level of Anglo-Irish topicality
and gives it a more universal meaning than Shaw's, which in
other respects (its wealth of ideas, its structure and the complexity
of its figures) is superior.

*

Any interpretation of *Purple Dust* depends on the understanding one has of the conclusion. It is perhaps possible to see the
ending as a mere conclusion of the realistic comedy-plot. The
flood that overtakes the mansion would then simply be the result
of the river overflowing its banks, finalizing the long-predicted
separation of Avril and Souhaun from Poges and Stoke and
contributing to the 'punishment' of the two obstinate Englishmen.
In such an interpretation, it would parallel the farcical interludes
of the rest of the play, serving as a climax to the series of unfortunate events around Stoke and Poges: after their art treasures have
been destroyed and their furniture broken, they lose their girls,
their beloved Tudor mansion is ruined, and they themselves
have to climb onto the roof in the cold and the rain to save their
own lives. Such an interpretation, on a superficial level, would
consider the ending as another farcical situation, employed as
an appropriate conclusion to the comedy-plot. Indeed, the
combination of the elements of farce and comedy, noticeable
throughout, is here especially successful.

Such an interpretation, however, leaves several questions
open. Why is the flood so devastating in this particular year after

the house has withstood similar catastrophes over the centuries? What is the function of previous references to the flood; why, for instance, can O'Dempsey predict in Act I (p. 36) that the waters will drive away the English? What is the relationship of the conclusion to the level of national satire in the play? How can one interpret the mysterious figure that apparently personifies the flood? Its description in a stage direction precludes any realistic interpretation:

[*The room has darkened; the wind rises; the one light in the room flickers . . . Then . . . a Figure of a man is seen standing at the entrance leading to the hall. He is dressed from head to foot in gleaming black oilskins, hooded over his head, just giving a glimpse of a blue mask, all illumined by the rays of flickering lightning, so that The Figure seems to look like the spirit of the turbulent waters of the rising river . . .*] (p. 115)

These questions have led to diverging answers by those O'Casey critics who do not evade an interpretation of the conclusion altogether. The mansion destroyed by the flood, for instance, is seen as a 'symbol of an Ireland which is past and gone', but also as 'ein abgelebtes bröckliges Empire, reif zum Untergang', and its decaying state as 'the rottenness of capitalist society'.[33] The flood appears as 'the end of middle class society', but also as the 'endgültige Vernichtung der für Irland steril gewordenen Kultur jenes Merry Old England . . .' [34] The river is seen as a 'Lebensstrom' or as 'the river of time that overwhelms a dead past to which it is futile and impossible to return'.[35] Possibly, it is not necessary to side with any one of these interpretations against another, because the flood as a symbol (like the symbol of the rose in *Red Roses for Me*) functions simultaneously on several levels of understanding.

The historico-political relevance of the conclusion is the most obvious one. If Lady Gregory in her best play likens the rising of the moon with the rising of the people, here the rising of the river again suggests analogies to the Irish movement of independence and its success in the early twenties. Poges and Stoke do not only intend to re-establish some of the externals of Tudor life, and for the rest to pass the time as modest guests in a foreign country. Their attitude is that of an ascendancy class that had preserved its often brutal dominion over several centuries. They treat the Irish workers not only with an employer's condescension, but with the thoughtless arrogance of the colonizer who believes that, if necessary, he can always enforce his orders. The workers' reaction is partly a flattering submission characteristic of such situations, but partly also a brusque rejection: O'Dempsey considers Poges 'and all Englishmen, as a rascal, a thief, and a big-pulsed hypocrite' (p. 72) and warns with Shane the Proud of 'the horns of a bull, the hoofs of a horse, the snarl of a dog, an' th' smile of an Englishman' (p. 71). At the end of the play the rising river washes away the Englishmen's pretensions to power. Even those corrupted Irish who have taken sides with them for a while (Avril and Souhaun) now reject them and turn to the Gaelic-Irish cultural tradition personified in O'Dempsey. The only Irishman to remain with the Englishmen is the postmaster, a slightly sinister official employed by them, who is characterized by his hawthorn stick with which his father had once tried to beat Parnell, 'th' scandaliser of Ireland's holy name' (p. 112). In his opposition to Parnell, the symbol of Irish self-confidence and independence, the postmaster takes the part of the enemies of Ireland and, like these, is expelled by the flood. The priest, however, who is treated with equal criticism, can escape the flood in time and remains unharmed, just as the Catholic Church was untouched by the struggle for independence and even gained in power at the end. In this context, the Tudor mansion symbolizes British dominion over Ireland, long insecure and now finally removed. It represents the Protestant Ascendancy, many of whose country-seats were burned down during the guerilla war and whose influence ended with the establishment of the Free State.

However obvious these analogies to the Irish struggle for political independence may be, this particular historical perspective is not the only noteworthy aspect of the conclusion. Any such interpretation is refuted by several references associating the decaying house with the status of Britain as a world power: '. . . in a generation or so the English Empire will be remembered only as a half-forgotten nursery rhyme!' (p. 74). (It is interesting to note that in *Purple Dust* O'Casey always speaks of England and the English, never of Britain and the British; otherwise he would include Celtic populations in his criticism.) Ireland accordingly is only an example of more extended world events. An exclusively 'Irish' interpretation is also refuted by several references to the beginning of the Second World War. Poges and Stoke have come to Ireland not only for their love of nature but also to escape the blitz in London, and Poges even takes advantage of this situation when he tries to buy cement shares because they 'are bound to jump, the minute the bombing starts seriously' (p. 84). Another topical reference has to be considered: O'Killigain has fought in the Spanish Civil War (for a positive O'Casey figure there is no need to explain on which side) and has been wounded there.

If the first symbolic aspect of *Purple Dust* could be defined as the Rise of Irish Independence, and the second as the Fall of the British Empire, the third could be termed the Rise of the Common Man. Numerous scenes serve to demonstrate O'Killigain's moral superiority. Like Poges, he is a self-made man; but while the Englishman has been intent on acquiring possessions and on social climbing, aspiring even to some pseudo-aristocratic status, O'Killigain has made himself instead familiar with the history of his country and with literature, and has remained a self-confident representative of the workers for whose rights he fought in Spain. The newly-won self-confidence of the common man is also evident in his resistance to the priest's attempts at repression, especially if the latter is seen not only as a representative of his church but also as a 'representative of middle class hypocrisy'.[36] O'Killigain, like Ayamonn in *Red Roses for Me*, is an idealized leader of those classes for whose equality O'Casey fought all his life. He incorporates O'Casey's belief in the world-changing and world-improving power of socialism. The symbolic flood underlines the superiority of those values, because it defeats the representatives of class-consciousness founded on material rather than on moral principles. In this respect, the conclusion of *Purple Dust* resembles the optimistic ending of *The Star Turns Red*, for it takes for granted that a capitalist order will be supplanted by a socialist one and it actually shows how this event occurs. If, however, one wants to bracket *Purple Dust* with *The Star Turns Red* and *Red Roses for Me* as O'Casey's three 'red plays', one would have to add that the socialist theme here is only a partial aspect of the whole, just as in the purple of the title the red of the two other plays has been mixed with other colours.

The fourth, and most comprehensive, thematic aspect of the conclusion can best be approached through a significant phrase from O'Casey's own analysis of his play, even though, as a whole, this analysis is rather sketchy and not entirely consistent. Poges and Stoke 'try to shelter from the winds of change but Time wears away the roof, and Time's river eventually sweeps the purple dust away.' [37] According to this quotation, the ending of the play cannot be seen entirely as the victory of the Irish independence movement, as the decay of the British Empire or as the rise of the working classes. O'Casey alludes to the apotheosis of new forms and contents of life as the result of a continuous struggle between the old and the new: *Purple Dust* 'hits . . . at the adoration of the old, outworn things, and leans towards new thought and young ideas'.[38] Such a universal interpretation is supported by the associations of the Deluge (p. 36). The 'sin' that in an O'Caseyan world can lead to a Deluge is the contempt or the neglect of that process of change which is identical with life: '. . . there is no doom in a change except for those who refuse, or who cannot accept, the change – those like Stoke and Poges who tried to live in the past till the present overthrew them.'[39] Each change causes loss. The mansion, a remarkable monument of a distant epoch, is destroyed, the valuable pieces of furniture are to be broken up to construct a raft, and even the two Englishmen, in O'Casey's eyes, are not entirely without attraction: '. . . they are comic, at times pathetic, and all through likeable, if not exactly loveable.'[40] The 'dust' of decay can have a 'purple' sheen – the title of the play characterizes the inevitability of change as well as the regret which may be felt when the past is broken up. But it is significant for O'Casey's optimistic attitude to life that he sees sacrifices not only as necessary but also as more than balanced by what is to be gained by the continuous change of life itself. It remains to be seen how one can define this gain.

At the end of the play, O'Killigain and O'Dempsey establish an anti-world to Poges' and Stoke's stuffy, materialistic, past-oriented sphere of life. This is the world for which Avril and Souhaun decide. They liberate themselves from the dominating influence of possessions, from petrified conventions and old-fashioned class distinctions. They gain a life in an almost mystical closeness to nature where natural events are not filtered through the protection provided by civilization, 'where the rain is heavy, where the frost frets, and where the sun is warm' (p. 106). This world is dominated by joy, expressed in the typical O'Caseyan manifestations of song and dance. O'Killigain is a poet; his first courting scene takes the form of a dance and thus contrasts sharply with the prosaic talk of the two Englishmen from which O'Dempsey's metaphorical, poetic language likewise differs. There is no better proof of the superiority of this attitude to life than the fact that it is condemned by the Priest who represents a world devoid of joy, surrounded by prohibitions, and dominated by fear. The contrast between Christian life-negation and pagan life-affirmation inherent in many O'Casey plays (it has been called O'Casey's 'Ossianic theme'[41]), is especially obvious here. Both the world of the Priest and that of the two Englishmen is characterized by the fact that it has no place for love. This is why

Avril and Souhaun follow the two workers 'where love is fierce an' fond an' fruitful . . . where there's things to say an' things to do an' love at the endings!' (p. 106).

In this respect, *Purple Dust* resembles Synge's *The Shadow of the Glen*. In Act I (p. 12) O'Casey parodied Synge's style to illustrate Avril's unnatural attitude to the workers. In Act III, however, the affinity to Synge is no longer one of parody.[42] Avril and Souhaun are in a situation not dissimilar to that of Nora Burke:

. . . what good is a bit of a farm with cows on it, and sheep on the back hills, when you do be sitting looking out from a door . . . and seeing nothing but the mists rolling down the bog, and the mists again, and they rolling up the bog, and hearing nothing but the wind crying out in the bits of broken trees were left from the great storm, and the streams roaring with the rain.[43]

Nora has to decide between a materialistically secure existence in the 'shadow of the glen', sharing the life of a cold and unimaginative man with farcical traits, who directs her thoughts to old age and death, and the exposed, insecure, natural existence on the heights of life, depicted in the Tramp's poetical language. While Pegeen Mike in *The Playboy of the Western World* fails to live up to such a situation and decides for a mediocrity that will leave her discontented for the rest of her life, Nora accepts the fate of the Tramp and thus becomes a model for the women in *Purple Dust*. Like Nora, Avril and Souhaun are in no way criticized for the fact that even before their final separation they have fled from the frigidity of the two Englishmen into the relationship with other men. Like Nora, Souhaun is haunted by the fear of old age, and in O'Dempsey she finds a companion who, like the Tramp, lives in harmony with the laws of nature and can, therefore, allay her fears. Several other details, for instance the rain reminiscent of the Deluge and the intrusion of farcical traits, confirm these similarities between *The Shadow of the Glen* and Act III of *Purple Dust*; but the decisive element is the pagan pantheism and an almost romantic nature-mysticism, unusual in O'Casey, that establish *Purple Dust* as one of the few points of contact between the two dramatists who otherwise are so very far apart. This relationship may also be responsible in part for the symbolic transformation of the conclusion of *Purple Dust*.

If one considers these various levels of meaning and their faultless fusion with the elements of comedy, farce and satire, as well as the integration of literary influences within the play, it is easy to agree with those critics who see *Purple Dust* as 'O'Casey's finest structural achievement since *The Plough and the Stars*' and as 'a triumph of theatrical ingenuity.' [44]

# 15. RED ROSES FOR ME

*Red Roses for Me*[1] is the most clearly autobiographical of all O'Casey plays. It was written at about the same time as *Pictures in the Hallway* (both works were published in the same year), which explains why it deals with events described in this volume of the autobiography (approximately 1891-1904). The models and events in question have been discussed elsewhere,[2] and it will be sufficient to summarize them briefly here.

As in his early plays, the *milieu* of *Red Roses for Me* is the Dublin tenements, the life sphere of the young O'Casey. In the setting of the first two acts, the dramatist attempts to recreate the atmosphere in which he lived with his mother until her death. Thus the church of St. Burnupus in Act IV is his local Protestant parish church of St. Barnabas, and the historical stratum of the play, the general strike and lockout of 1913, comprises some of the most influential events of O'Casey's early life. The play underlines repeatedly that this strike originated with the transport workers: Ayamonn, the central character, and his comrades are shunters; the two blacklegs of Act IV appear in the uniforms of railway foremen; and during the first two acts one can see outside the window of Ayamonn's room '*the top of a railway signal, with transverse arms, showing green and red lights*' (p. 127).

Each of the more important figures in the play can be traced to a biographical model. The uneducated but wise Mrs. Breydon, distinguished by her courage, her willingness to help others and her love for her flowers seems to be a faithful portrait of O'Casey's mother. Sheila Moorneen is modelled on the girl Maura (called Nora in *Inishfallen, Fare Thee Well*) whose love for O'Casey was not strong enough to set aside the barriers of social and religious prejudice.[3] Roory O'Balacaun is the patriotic tram conductor whose comments in the autobiography accompany the path of young Casside. O'Casey met the model of Brennan o' the Moor in the market square of Totnes in Devon where he lived from 1939 onwards,[4] while Rev. Clinton combines traits of two Protestant clerics who for a long time influenced O'Casey's attitude to religion. Ayamonn Breydon, however, is not a reliable self-portrait of the dramatist. One would rather call him a wishful

175

impersonation, the image of young O'Casey as his older self
would have liked to see him, incorporating traits of Jim Larkin,
the strike leader of the Dublin workers heroized by O'Casey. It is
true that Ayamonn betrays a number of O'Casey characteristics:
his memories of childhood are identical with those of the
dramatist, his love of painting and literature, his relationship
with his mother and his sweetheart, even the theatrical rehearsal
of the opening scene find parallels in the autobiography. Yet
Ayamonn's tolerance and self-confidence, his heroism and readiness for sacrifice are not identical with the character of young
O'Casey as it is reflected in the autobiography.

If more biographical facts from the first half of O'Casey's life
were known, it is probable that even more details could be traced
back to the author's personal experiences. It is much more
important, however, to discuss the consequences that such an
accumulation of autobiographical elements can have on the
drama as a literary work of art. In drama, as opposed to the novel,
such close correspondences to the author's life are not frequent,
and the dangers attendant on them are obvious. The drama, more
than the novel, has to rely on a careful balancing of its proportions.
Such a balance is easier to achieve if the author finds his material
outside his own life or if he invents it; because personal material,
involving him emotionally, makes it more difficult to distinguish
between what is privately important and what is relevant for the
theme of the play. The following interpretation will therefore set
out from the question: what structural elements did O'Casey
employ to counter-balance the danger of formal disintegration
and to preserve the unity of his play? An answer to this question
will provide insights into O'Casey's technique and will help
towards an evaluation of the play.

*

It has been suggested above that O'Casey did not introduce his
private experiences unchanged. Ayamonn Breydon is not a
complete self-portrait; Rev. Clinton combines the memories of
two clergymen; O'Casey did not come across the model for
Brendan o' the Moor until several decades after the other events;
at the time of the general strike he did not live alone with his
mother; even his friendship with the model for Sheila belongs
biographically to a different period from that of the 1913 strike
and this again was not an event of his youth. O'Casey, therefore,
changed the chronological order of events to achieve a higher

degree of concentration. The strike itself is the best example of this: whereas the Dublin labour conflict had lasted several months, O'Casey concentrates these events into a few (probably three) days, and his indeterminate stage direction 'TIME. – A little while ago' (p. 126) explicitly foregoes the claim to depict historical events. Obviously O'Casey was conscious of the problems created by the inclusion of autobiographical elements, and he just as consciously attempted to counteract these problems and to preserve the unity of his play.

If one tries to summarize those elements that make for unity in the play, one will be surprised to notice that the most likely of such elements, the plot, contributes very little to the play's coherence. In this respect *Red Roses for Me* differs radically from the 'normal' type of drama whose unity is based predominantly on a logically developing sequence of events. It is true that O'Casey's play has a certain number of plot elements, but they are far too weak to unify the numerous scenes, figures and motifs. As in the earlier plays, it is necessary to distinguish between a stage action centering on the private fate of the hero, and a series of historical background events intervening at various moments in that action. The action itself can be summarized in one sentence: Ayamonn renounces all personal interests, even his girl, to concentrate on his worker-comrades' struggle, and he is killed during a demonstration. In addition, there is a rudimentary subordinate action, beginning in a few scenes of Act I and concluded as early as Act II: Brennan takes the faded statue of Our Lady of Eblana's Poor to give it a new coat of paint, and he replaces it without being seen.

Several parts of the play remain untouched by these two 'actions'. This holds equally true for the background events, the preparations and the beginnings of a strike with the climax of a mass demonstration. Its links with the stage actions are infrequent: in Act I a strike is mentioned by Mrs. Breydon and Sheila; in Act II, two emissaries of the workers come to see Ayamonn; in Act III the sound of the marching soldiers announces certain countermeasures; in Act IV two 'scabs' take refuge from the strikers in the parish church; then, off-stage noises suggest the troops' attack on the demonstrators; some of them, fleeing from the soldiers, arrive at the church, as does the police officer who gave the order to fire. Even if one adds to these plot elements a few premonitions that serve to direct the audience's expectations in a certain direction (Mrs. Breydon predicts Sheila's future attitude; Mullcanny's personal danger is suggested repeatedly before he is actually attacked; Ayamonn's death becomes predictable after the counter-measures of the police have been repeatedly discussed) the plot structure of the play remains loose indeed. It should also be considered that a great deal of the plot is concentrated in Act IV, while Acts I and II, more than half of the play, are chiefly expository in character and Act III contributes little to the development of external events. It is understandable that the structure of the play has been criticized repeatedly, culminating in one critic's dictum: '. . . the story is not the material for a full-length play.' [5]

If, however, such criticism leads to a generally negative evaluation of *Red Roses for Me*, it has to be countered by the observation that O'Casey employed other structural elements to preserve the unity of the play. Two of them are dominant: the character of Ayamonn on the one hand, a number of symbols closely linked together and suggesting the thematic coherence of the play on the other.

Ayamonn is certainly the central character; in older plays his name would be used in the title. He provides the decisive link between the various elements of the play. This is achieved, first, by his personal attitude to all the other figures. Not only Mrs. Breydon as his mother and Sheila as his sweetheart, but also Brennan, Roory, Mullcanny and Rev. Clinton as his friends enjoy a close relationship of trust with him, as is likewise expressed in the respect of the neighbours and of his working comrades. Dowzard, Foster and Inspector Finglas, like him, are vestrymen, Finglas, moreover, is a devotee of Sheila's. All the other characters, therefore, are somehow linked to Ayamonn; as will be shown later, this predisposes them to represent partial aspects of the central theme of which Ayamonn represents a synthesis.

His central position is, secondly, stressed by the fact that in the first three acts he is almost continuously on stage. The other characters come to him to ask for advice or assistance, problems suggested by him are discussed, his authority settles quarrels, and it is he who takes the important decisions, especially the final decision to go on strike. In Act III Ayamonn points out the transformation the city undergoes at sunset and thus makes possible the vision of a better future. In Act IV, where Ayamonn appears only in one short scene, his central position is nevertheless preserved because he is continuously present in the discussions of the stage characters and consequently in the consciousness of the audience: the farcical discussion between Clinton and the verger Samuel concerns the cross of flowers made by Ayamonn;

Mrs. Breydon and Sheila visit Clinton to persuade him to keep
Ayamonn from the demonstration; after Ayamonn's short scene,
Samuel discusses Ayamonn's cross with Brennan; following the
demonstrators' song against the scabs two of them (who have not
resisted the temptation with which Ayamonn was confronted)
appear on stage, both demand Ayamonn's removal from the
vestry; Samuel secretly gives them Ayamonn's cross; the sound
of the attacking troops reminds both the audience and the stage-
figures of the danger for Ayamonn; Eeada curses Ayamonn's
decision to strike; then the injured Finnoola brings the news of
his death and his last message for Clinton; after the curtain his
corpse is carried in, introducing the conflict over Clinton's right
to admit him to the church; the dialogue between Sheila and
Finglas clarifies the meaning of Ayamonn's sacrifice; Mrs.
Breydon asks to have the light left on for Ayamonn throughout
the night; finally Brennan sings Ayamonn's own song in farewell.
Ayamonn thus links together the figures as well as the scenes of
the play. It will have to be shown that thematically, too, he is at
the centre of the play. Before this, however, it is necessary to deal
with those symbols that likewise contribute to the unity of the
play.

Most important among these is the symbol of the rose, because
it is effective on several levels of the play.[6] It becomes actually
visible when, in Act IV, Sheila lays a bunch of crimson roses on
the dead Ayamonn's breast. The reference to the title is obvious.
The personal pronoun may refer to the autobiographical material,
but it finds its natural justification in the chorus of the central
song. This, again, is not introduced as a mere device of acoustic
embellishment. Ayamonn has written it for the strikers' variety
show which has been planned to collect money for the strike
funds. This show, initially referred to in the Shakespeare rehearsal
of the opening scene, justifies the rehearsal scene with Brennan
and the Singer. It is through these external circumstances that the
song is initially linked both to Ayamonn and Brennan as well as
to the imminent strike. The text of the song, quoted in *Pictures in
the Hallway* as 'a gay Dublin ditty',[7] confirms its central position.
On the most superficial level it describes a girl whose beauty is
not impaired by her poverty and whose capacity for love makes
up for her lack of finery.

The song thus presents a direct reference to the events involving
Ayamonn and Sheila. Ayamonn, quoting from the song, believes
of Sheila: 'A sober black shawl on her shoulders, a simple
petticoat, and naked feet would fail to find her craving finer

things that envious women love' (p. 134). His mother's scepticism is later justified when Sheila ridicules precisely this idea: 'Now, really, isn't it comical I'd look if I were to go about in a scanty petticoat, covered in a sober black shawl, and my poor feet bare! [*Mocking*] Wouldn't I look well that way!' (p. 171). Even before this, Ayamonn has intellectually realized his distance to Sheila. She appears to him 'like a timid little girl ensconced in a clear space in a thicket of thorns – safe from a scratch if she doesn't stir, but unable to get to the green grass or the open road unless she risks the tears the thorns can give' (p. 142). He himself would rather live 'where the redder roses grow, though they bear long thorns, sharp and piercing, thick among them' (p. 143). Yet his love for her makes her still appear like 'a bonnie rose, delectable and red' (p. 144), until Sheila finally estranges herself from him by her suggestion that he should become a blackleg. This is taken up in Act IV when Sheila remembers: 'He said that roses red were never meant for me; before I left him last, that's what he said' (p. 226). The roses of the song, as the traditional symbol of love and passion, therefore, first of all refer to the love between Ayamonn and Sheila. If initially this love is not strong enough, the bunch of roses in Sheila's hand finally suggests a change in her attitude. This is confirmed when Sheila rejects the Inspector in spite of the bourgeois respectability that he can offer her, and it is underlined when Sheila is left to speak the words that give a final meaning to Ayamonn's death. To the Inspector's belittling remark, 'It wasn't a very noble thing to die for a single shilling', she replies: 'Maybe he saw the shilling in th' shape of a new world' (p. 225). In spite of her remaining doubt ('Maybe'), Sheila's understanding love, visible in the bunch of roses, is here greater than at any previous time.

It is, however, not the only function of the song to establish a link between Ayamonn and Sheila on the one hand and the strike motif on the other. While on one level the song refers to Sheila, on another it describes Cathleen ni Houlihan as an allegorical personification of Ireland, a level of meaning that appears in Act III, when Ayamonn discusses the Dublin poor with the nationalist Roory:

ROORY [*hotly*]. An' d'ye think talkin' to these tatthered second-hand
    ghosts 'll bring back Heaven's grace an' Heaven's beauty to Kaithleen
    ni Houlihan?
AYAMONN. Roory, Roory, your Kaithleen ni Houlihan has th' bent
    back of an oul' woman as well as th' walk of a queen. We love th' ideal

Kaithleen ni Houlihan, not because she is false, but because she is beautiful; we hate th' real Kaithleen ni Houlihan, not because she is true, but because she is ugly (p. 197).

The reference to Yeats's plays is significant because the image of Ireland that it projects had become a basic concept of the Irish nationalists. It is, of course, easier to see a personification of Ireland in a venerable old woman from an almost mythical past who without difficulty turns into a girl of royal beauty, than to admit that the dirty and ragged proletariat of present-day Dublin is equally representative of the country. O'Casey in Ayamonn's words denounces the grandiloquent patriotism that is directed at an ideal but ignores reality. In O'Casey's view, the Dublin poor, *'dressed so in black that they appear to be enveloped in the blackness of a dark night'* (pp. 185-186), are to be equated with the Cathleen ni Houlihan of the song. The ugliness of their external appearance hides the beauty of the rose, and it is Ayamonn's chief object in life to make this visible again. He succeeds for a while when, during the vision scene, he admonishes them: 'Take heart of grace from your city's *hidden splendour'* (p. 198).[8] The reference to Cathleen ni Houlihan is underlined by further literary references, when, in Act III, O'Casey uses quotations from James Clarence Mangan's 'The Dark Rosaleen'. Ayamonn blesses young Finnoola with the words: 'May you marry well, an' rear up children fair as Emer was, an' fine as Oscar's son; an' may they be young when *Spanish ale* foams high on every hand, an' *wine from th' royal Pope's* a common dhrink!' (p. 202). And Roory believes of the poor: '*Gun peal an' slogan cry* are th' only things to startle them' (p. 197).[9] Mangan's moving poem, based on a Gaelic original, describes Dark Rosaleen as the personification of Ireland, banished from her golden throne, but it also betrays the speaker's feverish patriotism whose visions of a better future for Dark Rosaleen as well as his own unlimited self-sacrificing devotion have their parallels in O'Casey's Ayamonn.

The symbol of the rose, introduced through the song in the rehearsal and associated both with Sheila and with Cathleen ni Houlihan, has an additional, more comprehensive meaning. The theme of the song is the presence of hidden beauty under an unattractive exterior, a bright colour (likened to 'jewel'd desire') shining all the more radiantly from the surrounding darkness. This theme affects several parts of the play. Brennan o' the Moor, for instance, hides his secret compassion for the fate of the poor, his reticent generosity, under the shabby cover of avarice. Not only does Brennan buy flowers for little Ursula which, as he knows well enough, are destined for the statue of the Virgin, but he also carries off the statue itself to return it with a fresh coat of paint without giving the poor a chance to thank him.

This statue deserves special attention in the present context because it is one of those additional symbols subordinated to the symbol of the rose and employed to ensure the play's coherence. This becomes clear in a stage direction:

*The figure was once a glory of purest white, sparkling blue, and luscious gilding; but the colours have faded, the gilt is gone, save for a spot or two of dull gold still lingering on the crown. She is wearing a crown that, instead of being domed, is castellated like a city's tower, resembling those of Dublin; and the pale face of the Virgin is sadly soiled by the grime of the house. The men are dressed in drab brown, the women in a chill grey, each suit or dress having a patch of faded blue, red, green, or purple somewhere about them* (pp. 136-137).

The statue preserves only a few traces of its past beauty, just as the inhabitants of the slums wear only a few patches of faded coloured material on their drab clothes, and the face of the statue is soiled like that of its people. The statue thus becomes a representative of the poor who carry it in. Its crown, castellated like the Dublin coat of arms, suggests that it represents not only the inhabitants of this one house, but the whole of the city, once rich, now soiled by poverty and misery. Its name, Our Lady of Eblana's Poor, which refers to an earlier name for Dublin, supports such an interpretation. If the statue is restored, this anticipates a change in the life of the slum people; from now on it shines, 'Bright and gorgeous' (p. 176) like the song's bunch of red roses, from the surrounding darkness. The events concerning the statue are paralleled by the vision scene of Act III which likewise points forward to a better future and a brighter city. It should be stressed, however, that, although the poor see the transformation of the statue as a divine miracle, embellishing its return with vivid imagination, in reality its restoration is due to human activity, as the audience well knows. O'Casey, as some critics have not realized, has distinguished quite clearly between these two different points of view. If the city is to be redeemed, this will not happen by a sudden miracle, but it will have to be attained by hard work and perhaps paid for by sacrifice. It is Ayamonn who works for such a redemption, trying to introduce joy and beauty into his own poverty-stricken life as into that of the other poor: he paints, reads, writes songs and stages a show. His endeavours are visualized right at the beginning when, with his mother, he rehearses a scene from *Henry VI* (Part 3, V, vi) to bring Shakespeare closer to the poor (and the War of the Roses in this scene is, of course, also associated with the dominant symbol). Ayamonn and his mother wear colourful costumes over their drab everyday clothes, shining against the gloomy background of the room like the roses of the title song. Although realistically based on the rehearsal situation, they serve to underline the heroic character of the two figures: 'The hobnailed boots and shabby skirt beneath the costume relate them to their material environment, but the Shakespearean costume symbolises the transcending of this environment through spirit and imagination.' [10] In a similar way, in Act III the clothes of the poor are transformed as an image of the (short-lived) moment in which they overcome their misery. It is not justified, therefore, to criticize O'Casey for the 'laying of fancy dress over modern clothes' and to see in it an evasion of reality.[11] O'Casey anticipates possible changes in a reality that he considers as unacceptable; the show as a preparation for the strike will be the first step in this direction. In the vision scene as well as in the 'miracle' of the statue the transformation is seen to be attainable, but it cannot be achieved without a struggle. The strike, therefore, is a first step in the process of liberating the poor from the darkness of their present-day existence.

Whereas the hope for a religious miracle in the action of the statue is revealed as superstitious, the struggle itself takes on religious overtones. This, again, is made explicit through the rose symbol. The symbolic meaning of the rose, suggesting love and passion, is not limited to the private sphere but includes religious Passion as well. The death of Ayamonn resembles the sacrifice of Christ inasmuch as he attempts to liberate his fellow human beings from the darkness of their present existence, with this difference only, that his liberation concerns this world. Such an interpretation is supported by various textual images. In the final scene, the bunch of roses in the church carries certain religious overtones. The colour symbolism in the clergyman's apparel, '*a thick black cassock lined with red cloth*' (p. 205), underlines the relationship between the rose symbol in Ayamonn's song and the religious meaning of his sacrifice. Again, the events of the play take place during Passion Week; Ayamonn is carried into a church decorated for the Festival of the Resurrection. And Rev. Clinton places on the altar another religious symbol which deserves special attention: the cross of daffodils made by Ayamonn. This additional flower symbol, reinforcing the symbol of the roses, is interpreted in the text itself:

RECTOR. The daffodils? But they simply signify the new life that Spring gives; and we connect them in a symbolic way, quite innocently, with our Blessed Lord's Rising. And a beautiful symbol they are: daffodils that come before the swallow dares, and take the winds of March with beauty. Shakespeare, Sam (p. 208).

Here the resurrection of Christ is linked to the rebirth of life in Spring and to a quotation from Shakespeare, thus giving Ayamonn's death a higher meaning. In addition, it should be noted that the cross is a Celtic cross, *'the shafts made of the flowers, and the circle of vivid green moss'* (p. 219), associating Ayamonn's national aspirations with the religious context.

The 'vision' of Act III, a symbolic *scene* in contrast to the symbolic *objects* discussed above, takes up a special position among the symbols of the play. It can be understood as a direct answer to the people's prayer-chant at the end of the previous act. This scene, like the other symbols, is not entirely dissociated from reality. Initially the bridge across the Liffey with the surrounding houses, a church spire and Nelson's column in the distance and with its entourage of unemployed and beggars is depicted quite realistically. Even the transformation of the scene has some factual basis in that it is due to the Dublin sunset, described by O'Casey in *Pictures in the Hallway*.[12] Nevertheless, the scene, from its very beginning, is more stylized than the rest of the play. The stage direction is quite explicit: *'The sun shines on [Nelson's] pillar and church spire, but there is no sign of sun where these people are'* (p. 185). The process of stylization is continued in the grouping of the figures on the bridge and even more so in their language. From the beginning Eeada, Dympna and Finnoola speak in a rhythmical, alliterative chant; they express ideas inappropriate to their level of education, and they are even capable of irony. Eeada's first words serve as signature for the key employed here: 'This spongy leaden sky's Dublin; those tomby houses is Dublin too – Dublin's scurvy body; an' we're Dublin's silver soul' (p. 186). In a realistic context it would be unthinkable for the figures to express their own lethargy and resignation in such perfect figures of speech. This act, therefore, immediately stands out from the rest of the play. O'Casey here continues a technique suggested in Act II of *The Plough and the Stars* and fully developed in Act II of *The Silver Tassie*: in one section of the play the implicit meaning is made explicit by unrealistic presentation. The act therefore deserves special attention.

It has several functions. It enlarges, quite literally, the audience's circle of vision. So far, the audience had observed the situation of the poor in one house, now they realize that this situation is typical: the whole of Dublin is covered by the spongy leaden sky of misery, the poor of the city itself are untouched by the rays of the sun. This makes it more understandable why Ayamonn is ready to give up Sheila to fight against these conditions. The act also provides an opportunity of showing various figures, representatives of certain modes of thinking or social groups, in their attitudes to the poor. Rev. Clinton, the Inspector, Brennan and Roory all leave the surroundings in great haste; Sheila typically does not come here at all. Only Ayamonn does not evade the confrontation with the poor, he has not given up the hope of a better life for them and at the same time points a way to it: 'Rouse yourselves; we hold a city in our hands!' (p. 196). It is Ayamonn, too, who associates this scene with the strike: 'Friend, we would that you should live a greater life; we will that all of us shall live a greater life. Our sthrike is yours' (p. 198).

The connections between the vision scene and the strike are underlined by a short scene added in the third version of the play. In it, three workers appear on the bridge; they report that the readiness to strike is spreading, and confirm their determination to resist the counter-measures of the police and the military. This scene stresses the function of Act III as a bridge between the decision to strike at the end of Act II and the demonstration in Act IV, and it also underlines the meaning of the vision scene. Ayamonn sees the strike as a first step on the path to a life that had become visible for a few moments in the vision scene. His object is not material gain alone. The determining elements of that transformation are beauty and joy, the one visible in the outline of the riverside houses *'decked in mauve and burnished bronze'* (p. 199) from which the men stand out like statues of bronze, the other embodied in the dance of Ayamonn and Finnoola. The transformation not only changes the city but also the people; the scene therefore corresponds to Ayamonn's endeavours to make the poor familiar with Shakespeare as well as to provide them with a better income. Yet the vision not only projects a new life but also arouses the motivation to fight for it. The central song (this time not introduced realistically) expresses the changing attitude of the people:

We swear to release thee from hunger an' hardship,
From things that are ugly an' common an' mean;
Thy people together shall build a brave city,
Th' fairest an' finest that ever was seen (p. 201).

This stanza, intensified by the repetition at the end of the act,
establishes one pole of the following conflict, the other being
introduced through the *sound of many feet marching in unison*
(p. 202). The vision act, by establishing the object of the ensuing
conflict as well as the conflicting parties' determination to fight, is
not a static interpolation, but has considerable dynamic potential
for the play; by no means is it merely theatrical propaganda.[13]

An additional function can easily be overlooked, although it is
relevant for an evaluation of Ayamonn. The whole act is shot
through with references to figures of Irish myth, legend and
history. The starting point, again, is the shabby present-day
reality of the Dublin poor: Eeada mentions the golden harp of Brian
Boru, the important Irish high-king from pre-Norman times, an
emblem visible today only on the Guinness bottles. Soon after
this the Inspector remembers that in the vicinity of the bridge
were the living quarters of Henry Grattan, who fought for Catholic
emancipation and against the Union, and also of Jonathan Swift.
These names are followed by many others that in Ireland have
undergone a fusion of historical reality and legendary glorification,
among them Conn, the ancestor of the Irish high-kings, and
Osheen who embodies the conflict between Christianity and
the pagan cultural tradition. This sequence terminates in the
description of Ayamonn whose *'head set in a streak of sunlight'*
appears like *'the severed head of Dunn-Bo speaking out of the
darkness'* (p. 198). By associating Ayamonn with the legendary
singer Dunn-bó who was killed in a battle for the King of Ireland
and nevertheless in the evening sang before his King, Ayamonn
is placed among those legendary figures of a living popular
tradition who either represent the image of a more beautiful and
happier Ireland or who fought for its re-establishment. *Red
Roses for Me* thus acquires an historical-cum-mythological
perspective.

*

So far, this interpretation has been chiefly concerned with the
unity of the play. Despite the scarcity of coherent plot elements,
the central character and several related symbols establish a

complex network of relationships between the various structural elements and thematic levels. An analysis of the manifold functions of the symbols also permits important insights into the play. But only if it can be shown that the individual scenes and figures are related to a common theme, will it finally be possible to judge the play's coherence.

In several works, especially in *Hall of Healing*, O'Casey depicts the miserable living conditions of the Dublin proletariat. In *Red Roses for Me*, however, he not only shows the situation of the poor: his prime concern is with the means of altering that situation. All the structural elements of the play are subservient to this theme. In the first two acts, the atmosphere of the tenements is exemplified in the living room of the Breydons and in the other inhabitants of the house who enter it. This is supplemented by the depiction of the loungers on the Liffey bridge, who, in the unrealistic Act III, analyze their own life. Metaphors like 'Sorrow's a slush under our feet, up to our ankles, an' th' deep drip of it constant overhead' and the description of Dublin as 'A graveyard where th' dead are all above th' ground' (p. 186) summarize the present situation.

In the scenery of Act III, the shadow-like existence of the poor is dominated by two sunlit edifices, Nelson's column and a church spire. Both represent the powers that will resist any alteration in the living conditions of the people because this would reduce their own influence. Both have their analogues in the figures of the play. Inspector Finglas of the mounted police represents the power of the (British) state. He sees the poor as 'flotsam and jetsam' (p. 190) and Ayamonn as 'but a neat slab of a similar slime' (p. 191). He has no understanding for the demands made in the strike (p. 225) and therefore considers it his duty to defend the existing order (p. 212). He effectively combines his occasional willingness to help others with his own interests: when the firing order is given, he seeks to protect Ayamonn because this may impress Sheila. When in the final act he is rejected by Sheila, his attitude, in the scale of values represented by this play, is repudiated. Finglas, the representative of British dominion, the enemy of the poor and the adversary of Catholicism is ultimately completely isolated, as can be seen from stage directions in both parts of Act IV: Finglas *'stands a little apart, nearer the hedge'* (p. 210), *'Partly behind the tree, the Inspector is standing alone'* (p. 222).

The Catholic Church is personified in several figures in the play. Roory O'Balacaun is not only a radical nationalist but also a

Catholic. He immediately feels and resents the erotic associations in Ayamonn's song (p. 152), he reverses Brennan's fanatic exclamation: 'You damned bigot – to hell with th' King, an' God save th' Pope!' (p. 167), and soon after sides with Brennan to prevent Mullcanny from explaining the ideas of Haeckel's *Welträtsel* to Ayamonn. In a farcical scene in which he, together with Brennan and Mullcanny, reduces religious-ideological fanaticism to absurdity, he demonstrates his arrogant conscious-ness of his own elevated position: '. . . men o' goodwill we are, abloom with th' blessin' o' charity, showin' in th' dust we're made of, th' diamond-core of an everlastin' divinity!' (p. 175). The consequences of such an attitude are shown in Sheila. Her anti-Protestant, anti-sensuous, class-conscious family forces her to attend the exercises of a group with the significant name 'Daughters of St. Frigid' (p. 141), thereby estranging her from Ayamonn. Her family has no understanding for the objects of the strike and therefore expects Ayamonn to turn blackleg; respectability in their eyes can be achieved only by deserting the ranks of the workers. The attitude of Catholicism to the strike can also be gauged from the action around the statue of the Virgin. The best the poor can do is to beg for some soap to have their statue cleaned, just as their begging on the Liffey bridge merely serves to maintain their present living conditions. If any basic change occurs (the restoration of the statue) they immediately see this as a miracle, elaborating it with the exotic imagination of superstition. Their superstition is even more discredited because it is paralleled by their hope for another miracle when they put some money on a horse (p. 187). Catholicism as presented in this play substitutes an ineffective belief in miracles for the confidence in one's own ability to change existing conditions, and at the same time it resists all attempts to alter the *status quo*.

These two static attitudes are contrasted with four ideological tendencies, all of which, in their different ways, aim for certain alterations, none of them, therefore, appearing entirely negative in the play's scale of values: they are Protestantism, atheistic rationalism, nationalism and socialism. Protestantism is depicted in many different forms. The lowest position in the scale of values (even lower than Finglas) is occupied by the two vestrymen Foster and Dowzard, whose very external appearance is caricatured (pp. 215-216). Not only are they arrogant, cowardly and deceitful, but they also commit the (in the value system of this play) unforgivable sin of acting as 'scabs' in defiance of Ayamonn's hopes. Accordingly, their Protestantism does not spring from

belief but from the hatred of Catholicism. They represent a
radicalism typical of religious minorities and still prevalent in
Ulster (Foster speaks with an Ulster accent and wears the orange
insignia of Northern Protestantism). Brennan o' the Moor who,
when excited, also lapses into an Ulster accent, resembles them
in many ways. He too sees in Ayamonn's cross not the symbol of
re-born life but the image of popery; he too is cowardly and
hides as soon as there is trouble. In the farcical controversy of Act
II between Brennan, Mullcanny and Roory he is ridiculed in
O'Casey's mode of presentation, as are Foster and Dowzard later
on. On the other hand he overcomes his acute avarice in order to
mitigate people's sufferings by unrecognized acts of charity, and
he even supports the Catholics' hated worship of effigies when
this can procure them some pleasure. He owes his name to the
hero of an Irish popular ballad who, like Robin Hood, robs the
rich to help the poor.[14] The ending of the play is in this context of
special significance: Brennan gives the verger some money so
that he can once more sing Ayamonn's song for his dead friend.
Towards the end, therefore, he is quite close to those figures
who, next to Ayamonn, take up the highest position in the play's
scale of values: Rev. Clinton and Mrs. Breydon. Neither shares
Ayamonn's uncompromising attitude; moreover they warn him
not to take part in the strike because they fear for his personal
security, but they approve of his path and therefore do not hinder
him when he decides to go on:

MRS. BREYDON. . . . Go on your way, my son, an' win. We'll welcome
    another inch of the world's welfare.
RECTOR [*shaking his hand*]. Go, and may the Lord direct you! (p. 213).

The limits of their own willingness to fight for change have been
depicted earlier on in the play. Although on the Liffey bridge
Clinton feels the contrast between his own secure life and the
beggars' exposed existence, he only throws them a few coins and
tries not to take too much notice of them, because otherwise he
might find himself forced into some further action: 'Let us go
from here. Things here frighten me, for they seem to look with
wonder on our ease and comfort . . . Things here are of a substance
I dare not think about, much less see and handle' (p. 191). It is
doubtful, therefore, whether Clinton is really 'O'Casey's ideal
clergyman',[15] a role better filled by Father Boheroe in *The Bishop's
Bonfire*. Mrs. Breydon sees *caritas* as her duty to the point of self-
sacrifice, but she cannot achieve any real improvement. It is

typical that she devotes herself to a dying woman whose death she may render a little easier while she has not been able to improve her life. For Mrs. Breydon, too, the statue of the Virgin becomes a touchstone: she can give the poor some soap-powder to clean the statue from the dirt of the moment, but it is not in her power to recreate its original beauty. It is precisely these two irreproachable persons who underline O'Casey's thesis that it is not enough to live an exemplary private life.[16] According to O'Casey, it is only by joint action that life and its conditions can be changed.

Such a readiness for activity is shown by Roory O'Balacaun; his limitations are of a different kind. As a radical nationalist, Roory strives for the liberation of Ireland from British dominion. For all its inherent justification, this demand is, however, linked to a narrowness of opinion repeatedly criticized by Ayamonn (who here, as elsewhere, becomes the author's spokesman). On the one hand, Roory ignores the existence of social problems and despises the Dublin proletariat. His romantic image of Ireland has no room for the deplorable conditions of the present; his patriotism bypasses reality. On the other hand Roory believes it to be his duty to cling to a narrow-minded provincialism in all cultural matters. He has never heard of Angelico and Constable, he rejects Ruskin as a Scotsman, and even in the planned variety show he sees a lurking English influence. When such an attitude is joined to moral prejudice and religious intolerance, it does indeed contain the danger described by Ayamonn:

Roory, Roory, is that th' sort o' freedom you'd bring to Ireland with a crowd of green branches an' th' joy of shouting? If we give no room to men of our time to question many things, all things, ay, life itself, then freedom's but a paper flower, a star of tinsel, a dead lass with gay ribbons at her breast an' a gold comb in her hair. Let us bring freedom here, not with sounding brass an' tinkling cymbal, but with silver trumpets blowing, with a song all men can sing, with a palm branch in our hand, rather than with a whip at our belt, and a headsman's axe on our shoulders (p. 169).

This speech is significant beyond the dramatic context, because in post-revolutionary Ireland it was Roory's attitude that prevailed; O'Casey again and again denounced its religious intolerance, narrow morality, loud-mouthed patriotism and neglect for the emancipation of the lower classes. Ayamonn's speech can therefore be understood as a justification for O'Casey's own departure from Ireland.

Whereas O'Casey depicted in the figure of Roory the dangers of an attitude that became current in the early Free State, he draws Mullcanny as a representative of an equally dubious attitude that did not have a chance in Ireland. Mullcanny, a militant atheist, tries to free his fellow human beings from their religious views, which for him constitute the root of all evil. Unlike the other fanatics, Foster, Dowzard and Roory, he does not however forgo his opinions when they carry disadvantages for him: 'He's really a good fellow. Gave up his job rather than his beliefs – more'n many would do' (p. 156). Yet he is just as unsparing with others as he is with himself. His attempts to alter the world are purely destructive. Like the Atheist in *Within the Gates* he wants to expunge any and every form of religiosity ('superstition') without being able to put anything better in its place. Even if the belief in a better life after death is a mere illusion, his attempt to destroy it is more than doubtful as long as he can offer the poor no substitute for their last hope. He is dangerous precisely because the logic of his arguments is unassailable. Only once does Brennan, with one of O'Casey's marvellous strokes of comic relief, succeed in unbalancing him, when Mullcanny tries to argue man's evolution from the monkey by the monkey's preference for beer, which leads Brennan to ask: 'Did they get their likin' for beer from us, or did we get our likin' of beer from them? Answer me that, you, now; answer me that!' (p. 175). Mullcanny's position in the play's scale of values becomes clear when compared to Ayamonn: Ayamonn dies for his aim to build something new, Mullcanny is merely knocked down for his intention to destroy something old. The different outcome shows that the insistence on ideals is of higher value than the struggle against illusions.

These various dubious attempts to change the world are contrasted with socialism, which, given the circumstances of this play, is the only promising answer to the problems presented. As O'Casey depicts it, it strives for material improvements in the workers' situation as a precondition for an enlargement of their intellectual sphere of life. The present situation, as depicted in the play, can only be changed by a struggle with the conservative powers. The only appropriate means to achieve such an end is the strike which is effective only through the principle of solidarity. In such a scale of values, therefore, human solidarity is of the highest importance, and the highest offence is to break the strike, because to do so endangers the success of the struggle. It is for this reason that the two 'scabs' Foster and Dowzard take up the lowest position in the human scale of values, and the demonstrators' attack on them, unlike the violence on Mullcanny, is not criticized; for the same reason, Sheila's insistence that Ayamonn become a strike-breaker is reprehensible enough to lead to their separation.

For Ayamonn as the representative of socialism, solidarity with the other workers always ranks higher than personal interest. He unites in an ideal way the struggle for material progress with the endeavour for intellectual liberation. In the opening scene he declares with an almost Weskerian optimism that he wants to see the workers familiar with Shakespeare: 'Before I'm done, I'll have him drinking in th' pubs with them!' (p. 131). Ayamonn, however, is not only an ideal (and idealized) leader of the workers; he also incorporates a synthesis of all the intellectual attitudes depicted in the play. His links with Protestantism are obvious: his mother is a devout Protestant, he himself is a member of the vestry and has the rector for his fatherly friend, and after his death his body is not taken to his flat but to the church. Yet his belief is a type of Protestantism that does not shy away from contact with Catholicism and is even condemned by the more extreme members of the parish as 'popery' (p. 218); his cross of flowers is taken by Dowzard and Foster as 'a Popish symbol' (p. 219). As can also be seen in his treatment of the Catholic inhabitants of the tenements, he does not reject Catholicism, thereby putting himself into opposition to his mother who considers it a sin to have found the restored statue, even for a moment, beautiful. Ayamonn's attitude to Mullcanny is still more unusual. He is the only one who tries to understand him and reads with interest his 'Bible', Haeckel's *Welträtsel* (the effect of such reading on his beliefs, however, is not shown). Finally, Ayamonn also approves of Roory's nationalist ideas, as can best be seen at the end of Act I where Roory and Ayamonn together sing the Fenian song.

*Red Roses for Me*, therefore, does not simply juxtapose ideologies and propose one as superior to all the others; it endeavours to achieve some kind of synthesis, embodied in the person of Ayamonn. Ayamonn thus takes on prophetic, if utopian traits, mirrored in the vision scene of Act III. The synthetic nature of the play is confirmed when one observes the conclusions of the individual acts. Each of the four acts ends with a song. The endings of the first three acts each stress one of the ideologies represented in the play: the Republican battle song in Act I, the Catholic prayer chant in Act II, the socialist song, combining the belief in a better future with the promise to fight for it, in Act III. Act IV ends with the title song whose symbol of the rose, as has been shown, links all the various aspects of this play.

*

There can, then, be no doubt about the artistic unity of *Red Roses for Me*. A critic's view that there is 'no unity in the play other than the thin thread of the poorly told, grotesquely proportioned story of Ayamonn',[17] is based on a rather superficial consideration of formal elements alone and cannot be maintained. Equally untenable is the view that the play's unity derives only from its 'melancholy sweet-and-sour mood in which everything is enveloped.'[18] Nevertheless, the play is not without its weaknesses. Some of these have already been pointed out in previous analyses; since none of them decisively reduces the play's qualities, it will be sufficient to list them in brief.

The division of Act IV where, as in Act III of *Juno and the Paycock* and *The Star Turns Red*, the curtain indicates the passing of several hours, is certainly unfortunate. Quite apart from the fact that it will be difficult for the audience to grasp the time sequence, the dramatist here evades the necessity of showing on stage the transition from the passion of battle to the grief of death. He chooses a simpler way of evoking a new mood by visual and acoustic means. On the other hand, O'Casey's solution is preferable to that of many other plays (*Riders to the Sea* may be taken as an example) where the dead hero is brought in long before his corpse could even possibly have been found. Another subject for criticism is the fact that in Act IV, with Foster, Dowzard, Samuel and the Lamplighter, four new characters are introduced, at least two of whom attain considerable significance, while at the same time two other important characters from the previous acts (Roory and Mullcanny) have disappeared. Although in the theatre this may offer a welcome chance for double casting, it is unfortunate if the final act that should be moving smoothly to the play's climax, has again to take on expository functions. Foster, Dowzard and Samuel, moreover, are not only new characters, they also introduce a new thematic element, the criticism of Clinton's alleged popery. On the other hand, Dowzard and Foster as blacklegs are at least remotely connected with the Ayamonn action and the background events, and their attack on the cross of flowers has a parallel to the statue action of Acts I and II: if in the earlier acts the Catholic belief in miracles is revealed as superstition, here the Protestant rejection of religious symbols is equally reduced to absurdity.

The diction of *Red Roses for Me* has been criticized repeatedly.[19] It is true that O'Casey here, instead of searching for a compromise between 'poetical' and 'realistic' language in the manner of Synge, has again and again substituted an obviously 'literary' diction, distinguished by alliteration, complicated syntax, a massing of adjectives, involved metaphors etc., for ordinary everyday speech. Not only in the unrealistic Act III, where this would be quite legitimate, but also in other parts of the play can one frequently observe 'the lack of harmony between the speaker and the spoken words'.[20] Moreover, he sometimes chooses images that are neither particularly appropriate nor directly connected with the dramatic context. The alterations introduced in the second version have removed only a few such passages. The new version still contains sentences like: 'Who through every inch of life weaves a patthern of vigour an' elation can never taste death but goes to sleep among th' stars, his withered arms outstretched to greet th' echo of his own shout' (p. 179). The shortened article and the aspirated dental are the only indications in this cluster of confused images that these are the words of a character in this play. Such passages cannot be excused by reference to the 'superb Elizabethan energy'[21] often attributed to O'Casey's language; yet they are not frequent enough to injure the dramatic substance of the play.

Another objection has more weight, because it touches the limitations of O'Casey's creative powers or at least the limitations of the type of drama chosen here. In a play which carries so many different levels of meaning, it becomes difficult for the characters to preserve any realistic individuality. It is doubtful whether *Red Roses for Me* really offers 'a valid world of credible people who are capable of achieving symbolic stature because they live unmanipulated lives of their own.'[22] Since every figure represents certain social groups or ideologies, their freedom of individual development is limited. The only characters who stand 'between' the various groups and therefore do not have to behave 'representatively', are Brennan and Sheila. They alone, therefore, are contradictory in themselves (Brennan) or open to change (Sheila). This turns them into the most credible and also the most interesting figures of the play. Sheila, moreover, is the only one who has to endure an internal conflict, the decision between several, near-equal values (the demands of her bourgeois-Catholic society and her love for Ayamonn). If, at first, she turns away from her lover, her final actions and her justification of Ayamonn's attitude suggest that she has undergone a development of a sort that is not possible for any of the other characters.

Ayamonn himself has to carry the exceptionally heavy weight of his various dramatic functions. Not only is he supposed to represent socialism, but also a synthesis of all the other ideologies in a purified form. It is with some exaggeration, but not without all justification that Ayamonn has been termed 'a combination of Red Jim and Christ and the president of the local Browning society'.[23] Apart from a certain irritation towards his mother (p. 140) he never shows any weaknesses; even when he is angry, his anger is fully justified.[24] His temptation by Sheila who offers her hand for the price of his betrayal of the workers, and later his mother's and Sheila's attempts to persuade him not to take part in the demonstration, do not cause any conflict in him, they do not even make him hesitate, because in his world the values are distributed so clearly that there is no room for ambivalence. Ayamonn as an ordinary worker would be more convincing if he were not so super-humanly sure of his objectives, and reached them only after a longer search, yet this would make him less suited for his representative functions.[25] O'Casey has not been entirely successful in linking the symbolic character of his figures, especially Ayamonn, with the believable fate of individuals. *Red Roses for Me* is impaired by a lack of congruity, an insufficient integration of the realistic and the symbolic level.

Another objection is directly connected with this. Among the ideologies exhibited in this play, socialism is preferred to such an extent that the audience really is left with no choice. This, of course, is an objection to O'Casey's intentions, not to his dramatic power. Quite early in his career, partially influenced by Shaw, he reached the conviction that the author's opinions should always be visible in his work. His reply to Yeats's refusal to accept *The Silver Tassie* is well known:

It is all very well and very easy to say that 'dramatic action must burn up the author's opinions.' The best way, and the only way, to do that is to burn up the author himself.
What's the use of writing a play that's just as like a camel as a whale?[26]

Such an attitude presupposes that the audience either shares the author's opinions from the start or is 'converted' to them in the course of the play. If they do not share his views, they will not accept the play's peculiar scale of values and, although they may admire certain passages, will feel irritated by the author's distortions of reality as they see it. *Red Roses for Me* presupposes a belief in the changeability of the world through human action. It is only in this perspective that the death of Ayamonn can appear as a sacrifice and the dramatic conclusion be meaningful, especially as O'Casey does not show the outcome of the demonstration, let alone any tangible result of the strike. Success is to be defined in terms of the effect an action has on others: 'renewed courage and a resolve that his death shall not have been in vain.'[27] The death of Ayamonn strengthens the workers' solidarity; in the scale of values outlined above its purpose is quite clear. The more sceptical among his critics, who do not share O'Casey's belief in the possibility of a better future, greet the play, therefore, with little understanding:

. . . how can anyone believe that they are going to abolish 'hunger and hardship . . . things that are ugly an' common an' mean'. Hunger and hardship and envy and strife have always existed. Anger and envy are elements of human nature; hunger and hardship are conditions of human existence. It is possible to control the elements of human nature and to modify the conditions of human existence, but it is quite improbable that they will ever be abolished![28]

A literary interpretation, however, should not allow itself to be pushed aside by a quarrel over ideologies. If one accepts the author's premises, the death of Ayamonn is a meaningful sacrifice because it confirms the living in their struggle for a better world.

# 16. OAK LEAVES AND LAVENDER

The reception of *Oak Leaves and Lavender* was almost uniformly unfavourable. Although occasionally praised for individual traits, it is generally condemned as a whole.[1] This is probably due, at least in part, to the debacle of the first production (May 1947) at the Lyric Theatre, Hammersmith (i.e. outside the West End), 'one of the most thoroughly botched productions in the last decade'.[2] O'Casey is obviously referring to this production when he writes in *Sunset and Evening Star*:

Whenever he ventured to think of what was the worst production of a play of his, his heart's blood pressed into his head, and all the world became red. Even critics, often tolerant of things done badly, declared it to be a butchery of a play. And one had to bear it quietly, though the heart was stung. Never before had Sean seen such an assured and massive incompetency in a producer assigned to an English theatre or such managerial support given to incompetence. He was the cockiest clacking cod Sean had ever encountered, adazzle with iridescent ignorance of the drama; a fellow who should never have been allowed even to pull a curtain up from the stage of a tuppenny gaff, yet the manager clapped him on the back continually. The play, admittedly, was a difficult one, probably a clumsy one, possibly, even, a bad one; but the shocking production failed, in every possible way, to show whether it was one, or all, of these; failed to give the slightest guidance to an experimental playwright. The fellow's gone now, making his exit by way of a gas-oven, giving in a kitchen a better production than he ever gave on the stage.[3]

After such a production, O'Casey could hardly hope for a second chance on the English or American commercial stage, while the play's demands on stage technique were too high for the amateur theatre.

The failure of the Hammersmith production was not, however, the only reason for the play's poor reception among the O'Casey critics. The author's admission that the play was 'probably a clumsy one, possibly, even, a bad one' – an unusual case of self-criticism – shows his own doubts about it. These are underlined by the fact that he did not, apparently, consider *Oak Leaves and Lavender* worth a revision, but transferred the 1946 version

unchanged to volume IV of the *Collected Plays*, although this
play more than any other might have gained in effectiveness
from certain revisions. These factors are bound to influence any
analysis of the play, making it peculiarly difficult to separate
interpretation from evaluation. Nevertheless, the play requires
thorough consideration, as does any work by so important a
dramatist. Moreover, *Oak Leaves and Lavender* shows a number
of innovations that have not yet been fully appreciated by
O'Casey critics; and even those formal experiments that were not
fully successful indicate steps in the development of the author's
dramatic technique. In addition, the play provides certain insights
into O'Casey's attitude to a number of problems with which he
wrestled throughout his life.

*

O'Casey's subtitle, *A Warld on Wallpaper*, provides a suitable
starting-point for an interpretation. As several critics have noted,
this is a reference to a statement by Yeats in the *Silver Tassie*
controversy:

The mere greatness of the world war has thwarted you; it has refused to
become mere background, and obtrudes itself upon the stage as so much
dead wood that will not burn with the dramatic fire. Dramatic action is a
fire that must burn up everything but itself; there should be no room in a
play for anything that does not belong to it; the whole history of the
world must be reduced to wallpaper in front of which the characters
must pose and speak.[4]

In *The Silver Tassie* O'Casey had attempted to dramatize the
horrors of the First World War and its effects, reflected in the fate
of Harry Heegan. O'Casey, in contrast to Yeats, was convinced
that he had succeeded in this experiment. When he subtitled his
play about the Second World War, *A Warld on Wallpaper* (this
originally being intended as the main title[5]), he most certainly
did not intend to submit to Yeats's definition of a play. If one
critic supposes that 'he fulfills Yeats's prerequisites for a good
play',[6] he not only underestimates the degree of continuing
bitterness with which O'Casey had reacted to Yeats's rejection of
*The Silver Tassie*, but he also ignores O'Casey's different concept
of the play's purpose, and he disregards the irony of the subtitle,
implicit in the suggestion of Hiberno-English dialect. In *Oak
Leaves and Lavender* O'Casey did *not* intend to reduce the
'history of the world' to a decorative pattern on wallpaper 'in

front of which the characters must pose and speak'; he undertook to do for the Second World War what, in his eyes, he had successfully done for World War I. He particularly felt provoked to write such a play by Yeats's insulting remark that he had not shown any real interest in the earlier war. There are a number of parallels between the two plays which support this theory and form a suitable basis for an evaluation of the second play as seen in juxtaposition with the first.

Both plays share the background of a world war that decisively influences the stage events. It provides the situation in which the characters find themselves, and it determines their fate. In both cases, two central characters are killed or wounded in battle, while the others, as relatives, friends and nurses, are likewise concerned by the events of the war. In neither case does O'Casey provide a realistic representation of the fighting, which is shown primarily as mirrored in the soldiers' homes. This leaves room for the introduction of comic figures and farcical scenes, where battle with a real enemy is supplanted by a farcical struggle with comic objects. The structure, therefore, is loose, the various lines of the plot being interrupted and broken up by static scenes. O'Casey tried to counteract the danger of formal confusion inherent in this structure by introducing a number of non-realistic scenes in addition to his predominantly realistic events. In these parts – Act II in *The Silver Tassie*, Prelude and Epilogue in *Oak Leaves and Lavender* – he attempts to elucidate his central themes, providing a framework for the individual events of the other parts without which the realistic sections would be largely meaningless; moreover, in the form of certain symbolic elements, these non-realistic scenes also intrude into the realistic action.

Despite these parallels, the differences between the two plays are more significant than the similarities. While in *The Silver Tassie* Harry Heegan is undoubtedly the central character, clearly dominating the action, there is no such central figure in *Oak Leaves and Lavender*. Accordingly, it is difficult to recognize any unified action that integrates all the scenes and is determined by the fate of the central characters. Moreover, there is no such central symbol as the 'tassie' in the earlier play that could serve as a starting-point for an understanding of the play's meaning. Again, the themes dealt with in *Oak Leaves and Lavender* are much more diverse. Some of them are not, like the attack on war in *The Silver Tassie*, developed implicitly from the action, but are treated explicitly in discursive scenes which are not justified by the action, the author leaving no doubt as to his own preferences in the argument.

The common denominator to all these differences between the two plays is the second work's lack of unity, determining its inferior degree of thematic intensity. Any analysis of *Oak Leaves and Lavender* will have to follow up this problem, and it will have to discuss O'Casey's attempts to counterbalance what he must have observed as the essential weakness of his own play.

*

The characters in *Oak Leaves and Lavender* are a good example of this lack of coherence. At first glance, Feelim O'Morrigun, Dame Hatherleigh's loquacious Irish butler, appears to have the central role. He is almost always present, he dominates every scene through his position of authority as well as his verbose comments on every possible question, and it is to him that the final speech of the realistic action as well as the concluding song is given. It can be shown, however, that Feelim is not associated very closely with the action of the play. As is made clear in the exposition, he has obtained his position in Dame Hatherleigh's house only by chance, and his presence in O'Casey's play seems to be equally accidental – owing to the success of his literary models (especially Captain Boyle) rather than to any justification inherent in the text of the play itself. Like the 'Captain', he does not undergo any development, he does not influence the course of the action and he tends to dominate only in those static scenes which interrupt the progression of the events.

The second figure that stands out in some way from such a large range of characters is Monica Penrhyn, who shares with Feelim the exposition scene. She is the only one whose previous history is discussed, and, through her father's appearance, is even drawn into the stage events. Her mother died when she was ten years old; her death had been hastened by her father's puritanical fanaticism, dispelling any shred of happiness from the life of his family. Monica was brought up by Dame Hatherleigh, and her father could observe her only at a distance; this explains his appearance at the window after Monica has spent the night with Drishogue. Nevertheless, the character of Monica is necessary only for one facet of the play, and for long passages the audience lose sight of her altogether. This holds equally true for the other young people, Drishogue, Edgar and Jennie; although they are important for parts of the play, none of them is indispensable.

The only exception is Dame Hatherleigh, without whom it is difficult to imagine the play at all. Her structural significance lies in the fact that she serves to interweave its various elements, providing, above all, one of the few links between the realistic and the symbolic aspects of the drama, inasmuch as she has access to both spheres. As Edgar's mother and Monica's foster-mother she has a personal relationship to two of the play's most important figures; Drishogue, as Edgar's friend, and Edgar's girl-friend Jennie are included in this relationship; and as mistress of the manor she is in a position of authority over Feelim as well as over most of the other persons. Moreover, she possesses an unusual degree of personal authority which places her even above those who are not dependent on her. This is shown, for instance, in the comic scene in which she turns upon themselves the reproaches of the two policemen (in whom authority should be vested) and finally condescends to remit their punishment (pp. 68-70). Her natural superiority is also shown in the serious counterpart to this comic scene: she is the only one to calm down the excited Penrhyn who pushes his way into the house with an unexploded bomb in his arm (pp. 102-103). Her behaviour in the severest trials turns her into a kind of yardstick by which the others are measured. Her fixed idea that England, the 'British Israel' is the 'soul of the soul of the lost Ten Tribes of Israel' (p. 37), and her intention to rediscover the lost Ark of the Covenant on the Irish Hill of Tara, connect her to the symbolic meaning of the play, as does her position as the mistress of the manor-house that changes into a symbol of England. Finally, she is the only figure to come into contact with the shadowy figures of the frame-action. This particular aspect of her persona will have to be discussed below.

Dame Hatherleigh is also at the centre of one of the three rudimentary lines of action, where there is at least the suggestion of a development. Her husband is an officer at the front. After mysterious presentiments (Act I) she receives the news of his death (Act II), and soon afterwards her only son is killed when his aeroplane crashes (Act III). Finally, her ancient manor-house, which had appeared unchangeable to her, is turned into a factory, leaving her without a purpose in life. The second line of action includes Monica, Drishogue and Penrhyn; it is supported by Monica's previous history as mentioned above. Monica loves Feelim's son Drishogue who spends his last few days with her before he is prematurely recalled and, soon afterwards, killed. The catastrophe of his death is mitigated for Monica by the fact that she carries Drishogue's child, while for the puritanical

Penrhyn this means an additional catastrophe, after his earlier attempt to separate the lovers. His own life loses its meaning, like that of Dame Hatherleigh, when his farm is destroyed by fire – ironically just after he had been decorated for his exertions in fighting other fires. The third line of action (Edgar-Jennie) serves as a foil to the Drishogue-Monica action. Edgar undergoes the same training as his friend Drishogue and is killed like him. His relationship with Jennie, however, from the start not imbued with any degree of permanence, ends when Jennie vainly attempts to rescue him from the burning wreck of his aeroplane and is herself killed in the attempt.

This fragile fabric of the action is hardly sufficient to support the burden of the numerous farcical as well as didactic scenes that are loosely associated with it. It would, however, be wrong to characterize it as a 'structure of character',[7] for in contrast to *The Plough and the Stars*, the play does not intend to evaluate the varying behaviour of the individual figures. These, with the possible exception of Feelim and Dame Hatherleigh, are uninteresting as characters and are only important as representatives of opinions or as instigators of isolated events. There is only one possible justification for the loose structure of the play:

O'Casey introduces disorder to show the chaos that was created during the War. When men and women from different walks of life, with different outlooks and faiths assemble, even though to fight against a common enemy, harmony is impossible. If a dramatist wishes to show such an anomaly in life he has no choice but to introduce anarchy to the stage.[8]

But even a work of art that is meant to mirror chaos demands a strong degree of order, and it will be necessary to enquire to what extent O'Casey achieves such an 'ordering of chaos' in presenting the situation of the war. He attempts such a presentation on three levels, two of which, the realistic and the symbolic, take on dramatic form in the development of the play, while the third serves to provide a theoretical and abstract discussion of certain problems related to the material presented.

*

The *realistic* sphere in which the play moves is largely based on O'Casey's own war experiences. During the war he lived with his family in Totnes in Devon, and it is from such a vantage-point that the war in *Oak Leaves and Lavender* is seen. Although this part of England (with the exception of Plymouth) remained untouched by the horrors of the blitz, it suffered from the usual effects of war: food-rationing, the evacuee invasion, the blackout, the stationing of aircraft units, the mobilization of the Home Guard etc.; and moreover during the first years of the war, life in this area was overshadowed by the threat of a German invasion. In *Sunset and Evening Star* O'Casey effectively described some of his impressions from the period. In *Oak Leaves and Lavender* he transfers these experiences to Hatherleigh Manor, situated evidently somewhere in Cornwall.[9] This Big House is serving for the last time as a centre of established authority and therefore proves an excellent focus for dramatic activity of all kinds. The ancient manor-house has been turned into a home for evacuees from the cities threatened by the blitz, it is here that the fire-brigade and land-girls are stationed, its rooms are used for Red Cross courses, its park by the Home Guard, and finally it is transformed into an arms factory. The neighbouring farmers come here for help and advice, as they had always been used to do in what was still a semi-feudal society. They ask for help with filling in forms, they bring their complaints to Lady Hatherleigh, and even a demonstration for building air-raid shelters comes here rather than to the offices of the Rural District Council.

This presentation of the situation on the home front is effective and convincing. O'Casey succeeds in reproducing the juxtaposition of comedy and pathos, readiness for sacrifice and lack of confidence, disregard of death and desire to live, helplessness and improvisation that characterized this period in England.[10] The comedy is usually shown to arise from ordinary people's failing to understand the requirements of a war bureaucracy. The reading of gas and electricity meters offers insurmountable difficulties, and it remains an unsolved problem where to billet the hens kept in the school for whom officially no food is supplied during the school holidays. Some of the scenes are farcical when, for instance, the adjustment of the blackout screens causes a series of injuries. Even the training of the Home Guard has its comic sides: the honest fellows, who have to exercise with pikes, endanger their surroundings more than they ever would an enemy. The use of dialect, too, especially the constant repetition of certain idiomatic phrases, serves a comic purpose. O'Casey has been criticized for his inaccurate presentation of Cornish dialect.[11] It is true that he never had the same close relationship with West Country people as with the Dublin proletariat, and, of course, he did not find here the same favourable conditions of unobtrusive observation as in London. Yet this is not a major issue. Almost every English dramatist since Shakespeare has supplied the farmers among his characters not with an authentic regional dialect, but with a synthetic language that chiefly serves to characterize their position in society.

These comic elements are juxtaposed with the serious aspects of the play. If it is at all possible to speak of a central theme in *Oak Leaves and Lavender* (and a number of scenes are not related to any such theme), it is the constant presence of death and its effect on everybody living at such a time of war. Four times death interferes in the lives of the people assembled at Hatherleigh: the lord of the manor himself, his son Edgar, Drishogue and Jennie are abruptly torn from the circle. The constant threat of death is shown in the frequent handling of arms, and even more in the reports of the blitz, especially the death of Feelim's predecessor (p. 20) and the death of the five firemen. At one point, death itself threatens to appear on stage, when Penrhyn in his madness carries in a dud bomb that could explode any moment. With the Cornish legend of the scent of lavender, permeating the house whenever someone is going to die, O'Casey has found an effective symbol for this threat. Characters whose own death is imminent, or who are about to lose one of their relatives, repeatedly become aware of this strange, terrifying scent.

Under such conditions, people's lives begin to change. They are forced to consider the justification for their fighting, and they are confronted with the question whether they are ready to sacrifice their own security for a higher purpose. O'Casey provides a whole range of possible reactions. At the lowest end is Constant who wants to send his wife to the United States and would prefer to follow her himself.[12] Pobjoy, the conscientious objector, who rejects war without considering the possibility of its justification, is hardly treated with any more understanding. Edgar and Drishogue take up a position at the other end of the scale, but again their positions differ significantly. Edgar does not believe in any purpose in the war:

Oh, all causes are fair to those who believe in them: I believe in none. I have no cause to die for, such as you love; no principle; only an old, doting mother who's jutting close to death herself: my old and dying mother and myself, but I cannot die for him (p. 28).

He fears death because he wants to enjoy life. Perhaps his

readiness to fight ranks thereby even higher than the idealism of Drishogue, who knows exactly what he is fighting for: the destruction of Fascism. A special position is taken up by the three dominating women characters. Although they fear for the death of husband, son or lover, they do not attempt for a moment to restrain them. It is left to the audience to decide who makes the greatest sacrifice: Dame Hatherleigh who, with the loss of her husband and her son, has to give up all hope for the future of her family; Monica who will be alone to care for Drishogue's child; or Jennie who takes death upon herself. In contrast to earlier plays, especially *Juno and the Paycock* and *The Plough and the Stars*, the women are convinced of the necessity of sacrifice and are willing to take a share in it.

The dual love plot, too, can only be seen in the context of this constant looming of death. In such a situation, conventional morals are discarded. If the average life expectancy of an Air Force pilot is eight weeks (p. 26), traditional ideas of marriage lose their meaning. Sexual relationships cannot be postponed to a moment that in all probability will not occur at all. For the girls, intercourse almost becomes a patriotic duty; at least it loses all traces of the immoral. Such a change of attitude is particularly marked in the relationship between Edgar and Jennie. Young Hatherleigh does not have any illusions:

DRISHOGUE. Don't you ever get tired of walking or lying with Jennie?
EDGAR. Often; but with her the tiredness is always restful. She's grand for the time being.
DRISHOGUE. But you don't value her enough to want to spend a lifetime with her?
EDGAR. Well, hardly; in the cool of the evening, in the deep dusk of the night, she is lovely; but I shouldn't care to have to welcome her the first thing in the morning (p. 26).

Jennie, uneducated and vulgar, would hardly be the proper life-companion for the future lord of the manor, so long as the term 'life' is not reduced to a period of a few weeks. But even this shortlived relationship is not one of mere sensuous enjoyment, as is shown in Jennie's courageous attempt to save Edgar. It is one of the weaknesses of the play that both his and her death are highly improbable (Edgar's plane is brought down at the precise spot where Jennie happens to be, and she succeeds in reaching the wreck 'among the pile of German burnt-out planes around them' [p. 90]; further Monica claims that Jennie died 'calmly' beside her lover [p. 105]).

If O'Casey uses Jennie's sacrifice to stress that he does not favour irresponsible hedonism, he makes this even clearer in Drishogue's attitude to Monica. Drishogue is O'Casey's ideal character; he represents the dramatist's opinions, and his attitude serves as a corrective to his friend's behaviour: 'Take care, for we may have to wear out; so be fair to yourself in being fair to Jennie' (p. 27). His own love for Monica will last 'Till time has grown so old that things remembered lose their colour, and are growing grey' (p. 59). Repeatedly Monica and he defend their position to their respective fathers, who insist on certain moral conventions: where genuine love prevails, the young people say, formalities become irrelevant. Consequently, Monica does not hesitate at all to speak of the child she is expecting. Her admission, however, is invalidated by the sentence, added as an afterthought: 'Besides, we were married a month ago at a registry office; but his dad and my dad were so contrairy that we didn't say anything about it' (p. 107). Such a 'moral' solution of an apparently 'immoral' situation, as contrary to this play's system of values as it was to O'Casey's general opinions, can only be seen as a regrettable concession to the demands of a puritanical audience. It utterly subverts Drishogue's and Monica's intellectual independence as this is developed in the play. If in a new version of *Oak Leaves and Lavender* only a single sentence were to be omitted, it would have to be this one.

This is one of the points that make it so difficult to evaluate the play. Others are the frequent improbabilities, especially where the appearances and encounters of the characters are concerned. Time and again, the audience is forced to realize that it is witnessing mere stage events, however probable in their general outline these may be. Unlike Brecht, O'Casey does not employ improbability to make it less easy for the audience to identify with the stage characters, but he simply fails to co-ordinate disparate events. Another grave reservation concerns the language the characters use. Especially the four lovers employ a pseudo-Shakespearean diction that reduces their individual credibility without substituting any degree of universality for it. If Monica encourages her lover 'Why should you fear the taunt in the rosy hours spent with a girl you like?' (p. 59), or when sturdy Jennie pontificates, 'Though life's uncertain, we ought to edge its darkness with a song!' (p. 34), the effect is ridiculous, stressing the unintentional discrepancy between the spoken word and the speaker rather than any additional awareness of ideals or ideas that O'Casey may have wanted to transmit. Several critics have expressed their dissatisfaction with this aspect of the play: 'The love scenes have an artificial, stagy quality about them that ruins them. The lovers say words because O'Casey feels such words are necessary to his purpose, rather than necessary to their own believability.'[13] J. B. Priestley, despite his general respect for O'Casey, condemned these scenes even more harshly:

It is simply so much windy rhetoric that obscures the characters and blunts the situations. It does not, as it is claimed to do, bring back poetry into the theatre. I prefer, even for poetry's sake, the understatements and hesitations and mumblings of our stage characters. Too much has been lost here for the sake of Palgrave's *Golden Treasury* and sodawater. Landgirls and airmen who talk like this have, to my mind, sacrificed their own characteristic flavour and appeal for nothing. O'Casey-in-Dublin created literature, whereas O'Casey in Devon is merely being literary.[14]

That O'Casey was more concerned here with a poetic tradition than with innovations, can be seen from Jennie's quotations from literature which, completely at variance with her character, she introduces into her conversation. Such quotations range from nursery rhymes ('The sheep's in the meadow, the cow's in the corn!' [p. 33]) to Gray's 'Elegy Written in a Country Churchyard' ('. . . the curfew's tolled the knell of parting day . . .' [p. 33]) and Fitzgerald's translation of Omar Khayyam's *Rubaiyat* ('You'll find in me the loaf of bread, the jug of wine, the book of verse, and the maid singing in the wilderness' [p. 34]).[15] Even when one considers that Jennie cites these quotations ironically, she is still entirely unsuited to the display of such remnants of education, and O'Casey himself shows his awareness of this when he has her erroneously attribute her song to Shakespeare (p. 16). The closest approximation to Shakespeare can be seen in those embarrassing reminiscences of *Romeo and Juliet* in the scene where Monica and Drishogue philosophise on death while they are getting up, and Monica presses her lover to stay while he wants to depart because he fears the wrath of their fathers (pp. 57-62).

A further objection can be levelled at the failing coherence between the individual scenes and plot-elements in the play. Apart from the Prelude and the Epilogue, one can distinguish thirty individual scenes. Jennie and Edgar, two central characters, do not take part in more than four of them. In Act III, neither of them – and the same is true of Drishogue – is present any longer; and Edgar (with the exception of his short appearance near the end of Act II where he speaks a single sentence) only appears at all in three continuous scenes of Act I. On the other hand, Act III introduces two important new characters, Pobjoy and the Foreman. It is understandable that such a fluctuation of more than thirty characters should fail to ensure a logical continuity of action or a unity of theme.

★

O'Casey provided certain *symbolic* means to counteract this splintering tendency in his work, and these devices also serve his ambitious attempt to present in *Oak Leaves and Lavender* not only a specific segment of the war, but an overall view of England in wartime. His great problem was to integrate the realistic and the symbolic aspects of this picture. He succeeded, at least in part, in fusing them in the manor-house itself. On the realistic level it is, as has been shown above, the skilfully selected setting for all the events. In addition it is O'Casey's contribution to the theme of the decline of the Big House in England, those centres of culture, tradition and authority that lost their function with the end of the Second World War and were at best turned into museums. In this respect, *Oak Leaves and Lavender* might be compared with Evelyn Waugh's war-time novel *Brideshead Revisited*, although Waugh's cultural pessimism is directly opposed to O'Casey's belief in the future. However much O'Casey may regret the decline of established values, he sees the process of history not only as a necessity but also as a concrete chance to improve the situation of the people. Transferred to Ireland, this theme reminds one of his *Purple Dust* and of numerous other works (Lennox Robinson's *The Big House* immediately comes to mind) where the decline of the aristocratic manor is usually seen as a regrettable but unavoidable loss to the cultural tradition.

In *Oak Leaves and Lavender*, Hatherleigh Manor is not only an example of the destruction of the Big House – it becomes a symbol of the country as a whole at a time of unparalleled change. To achieve his purpose, O'Casey relies chiefly on scenery techniques. Act I shows the '*chaste and pleasing beauty*' of the big hall, but '*Its broad and beaded panelling runs across the walls in simple lines and ovals, so that a dreamy engineer might see in them the rods and motionless shafts of machinery*' (p. 5). This similarity with the machinery of factories, described in great detail, increases from Act to Act, until, towards the end of Act III,

*. . . the young foreman . . . blows a whistle sharply, and the room becomes alive with movement – the belts travel, the wheels turn, and the drop-hammer rises and falls . . . Through the window, the silhouette of the great crane's jib is seen, holding in its beak the silhouette of a tank that is swung by the window, down to the ground. The modified clank of steel touching steel is heard, accompanied by the sounds indicating the busy and orderly hustle of a factory* (p. 109).

Under the pressure of the war situation, England is turned into an arms factory, and the industrial age destroys the old order incorporated in the manor-house. The dissolution of the established social structure that runs parallel to the alteration of the house, is shown in the 'invasion' of people from all walks of life who populate and take over the building, and even more in the fact that the transformation proceeds without any regard for the lady of the manor who still believes: '. . . this house can never change . . .' (p. 88). At the end the Foreman, *'taking no notice of Dame Hatherleigh still standing rigid by the window'*, sets the scenery in motion. One should also notice that the family of the lord of the manor, with the death of Hatherleigh and Edgar, will die out, while Drishogue, the ordinary man with his socialist beliefs, will live on in his child.

The symbolic sense is further underlined by the contraction of time and space. Although Hatherleigh is situated in Cornwall, it is also near a big city ('Duxton') that is hit by the blitz (p. 55), and the Shadows of the Prelude and Epilogue can even see St. Paul's in London (pp. 10, 110). The contraction of time is still greater. The play apparently begins before the defeat of France and the evacuation of the British troops from Dunkerque (26 May – 4 June 1940), it encompasses the Battle of Britain (which English historians date from 10 July to 31 October 1940), it includes the bombing of London (beginning on 7 September 1940), has its turning point with the arrival of the first American arms deliveries, and ends with the entry of the Soviet Union into the war (22 June 1941). O'Casey, perhaps taking a suggestion from the beginnings of television, employs an unconvincing scenic device to make this historic process visible: the cloth panel in the wireless cabinet lights up occasionally, showing the swastika, accompanied by the voice of the German propaganda station, 'Germany calling, Germany calling, Germany calling' and the German national anthem, the volume of sound indicating the growing and receding German hope for victory. Later, this ridiculous emblem of menace is replaced by the V-sign and finally by the crossed British and Soviet flags. One really wonders how a dramatist who had repeatedly shown himself a master of sophisticated stage technique could here fall back on such naïve visual devices.

Another symbolic element is the figure of Dame Hatherleigh herself, her significance corresponding largely to that of her manor-house. She has been seen as the personification of British history,[16] and it is certainly true to say: 'O'Casey hat in vielen ihrer Züge ein überlebtes Zeitalter zeichnen wollen, doch nicht in negativem Sinn sondern als Epoche, die ihrer erfüllten Sendung bewußt, der folgenden den Platz räumt.'[17] She is the representative of the period in which her own social class dominated both politics and culture. Her belief in a 'British Israel', in realistic terms no more than an *idée fixe*, symbolizes the belief in the mission of her country that lay behind the imperialist tendencies of the epoch. Her resignation marks the end of this period. One has to ask, however, whether Dame Hatherleigh does not also incorporate certain autobiographical experiences of the author that conflict with her symbolic significance. For O'Casey himself stated in a letter[18] how he came into touch with the theory of a 'British Israel'. It is also relatively certain that O'Casey, when he created the character of Dame Hatherleigh, had Lady Gregory in mind, who lost her only son as a fighter pilot during World War I and whose 'Big House', Coole Park, was later torn down in 1941. The characterization of Dame Hatherleigh reflects the respect that O'Casey throughout his life evinced for Lady Gregory. If his attempt to commemorate her in one of his plays, is in itself wholly understandable, it is nevertheless questionable from an artist's point of view, for it introduces external tendencies into the drama that, without complete integration, endanger its internal logic.[19]

Towards the end, Dame Hatherleigh joins the procession of the powerless Shadows, acknowledging her renunciation of all authority. The two scenes in which the Shadows of the past populate the great hall of Hatherleigh Manor are an original – and partly successful – attempt to give the play both unity and universality. As Prelude and Epilogue they bracket the stage action and provide a historical perspective for present events. The Shadows, 'symbols of England's history',[20] are the eighteenth-century founders and inhabitants of the house. They had laid the foundations for Britain's international position that is now threatened. Their confrontation with the present indicates the downfall of the social order that they had created. They regret the disruption of their erstwhile power and face the 'dull and hangdog crowd' (p. 8) that encroaches upon their privileges without any understanding; yet they are also confident that 'The world shall never lose what the world has ever given' (p. 9), and Dame Hatherleigh is even more optimistic: 'Only the rottenness and ruin must die. Great things we did and said; things graceful, and things that had a charm, live on to dance before the eyes of men admiring' (p. 110). This is the essence of an optimistic view of history: only those values that are not viable will be destroyed. The worthwhile achievements of each period accumulate, every menace leads to better conditions for the people. The regret for the loss of old things is more than compensated by the confidence of gaining something new. This also characterizes O'Casey's attitude to the war that is at the centre of the play.

This symbolic framework serves to prevent the actual events from disintegrating. It has not, however, been completely transposed into the dramatic action. Instead it carries some rhetorical ballast that partly hides its dramatic function. And there is little justification for an allegorical figure, the Young Son of Time, in whose dress O'Casey wants to see symbolized '*youth's earnest and warm vigour*', '*the threat of old age bound to come*', and '*the remembrance of things past*' (pp. 6-7). His pseudo-profound utterances only repeat what the Gentlemen Dancers know without him; and it remains a mystery why in the Epilogue Dame Hatherleigh, a character from the realistic section of the play, takes up the position of this allegorical figure.

*

The tendency, observed in the frame-action, to discuss themes *theoretically* rather than transform them into dramatic action, can be seen throughout the play. Repeatedly, problems are set up for discussion without any contextual justification. In addition, O'Casey usually makes his preferences clear to such an extent that no unprejudiced consideration of pros and cons is possible. Both his tendency to substitute theoretical discussion for dramatic action and his lack of objectivity mark the distance between *Oak Leaves and Lavender* and his greatest plays. The crassest example is the episode of Deeda Tutting (pp. 46-54). She bursts into the house without any preparation or motivation for her appearance and attempts to convince Drishogue, whom she correctly suspects of Communist views, of the reprehensibility of the Soviet system. Her repellent appearance (described in detail) and her arrogant behaviour, as well as her comic name, are designed to predispose the audience against her arguments. On top of that, her position is weakened by her Mosleyan sympathies for National Socialism, an unforgivable position during the Battle of Britain. Her reproaches against the Soviet Union are thus refuted before she has even uttered them. Her personal experiences and the fact that her husband was arrested by the OGPU, are of much less weight than Drishogue's axiomatic conviction of the Soviet Union's material and moral superiority, because Drishogue is the likeable character and she is not. Even when Drishogue emotionally exclaims, 'Woe unto any nation making war on the Soviet Union! She will slash open the snout, and tear out of the guts of any power crossing her borders!' (p. 51), he is supposed to be in the right, although the audience may be embarrassed by such pseudo-arguments. It is not true by any means that O'Casey 'in a sharp dialogue . . . generously allows an attractive young Communist to get, or seem to get, the worst of it . . .'[21] A comparison with a parallel situation in *Sunset and Evening Star* shows that O'Casey here recreates a personal episode[22] in which he used the same pseudo-arguments as Drishogue and was perfectly convinced of their validity.

The Deeda Tutting scene is certainly an extreme case, but lack of objectivity or dramatic integration can also be observed in several other discussion scenes where the outcome is generally determined from the beginning. Drishogue especially, as O'Casey's ideal character, has always to be in the right. In the first great discussion on the meaning of war he preaches the struggle for 'the great human soul of England' (p. 29) while a little later he maintains '. . . I have no love for England! . . . I'm fighting for the people' (p. 61), and remains without opposition in either case. Another theme for discussion is the problem of conscientious objection. Pobjoy, generally ridiculed as a 'Conchie', is, like Deeda Tutting, made a mockery of by his external appearance even though his arguments are just as convincing as those of his opponents. Constant, who wants to send his wife to America, makes a fool of himself by claiming that he will be sent to a concentration camp because he has written several letters to the *Times*; this precludes any objective discussion of the problem of war emigration. Several discussion scenes are provoked by the fact that Feelim, Drishogue and the Foreman are Irishmen, although this is largely irrelevant in the context of the play. Ireland's war-time neutrality, the role of Ulster and De Valera's political strategies can thus be dragged into the play. Feelim delivers a passionate lecture on the role of Irish troops in all the

big battles of world history, reminiscent of Meredith's motto, '. . .
'tis Ireland gives England her soldiers, her generals too.'[23] This,
of course, was a subject of great emotional importance to
O'Casey.[24] When one adds those questions that, both in the
realistic and the symbolic sections of the play, have been
dramatized in one way or another one finds a multitude of ideas
each of which is put aside as quickly as it has been taken up. It is
precisely the cumulation of problems, none of which is taken to
any logical conclusion, that makes for the prevailing impression
of superficiality that the play presents.

Finally, one ought to consider the author's own position as it is
projected in this play. O'Casey obviously felt an urgent obligation
to the British dead of the Second World War. *Oak Leaves and
Lavender* was dedicated to one of them, whom he had known in
his youth.[25] He evidently admired the war-time attitude of the
British people. His hatred of Fascism led him to side with the
Soviet Union and Britain at one and the same time. It is an
exaggeration, but not completely wrong, if one critic calls *Oak
Leaves and Lavender* a 'mixture of jingoism and communist
rhetoric, the defiant mixture of an unreasoning and passionate
nature.'[26] In two of his characters O'Casey introduced personal
elements: 'In the character of Feelim there seems to be a personal
uniting; in the character of Drishogue . . . an ideological one'.[27]
Feelim is the ageing emigrant from Ireland who never forgets his
pride in being Irish and his condescension towards the English
('God must ha' had a rare laugh when He made a serious Englishman' [p. 21]); nevertheless he does his duty in the fight against
the common enemy. Drishogue shares Feelim's – and O'Casey's
– prejudices against the British; Monica makes him happy when
she declares: '. . . I'm not an English girl, but a thoroughbred
Cornish lass' (p. 62). Moreover, O'Casey embodied in Drishogue
his own ideological position. In his view, the menace of Fascism
is bound to lessen the conflict between Capitalism and Communism. Drishogue's embarrassing simplifications – 'In this
fight, Edgar, righteousness and war have kissed each other: Christ,
Mahomet, Confucius, and Buddha are one' (p. 29) – are O'Casey's.
There is no trace of O'Casey's uncompromising rejection of war,
as this was evident at the centre of *The Silver Tassie*. When
Monica asks: '. . . isn't it nobler to bring one life into the world
than to hunt a hundred out of it?' Drishogue answers: 'Depends
on the kind you kill' (p. 58). One critic has therefore called *Oak
Leaves and Lavender* 'surely the most blood-thirsty play ever
written by a congenital pacifist.'[28]

The clearest example for the difference between O'Casey's attitude in this play and his earlier works is Feelim's big revenge monologue, placed at the end of the realistic section. Its position, as well as its function, demands comparison with Juno's great prayer, which equally summarizes the thematic concerns of the earlier play. Juno is in a similar position to Feelim: she has lost her son in the war, and her daughter is expecting an illegitimate child. In such a situation she prays: 'Sacred Heart o' Jesus, take away our hearts o' stone, and give us hearts o' flesh! Take away this murdherin' hate, an' give us Thine own eternal love!' She has learnt to disregard differences of political opinion when seen against the loss of a beloved person. She herself is the first to follow her appeal when she takes on the responsibility for Mary's child. Feelim, on the other hand, is only shocked at the idea that he may have to care for Monica's child. He is obsessed by the idea of revenge and wants to take it into his own hands: 'Th' damned villains, bloodied all over with th' rent-out lives of child an' woman! They owe Feelim O'Morrigun a son; an', be Christ! old as he is, he'll help to make them pay to th' uttermost farthing in th' blood of their youngest an' their best!' (p. 106). These words do not, as one might suppose at first glance, imply criticism of Feelim's attitude; they sum up the play as a whole and reflect the author's position. More than any formal defects, such narrowness reveals the decisive flaw of *Oak Leaves and Lavender*.

# 17. HALL OF HEALING

*Hall of Healing* is the most underrated play in the whole O'Casey canon. The reasons for this neglect are not far to seek. On the one hand it is a short play that, considering the practices of the commercial theatre, has little chance of a professional production. Apart from occasional amateur performances, it has hardly found its way onto the English-speaking stage. It is thus automatically excluded from the field of vision of the influential theatre critics. On the other hand, *Hall of Healing* does not fit into the simplified period-*schema* of O'Casey's works to which many critics still adhere, the classification which sees his early works as 'realistic', and his later ones as 'symbolic', 'expressionistic', 'allegorical' or 'fantastic', i.e. unrealistic. It has already been shown in connection with *Kathleen Listens In* that such a division is not tenable; *Hall of Healing* is further proof of this. It was published in volume III of the *Collected Plays* (1951), and although the exact dates are not known, one can be fairly certain that it was not written before the late forties – for financial reasons O'Casey tended to publish his works as soon as possible. But *Hall of Healing* stands out from the predominantly unrealistic plays of this period, being similar, if anything, to the 'realistic' works whose period, so the critics maintain, terminated some twenty-five years earlier.[1] If one prefers neat categories, it is, therefore, easier to ignore *Hall of Healing* altogether. It is the purpose of this chapter to show why such neglect is untenable.

The theme of the play can be defined as the degrading conditions that determine the life of the poor. This formula contains three significant elements: the term 'condition' characterizes the predominantly static nature of the play, 'the poor' points to its generalizing tendency, 'degrading' suggests the author's own critical stance.

There is no proper plot in *Hall of Healing*. What movement there is on the stage is not due to a logical sequence of events but to the entrances and exits of individual figures. The only 'event' that leads to any change in the situation is the death of little Sheila, and this takes place off-stage: at the beginning the audience are informed of her illness, towards the end of the play they learn of her death. Apart from this, the situation of the people remains unchanged throughout the play. They visit a primitive parish dispensary for the poor, they are attended to or dismissed by the doctor and leave the room with the same ailments, sorrows, desires and illusions with which they entered it. Since the play lacks a central plot, the twenty or so small scenes take on a life of their own. What there is of external coherence is due to the unities of place and time. The setting, the waiting-room of the dispensary, with its various opportunities for entrances and exits, allows for a constant re-grouping of the stage figures without calling into question its realistic credibility.

Without being predetermined by the plot, the arrangement of the individual scenes is not however arbitrary. They are subordinated to a dominating principle, the contrast of comedy and pathos. The opening may be taken as an example. The farcical scene of Aloysius who, according to an age-old convention of that genre, is clumsy enough to hurt himself, thus provoking the audience's laughter, is followed by the scene of the old woman whose pitiable appearance, timid behaviour and hopeless submission turn her from the start into a personification of suffering, rousing the audience's compassion. This tension between two emotional extremes, established in the opening scenes, continues to dominate the play and determines its unusual impact.

The static nature of the play, ideally suited to the author's intention, can also be observed in the figures. None of them undergoes any development; no new insights are gained or attitudes changed to self or world. This holds true not only for the Doctor, who makes his patients suffer for his Sunday drinking-bout, and the Apothecary, who resembles him in his contempt for the sick, but also for the poor themselves, who are at the centre of O'Casey's interest. With one exception they do not even have names, being distinguished merely by age – Old Woman, Young Woman – or by an article of clothing – Green Muffler, Black Muffler, Red Muffler, Grey Shawl. Accordingly, the audience learn next to nothing about their life, about the sphere they leave when they enter the waiting-room. For a short moment they step out of their grey anonymity and then return to it.

This is not to say that the characters are indistinguishable. It has even been maintained that *Hall of Healing* is 'easily the best among O'Casey's one-act plays', containing 'a wealth of characterisation, so rich, so manifold, so individual that one is left dazzled.'[2] It is, however, a simplifying technique of characterisation, employing distinctions of dress and gesture to distinguish the characters without obliterating their common fate of being poor. Thus the Old Woman's back is bent by the weight of life and, against all probability, she still hopes to cure it; the Young Woman's dry cough emphasizes her fear of being sent to the consumptive ward and thereby of losing her job. Mr. Jentree (= *gentry*) attempts to simulate past respectability in his clothing; his constant shaking, produced by excessive drink, makes him a centre of interest for the others. Green Muffler shows himself to be a newcomer by his unfamiliarity with the regulations. These and all the other characters are described in the stage direction: *'The other patients are but variants of the others in feature and colour of clothing'* (p. 249).

Red Muffler is the only one who stands out from the group of the poor in more than formal qualities. The death of his daughter and the suffering of his wife provide a few hints at a personal life-history. He is also the only one to make any attempt to act; he does not accept authority simply as God-given, and he is the only one who for a moment seems able to change the direction of his life. Moreover he is the one who can put into words the criticism of these people's life conditions, a criticism that for the rest of the play is only implied; he thus personifies the author's social protest. Nevertheless, he remains an individual character and is not reduced to an abstract embodiment of opinions, inasmuch as he combines both positive and negative character traits. It is therefore not true to say that he is 'a brother of Red Jim' in *The Star Turns Red*.[3] His first entrance demonstrates his ambiguous personality. On the one hand he encourages the Old Woman to disobey Aloysius' senseless regulations and to seek shelter from the weather in the waiting-room before the time of opening: 'Aw, go and sit down, woman. I'll know how to deal with this Alleluia of yours when he shows himself' (p. 240). But when both of them are driven out, he resists only for himself and permits the Old Woman to be roughly expelled: *'During all this Red Muffler has taken no notice, making no effort to defend the Old Woman; but has turned his back on the other two, and is now staring hard at one of the posters'* (p. 244).

This discrepancy continues to mark his behaviour. He is the only one among the poor capable of rebellion against existing conditions. His attitude is sharply contrasted with that of the Old Woman:

OLD WOMAN. Arra, be sensible, son! Let what they give kill or cure us, there's ne'er a one for us to appeal to, bar the good God Himself! The poor who refuse to be patient, die young.

RED MUFFLER [*fiercely*]. We've been too patient too long; too damned
    long; too god-damned long, I'm sayin'! Patience is only th' holy name
    for suicide! (p. 264).

Not only does he have an insight into the inhuman conditions
under which they all live, but he also knows that they can
be changed only by abandoning patience and submission. He
becomes the central figure of a small private tragedy, not so much
because he loses his beloved child but because his rebellion
bears no fruit whatsoever. At the very first meeting he could have
induced the Doctor to visit his sick child if he had not submitted
too quickly to his authority. And later his indignation fizzles out
in a few angry speeches without any effect and, what is more,
without any concrete aim:

Even with the best docthor in its bosom, what kind of a kip is this place?
I deny that this is all that God has got to give us! Even with the best
music of a church organ, what betther could we do here but dance a
dance of death! I won't do it; I won't do it! By God, if that fella inside
refuses to come to our sick kid, I'll know th' reason why! (p. 261).

With the failure of his rebellion Red Muffler falls back into the
group of the other patients, and it becomes evident that he is
simply the exponent of these people, characterized by a slightly
higher degree of consciousness. *Hall of Healing*, therefore, is not
the drama of Red Muffler but the drama of the poor. Just as he
represents the other figures, these represent all who live under
similar conditions. When street names, districts and distances
are mentioned, this does not serve so much to localize the play in
Dublin as to suggest an immense group of similar people behind
those who are shown on stage.

How does O'Casey see the poor? Their first noticeable characteristic is their constant fear of authority. The upper end of the
scale of authority is taken by God, the lower by the caretaker
Aloysius, and between them are placed the Doctor, the Apothecary
and, probably, any person even ever so slightly raised above the
lowest social status. In spite of their desperate position it is
considered dangerous to doubt the grace of God: 'We're too poor
to take th' risk of sayin' serious things. We're told God is good,
an' we need every little help we can get' (p. 241). In a similar way
it is not advisable to question the arbitrary rules of Aloysius; the
Old Woman permits herself to be led out into the rain, and later
the patients submit to the ridiculous regulation of toeing a chalk
line drawn across the waiting-room. Their respect is the more

ominous because it is acted out in mime: not even words are necessary to put the regulation into effect. The reverse of this submission is the abuse of power on the part of those whose position gives them a chance to do so. Aloysius, hailing from the same walk of life as the patients, enjoys his freedom to boss them around, and his behaviour arouses the suspicion that his victims would behave in a similar way if only they had the chance. The renunciation of resistance on the part of the poor stands for a more comprehensive resignation, as it is expressed in the words of the Old Woman, 'Fightin' only makes things worse' (p. 241).

Such a situation favours superstition and illusion. Partly from fear of the omnipotent Aloysius, but partly also in the hope of purchasing a better future, the poor pay their pennies to the caretaker 'to help the Holy Souls outa purgatory . . .' (p. 267). What their religiosity really amounts to is shown in their superstitious belief in the effect of medicines. A garish blue or red mixture in a bottle offers the same illusory hopes for a better life in this world as does the observance of church regulations for the after-life. The patients' only criticism of the previous Doctor, whom they worshipped, is directed at his remark '. . . you can't expect to dhrink health into you out of a bottle' (p. 250), and the only positive trait they can see in the present Doctor is his unscrupulous readiness to prescribe any kind of medicine for them to get rid of them more quickly. Their lack of understanding is evinced, too, in the scene where Green Muffler hands the Apothecary his three empty bottles and, instead of the expected medicine, receives a small box of tablets. Green Muffler works himself up into a hysterical rage, but his protest is not directed at the degrading regulation of the Poor Law that did, in fact, force each patient to provide himself the bottles for the medicine that was issued free (as Lady Gregory reports, O'Casey still felt this regulation in 1923[4]), but against the suggestion that he should swallow unsightly tablets instead of colourful medicine. He does not even consider the idea that the tablets could be the right remedy for his disease.

This scene, in its combination of farce and pathos one of the most effective in the play, contributes significantly to O'Casey's analysis of the situation and the mentality of the poor. If they for once vent their indignation, they do so in front of the wrong listeners and turn it on an inappropriate object. While Green Muffler rages over his tablets before the other patients, events that would have deserved the strongest protest remain unheeded: Jentree in his despair is repulsed by the Doctor, the Young

Woman is got rid of to the consumptive ward although this will lose her her job, and the Boy who seeks help for his sick mother is treated by Aloysius with arrogant irony after he has talked him out of one of his two pennies for the Holy Souls. The predominant impression of the poor in this play is that of their wretchedness. Fear of authority, superstition, lack of judgement, egotism, lack of self-control and unpredictability are the constituents of this depressing analysis.

The melancholy impression is relieved only occasionally by a ray of helpfulness, when, for instance, the Old Woman attempts to console the despairing Young Woman, promises to accompany her home, and one finally sees that '*The Old Woman has an arm around the young one, though she needs support herself*' (p. 271). Similar in effect is the gesture of Grey Shawl who brings the news of the death of little Sheila: '*Her hand steals forward to cling to a hand of Red Muffler's, and there is a silence for some moments*' (p. 271). But her attempt to soothe her husband is partly due to her fear of the Doctor's authority, although he, the Doctor, has just failed them completely. Even these occasional, helplessly moving gestures of affection still have something depressing about them.

O'Casey therefore (and this is important for an evaluation of the play) does not heroize the poor. He employs the very wretchedness of their present situation to rouse the audience's sympathy. It becomes quite plain that these people will not be able to help themselves, that they will need help from the outside to improve their situation. If the play has no hero, it has no villain either on whom responsibility could easily be devolved. Aloysius is completely unsuited for such a part, because he is entirely dependent on the Doctor ('He has th' life frightened outa poor oul' Alleluia.' [p. 240]) and persecutes the patients with the vague intention of doing his superior a favour. The Doctor himself is certainly not an agreeable representative of his profession. He is callous, egotistical and without any understanding; moreover he shows a discouraging inability to learn from his errors when, having just heard of the death of little Sheila, brought about by his delay, he nevertheless has the visiting ticket for the Boy's sick mother put on his desk, where he will not see it before the next day. Yet even the Doctor is a victim of circumstances and is not responsible for them. This is shown in the comparison with the earlier, 'good' Doctor who is constantly present in the patients' conversations. He has killed himself in his devotion to the sick, has attempted to relieve their ailments as his successor fails to do, and has sacrificed himself despite his own illness. Nevertheless he was not in a position to improve their situation. He could neither straighten the Old Woman's back, nor could he provide Black Muffler with 'Betther food, a finer house to live in, an' a lot more enjoyment' (p. 250), the only remedy for his disease.

O'Casey takes great pains to minimize the responsibility of individuals, because otherwise the audience could satisfy themselves with the idea that the exchange of a few benevolent for a few malevolent characters could alter the basic situation. He provides an objective analysis and leaves it to the audience to draw their own conclusions. Nevertheless, he clearly indicates his own position in three respects. First, some of Red Muffler's utterances, for instance 'Yous are afraid to fight these things. That's what's th' matther – we're all afraid to fight!' (p. 272) or 'I deny that this is all that God has got to give us!' (p. 261), reflect the author's programmatic position. Second, the ironic title that is in complete contradiction to the stage events implies the dramatist's own critical stance. Third, his ironic attitude is reflected in certain posters that O'Casey wants to see displayed in the waiting-room; the slogans 'DIPHTHERIA: BEWARE!', 'TUBERCULOSIS: BEWARE!' and 'CANCER: BEWARE!' (p. 235) are reduced to absurdity by the stage proceedings. O'Casey makes it clear by his stage directions that he wants the audience's attention directed to these posters, for instance by having Aloysius fix one of them, or (p. 271) by the grouping of the figures. Like *The Silver Tassie, Hall of Healing* could paradoxically be called an 'objective play with a purpose', a play in which, quite unlike *Oak Leaves and Lavender,* the author succeeds in dramatizing his own views of the necessity of social change without manipulating the figures and their scale of values. It is precisely the static portrayal of a situation that provokes the audience to criticize this situation and effects the desire to alter it. Although *Hall of Healing* is based on O'Casey's personal experiences,[5] he has objectified these and kept his own ideological opinions out of them. It is interesting only for his biography, but not for an interpretation of the play, that he was able and willing to utilize his own experiences even after several decades.

*

*Hall of Healing* as it has been described so far, suggests a surprising proximity to the forms and contents of the drama of Naturalism. Although it was not published until 1951, it is closer

to Naturalism than any other O'Casey play, including his early
works which at the beginning were often noticed for their slice-
of-life technique.[6] This is not to say that *Hall of Healing* is
particularly close to the Anglo-Irish version of Naturalism, marked
by such plays as Padraic Colum's *Thomas Muskerry* or Lennox
Robinson's *Harvest*, for these concentrate almost exclusively on
the problems of the Irish peasant population, leading to that host
of harmless peasant comedies that contributed to the decline of
the Abbey Theatre. It is equally distant from the Manchester
school of dramatists (Houghton, Monkhouse, Brighouse, Elizabeth
Baker etc.) who, under the influence of English disciples of Ibsen
(Galsworthy, Hankin) and with the help of techniques of the
*pièce bien faite*, tried to establish the play of ideas in the
working-class and bourgeois milieu of the North of England. It
is, however, closely related to the drama of Continental Naturalism;
these similarities deserve to be briefly summarized here, because
it will be possible, from this, the closest point of their contact, to
gauge O'Casey's general attitude to the ideas and dramatic
techniques of Naturalism.

The most obvious parallel to Continental Naturalism is the almost
documentary accuracy of O'Casey's reproduction of reality. It is
manifest, for instance, in the play's long introductory stage directions (almost five pages); not only do these describe the setting in
great detail, but also the stage characters in their looks, gestures and
idiosyncratic behaviour, sometimes to an extent far beyond the
capabilities of the stage itself. O'Casey's attempt to create true-
to-life characters can also be seen in their language, a reliable
reproduction of the Dublin city dialect in the form spoken in the
slums, with its grammatical and phonetic irregularities, and also
with its wealth of imagery and rhetorical figures. In this respect, the
two groups of characters in the play, the poor on the one hand,
Doctor and Apothecary on the other, are clearly differentiated.
The unity of time and place contributes to the audience's illusion
of witnessing 'real' events, as does O'Casey's attempt to avoid all
'theatrical' devices. It is also typical of Naturalism that O'Casey
should choose a city setting dominated by poverty and misery.
For all its intended objectivity, his drastic portraiture of the
situation of the poor reveals his own social sympathies and
suggests their radical tendency, just as the drama of Naturalism
is frequently characterized by the conflict between a sober
reproduction of reality and the social criticism of the dramatist.

O'Casey's image of humanity, too, corresponds to the deter-
ministic views of Naturalism. The conditions under which his

poor live are largely determined by milieu, by social and economic factors that lie beyond their control and quite often also beyond their understanding, and therefore condemn them to a life in bondage. Their existence is a desperate struggle for survival that might well be described in the jungle metaphor so often used by Naturalists. Even the separation from a religious or metaphysical background is reflected, at least in part, in O'Casey's play.

The fact that O'Casey dispenses with a central character suggests specific parallels to certain group dramas of Continental Naturalism that are concerned not with individual life histories but with the situation of a larger group of people: Gorki's *The Lower Depths* and Hauptmann's *The Weavers* are typical examples. Even though these are full-length plays, the similarities to *Hall of Healing* are remarkable. O'Casey, who in 1926 had seen an English production of *The Lower Depths*,[7] called Gorki in 1946 'by far, a greater dramatist than the towering Tolstoy' and placed him beside Strindberg, Ibsen, Hauptmann and Chekhov.[8] He appears to have seen connections between Gorki's life-history and his own; and it is possible that Gorki's play provided the essential stimulus for him to do for the Dublin poor what the Russian playwright had done for the outcasts of his society, portraying them not in the exceptional situation of the struggle for national independence and civil war, but in the desolate hopelessness of ordinary day-to-day existence, where there is no chance of alteration, no development, and therefore no dramatic action, and where only death allows an occasional hiatus.

Even more remarkable are the similarities to *The Weavers* although, apart from O'Casey's reference to Hauptmann mentioned above, no influence can be substantiated from O'Casey's biography.[9] Like Hauptmann's play, O'Casey's is set in the past, for, despite O'Casey's words,[10] *Hall of Healing* is not a play of the fifties; rather, it looks back in its subject matter to the turn of the century, just as the events of Hauptmann's play had become historical by the time he wrote it. Moreover, Act I of *The Weavers* is, in its structure, so similar to *Hall of Healing* that a direct influence seems more than likely. Both plays show a waiting-room where the poor crowd together in an atmosphere of fear and submission. They are tormented by Aloysius and Pfeifer, both of whom are members of their own class newly promoted to a position of authority. The dominant impression in both cases is that of wretchedness, of stupidity and clumsiness, of an obsequious respect for those in authority and of a tenacious clinging to illusions that are in no way justified. Two characters stand out from this group, Red Muffler and Bäcker (who is sometimes called 'Red' Bäcker); they alone make a short-lived attempt to rebel against existing conditions. While Hauptmann, in the following Acts, shows the ill-fated revolt that arises from this situation, the rebellion in *Hall of Healing* is even briefer, but in both cases failure is certain from the start. Both dramatists were successful, as few others were, in combining an objective presentation of conditions with their own emotional commitment to the outcasts of their society.

It is in no way surprising that these Naturalistic tendencies should have appeared as late as 1951, for they have repeatedly surfaced in European and American drama right into the second half of this century. What is remarkable, however, is that O'Casey, who in his early work had not by any means been a Naturalist, and who later on had experimented with various unrealistic techniques, should now approach this movement in one individual play. His reasons may have been personal – the writing of his autobiography was among other things an important stimulus for his dramatic work – as well as literary, for certain literary influences reached O'Casey much later than they did other writers. It should finally be pointed out, however, that even this 'most Naturalistic' of his plays deviates in certain important respects from its literary models. When O'Casey abandons individual names and identifies his figures by objects or colours, he goes beyond the de-individualising tendencies of Naturalism; indeed his technique here is almost Expressionistic. His dialogue, too, occasionally transcends the framework of Naturalism: certain poetic images, expressing the essence of a situation, seem to belong to the author rather than to the characters who utter them. Thus the Old Woman complains of 'th' chatther of th' interferin' wind outside' (p. 240) and believes '. . . God's thought is roomy with anxiety for the very young' (p. 242), while Red Muffler expresses the fate of the poor in the words: 'Such as us have barely time to glimpse a gleam that's kind before it hurries to the dark again' (p. 242).

Unusual for a Naturalistic context is also the use of comic elements and their juxtaposition with the basic seriousness of the play, as occurs, for instance, in the subtitle, *A Sincerious Farce in One Scene*. These comic elements range from the farcical introductory scene to the bitterly ironical counterpointing of the stage events with the background-music of an organ; this serves to preclude any kind of sentimentality, but it also suggests an element of affirmation that is quite untypical of the earlier

Naturalists. If the serious and the ridiculous, the sublime and the commonplace stand side by side, even the wretchedness of the poor may not be absolute but demands, at least in the audience's imagination, a similar complement. It is in this way that O'Casey implies the possibility of a better life. O'Casey contrasts the uniformly grey world of Naturalistic drama with a picture in many shades, in which the dark tones certainly predominate but are not the only ones. Precisely here, at the point of his closest approximation to the forms and literary modes of Naturalism, the playwright therefore reveals his artistic individuality.

# 18. BEDTIME STORY

The short play *Bedtime Story*, published in the same year, forms a decided contrast to the small-scale masterpiece *Hall of Healing*. Critics have hardly noticed this play. Here as elsewhere O'Casey's inventiveness in the field of comic situations guarantees the play's effectiveness on stage, but, in contrast to *A Pound on Demand*, the perfection of the dramatic form does not compensate the lack of thematic substance.

*Bedtime Story*, despite the unity of setting and plot, is clearly divided into two separate sections. Part I (pp. 227-248) shows how, in the middle of the night, the clerk John Jo Mulligan tries to get rid of the girl Angela Nightingale whom he had brought into his flat the previous evening. In his fear of discovery by his neighbour and his landlady he permits Angela to talk him out of a large sum of money and various valuables, and he is completely dejected when she finally leaves him. The second part (pp. 248-257) presents the misunderstandings that result from his confrontation with his neighbour Halibut and his landlady Miss Mossie; eventually Mulligan is taken into custody for dangerous sleep-walking.

Part I is predominantly satirical with occasional farcical elements. It is based on the contrast between Mulligan and Angela, Mulligan's attitude being persistently criticized in the dramatic presentation: '. . . O'Casey contrasts the essential freedom that honesty provides with the everpresent fear that accompanies hypocrisy . . .'[1] Mulligan is a fearful, bigoted bachelor, full of complexes and bound by moral conventions, who has always tried to keep to the path of virtue, but only in order to preserve his reputation with those in spiritual and secular authority. His pangs of conscience after the night he has spent with Angela are due solely to his fear that somebody might hear about it. When they both describe the events of the previous evening, Mulligan's version sounds more likely than Angela's, for it seems more probable that he should invite her to read Yeats's poetry and then be surprised by her initiative rather than that he should from the beginning have had ulterior motives.

Angela is in every way a contrast to Mulligan. She is attractive and free from inhibitions, capable of rejecting prejudices and unable to see anything wrong in the enjoyment of the senses. Significantly, it is stated that '*She is something of a pagan*' (p. 230). She is also more intelligent, and therefore succeeds in duping Mulligan time and again: she cleverly acts the part of seduced innocence only to be able to demand a higher compensation, she invents the existence of a handbag only to be paid for it, and under some pretence swindles him out of his valuable ring. All the same, this does not for a moment make her less loveable. O'Casey manipulates the audience's reaction to such an extent that Angela (whose name is indicative of the author's opinion of her) remains uncriticized, while her opponent's defeat produces nothing but delight. The only reservation concerns her decision to take up Mulligan at all. O'Casey's attitude can be documented by a comparison of two short speeches. Mulligan complains in comic despair:

You know you did wrong to practise on a body who didn't know enough. Situated as we are, without divine warrant, it's not proper. We're in the midst of a violent sin, and you should be ashamed and sorry, instead of feeling sinfully gay about it. It's necessary to feel sorry for a sin of this kind (p. 231).

Angela, on the other hand, presents the views of the author in typical O'Caseyan phraseology:

Sometime or other, we have to face out of all we get into: face out of getting into bed with a woman no less than face out into silence from the glamour of prayer; face out of summer into winter; face out of life into death! (p. 235).

O'Casey reverses conventional moral values: the frivolous girl with her dubious way of life is shown to be superior to her virtuous victim. The author succeeds in this reversal by stressing the egotism of Mulligan who, after his short sensual intoxication is over, can only see the danger to himself and is incapable of understanding Angela's position. Part I of *Bedtime Story* can therefore be placed under the heading of a theme, prominent throughout O'Casey's work, which has been defined as 'la dénonciation de l'hypocrisie morale qui empoisonne la vie des Irlandais et développe leur inaptitude au bonheur'.[2] His sympathy is with Angela as with those other outsiders of society, Nannie (*Nannie's Night Out*), Rosie Redmond (*The Plough and the Stars*) and Jannice (*Within the Gates*), all of whom live beyond the pale of bourgeois prejudices. He criticizes the hypocrisy that considers an action immoral only when it becomes known to the neighbours, and he rejects the repression of affirmation and the enjoyment of life through the negative demands of the Catholic Church, resulting in a negation of life. Mulligan *'can never become convalescent from a futile sense of sin'* (p. 228). It is typical for such an attitude that rational control is occasionally overwhelmed by the repressed physical functions, providing ample occasion for regret and contrition. This aspect of *Bedtime Story* is foreshadowed in the scene of Joybell, the strange young man in *The Star Turns Red* who, in his ineffective talk of bishop and priest, tries to avert the temptation of watching Julia's undress, then suddenly clasps her fiercely to him, kissing her madly, and, in his shame at having forgotten himself, puts all the blame on her. O'Casey found himself confirmed in his criticism of bourgeois hypocrisy, 'the drab and malicious menace of puritanism', when the Essex Education Council banned a production of *Bedtime Story* from an amateur theatre competition.[3]

Partly due to the form of the short play that makes it impossible to analyze Angela's past and her conditions of life, this theme, however, is not taken very seriously in *Bedtime Story*. It is therefore not clear to what an extent Angela is consistent in the life-affirming attitude that O'Casey prefers. In addition, the second part of the play leads away from the conflict between affirmation and negation and remains purely farcical.[4] Mulligan here becomes the victim of simple misadventure. Halibut and Miss Mossie are not individual characters, they merely assume certain functions in the developing confusion. This is why the misunderstandings remain comic; the characters' misjudgement of truth makes no emotional demands on the audience. At the same time, O'Casey handles all the conventions of farce with his customary mastery. When everybody misunderstands everyone else, this leads to a perfect misreading of reality, all the characters taking each other for dangerous lunatics. In the end Halibut can even say to Mulligan: 'And, now, you'll have to admit that these things couldn't have happened to you if you had had a girl with you tonight' (p. 253). This section reminds one more of the tradition of *Box and Cox* than of the theme suggested at the beginning of the play.

In a programme note for an American production[5] O'Casey put down his own view of the play. He sees it as a 'battle of wits', in which 'the child of this world' proves 'far cleverer, wittier, and more alive, than the child of light'. Angela 'is more honest, too, as wickedness is as often as virtue, for piety is often stained with pride, while wickedness is in too much of a hurry to bother about it.' He emphasizes the contrast between the chief characters: 'She is forthright about her fault, he bothered with anxiety about pretence; eager to keep, not himself, but his little name unspotted from the world.' He does not, however, want to see *Bedtime Story* taken too seriously, calling it 'a little play in which there are neither good nor bad judged seriously, with a laugh at the beginning and another at the end.' He is not writing critically, so it is not surprising that he should not comment upon the unbalanced combination of satire and farce. What is surprising, however, is his insistence on an alleged literary relationship that he had already suggested in the subtitle, *An Anatole* [sic] *Burlesque in One Act*, and that he repeats here in the description of the play as 'an unconsidered trifle in the fashion of a Schnitzler *Anatole [sic]* play in the O'Casey style'. Since he seems to have been acquainted with Schnitzler's sequence of 'Anatol' scenes, this can only be taken as an example of the questionable literary judgement that he evinced repeatedly, both where his own and where other plays were concerned. Schnitzler's faintly sentimental world, dominated by *ennui* and fatalism, is so entirely different from the atmosphere of *Bedtime Story* that one can find no similarities whatsoever beyond the simple fact that they are both short plays. Not even the erotic background can suggest any comparison; in O'Casey it is the occasion of satire and farce, while in Schnitzler it serves as a subject of weighty discussions and the source of serious emotions. The present-day reader will probably prefer O'Casey's play, feeling, perhaps, more at home in the every-day reality of a dramatist who reacts to people's weaknesses with laughter than in the stuffy drawing-room atmosphere of the *fin de siècle*.

# PART IV

# Ireland as a Microcosm

I will show you hope in a handful of life.

(Sean O'Casey)

# 19.  PREFATORY

In contrast to O'Casey's other plays with their pronounced individuality, *Cock-a-doodle Dandy* (1949), *Time to Go* (1951), *The Bishop's Bonfire* (1955), and *The Drums of Father Ned* (1958), show remarkable formal and thematic correspondences. Critics have usually ignored the similarities between these plays,[1] which is surprising when one considers how relatively superficial parallels between O'Casey's early Dublin plays have led to their being bundled together into a 'trilogy'. It has, for instance, been entirely overlooked that the three full-length plays of this period do form a clear seasonal trilogy: *Cock-a-doodle Dandy* takes place in the summer, *The Bishop's Bonfire* in autumn, *The Drums of Father Ned* in spring, the mood and atmosphere being in each case closely associated with the season depicted. Significantly, there is a definite progression to the optimistic 'spring' play, *The Drums of Father Ned*. It will be easier to understand these plays if one sees them as facets of a single intellectual world, for which Ireland serves as a microcosm. Alone among O'Casey's plays they present an opportunity for general description as well as, and prior to, individual interpretation. Such an introduction is all the more necessary in that O'Casey has here developed a new form of the drama, characterized by the heterogeneity of its structural elements. Critics are hardly to blame if they find the conventional tools of dramatic criticism next to useless when confronted with the originality of these plays, but they are to be criticized when they simply ignore certain factors in order to make the plays fit into their traditional categories. The following summary description focuses on the similarities between the plays, while the subsequent chapters concentrate on their individual traits.

All of these plays are set in Ireland; they take place in a village or small town remote from all centres of culture and civilization and isolated to an unusual extent, a place where the inhabitants are both dependent on and informed about each other. The action in each case is confined to a single day. The time is the present,

with the War of Independence, the establishment of the Free
State and the Civil War as concrete points of reference in the past.
Although the season in each case is different, the progression of
seasons clearly links the plays with each other.

The *dramatis personae*, too, are similar to an extent that is
unusual in O'Casey's work. It is hardly possible to follow the
conventional distinction between central and minor characters,
for what is represented here are certain population groups which
in turn represent certain ways of thinking and attitudes to life.
One can distinguish five such groups. One of them comprises
the local dignitaries, businessmen, inn-keepers and land-owners,
who as Members of Parliament, mayors and councillors control
the political power and at the same time occupy positions of
honour in the Catholic Church. They are representatives of the
dominant class of an independent Ireland that has absorbed the
political influence but not the cultural tradition of the Protestant
Ascendancy, a class frequently criticized by O'Casey. They are
characterized as materialistic, cunning, deceitful and insincere:
while they preach patriotism and subservience to the Church,
they are unscrupulous in their business transactions for which
they even exploit their honorary positions. Their central role in
these plays is emphasized by the fact that the events always take
place inside or in front of their houses. Their adversaries are
usually their own children who, together with other members of
the younger generation, are seriously concerned about intellectual
liberation from Church regulations and narrow-minded morality,
fighting against censorship and pleading for a natural relationship
between the sexes based on affection rather than on business
profits. O'Casey quite explicitly invests all his optimism in these
members of the younger generation. The third group consists of
certain workmen, who, under more difficult conditions, struggle
for social and intellectual emancipation, but who are frequently
not courageous enough to enforce their demands in the face of
militant opposition. The strongest adversary to change is the
village priest who is shown as an absolute ruler over the life and
opinions of his parish. His mental terror suppresses all liberal
tendencies, reducing his subjects to hypocrites who constantly
act against their natural impulses. Even in *Time to Go*, where the
priest does not personally appear, a similar role is attributed to
him in the conversations of the villagers.

The priest, therefore, is the constant object of O'Casey's satire,
hilarious or bitter according to the general mood of the play. This
clear-cut confrontation between different groups of figures is

mitigated by the presence of certain farcical villagers, descendants of Seumas Shields and 'Captain' Boyle. Although they occasionally become involved in the central conflicts, their partisanship cannot be taken seriously, and they simply become comic victims of the confusions they themselves help to create.

With the exception of the short (and irrelevant) Julia-episode in *Cock-a-doodle Dandy* and the Prelude to *The Drums of Father Ned*, all the characters in these plays fall into one of the categories mentioned: the 'dignitaries', the 'younger generation', the 'workmen', the 'priests' and the 'farcical figures', although a few of them sometimes cross the boundaries between the different groups. It should be stressed that all these figures differ in individual traits; they are not interchangeable. Nevertheless, the overall pattern can serve to illustrate the conflicts of these plays and to demonstrate their formal variety. The individual interpretations will be concerned largely with the deviations from the pattern as it has been outlined here.

Thematically the plays cannot be reduced to one single 'dramatic idea'. It is typical of these plays that in each of them several themes run side by side, overlap and intertwine; at the same time each play reflects a similar set of basic ideas, just as each play shows the same basic life-affirming attitude of the author, even if there are clear differences between the pessimistic tendencies of *The Bishop's Bonfire* and the unmitigated optimism of *The Drums of Father Ned*. In comparison to most of O'Casey's earlier works (with the possible exception of *The Star Turns Red*) his ideas are more evident and are frequently formulated as theses, preserving intellectual clarity despite the multiplicity of themes. The basic conflicts result from the confrontation of the groups of figures described above, the representatives of the 'younger generation' facing the 'dignitaries' and the 'priests', while the 'workmen' vacillate between the parties and the 'farcical figures' create additional confusion. These conflicts are based on the struggle between good and evil, most of the figures being quite unambiguously associated with one side or the other. 'Good' is not identical, however, with the traditional ethical category; it signifies the joy of life, the affirmation and conscious appreciation of this world in its beauty. Sexual love, a close relationship with nature, the inspiration bestowed by alcohol, an openness for the colourfulness and variety of life and an understanding for a living cultural tradition are positive values as opposed to puritanism, hypocrisy, prudishness, and ignorance. This is not to say that O'Casey supports any sort of hedonism: for him the beauty of this world is a manifestation of the divine. It is, of course, a most undogmatic form of religion that can turn the representatives of the Church, who believe themselves to have an unimpeachable relation with the divine, into representatives of evil (the force that opposes the joy of life). This conflict between the O'Caseyan versions of good and evil (ending variously with the victory of the one or the other) is linked with O'Casey's plea for tolerance, helpfulness and an uncomplicated, undogmatic and practical humanity.

This is a universal theme independent of any regional links, and in this respect it is unjustifiable to consider these works as provincial 'Irish plays'. The following quotation, typical of O'Casey criticism, evinces its own attachment to the surface of things: '. . . this type of play is limited in its appeal to those who can appreciate the significance of what to those unfamiliar with Irish temper and idiom might seem a rambling and parochial allegory.'[2] O'Casey himself refuted the critics who emphasized the parochialism of these plays when, for instance, he wrote of *Cock-a-doodle Dandy*:

> The action manifests itself in Ireland, the mouths that speak are Irish mouths; but *the spirit is to be found in action everywhere:* the fight made by many to drive the joy of life from the hearts of men; the fight against this fight to vindicate the right of the joy of life to live courageously in the hearts of men.[3]

The tension between specificity of place and universality of theme is characteristic of almost every play, unless it is completely abstract or allegorical. It is unfortunate that Anglo-Saxon critics should always accept a play that is set in England or America as universally significant, while they hesitate to attribute the same degree of universality to a play that is set anywhere else in the world.

It should be added at once, however, that O'Casey himself gave a semblance of truth to those who view his later plays as regional works, by introducing (not always in a fortunate way) specific problems of contemporary Ireland[4] into the universal conflict of good and evil. These concern, in particular, two themes, the social and the political. In the field of social relationships, O'Casey makes concrete demands: a juster distribution of property, and emancipation for the workers. One of his basic concerns is to overcome the rigid social barriers between the classes which he repeatedly shows to exist when he portrays love

affairs between people from different strata of society. He condemns the numerous obstacles – the Church's view of sin as well
as class prejudice – that in the Ireland of his time still impeded
marriage and led to the high marriage age of this country. When
he regrets the unwarrantable influence that priests and parents
exercise in the choice of partners, he takes up one of the central
themes of twentieth-century Irish drama. O'Casey, however,
connects this with his satire on the clergy and the dominant class
of small parochial politicians, with their eagerness for titles, their
materialism and their hypocrisy. In the field of politics, his criticism is directed at the failure of the contemporary Ireland to
assimilate its past. It is a crime of the present not to have justified
the optimistic hopes of the struggle for independence, and to
insist on a barren piety for the dead instead of realizing their
ideals. In the form of a motif O'Casey touches on another
immediate problem of the Ireland of his time that for him had a
bitter immediacy: the motif of exile. In each of these plays there
are figures (and it is noticeable that they are usually among those
favoured by the author) who are confronted with the decision as
to whether they should leave the country, because they can no
longer struggle against the superior strength of materialism,
morality and greed for power. They frequently depart for England
or America where, according to O'Casey, life seems more tolerable
although not by any means ideal.

If O'Casey sees such idealistic reasons behind the Irish rural
exodus and emigration, it is clear that his image of Ireland is
subjective. In fact, after his departure from Ireland in 1926, he
returned only a few times, and even if he kept himself informed
through newspapers and visitors, an impression gained in this
way cannot do service for reality. Irish critics, therefore, have
been unanimous in maintaining that O'Casey misinterpreted
the facts and gave the world an unreliable, if not faulty impression
of the conditions in his native country.[5] On the other hand there
is no denying that O'Casey took up some of the central problems
of Irish life in the forties and – possibly – in the fifties, the high
marriage age, mass emigration, literary censorship and the
influence of the Catholic Church; nor, indeed, that he was justified
in criticizing it. It is not the primary task of literary criticism to
determine to what degree the author's personal image of his own
country is correct. All that can definitely be stated here is that
O'Casey based his plays on undeniable facts, but at the same
time he isolated and sometimes exaggerated them, making of
them a whipping-boy he could then attack for hypocrisy and

materialism, intolerance and general inhumanity. It is precisely this tendency, however, that supports the present thesis of the validity of O'Casey's plays beyond the shores of Ireland.

The variety of themes is reflected in the formal structure of these four plays. If the whole history of modern drama can be seen as a conflict between realistic and unrealistic tendencies, these plays are firmly based in the movement away from, or counter to stage realism. They are subdivided into numerous scenes, sometimes skilfully linked, but sharply contrasted in mood and theme. Not many of them are connected with 'lines of action' in the traditional sense; what plot there is usually concerns the love between young people whose affection is threatened from outside. Such action is broken up by numerous other scenes, and it would be better to speak of a few remaining scraps of action than of a continuous development of plot.

The style of the individual scenes varies between a true-to-nature imitation of reality and symbolic or allegorical stylization. In particular the conflict between good and evil sometimes appears as an allegory, the exponents of both positions being clearly identified as such. In consequence, these plays occasionally resemble the morality play, but (as opposed to *Within the Gates*) such similarities are eclipsed by other structural devices. O'Casey especially uses the whole range of comic elements, from the extreme of farce to that of satire. Farcical scenes, emphasizing physical confrontation, the malice of inanimate objects and various confusions of misunderstanding, serve not only as comic relief but also to give the plays a firm basis in every-day life (as in *Purple Dust*, O'Casey frequently uses craftsmen or workmen scenes for such farcical effects). Moreover, they serve as a foil to more serious events, the breaking of confidence, disease, death and banishment, setting off the darker shades of disappointment, fear and despair. O'Casey's criticism of certain human activities also takes on the form of satire. The 'dignitaries' and the 'priests', for instance, are treated satirically throughout, their unfavourable characteristics being exaggerated to comic effect. Their lofty claims, embracing patriotism, church allegiance, unselfishness, fearlessness and charity, are constantly exposed by their own behaviour, and their true motives become visible again and again like a skeleton under the enveloping coat of virtue.

For such exposure scenes O'Casey frequently employs elements of fantasy or fairy-tale, because the confrontation with the unreal or the non-rational tends to show up the motives of human behaviour with particular clarity. The introduction of these fantastical elements in the form of figures or objects is the real innovation in these plays – all other elements have already been tried in earlier works and have only been re-combined here in different ways. O'Casey utilizes the ideas of popular superstition, shaping them to suit his purpose. These fantastical elements often make high demands on stage technique, but their combination with the basic tendencies of these plays, partly realistic, partly allegorical or symbolic, is surprisingly successful. 'Fantasy', 'das von der poetischen Phantasie inszenierte freie Spiel mit Elementen der Wirklichkeit und des Theaters',[6] seems therefore the most appropriate term to characterize these plays as a whole.

At the same time, in each of the plays one figure or object from the realm of the fantastic serves as a means to preserve dramatic unity. In *Cock-a-doodle Dandy*, the supernatural cock is a symbol of vitality and of the joy of life; in *Time to Go* the blossoming trees emphasize the fairy-tale nature of the events; in *The Bishop's Bonfire* the statue of the rather odd St. Tremolo is a comic symbol for the life-denying forces that dominate this play, while in *The Drums of Father Ned* the invisible and ubiquitous title character beats his drums for a better existence. A second element that makes for dramatic unity is more concerned with the action: the recurrent motif of a festival or celebration focusing the divergent happenings on one point: in *Cock-a-doodle Dandy* it is the imminent arrival of the President, in *Time to Go* the market-day that is just over, in *The Bishop's Bonfire* the Bishop's expected visit to his native town, in *The Drums of Father Ned* the Tostal (local festival) that dominates the stage activities and makes for some kind of external coherence. The inner unity of the plays, on the other hand, is established by the technique of contrast that juxtaposes gay and serious, realistic and fantastic elements, viewing the same theme from different angles. This principle dominates each individual scene to an extent that could only be demonstrated by a line-by-line analysis; the multiper-spectivity of these plays is thus revealed in the simultaneous presentation of contradictory elements.

It is difficult indeed to find any direct literary models for this type of play. Even the unconventional extravaganzas of Bernard Shaw's later work cannot have provided O'Casey with more than an occasional suggestion. If one looks beyond the field of drama, James Stephens comes to mind, for to him O'Casey had dedicated his first play of this kind, *Cock-a-doodle Dandy*.[7] Stephens's symbolic-allegorical volume of narrative prose, *The Crock of Gold* (1912) presents a similar complex mixture of various elements as

O'Casey's plays of this phase. Fairy-tale, philosophical tract, animal fable, prose poem, satire, allegory and fantastical burlesque in an Irish setting have here been fused into a work of astounding artistic coherence. *The Crock of Gold* may have suggested to O'Casey the possibility of linking such disparate elements. It is without doubt, too, that O'Casey must have sympathized with Stephens's attitude as evinced in this work, and that in certain phrases he must have found formulated his own views, for instance: 'It has occurred to me, brother, that wisdom may not be the end of everything. Goodness and kindliness are, perhaps, beyond wisdom. Is it not possible that the ultimate end is gaiety and music and a dance of joy?'[8] This kind of attitude found its valid dramatic personification in Codger Sleehaun.

O'Casey himself defended his new type of play against a great deal of hostile criticism and at the same time justified his departure from his earlier dramatic forms:

... the drama must change and develop a new outlook, a broader scope, and a fresh style, if it is to live as an art alongside the art of architecture, of painting, and of music. In my opinion, the time has passed for a drama to devote its expression to one aspect of life alone, and to consider that aspect of life as dominant for the time the play takes to unfold itself; that in one play one aspect of life must be the beginning, the middle, and the end of it. Consistency of mood and of manner isn't always, indeed, not even often, found in life, and why should it then be demanded in a play? ... A jewel moved about in the hand shows many flashes of light and colour; and the human life, moved about by circumstances of tragedy and comedy, shows more than many flashes of diversity in the unity of its many-sided human nature.[9]

Two of the best O'Casey critics agree with this view and at the same time testify to the success of O'Casey's search for new forms: 'O'Casey's later plays have not lack of form, but the tremendous formal complexity of one of the few still growing and experimental talents of the modern theatre.'[10] And:

O'Casey has decided to ignore any strengths the Irish may possess, but from his constricted vision he has made at least three recent plays which attain universal relevance. In his eighties as in his forties he is the involved spectator of a battle between corrupt age and untarnished youth, between the lie and the dream, between death-in-life and life. He remains our only proven living master, if, that is, we accept the theatre as the arena of opposing moral forces.[11]

To counterbalance this discussion of the similarities between these plays, the following interpretations will stress their individual traits. When the general survey and the individual analyses are taken together, it will be easier to assess the originality and the artistic rank of these works.

# 20. COCK-A-DOODLE DANDY

Among O'Casey's later plays, *Cock-a-doodle Dandy* is the best known; it has also found some interest with the critics. After an early amateur production in Newcastle-on-Tyne (1949), it became known to a wider public through the Edinburgh Festival production in 1959 and performances in Toronto and New York (1958) as well as London (1959). It was published in 1949. O'Casey himself always emphasized his feelings for this work: 'It is my favourite play; I think it is my best play . . .'. He stressed two factors: on the one hand the play is set in Ireland ('. . . like Joyce it is only through an Irish scene that my imagination can weave away . . .'), and almost all the events have a factual basis in present-day Ireland; on the other hand his themes are relevant to any country and any time.[1] The second factor is the more important one; only if an interpretation can show that the play, in contrast to the mass of Irish drama of the forties and fifties, is relevant beyond Ireland, can it make a case for its being among the most significant works of this century.[2]

A first glance must take account of the scenery, described by O'Casey in great detail. It suggests parallels to *Kathleen Listens In*, which is also set in a garden outside a house representing Ireland. Accordingly, the scene of *Cock-a-doodle Dandy* has been seen as 'an Irish microcosm'.[3] Closer scrutiny shows, however, that, in contrast to the earlier work, the Irish Tricolour is the only element suggestive of an Irish setting. The barren, uncared-for garden with its yellow grass and its clump of hostile flowers, enclosed by a rough stone wall and the twisted framework of the house, is an 'every-town' scenery that symbolizes a state of affairs by no means limited to Ireland. This holds true for the name of the place, too, for Nyadnanave 'means in Gaelic, Nest of Saints; and the name also contains the ironic pun, Nest of Knaves.'[4] The events, too, are not confined to one particular region. It is true that the two central characters quarrel pertinaciously over the price of carting the peat from the near-by bog, but the quarrel could be transferred to any other country by changing a few details. In contrast to the other plays of this period, O'Casey has here avoided everything that would substantiate an

242

exclusively 'Irish' interpretation.[5] Like *Within the Gates, Cock-a-doodle Dandy* could be transposed without difficulty into other milieus. To do so, it would only be necessary to observe the symbolic-allegorical traits of the individual figures, which are almost as explicit as in the earlier play.

Any analysis of *Cock-a-doodle Dandy* has to concentrate on the figure of the Cock. He has three important functions: (1) he sets the action in motion and triggers off all the individual events; (2) he is a central symbol for the attitude the author supports; (3) he serves as a touchstone for the persons in the play. It is significant that the external action and the inner theme are determined by the same centre, which makes for the play's unity despite the variety of its elements. In this respect *Cock-a-doodle Dandy* is far superior to the other works of this phase.

With two exceptions, the Cock actuates all the events of the play. As a dynamic force he enters the paralyzed world of Nyadnanave and makes possible the colourful sequence of surprising developments that constitute the play. The very first entry, that of Michael Marthraun and Sailor Mahan, who have left the house because something mysterious is going on in it, is later explained by the presence of the Cock. He creates such confusion that even Marion flees from him and only the Messenger can quieten him down. All the 'supernatural' events (a whiskey bottle being transformed, chairs collapsing etc.) are somehow connected with his presence. When the Porter brings in a top hat with a hole shot through it, the explanation is provided by the Sergeant who reports that the Cock transformed himself into this hat when he was shot at. Now the Bellman's warnings of the Cock have to be taken seriously, too. When the three women entice the men to dance, their behaviour can only be explained by the confusion that the Cock has created, and it is he to whom everybody drinks at the climax of this scene, until Father Domineer appears, accompanied by a clap of thunder, to remind everyone of the Cock's dangerous omnipresence. Act III[6] begins with the hunt for the Cock, the police and the military searching for him, accompanied by their respective bands. Father Domineer himself, with his dubious followers, attempts to expel him from Marthraun's house. The villagers' attack on Loreleen seems to be immediately connected with this hunt, because she appears more and more as a complementary figure to the Cock, and even the burning of her books is an extension of the fight against the Cock. Eventually he himself dances through the garden (as he had done previously at

decisive moments), sparking off a pandemonium of comic confusion, with Michael and Mahan being struck by cigar-shaped
bullets and Father Domineer being whisked away through the
air. The rising storm brings additional danger for all the pursuers
of the Cock. As the first proof of his defeat, announced by the
triumphant Father Domineer, the frightened Loreleen is dragged
in. Her banishment, in which she is joined by Lorna, Marion and
the Messenger, is an expression of the desire to expulse the Cock
himself, and is considered as part of his defeat. Almost every
movement in this play can therefore be explained in terms of the
actions of the cock or the reactions to his presence.

Only two scenes form an exception. In one of them, Father
Domineer knocks down Jack the lorry-driver, who lives with a
woman without clerical sanction, killing him in his fury. In the
other, Julia, Lorna's paralyzed sister, departs on a pilgrimage to
Lourdes; towards the end she returns uncured and without
hope.[7] Both episodes have been criticized as irrelevant,[8] and with
some justification. While the first of them is at least joined to the
rest of the play by the figure of the Priest, O'Casey requires a
complicated recapitulation of previous events to make the two
Julia scenes comprehensible. Julia's and Lorna's father, a poor
farmer, had sold his bog to Marthraun to obtain the money for
Julia's pilgrimage, and he also persuaded Lorna to marry
Marthraun to make him favourably inclined to him. This proved
a double bargain to Marthraun, because he gained a young and
attractive wife and a bog that soon became a goldmine, while
Lorna's father was left destitute and alone with his paralyzed
daughter. If such an explanation is required, the Julia scenes can
have little contact with the rest of the play; moreover O'Casey
marshals several figures for Julia's departure who are never used
again. It will be considered later whether these two scenes
nevertheless have a certain thematic function, but this does not
make up for their separation from the Cock.

The Cock's second function, besides his role as an integrating
element in the plot, is to serve as a central thematic symbol.
O'Casey utilizes certain widespread ideas of popular belief that
see the cock as an emblem of virility and vitality. In addition, he
probably took up a suggestion from Yeats's *The Dreaming of the
Bones*. The chorus of musicians in this play repeatedly evokes
the 'Red bird of March' as a personification of daylight and
unambiguous clarity in contrast to the ambiguous, mysterious,
ghost-haunted twilight:

> Up with the neck and clap the wing,
> Red cock, and crow![9]

At the end of his short article on *Cock-a-doodle Dandy*, O'Casey slightly misquotes these lines:

> Lift up the head
> and clap the wings,
> Red Cock, and crow![10]

For *Cock-a-doodle Dandy*, he seems to have consciously changed it again, giving the Messenger the words: '[*To the Cock*]. Go on, comrade, lift up th' head an' clap th' wings, black cock, an' crow!' (p. 144). Obviously O'Casey wanted to associate the Cock with the enemies of the powers of darkness.

In the whole of O'Casey's work, the Cock is the most perfect personification of his idea of a positive life-force (which, however, should not be confused with Shaw's philosophical concept of the life-force). His shining colourful plumage makes him appear as the symbol of visible beauty, his graceful dances represent affirmation and joy of life; his facial expression, that of a '*cynical jester*' (p. 122) suggests a critical attitude that finds expression in capricious, *Eulenspiegel*-like pranks rather than in moral sermons. When he attacks the Marthrauns' domestic altar, tears up pictures of saints and damages the top hat, status symbol of the dominating bourgeois class, he proves to be the enemy of all life-negating and authority-worshipping forces. In the words of the Messenger, who is at first the only one able to control him, he also appears as the embodiment of a sexuality that is equally free from prudishness and licentiousness: 'Just a gay bird, that's all. A bit unruly at times, but conthrollable be th' right persons' (p. 144), and (to Lorna): 'Instead of shyin' cups an' saucers at him, if only you'd given him your lily-white hand, he'd have led you through a wistful an' wondherful dance' (p. 143). Marion is the first to recognize this meaning: 'Sure, he's harmless when you know him' (p. 144), and she adds with admiration: 'Wasn't it a saucy bird! . . . God forgive me, but it gave us all an hilarious time . . .' (p. 145). She owns up to him just as, in the same action, she openly demonstrates her love for the Messenger: '[*kissing the Messenger*]. Bring him here first, Robin, an' I'll have a wreath of roses ready to hang round his neck' (p. 162). Finally, the Cock quite convincingly symbolizes the principle of freedom from all repression. He appears without motivation and can neither be conjured away by exorcism nor destroyed by force. He confronts the united power of State and Church with his nimble dance and arouses confusion without losing himself. It is significant that in the end the people who have confessed themselves his followers can be expelled from the town, but the Cock himself remains untouched and, one supposes, will reappear in Nyadnanave until he is permitted to stay.

The characters in the play can be distinguished by their varying behaviour in their confrontation with the Cock. They can be subdivided into his supporters, his foes, the undecided and the uncomprehending; within these groups, however, one can find various shades of attitude.

The person most clearly associated with the Cock is Loreleen. Superficially, she is nothing but a natural girl, Marthraun's daughter from his first marriage, who has returned from London to her Irish home, dares to dress attractively, is therefore persecuted and even stoned, is persuaded by Sailor Mahan to a tête-à-tête to obtain the money for her return journey to England, and is finally banished for seducing a married man. But at the same time, Loreleen demonstrates the ideals that are embodied in the Cock. She is, of all the people in the play, most clearly his counterpart, and is therefore O'Casey's key figure.

In the course of the events, she is variously related to the Cock. Even at the beginning, Marthraun links with her presence those disquieting events in his house that are due to the Cock, and reports that she often dances on her own in her room, just as the Cock had opened the play with a dance. When Loreleen appears for the first time, a cock crows loudly, and her dress is decidedly reminiscent of the plumage of a cock. When the two Rough Fellows are about to follow her admiringly, they notice to their horror that Loreleen is changing: 'Jasus, she's changin' into th' look of a fancy-bred fowl! It's turnin' to face us; it's openin' its bake as big as a bayonet!' (p. 132). When the Cock begins to cause tumult in Marthraun's house, even Marion associates this with Loreleen (p. 139). In Act II Loreleen enters after the Bellman has announced that the Cock is abroad in the shape of a woman. In Act III the hunt for the Cock ends with Loreleen being caught, and this seems to satisfy his pursuers. During the whole play, Loreleen and the Cock never appear simultaneously, and occasionally their identity is suggested in the stage directions: '*As Loreleen disappears, the Cock suddenly springs over the wall . . .*' (p. 202). The reason, of course, is that 'essentially the two are indivisible, one is the body, the other the spirit. Each represents the other.'[11]

Loreleen attempts to transpose those values embodied in the Cock into the reality of human existence. She does not hide her attractive figure and believes, 'When you condemn a fair face, you sneer at God's good handiwork' (p. 216); she enjoys dance and song; she refuses to obey Father Domineer, and she reads books that have been banned, among them one about Voltaire and another that One-eyed Larry identifies as 'Ullisississies, or something' (p. 201). To the end she remains O'Casey's ideal character; only by force can she be brought before Father Domineer's pseudo-tribunal and only by compulsion can she be expelled. In the system of values that this play presents, Loreleen's sentence is the judgement of Nyadnanave. Yet *Cock-a-doodle Dandy* is essentially an optimistic play, because Loreleen remains undefeated.

Lorna, her young step-mother, and her servant-girl Marion find it much more difficult to struggle through to the attitude embodied in the Cock. Although they share Loreleen's life affirmation, they repeatedly submit to the life-denying forces. Marion is frightened by the first appearance of the Cock, Lorna even wants to put him into custody and pleads with the Messenger: 'Robin, will you take that damned animal away, before things happen that God won't know about!' (p. 144). She mistakes the Cock, as do most of the others, as an emissary of the Devil. Her 'conversion' to Loreleen's position is first intimated in apparently insignificant details like the sentence 'An' th' Devil's not a bad fella either' (p. 156) with which she shows that she no longer accepts Father Domineer's primitive God-Devil dichotomy. Together with Loreleen, Marion and Lorna encourage the men to an ecstatic dance, but submit with contrition when the Priest appears. In the 'exorcism' scene it becomes clear that they by have no means overcome their fear of the demons who bear such promising names as 'Kissalass, Velvethighs, Reedabuck, Dancesolong, an' Sameagain' (p. 198). On the other hand, nothing will deter them from their preparations for the fancy-dress ball, and their costumes of a gipsy and a 'Nippy' (a waitress in a Lyon's Corner House) betray their growing independence. The tribunal scene finds them once more wavering between independence and submission: '*Marion and Lorna have started to come to Loreleen's assistance, but have been imperiously waved back by Father Domineer, and have retreated back towards the house . . .*' (p. 213). When, however, Loreleen is banished, they accept her fate as their own: '*Lorna shoves Father Domineer aside at the gateway, nearly knocks Shanaar over, and hurries to Loreleen*' (p. 217). Both will

go to a place 'where life resembles life more than it does here' (p.
220). They place their personal freedom above material security,
taking up a position which Souhaun and Avril in *Purple Dust*,
following Synge's Nora, had also chosen.[12]

Marion is distinguished from the more sceptical Lorna by her
love for the Messenger, a love that she admits quite openly despite
the dangers bound up with such a confession. These two lovers
are distinguished by the literary associations of their names
(Maid Marion and Robin Adair). Maid Marion from the complex
of Robin Hood myths embodies self-sacrificing faithfulness, the
willingness to accept dangers and privations to be near her lover.
Robin Adair is the title character of the well-known folk song that
sings of the change the world will undergo when the lover has
been separated from his lass:

> What's this dull town to me?
> Robin's not near.
> What was't I wish'd to see,
> What wish'd to hear?
> Where all the joy and mirth
> Made this town heav'n on earth?
> Oh, they're all fled with thee,
> Robin Adair.[13]

The Messenger's name suggests the fate that Marion would
undergo if she left the party of the Cock. At the same time the
song describes the situation as it will be at Nyadnanave when
Robin Adair and his friends have left it.

O'Casey uses the Messenger not only as the bearer of telegrams
but also as the bearer of his own message, having him pronounce
in so many words what has been dramatized in the other figures.
Not only does the Messenger reveal the meaning of the Cock, as
indicated above, he also lays bare the clergy's unchristian
attitude: 'Honour be th' clergy's regulated by how much a man
can give!' (p. 159), and he exposes the dubious religiosity of the
villagers: 'Faith, your fathers' faith is fear, an' now fear is your
only fun' (p. 161). He cites, as an example, the disregard of the
'holy spots' by the 'faithful' (p. 160), a theme that is taken up
again in *Time to Go*. He rejects the idea that films, theatre and
books have made the world more accessible to the Devil (p. 184),
and he reminds the Priest how much he himself is in need of
divine grace. In the end, he is the only one to defend Loreleen
and to rescue her from the hands of the mob. His words to the
Priest, '. . . Thry to mingle undherstandin' with your pride, so as

to ease th' tangle God has suffered to be flung around us all' (p. 215), formulate one of O'Casey's life-long maxims and could serve as a motto for most of his work. This holds even more true for the Messenger's 'blessing' with which he greets the returning Julia: 'Be brave' and again: 'Evermore be brave' (pp. 220, 221). For Marthraun, on the other hand, he has only the crushing advice: 'Die. There is little else left useful for the likes of you to do' (p. 221). If, in addition, one remembers that the Messenger is a 'singer', it becomes clear that, even more than the Dreamer in *Within the Gates*, he represents the dramatist on stage. The multi-perspective structure of this play, however, makes if much easier to accept such an autobiographical message-bearing figure. The Messenger is probably O'Casey's closest approximation to the wide-spread tendency in modern theatre to introduce a mediator – speaker, stage manager, compère – between the stage events and the audience. It is characteristic of O'Casey's later works that this figure openly pleads the dramatist's views.

If the central symbol, the autobiographical mediator, and all the positive characters are on the same side, the opposing side can expect little sympathy. Father Domineer – *dominus* perverted into *domineering* – embodies a position against which the Cock and his adherents fight. Whenever he appears, he characterizes himself, both in word and action, as a despot who demands absolute obedience, condemns joy and beauty and is not even just according to his own precepts (he convicts Loreleen for her meeting with Mahan while he acquits Mahan). His every action is destructive: he interrupts the dance of the three couples and forces them down on their knees, he knocks down Jack, inadvertently killing him, relegates the women to the position of lower servants, burns books and banishes Loreleen. His opposition to the Cock is marked most clearly when, like his adversary, he attempts to produce a miracle. He sends Julia on a hopeless journey to Lourdes and promises: 'Julia will bring us back a miracle, a glorious miracle!' (p. 155). When she returns uncured, he is prudently absent. He threatens Jack: 'Isn't it a wondher God doesn't strike you dead!' (p. 188), and he makes up for such an 'omission' on the part of God by producing the 'wonder' himself. In contrast to the gay fantastic and harmless 'miracles' of the Cock, Father Domineer's 'miracles' have always grave and cruel consequences. It would be quite inappropriate to try to upgrade his character, quoting in his favour the sentence 'We'll follow some of the way to prevent anyone from harming her [Loreleen]' (p. 217).[14] In reality, he is not concerned about Loreleen's safety but about his own dominion; he wants to prevent the seduction of her attitude to life from affecting the others. If Father Domineer were supposed to be a realistic character, O'Casey would have to be criticized for blatant black-and-white caricature; however, *Cock-a-doodle Dandy* is not a confrontation of characters but a juxtaposition of attitudes, and this gives the Priest his firm position at the one extreme. It need hardly be stressed that he represents more than the Catholic Church. Every life-denying force is embodied in him.

This becomes quite clear in his followers. They consist of members of the leading bourgeoisie as well as representatives of secular power and perversions of devoted church membership. All of them are caricatured to some extent, but the difference between them lies in the degree of their dangerousness. The Bellman, the Sergeant and the Porter are comic in a harmless way. But even their harmlessness contributes to threaten the Cock and his party, because the Bellman, representative of the local politicians, and the Sergeant, representative of the secular principle of order, are willing tools in the hands of Father Domineer. The climax of the comic events surrounding them is the storm which the Cock conjures up. It is a beautiful illustration of the conflicting powers when the storm pulls down their trousers while they desperately cling to these emblems of a Domineering respectability.

Shanaar and One-eyed Larry are more dangerous. Although one can enjoy Shanaar's comic bog-Latin which he uses to exorcise the Devil, one should not overlook his power over the inhabitants of Nyadnanave, who revere in him a wise old man and take his hocus-pocus very seriously. Like Father Domineer he is responsible when Marthraun considers his nearest relations as possessed, and his influence finally contributes to the banishment of the three women. The clever One-eyed Larry has the makings of a second Shanaar. Even now he cannot clearly distinguish between his imagination and reality; he will repeat his cleverly invented story of how he lost his eye to the demonic cock until he believes it himself, and then his seeming honesty will help him to obtain an influence similar to Shanaar's. That he is a parallel figure to Father Domineer, and therefore a dangerous man, becomes evident when the Priest returns from his 'exorcism' with a '*black eye*' (p. 199) and is greeted by Larry, who, where his eye should have been, has a '*black cavity*' (p. 192).

Finally, the dignitaries are on the side of Father Domineer, too. Michael Marthraun who has risen to his present position through skilful financial manipulation, prepares for the honour of receiving the President. The extended theme of the damaged top hat not only serves as comic relief, it also emphazises Marthraun's position as the owner of such a status symbol. Considering his status, it is all the more shocking to see how easily he succumbs to any superstition, how quickly he sacrifices even his closest relations and how submissively he accepts the Priest's authority. His view of life, like his house, is twisted, as becomes clear from his surprising conclusions: '. . . I seen the way th' eyes of young men stare at her [Lorna's] face, an' follow th' movements of her lurin' legs – there's evil in that woman!' (p. 125). O'Casey uses Marthraun to diagnose a danger that is familiar from many countries: when a class rises to power without being prepared for it, it will believe any charlatan and follow any demagogue. It is mere poetic justice when Marthraun in the end remains lonely and without a purpose in life, for to be banished from Nyadnanave is still better than to be privileged to stay there.[15]

These unfavourable traits in a representative of political power are complemented by his attitude to his workers. In this respect he agrees with Sailor Mahan with whom he quarrels throughout the play. Both refuse to pay just wages, thus inadvertently endangering their own positions, as is shown in the bog-labourers' strike. Apart from this, however, Mahan is decidedly different from Marthraun. He is much closer to those O'Caseyan workers who struggle for intellectual and moral emancipation but repeatedly lapse into submission. From the beginning he wavers between the positions of the Priest and the Cock. He dares to doubt Marthraun's belief in demons and is even sceptical towards Shanaar: 'Aw, th' oul' fool, pipin' a gale into every breeze that blows! I don't believe there was ever anything engenderogically evil in that cock as a cock, or denounceable either!' (pp. 148-149). He is responsive to the beauty of Loreleen and Marion, but kneels down before Father Domineer when he has been caught dancing. He even comes to Jack's defence but does not forget his personal interests, because Jack is his best worker. Sometimes he gains an insight into an O'Caseyan truth: 'It'll take a betther man than Father Domineer to dhrive evil things outa Eire' (p. 193), then again he proves himself to be far from it: 'What do people want with books? I don't remember readin' a book in me life' (p. 201). The ambiguity of his character is expressed quite clearly when he offers money to Loreleen, his desire to help a girl in distress and his hope of deriving his own amusement from it clearly complementing each other. When they are caught in their tête-à-tête he does not defend her but hides in his own house. Mahan is a carefully balanced representative of the average man, who is not disinclined to support 'higher things' if these are connected with personal advantage and do not produce any inconveniences, but who quickly returns to his world of bondage, fenced in by prohibitions, whenever independence and sacrifices are expected of him. If he (in addition to the Messenger and the women) is said to be 'the only other person in Nyadnanave who is capable of being saved'[16] one ought to add that his chances of falling into an O'Caseyan damnation are equally great.

This holds true, too, for the two Rough Fellows, who, when they first meet Loreleen, are quite ready to forget Father Domineer's rules, but who later, with redoubled eagerness, drag her in to demonstrate their own righteousness. O'Casey uses them, with perhaps an exaggerated degree of emphasis, to show that the freedom he propagates in *Cock-a-doodle Dandy* is not one of sexual licence. Jack, on the other hand, who lives in 'sin' with a woman, has sided with the Cock. Like other workers in O'Casey's plays, however, he is not independent enough to take the consequences of such an attitude, i.e. to confront Father Domineer decisively or to leave the country. His indecision is the final cause of his death, just as, in this phase of O'Casey's work, those characters suffer most who stand between the fronts.

Those who give their allegiance to Father Domineer cannot be helped. Figures like Marthraun or Shanaar, therefore, do not demand compassion. Whoever maintains his independence, on the other hand, does not need compassion: Loreleen, Lorna, Marion and the Messenger are strong enough to convert the apparent defeat of their banishment into a victory and to build up a world of their own, a counter-world to that of Father Domineer, infused with joy and affection. Compassion is due to those who have caught sight of this other world without being strong enough to join it. This is the reason why Sailor Mahan becomes at once the most impressive and the most interesting character of the play. Had the episodes of Julia and Jack been integrated into the rest of the play, they would demand more attention and perhaps would darken the general impression the play conveys. As it is, however, *Cock-a-doodle Dandy* remains an optimistic work, because the symbol of life affirmation proves itself indestructible and because with its help those people who join the world of the Cock remain victorious.

# 21. TIME TO GO

Like all of O'Casey's short plays, *Time to Go* has received little attention from the critics. But while such disregard is utterly unjustifiable in cases like *Hall of Healing*, it is in this instance more readily understandable. Even when seen in the context of this particular phase in O'Casey's career, *Time to Go* is no masterpiece. It becomes evident that the new type of play evolved by O'Casey with *Cock-a-doodle Dandy* cannot easily be compressed into the form of the short play. Despite a variety of techniques, the short play always aims for singleness of effect; it isolates a single situation and elucidates one significant event, one human character trait, one emotion.[1] It is thus in sharp contrast to the kaleidoscopic form of O'Casey's plays from *Cock-a-doodle Dandy* to *The Drums of Father Ned*. The time span available in a short play is not sufficient to comprise O'Casey's wealth of characters, themes and dramatic effects and to weld them into a unified whole. Nor does the fact that the subject matter of *Time to Go* is based on an Irish folk-tale[2] contribute to a concentration of elements. In addition, the play lacks a dominating and unifying symbol like the Cock in the earlier play, and the after-effects of the past market-day contribute less to the play's unity than do the preparations for future events in *The Bishop's Bonfire* and *The Drums of Father Ned*. Even the comparison with *Kathleen Listens In* is unfavourable to *Time to Go*, for in the earlier play all the elements are oriented towards the central character and are integrated into the unifying concept of allegory. In the case of *Time to Go*, an interpretation can do no more than demonstrate in what ways the various themes of this period are presented.[3]

Central to this play is the theme of all-consuming material interest. Michael Flagonson and Bull Farrell, the small-town owners of a tavern and a general stores, have filled their tills on the market-day; *'the sound of coins jingling together'* (p. 272) resounds into the street. Several episodes serve to show that they draw their own business advantage from the distress of their fellow human beings: Farrell refuses to sell Barney O'Hay a sack of phosphates on credit although he needs it for his miserable fields; Flagonson offers the tourists a shabby meal for a usurious price; even the papal flag that Farrell has hoisted outside his shop has not cost him a penny: 'I nailed that off a kid bangin' the window with it to th' point of breakin'; and when I threatened the police on him, he was damned glad to get away without it' (p. 263). These two despicable figures are paralleled by the farmers Conroy and Cousins who have bargained for twelve hours over the sale of a few head of cattle, Conroy forcing Cousins into financial concessions because he is the richer of the two. Farrell's description of Conroy holds equally true for the other three: '. . . Conroy ud take the gold from a holy saint's halo an' shove it in th' bank!' (p. 264). Each of them is typified in character and behaviour to such a degree that he remains uninteresting as long as he is not confronted with persons of a different kind.

The play gains in colour when these four are juxtaposed with Widda Machree and Kelly from the Isle of Mananaun, two fairy-tale figures who stand in opposition to their business egotism. Their appearance triggers off a rudimentary plot. Widda Machree is looking for Kelly because she believes she has demanded an excessive price for her cow; he searches for her because he thinks he has given her too little. Neither can shake off his 'deadly sin' until they finally meet. It is part of the other figures' characterization that Kelly and Widda Machree are conceived as fairy-tale figures who are distinguished from the rest by their personal beauty, their antiquated dress, their illogical behaviour, but also their supernatural faculties and their insight into the others' characters. Subordination of personal interests to a concern for one's fellow human-beings in this town is a fairy-tale affair. Their unselfishness liberates Kelly and Widda Machree from the ties that fetter the others. When they are led off in handcuffs, they mysteriously succeed in shaking them off. They repeatedly sing a bitter-critical version of the Christmas carol 'Jingle Bells' and thus provide a concentrated analysis of the prevalent situation in this town:

> Jingle coins, jingle coins, jingle all th' day,
> Jingle them at night again, for coins have come to stay.
> Jingle coins till silent Death comes in his frozen sleigh
> To gather yous an' all your coins, an' jingle yous away! (p. 282)

The critical attitude embodied in these two persons is visualized in the remains of two trees that dominate the scenery: '*Their branches are withered, and they look as if they had been blasted by lightning*' (p. 261). Kelly later links them to the avaricious businessmen and farmers: 'Soon yous'll all be no more than are these two barren, deadened trees. Then when yous are silent stiffs, others will count your coins' (p. 289). The two fairy-tale figures effect the 'miracle' that for a while seems to make the alternative of a more beautiful and more fertile life possible. While *The tune of "Jingle Coins" played on trumpet and drum becomes loud and clear now . . .'*, the two ruined trees begin to change, they *'suddenly flush with blossom, foliage and illuminated fruit'* (p. 291). For a moment the men bend their knees before this apparition. But when Mrs. Flagonson enjoins her husband, 'Come in, Michael, an' help me tot up th' takin's' (p. 292), their enthusiasm evaporates and simultaneously the vision disappears; the thought of the day's takings defeats the vision of a world redeemed by altruism.

Such over-accentuated contrasts underline the naivety of the plot, which would indeed be embarrassing if it were not mitigated by the fairy-tale character of the business-people's opponents. Thus O'Casey does not juxtapose two equally viable attitudes to life, but contrasts reality with an ideal that cannot materialize. While reality, the business-people's attitude, is criticized, the position of Kelly and Widda Machree is shown as unattainable and perhaps not even desirable.[4] An attitude that is both attainable and desirable lies *between* egotism and self-denial, between rapacity and total renunciation. This would be an effective conclusion that could be encompassed even within the limitations of the short play. Yet in *Time to Go* O'Casey does not aim at a compromise between the two extremes; instead he touches upon a number of other themes that water down the play's intellectual content. He suggests, for instance, occasional allegorical inter- pretations for the figures of Kelly and Widda Machree that on closer inspection cannot be verified. Furthermore, it is possible to identify five other themes that have no more than superficial links with the central theme and cannot be more than touched upon within the scope of the play.

First, the character of the small farmer Barney O'Hay is utilized to demonstrate the degree of hypocrisy and submission that results from financial dependence and social degradation. Barney attempts to flatter Farrell, then to defend Conroy, is pushed aside in both cases and thus experiences his own despicable situation. — Second, the property-owners' dependence on the Catholic Church is demonstrated drastically. Although Farrell and Flagonson polemicise against the clergy's avarice, they have decorated their houses with church flags, and Farrell, who

repeatedly emphasizes his militant opposition to the influence
of the priests, has even secretly donated a large sum of money to
the local priest. Religion for these people is not a living and life-
determining relation to the supernatural, but only the dominion
of the clergy, accepted in fear rather than in conviction, as is
shown in Barney's words, '. . . to bring in th' topic of religion outa
hours shows a quare mind' (p. 283), and Flagonson's advice for
the treatment of the young: 'The polis is the only ones to put th'
fear o' God in them' (p. 263). — Third, it is shown that, for such
people, the conception of sin is restricted to sexual misbehaviour.
While they are constantly guilty of the sins of avarice and envy,
they suspect their opponents of immoral behaviour in order to
get rid of them more easily (pp. 273, 280). — Fourth, the theme of
the relationship between past and present (that O'Casey was to
present so effectively in *The Drums of Father Ned*) is touched
upon. Two tourists, who have apparently been introduced only
for this purpose, are looking for the remains of an old Abbey, 'A
lovely crypt with groined arches, supported by lovely semi-
columns, decorated with lovely foliage an' faces' (p. 267).
Allegedly there is still a pathway to this symbol of an artistic and
less materialistic past, but Farrell who speaks for the present
remembers only an 'oul graveyard with th' ruins in it . . .' about
which nothing is known except that 'th' whole thing's lost . . . in
thickets, brambles, an' briars' (p. 267). Later, Brian Boru, the
semi-legendary Irish king, and the Fenians are referred to in
order to point up the contrast between a remarkable past and a
despicable present. This purpose is served, too, by the traditional
national costumes of the two 'positive' characters. There is also
an ironical reference to the ideals of the participants in the Easter
Rising: 'Where's th' freedom our poor boys died to get, if a body
daren't ask for what he wants for a thing he's sellin'?' (p. 285). —
Fifth, in several places, as in the title, the motif of exile is referred
to. Farrell and Flagonson regret the depopulation of the country
(pp. 264-265); the two tourists, the last in this play's world who
know about the greatness of the past, want to visit the Abbey
'before we go away' (p. 267); and Kelly and Widda Machree
affirm repeatedly: 'It is time to go . . .' (pp. 271, 289). The 'positive'
characters leave the country, and no one is left except the
unscrupulous businessmen, the hypocrites and the tale-bearers
of the clergy.

There is obviously a relationship between this last theme and
O'Casey's personal life history. In *Inishfallen, Fare Thee Well*,
the volume of his autobiography that deals with his departure

from Ireland the final chapter (also called 'Inishfallen, Fare Thee Well') employs the sentence 'It was time for Sean to go' as a *leitmotiv*.[5] When he looked back (*Inishfallen, Fare Thee Well* was written more than twenty years after his departure from Ireland) he saw his decision to go as a liberation from intolerable restrictions: 'It was getting dark in Ireland, so his flight to London would be a leap in the light.'[6] *Time to Go*, published two years after *Inishfallen, Fare Thee Well*, seems to have been an additional, less subjective attempt at justification for his departure from Ireland. The themes listed above can serve as a catalogue of O'Casey's reasons for leaving Ireland, as he saw them in 1950. *Time to Go*, then, can be considered as a portrait of a country in which a person like O'Casey cannot exist. If his purpose in this play is understood as an act of personal apologia, it is easier to realize why it is not an artistic success..

# 22.  THE BISHOP'S BONFIRE

*The Bishop's Bonfire* is the only one of O'Casey's later plays to have received its première in Dublin. The doors of the Abbey Theatre remained closed to it; but in 1955, on the initiative of Cyril Cusack who also took the role of Codger Sleehaun, the play was produced by Tyrone Guthrie for the Gaiety Theatre.[1] Lively public interest justified the risk of producing a new work by O'Casey in Dublin (its five weeks' run is said to have set a new record for the Gaiety) and the verdicts of English and American critics were predominantly favourable; Irish critics, however, were almost unanimous in condemning the play. Again, they showed their consternation at O'Casey's image of Ireland and his criticism of his native country; and they proved themselves incapable of distinguishing between artistic quality and dramatic effectiveness on the one hand and O'Casey's opinions on the other. If one observes the degree of national criticism and even abuse that have, for instance, been heard on the American or the German stage during the past two or three decades, the intolerance by which the greatest Irish dramatist was for a long time virtually excluded from the theatres of his country, is even less understandable.

It must, however, be admitted that the Irish references in *The Bishop's Bonfire* are more explicit than in *Cock-a-doodle Dandy*.[2] A number of utterances, for instance 'The one thing increasin' in Ireland – the population of stone an' wooden saints' (p. 52),[3] are aimed at the country's contemporary situation, while others are only intelligible in an Irish context: 'You've escaped from the dominion of the big house with the lion and unicorn on its front; don't let yourselves sink beneath the meaner dominion of the big shop with the cross and shamrock on its gable' (p. 77). Several of the problems touched upon – the high marriage age and the tradition of match-making by the parents, the omnipotence of the clergy, the requirements of national defence and even the topical problem of rural dance-halls under church control – cannot immediately be transposed to other countries. Ballyoonagh in *The Bishop's Bonfire* is not Everytown to the same extent as Nyadnanave in *Cock-a-doodle Dandy*. Yet it is not correct to claim that 'Even the best and most human of his plays written in exile, *The Bishop's Bonfire*, would be largely meaningless before an audience unfamiliar with the religious framework and practice in Ireland'.[4] One would be equally justified in considering O'Casey's early plays as unsuitable for an audience outside Ireland. A more balanced verdict is: 'The author and the Irish people may believe that this play has special relevance to "problems of modern Ireland", but its greater relevance is to what will go on existing in the world, even when the Irish marriage-rate is high and the emigration rate low, and O'Casey and the priests he hates with such disproportionate ferocity, have passed on.'[5] In *The Bishop's Bonfire*, as in *Cock-a-doodle Dandy*, the universal traits are clearly more important than the regional ones.

*

In contrast to *Cock-a-doodle Dandy*, *The Bishop's Bonfire* lacks a central unifying symbol. In this case, therefore, the continuous development of the plot is of greater importance. Three plot lines can be distinguished: the preparations for the Bishop's visit, the love affair between Keelin Reiligan and Daniel Clooncoohy and the relationship between Foorawn Reiligan and Manus Moanroe. Although these lines are intertwined and permanently influence each other, they will here be considered separately. Subsequently it will be asked what they have in common, which question will necessarily lead to the central themes of the play.

The preparations for the Bishop's visit in his native town dominate the stage events for most of the play. To Councillor Reiligan and Canon Burren, the representatives of secular and spiritual power, no extravagance is too great. Of Reiligan, the wealthiest man of the region, it is said: 'You own the land, own the tavern, own the shirt factory, own the dance hall, own the store, an' God help us, you own the people too. You're a menace to the world, Reiligan' (p. 37). His house, furnished with the status symbols of the *nouveaux riches*, is to serve as the Bishop's lodgings and is therefore equipped with additional valuables. Canon Burren, together with Reiligan, supervises with indefatigable attention these secular preparations for the spiritual dignitary's visit. He is highly aware of his power over the people in Ballyoonagh; just as he can force Reiligan to plant ivy instead of roses or to dismiss his best employee, he can also separate lovers and prevent or arrange marriages. His figure may be less remote from reality than has been maintained by O'Casey's Irish critics. Even a highly favourable report about the 'new' Ireland of the early sixties still confirms that, at the time, Canon Burren's attitude was far from exceptional:

The wind of change that is blowing through the Vatican and through Maynooth has yet to reach some of the farflung outposts of the Church in rural Ireland. Most of the parish priests are old and set in their ways. Many of them are firmly and irretrievably cast in a mould that is familiar from the works of Irish writers and playwrights: complacent, ignorant, dogmatic, puritanical, obsessed with certain mechanical aspects of sex, and hopelessly ill-equipped to deal with young people in a society that can no longer be isolated from the rest of the world.[6]

The Canon represents an attitude that condemns everything foreign to it, and exploits people's fear of the supernatural to enforce his own views.

The only tangible result of the hectic preparations is the fact that Reiligan and Burren receive the titles 'Count of the Papal Court' and 'Monsignor': secular activities are requited with secular honours. The Bishop himself does not appear; but the big bonfire is lit on which, for his reception, 'evil' books and pictures are to be burned. On stage the Bishop is represented by the statue of a saint that accompanies him wherever he goes and that serves to characterize him. It is the effigy of a Roman legionary, an emblem of the power still wielded by the Pope. This strange figure is capable of emitting blasts from its buccina: 'The buckineeno boyo is the private patron of the Bishop, and his statue always fronts him while he's thinkin'. If he's thinkin' right, the buckineeno blows a steady note; if his thinkin's goin' wrong, the buckineeno quavers' (p. 53). In other words, the Bishop has replaced his conscience by a statue to which he has delegated his own decisions on right and wrong. In the system of values of an O'Caseyan play this suffices to indicate the type of person he is. The negative impression is completed by the fact that the statue is hollow. It is not, however, as dramatically effective as it could be because O'Casey does not use it quite consistently. While several times the saint emits shrill blasts as soon as 'improper' thoughts are being thought in his vicinity or the joy of life is expressed in a dance, on other, similar occasions, he remains silent.

Like the events surrounding the statue, large parts of the main plot are confined to the realm of the comic. The preparations for the Bishop's visit provide O'Casey with another opportunity of creating comic craftsmen or labourers scenes. Whenever walls are to be built, plants to be carried or potatoes to be peeled, such moments offer a chance to argue, to quarrel, to do mischief, in other words to shirk the work and to contribute by 'inspired buffoonery'[7] to the rising chaos. The builders quarrel over bricks; a keg of gin is discovered, rendering any future work unthinkable; a bag of cement is emptied on Reiligan's new carpet; furniture is damaged; the Bishop's brandy bottles are emptied: as in *Purple Dust*, the destruction almost keeps pace with the preparation of the house. Reiligan, infected by the growing confusion, coins an appropriate motto for all these scenes: 'From this out, there's to be no talkin'; and if anyone does talk, everybody is to listen to nobody. Anyone – no one – mind yous! [*The three men stand mute*.] Damn it, are yous listenin' to me?' (p. 59). The labourers Richard Rankin and 'Prodical' Carranaun and the two workmen Daniel Clooncoohy and Codger Sleehaun form a comic quartet that, in its variety of grotesque ideas and its wealth of invective, is equal to any similar group in O'Casey or anywhere else. It is significant, however, that each of these figures not only arouses laughter but also contributes to the play's central themes, the comic scenes deepening the serious effect.

There is one exception. One episode (pp. 54-58) is neither part of the main plot, nor can it be seen as belonging to one of the two 'private' plot lines, and it shows no thematic links to the other scenes. In this episode, Prodical, Daniel and Codger, together with Lieutenant Reiligan (whom O'Casey appears to have introduced for the purpose of this scene only) discuss the dangers of a Soviet invasion in Ireland, and the measures necessary to prevent it. Their analysis of world politics, in which O'Casey parodies the blatant anti-communist propaganda in his native country, is just as absurd as the preventive measures they suggest, to people all Irish roads with swarms of American jeeps. O'Casey seems to have enjoyed this scene so much that he published it twice before its appearance in *The Bishop's Bonfire*.[8] It is not surprising that, despite its comic potential, it should be an alien element in the play.

In contrast to the predominantly comic main plot, the other two plot lines are almost devoid of comic effect. They convey the bitter-pessimistic atmosphere that characterizes the play as a whole. Daniel, the unskilled labourer from a poor home, and Keelin, Councillor Reiligan's daughter, are thrown into deep unhappiness because of their love for each other. At the beginning it seems still possible for them to overcome the social barriers that separate them. The preparations for the visit give them an unhoped-for opportunity to work together. Daniel succeeds in

262

*O'Casey the Dramatist*

persuading Keelin to confess that she loves him, and he even convinces her that he is determined to overcome all future obstacles: her father, the Canon and the opinion of the whole town:

What's it matter whether a man's born under turrets or under a thatch? It's the man with the gay heart that rides the waters an' the winds; who shakes life be the hand when life looks fair, an' shakes her be the shoulder when she shows a frown (p. 71).

With great eloquence he pictures their emigration to England. But when Father Boheroe surprises them, he begins to look for excuses. And when, a little later, Reiligan and the Canon discover them dancing, he does not dare to confess his love, and declares, '[*frightened*] I didn't mean it, I didn't really. I musta been mad, sir' (p. 78). He even repulses Keelin who takes his part, and submits to the priest's commands. It is psychologically consistent if he afterwards protests his courage but rejects Keelin when she overcomes her pride once more and asks him to take her to England. He cannot return to her because she will always remind him of his defeat. Since Daniel is not shown in an unfavourable light, the reader's or spectator's criticism is directed to the conditions under which a likable ordinary person like Daniel is so pushed as to fail both his own principles and the person he loves.

The situation for Keelin, after she has overcome her pride and confessed her love for a person of lower social standing, is even less favourable. She is left behind both with the conviction of her lover's failure and the stigma of having been rejected by a mere labourer. Her despair is complete when her father and the priest reveal their plans to marry her to a farmer aged 58 who has the dubious advantage of being the Bishop's brother but himself fights shy of married life. The outcome of this 'courtship' remains undecided, but it is doubtful whether Keelin will find the strength to resist the combined authority of her father and her priest. In any case, she will not escape a thoroughly unhappy life.

Her fate will thus be similar to that of Manus Moanroe, her sister Foorawn's former lover. In contrast to Keelin and Daniel, there is hardly any hope for Foorawn and Manus right from the start. It is part of their previous history that Manus left the seminary when he realized that he did not have a vocation to the priesthood, that he in vain sought forgetfulness and death in the British Airforce and finally returned to Ballyoonagh in the desperate hope of regaining Foorawn. She, however, clings to her vow of perpetual chastity and does not dare to admit that she is still in love with Manus. Hers is a tragic conflict for which there is no solution. Her natural joy in life, intimated in her short dance with Codger, will urge her to a life with Manus; but her belief, intensified by her religious education, prevents her from breaking her vow. The will of God seems to be accessible to her only in its interpretation by the Canon and the Bishop, who would never accept her liberation: 'How could I ever possibly know that God wouldn't be angry with me for breaking my vow?' (p. 112).

If Foorawn suffers from an overdose of the fear of God, Manus has lost all belief and has retreated into an attitude of cynical disdain from which Foorawn alone could redeem him. Even his external appearance shows his deterioration: '*Manus Moanroe is thirty or so, tall and well built. He looks slovenly now, with a beard of a week's growth, and a face lined more than his years warrant, warped by a sad and sullen look*' (p. 9). His intelligence finds expression in his irony with which he confronts the world. As Reiligan's assistant he seems to derive a perverse enjoyment from proving his superiority by fulfilling his tasks (for which he feels nothing but contempt) with a high degree of efficiency. His future path through life is clearly marked. If, as he says himself, he steals some money 'for Manus and his doxies now' (p. 116), he not only suggests the dissipations of his future life but also the contempt with which he will increasingly regard himself. This inconsistent and highly credible character, half repulsive, half likable, suffices to invalidate the thesis that the later O'Casey draws his figures according to a simple black and white scheme: 'His young people, especially his lovers, have no individuality either; they "succeed", i.e. defeat the Canons, or "fail", i.e. are defeated by the Canons, as the striker succeeds or fails against his boss.'[9] One wonders how familiar such critics are with the actual text of the plays.

Only towards the end of the play is there any development in the plot line around Foorawn and Manus. Foorawn's enforced reticence and Manus' growing bitterness preclude any understanding between the two lovers. The violent conclusion that puts an unexpected end to Foorawn's life is all the more surprising. Manus takes the money collected by Foorawn for the missions, is surprised by her and shoots her when she is about to call the police; in her letter written in the moment of death she accuses herself of suicide. The unmotivated planting of the revolver required for this purpose suggests the over-explicitness of Victorian melodrama, while the killing of Foorawn and her final

letter are even more suggestive of Boucicault and his contemporaries. It is true that Manus' theft is a credible step in his
development, and Foorawn's confession of her love at the
moment of death is not surprising. Even her decision to simulate
suicide may be acceptable, for she commits a mortal sin only in
the eyes of her family, not in the eyes of God. It is, however, quite
incredible that she should be able to take this decision with no
hesitation whatsoever, and it is even less likely that Manus
should find no other way of preventing her from using the
telephone than that of shooting her. Such a 'realistic' view of
the scene is in order because, despite O'Casey's subsequent
explanation that it was to be seen symbolically,[10] it in no way
deviates from the psychological realism of the Foorawn-Manus
plot. O'Casey, like Boucicault, tries to arouse the audience's
emotions by violent motivation and at the same time to lead the
plot to a definitive conclusion. Since the fate of Daniel, Keelin
and Manus remains undecided, it would have been more in
keeping with the atmosphere and the themes of the play to have
shown Foorawn, after the loss of her lover and the additional
disappointment of his sacrilegious theft, facing a joyless future
in the house of her uncomprehending father. Critics are therefore
wholly justified in deploring this scene. It is, however, incorrect
to condemn the whole work because of this one scene, since the
death of Foorawn is *not* characteristic of the play as a whole.

All three plot-lines find their conclusion when the bonfire
blazes up in the distance, announcing the Bishop's arrival. It is
not only a symbol of literary censorship which, both in its
institutionalized and unofficial forms was still active in Ireland at
the time; it also underlines most effectively the central characters'
fate. Naturally, it is less of a bonfire than a funeral pyre: when it
blazes up, Keelin loses her lover, Daniel his home, Codger his
employment, Foorawn her life, and Manus his last hold on the
world. All this is predicted by Manus: 'And in the ashes that the
fire will leave will be the ashes of our love; of mine for you, of
yours for me; and Daniel's love for Keelin and hers for him'.[43]

*

The pessimistic tone of this play prevails not only because the
positive characters suffer through the influence of forces from
outside, but also because they are unfaithful to themselves,
betraying the ideals that O'Casey supports. This is least true of
Keelin, who fails in her endeavour to gain the love of Daniel but

still does not abandon her own outlook on life. Her final submission is only hinted at in Canon Burren's confident assertion that she too will give up in the end (p. 87). Foorawn's betrayal is, according to O'Casey's criteria, much more explicit. She represses her impulse to live, and therefore shares in the responsibility for her own death as well as for Manus' despair. Manus puts himself in the wrong by his spontaneous act of manslaughter, and even more so by his planned theft of the mission funds. He thereby provides the enemies of life-affirmation with welcome arguments for their repressive measures: it is easy to imagine that Canon Burren will, for years to come, present him as a warning example whenever he tries to justify the restriction of personal freedom. And Daniel, finally, is the best example of a person who deserts the ideals that he, and with him the dramatist, has hitherto supported, losing both respect and self-respect in the process. In this regard, *The Bishop's Bonfire* differs principally from *Cock-a-doodle Dandy* where the positive characters' apparent defeat is really their moral victory. It should be noted that in *The Bishop's Bonfire* the motif of betrayal of one's own objectives is reflected on the comic level, Prodical twice breaking his solemn pledge to give up drinking.

This pessimism is reinforced by the fact that the play's events take place in a barren countryside devoid of all vitality: the fields are overgrown with weeds, the hay turns into dust, the cattle are half-starved and painfully produce a minimum of thin milk (pp. 24, 27, 29, 36-38). In such surroundings it is impossible for healthy human relationships to thrive; thus it is not surprising that Keelin should be doomed to intellectual and biological sterility and that Foorawn should freely impose such a state upon herself.

O'Casey confronts the sombre atmosphere of this play, whose bitterness is hardly mitigated by its comic scenes, with two counter-images, two characters who may be seen, in their different spheres of life, as the embodiment of his own ideals. Their special position may be gathered from the fact that they stand above the three plot-lines, sharing in all of them and contributing to their artistic unity. The Codger is *'eighty-four years old; but carries his age about with him in a jaunty and defiant way'* (p. 16). These two adjectives serve to characterize him. He is defiant and ready to resist whenever he feels a threat to his independence, but also 'jaunty' and carefree in his design to enjoy life to the last. He is the only one who does not permit himself to be intimidated by Reiligan and Canon Burren and who even accepts his dismissal in order to preserve the directness of his language and the gaiety of his songs. Drink, for him, is not evil; it stimulates him to a 'tait-a-tait talk about the woes an' wonders of the world' (p. 120), inspiring him to use an imaginative and poetic language that expresses his pantheistic relationship to the Deity:

What are the things that God gives to one man to the things God gives to all? What's the gold on a bishop's mitre to the gold on the gorse? The sheen of his satin shoon to the feel of a petal on the wildest rose? What's a bishop's purple to the purple in the silky plume of the speary thistle?' (p. 28).

He is capable of infecting even Foorawn with his cheerfulness and to lead her through a happy dance (p. 68). He shows a shy and tender understanding for Keelin's situation, inducing her to exclaim: 'Oh, Codger, dear Codger, I wish to God that you were me Da!' (p. 85). He is skilful in his handling of the cattle and knows the soil in every field – in other words his relationship to nature is direct and uncorrupted. When shortly before his dismissal, he appears '*carrying a branchy, big geranium, topped with many lovely clusters of scarlet flowers*' (p. 100), O'Casey has conferred on him one of the highest honours available in his world. O'Casey always associated the geranium with his adored mother whose favourite flower it was; it became for him a symbol of life lived under difficult conditions with joy and confidence, a symbol of the determined acceptance of this world which characterized his own attitude.

Occasionally the Codger has been seen as a self-portrait of the ageing O'Casey.[11] This is not entirely true, for the Codger lacks the bitterness that has impressed itself on so many of O'Casey's writings – for he was continually engaged in controversy of one sort or another – and that has also found expression in *The Bishop's Bonfire*. It is much more correct to see in him 'a composite figure of the Synge Tramp, the old bard Oisin, and the octogenarian O'Casey himself',[12] because this permits one to regard the Codger as the author's wish-image, combining traits of the inspired singer and the uncomplicated human being, living in harmony with nature and with himself. As the singer, the Codger figures in many songs in which he concentrates the atmosphere of a scene. This is true, for instance, for the mood of departure of the final act:

Ah, where is the laughter rich of children mad at play?
Gone, too is the lover and his lass

From all the hawthorn's fragrance in the month of June or month of May.
Where, where is the time when life had something fine to say? (p. 100).

In one of these songs the Codger expresses the motif of exile that
pervades the whole play and has special relevance for him (his
children have left the country, pp. 26-27), when he modifies the
well-known song to 'My Bonnie's *gone* over the ocean . . .' (p. 45).
At the end of Act III, this song is taken up again, forming the
melancholy conclusion of the play:

Last night as I lay on me pilla, last night as I lay on me bed
Last night as I lay on me pilla, I dreamt me dear Bonnie was dead (p. 121).

Father Boheroe confirms the intensity which the Codger instils
into his songs: 'I wish I could put into my prayers the spirit he
puts into his songs. I'm afraid, Monsignor, God listens more
eagerly to the songs of the Codger than He does to our best
prayers' (p. 105-106).

Father Boheroe is O'Casey's second ideal character in this
play. While the Codger lives from a spontaneous and unreflected
joy of life, the priest endeavours to come to terms intellectually
with the problems surrounding him. If this renders him less
impressive as a stage character, it makes him more suitable for his
task as a chorus-figure voicing the views of the dramatist. In this
respect, as well as in his character, he resembles one of Shaw's
most impressive figures, Father Keegan in *John Bull's Other
Island*. Father Boheroe, '*A man of the world as well as a man of
God*' (p. 24), sees the ideal relationship to God in other terms
than those of a total denial of the joys of life. When the labourers
concentrate on their keg of gin, he excuses them as 'trying to get
a glimpse of heaven through the wrong window' (p. 24). He
repeatedly resists the repressive measures of his superiors
although he is taken to task for it. He supports Keelin's and
Daniel's attempt to overcome the barriers of class and material
wealth, and he even urges Foorawn to obtain an exemption from
her vow. 'Be brave' (p. 112) is his decisive advice to her, the
same advice that is the Messenger's blessing in *Cock-a-doodle
Dandy*. Being brave: in the views of Boheroe and O'Casey this
means facing up to the world with its problems: 'God is unhappy
when we don't do what we can with what He gives us' (p. 27). A
compilation of his sayings reads like a brief profession of faith of
the ageing O'Casey. Some of his unorthodox utterances sound
surprising from the lips of an Irish priest:

Ah, Foorawn, it is easy to turn one's back on things, but it is better and braver to face them. I shall never turn my back on a beautiful world, nor on the beautiful flesh of humanity, asparkle with vigour, intelligence, and health; and as for the devil, what we often declare to be the devil is but truth who has at last mustered the courage to speak it (p. 112).

But if one accepts the double premise that Boheroe possesses the intellectual independence of such views and the courage to voice them, they are dramatically highly relevant. They lead the other characters to take decisions and usually show the alternatives which they do *not* choose. For it is important to realize that Father Boheroe, in the world of this play, has no chance of putting his views into effect. Like the other characters, he too fails:

FOORAWN . . . You have tried, and failed, Father. You have failed poor Keelin.
FATHER BOHEROE. I did my best.
FOORAWN [*bitterly*]. You have given no help to me, Father.
FATHER BOHEROE. I did my best.
FOORAWN. Or to Manus either.
FATHER BOHEROE. Or to him, though God knows I'd dearly like to help you both (p. 114).

In this respect he differs from the Messenger in *Cock-a-doodle Dandy* for whom the possibility of failure is unthinkable. This is the final measure of the play's pessimistic tone: O'Casey refuses his own representative, the character who embodies his creed, any hope of success.

*

The discussion of the bonfire, of the central characters' failure and of O'Casey's counter-images has already revealed certain devices guaranteeing the unity of the play. It is important to note that each of these three features is associated with all three plot-lines. A brief analysis of the central theme will underline the play's homogeneity, for it can be shown that this theme finds a place in each of the scenes. The play's central theme can be defined as the question of the right attitude to God. Only when the centrality of this theme is recognised, will it be possible fully to appreciate O'Casey's masterly skill in the play: he succeeds in displaying a multiplicity of possible answers without leaving the framework of a credible and continuously progressing sequence of events.

It is appropriate to the play's pessimistic atmosphere that O'Casey gives much more room to an (in his eyes) wrong attitude to God than to its positive alternatives. Certainly 'wrong' are the views of Reiligan who prepares for his meeting with the Bishop not by meditation but by additional excesses of material luxury, inducing Father Boheroe to speak of 'all the gilded foolishness claimed to come so gleefully from God' (p. 110). That Reiligan has not grasped the essence of Christianity becomes evident when he drives away Rankin from his daughter's *prie-Dieu*: even in prayer he expects social grades to be observed. He is encouraged in his consciousness of his special position by Canon Burren who disqualifies himself right from the start as a mediator of God's will when he says: 'When you are working for the Councillor, Rankin, however menial the job may be, you are serving God' (p. 5). This attitude is parodied in the subsequent scene when the bricklayers quarrel over the bricks: 'Remember what your Canon said that when you served oul' Reiligan, you served God; so as I'm servin' Reiligan, by servin' me, you're servin' God, too' (p. 7).

Reiligan believes himself to have done his duty to God when he permitted Foorawn to retire into a life of prayer, dispensing with her help in the house. He is all the more ruthless, however, in his demands on his other daughter. He expects her to do work that a machine could do much more quickly (pp. 32-33), and his refusal to permit her to marry is also bound up with his reluctance to do without her as an unpaid servant. To O'Casey this is just as much a falsification of the will of God as is Foorawn's rejection of the world: 'Too much work misfits a soul for heaven and for here . . .' (p. 26). Reiligan's misplaced attempt to separate the two fields of prayer and work is emphasized when he scolds Foorawn: '. . . go on, you, for prayers are no use here now' (p. 35), or when he swears at Rankin:

Oh, you menacer, turn your face to where the trouble is, an' not be lardin' your skimpy soul with maudlin mumbles, settin' the saints above wonderin' why they aren't deaf. Come outa your booze of prayin' for a minute to help our christian humanity on its way! (p. 34).

In the comic sphere of the play, Rankin corresponds to the figure of Foorawn. Not only is he a fanatic at prayer, but he has also developed a hysterical hatred of women, for in every confrontation with the other sex he senses the dangers of Hell. When Keelin tries to confuse him with a view of her attractive legs, he sees no other escape than to spit in her face (p. 23). Canon Burren supports him in this attitude when he credits the Codger, who sings the song of 'the lover and his lass', with 'a filthy mind' (p. 100). But also Foorawn's apparently harmless self-isolation is none the less dangerous, as can be seen from its direct result, Manus' bitterness. Father Boheroe, therefore, is justified in criticizing the 'vainglory of her chastity' (p. 43). Whereas she hopes to approach God by dissociating herself from other human beings, he believes: '. . . a man in a woman's arms may indeed be close to God' (p. 75).

Another erroneous attempt to improve one's relationship with God can be seen in Prodical's ineffective endeavours to give up the drink. The first of them leads to one of the most successful comic discussion-scenes in the whole of O'Casey's work, Rankin's and Prodical's quarrel about the validity of his vow, which is soon transferred to the level of their respective guardian angels. While Rankin warns: 'My angel's tellin' me to urge you to listen to your own angel's warning!', Prodical replies in comic despair: 'I'm not goin' to have your angel interferin' with my angel!' (p. 19). The second attempt, when the bottle of whiskey is hidden under the Bishop's hollow saint and is subsequently retrieved, shows that Prodical, as opposed to Rankin, is not hopelessly on the wrong track. In the last scene of the play, he appears in friendly companionship with the Codger – the only human being who constantly embodies the 'right' attitude to God. Prodical also voices a parodistic exaggeration of those warnings that he, and most of the others, normally tend to take so seriously. Acting the Bishop in a farcical scene, he emphasizes the opposite of what he says:

Dan, me son, take me epicpiscopal advice, an' keep your young innocent puss outa the whiskey-tumbler, out of a bad book, an' keep far from the girls, for a young bitch's enfiladin' blessin' is the devil's choicest curse! (p. 82).

The central question behind all these various demonstrations of a questionable attitude to God is voiced by the Porter, a strange figure who, after his trouble with the statue, suddenly breaks out into a blasphemous appeal to reason: 'I'm askin' yous something, Is prayer good for you? I don't mean the odd nod of the head most of us give to God, but the prayer that's the real McCoy – does it lift a man up, or does it cast a man down?' (p. 63). Previously he had given an answer to his own question when he complained of those 'holy men an' holy women' like Foorawn who approach

ordinary human beings: 'Give one of them ones a chance to get
a grip on you, an' he'll have you worryin' God for help to do what
you should be damn well able to do yourself without botherin'
God at all' (p. 62). A second answer is provided by Father
Boheroe: 'Too much formal prayer . . . sometimes makes a soul
conceited; and merriment may be a way of worship!' (p. 26).
Boheroe also voices the dramatist's view of a fruitful synthesis of
prayer and work, as opposed to those many attempts in the play
to separate the two spheres:

All places are sacred, man; the church we pray in, the homes sheltering
us, the shops where we get the things we need to go on living, the halls
we dance in; yea, the very place we walk on is holy ground. Work, too,
is holy, but only when it's reasonable (p. 25).

The best way to serve God is to make use of all the opportunities
offered by God to mankind, not to reject them. The joy of life, not
asceticism; tolerance, not repression; mutual assistance, not self-
isolation are the central terms for such an attitude that is put into
practice only by the Codger.

In *The Bishop's Bonfire*, the difficulties of effecting such an
ideal seem almost insurmountable. This is underlined by the
emotional mood of the play. It takes place on a warm, sunny
autumn day *'when nature gives a last rally and sings a song of
colour before winter brings death to flower and field'* (p. 2).
References to the impending death of nature and, in the human
sphere, to the problems of old age and inescapable death abound
throughout the play and contribute to its melancholy mood. *The
Bishop's Bonfire* seems to mark the final point of a development,
the pessimistic epilogue to an ageing dramatist's life-work. It is
all the more surprising to find O'Casey's next play shot through
again with a youthful, spring-like optimism.

# 23. THE DRUMS OF FATHER NED

The controversies over the Dublin première of *The Drums of Father Ned* came like a confirmation of the pessimistic prognosis for Ireland that O'Casey had voiced in *The Bishop's Bonfire*. The play was initially accepted for the Dublin International Theatre Festival in 1958, together with a dramatization of *Ulysses* by Alan McClelland and three short plays by Beckett, but was subsequently dropped from the programme in circumstances that have never been fully explained. It seems, however, that both political and religious pressure was exerted on the organizing committee, with the Archbishop of Dublin finally tipping the scales, providing O'Casey with a real 'Bishop's Bonfire'. The details of the affair, in the course of which McClelland's adaptation was rejected as well, while Beckett withdrew his plays in protest so that the Festival had to be cancelled, need not be repeated here.[1]

Two results of this controversy, however, had decisive consequences for the future stage history of O'Casey's plays. On the one hand O'Casey, in a rash and spontaneous act of defiance, banned all his plays from performance in Ireland. This prevented his early works, which until then had formed an important part of the Abbey's repertoire, from being produced for years (only amateur productions were exempted because O'Casey, in a financial emergency, had sold the amateur rights of his plays). Soon, younger Irish actors began to lack the experience necessary for the performance of O'Casey's works. The disastrous consequences of this discontinuity were still apparent when *The Plough and the Stars*, produced for the opening of the new Abbey Theatre, was a total failure. And then, in a second act of defiance, O'Casey permitted his new play to be premièred by the Little Theatre of Lafayette, Indiana, in a production by the O'Casey critic Robert Hogan. It is doubtful whether this production, however meritorious, improved the play's chances of a future stage career. A provincial little theatre production of such a complicated play may easily come up against insurmountable problems of casting and stage technique which will make the faults of the play all the more glaring and will at the same time hide its good qualities. Neither Broadway nor the West End showed a subsequent interest in the play, the first English production taking place at the small Repertory Theatre in Hornchurch, Essex. Even a later production in Dublin (Olympia Theatre) did not promote the play's international stage career although it again proved its effectiveness in the theatre.

One of O'Casey's sources for *The Drums of Father Ned* was his early, unproduced play *The Harvest Festival*. In *Inishfallen, Fare Thee Well* he links *The Harvest Festival* with the name of the Sligo Priest Father O'Flanagan to whom, among others, *The Drums of Father Ned* is dedicated.[2] Another source is to be seen in his article 'Bonfire Under a Black Sun' where O'Casey takes the Irish critics of *The Bishop's Bonfire* to task. At the end, he enumerates the encouraging indications of a more hopeful future for Ireland, and he mentions

. . . the cheeky and gallant town of Wexford, a little less in size than Littlehampton in Sussex, holding its annual Festival of the Arts, with opera flourishing, the finest of film shows, chamber music, and an art exhibition, with Trinity College students flaunting themselves in the poetic plays of Yeats, Continental eminence present, and Glyndebourne giving the town a bow. The Boys (and Girls) of Wexford are beginning another Rising . . .[3]

He thereby outlines the theme of the play of his that was to follow on *The Bishop's Bonfire*: his hope for a new struggle for liberation by the young, fighting now for intellectual independence after Ireland has achieved political autonomy. *The Drums of Father Ned* depicts the liberation, wholly utopian at the time, from those fetters which *The Bishop's Bonfire* had observed in every sphere of life.

*

The form of *The Drums of Father Ned* corresponds directly to the utopian character of the play. It is far less confined by the limits of probability and reality than was the preceding work. A certain stylization is immediately evident in the scenery. Acts I and III show the Binningtons', Act II the McGilligans' drawing-room, both of them distinguished only by a few details:

*McGilligan's drawing-room, looking almost exactly like the one in Binnington's except that the curtains and sashes are of reverse colours . . . and the palm tree has long yellow leaves with blue stems and trunk, the reverse of the palm in Binnington's* (p. 47).[4]

Another unrealistic device is the echo that ironically emphasizes important sections of the dialogue. The central characters are arranged in strict symmetry: the two Binningtons and their son Michael confront the McGilligans and their daughter Nora, Bernadette Shillayley is opposed to Tom Killsallighan. This deliberate symmetry is carried to the point where the maid Bernadette works three days for the Binningtons and the other three for the McGilligans. The characters resemble the flowers that are being planted to decorate the town: they are '*all much larger than life, and fashioned in a stylised way*' (p. 47). Equally, the stage figures are stylised, reduced to a few character traits, and far remote from the complexity of a Manus Moanroe or Codger Sleehaun. All of them can be identified with one of two clearly distinguished groups, whose chief difference is their positive or negative attitude to the Tostal. Among its opponents are the representatives of the small-town establishment, as Mayor Binnington declares himself: '. . . I'll go against it! McGilligan's again' it, Father Fillifogue's again' it, all men with a stake in the townland's again' it' (p. 18). Its supporters are the young and the working-class people as well as Mr. Murray the organist who fights for an 'international' attitude in the field of culture.

If there are no genuine characters in *The Drums of Father Ned*, there is little logical plot development either. Instead, a number of events connected with the Tostal have been arranged side by side. The only progression is to be seen in some rudimentary sub-plots. These contain some hints at a love relationship between Michael and Nora as well as between Tom and Bernadette. Furthermore, some kind of development is connected with the shipload of timber that has been imported from Siberia, is condemned to be burnt as 'red' timber and is eventually saved. And finally, the preparations for the parliamentary elections indicate a certain development, for it is repeatedly pointed out that Binnington and McGilligan have not yet handed in their nomination papers, and it becomes clear in the end that Nora and Michael will oppose them. What these snatches of plot have in common is that their outcome is determined from the very start. The victory of the young people is never in danger, because their opponents' influence is not to be taken seriously; this, more than anything else, indicates the play's utopian character. In general, however, plot-progression has been replaced by a functional juxtaposition of scenes which are differentiated by their varying emotional atmosphere, each of them dealing with another aspect of the same theme. Tension and suspense have been superseded

by the colourful movement of individual scenes which, in their
varying degrees of comic potential, guarantee the play's stage
effectiveness.

Special mention has to be made of the two most conspicuous
formal innovations in this play, the 'Prerumble' and the strange
title character. They are each linked respectively to one of the
two themes, the politico-historical and the religious theme, and
will be discussed in this context. Finally, it will be necessary
to analyze the various functions of the Tostal, for any evaluation
of the play will depend on the conviction and the dramatic
effectiveness of the values embodied in this festival.

*

The 'Prerumble', 'one of the sparest, most telling and grimly
grotesque single pieces that O'Casey has ever written',[5] has been
devised as a flashback to the period of the War of Independence
in 1920. A unit of the brutal Black and Tans, auxiliary forces of the
British police, has set fire to a small Irish town. They persecute its
inhabitants and are finally forced to retreat by the insurgents. Yet
this scene, in contrast to *The Shadow of a Gunman*, is not
concerned with a realistic representation of the historical events;
it appears '*like a sudden vision of an experience long past conjured
up within the mind of one who had gone through it*' (p. 2). In
other words: the present is the starting-point of the play, one of
its themes being the relationship of the contemporary scene to an
undigested past. Mrs. Binnington makes it quite clear that the
aims of the struggle for independence have not yet been realized:

We've done our best for our glorious dead with murmurin' of thousands
of Rosaries, hundhreds of volleys fired over where they lie, an' th' soundin'
of hundhreds more of Last Posts. All that can be done for a dead hero is
to put a headstone over his grave, an' leave him there (p. 17).

The insurgents are glorified as heroes, but the intellectual revival
that the best among them had fought for has not yet been
achieved. The dead are little more than a burden for the living;
the responsibility to continue fighting for their objectives has
been evaded by the substitute of memorial services.

The two central characters, Binnington and McGilligan, are
utilized to show that the War of Independence has not yet come
to its end. In the Prelude, they appear as victims of the Black and
Tans. Although they have grown up under identical conditions,

they are separated by an irrational hatred and almost prefer to be
shot than to be reconciled. They represent the inner strife of the
country that was largely responsible for the centuries of foreign
domination. When they are to be shot, the officer intervenes
with a wholly convincing argument: 'Can't you see that these
two rats will do more harm to Ireland living than they'll ever do
to Ireland dead?' (p. 10). The rest of the play justifies his decision.
Alderman Binnington and Councillor McGilligan, as mayor and
deputy mayor as well as T.D.'s in influential positions, have
learned nothing whatsoever from the past. They do not use their
offices to further the interests of the town but to engage in personal
rivalries. Their mutual hatred has remained unchanged, but they
set it aside when it would prevent them from carrying out shady
business transactions. Whereas at the time of the struggle for
independence they were at least prepared to risk their lives
for their mutual hostility, now they do not even sacrifice their
business interests to it. Their antagonism has naturally led them
into the two opposing factions in the most controversial question
of recent Irish history, the decision for or against the Treaty of
1921 that confirmed the separation of Ulster. Binnington criticizes
McGilligan as 'A Gael who betrayed the dead when he took th'
threaty, gave away Ulsther, an' took an oath of allegiance to an
English King' (p. 25). McGilligan, on the other hand, rages over
the equally questionable attitude of the Republican T.D.'s who,
after two years of bloodshed and four additional years of political
controversy, returned to parliament without having achieved
their object, to abolish the oath of allegiance to the British
Crown: 'An' when you and your gang found yous would lose th'
pay if yous didn't enther th' Dail, yous ran to th' registherin'
Officer, an' all Ireland heard your mouth smackin' th' Testament
takin' th' oath!' (p. 25). Binnington's answer parodies the dubious
reason that De Valera gave when he changed his own attitude:

A mottled lie! I'll take no oath, says I to th' officer attendin'; no oath,
sorra one, says I, or any words that might fashion a similarity to any oath
either, says I. You can take it or leave it, says he, for all I care, says he;
right, says I, so sign here, says he, an' fit yourself to take your seat (p. 25).

This quarrel reflects the stubbornness with which this question
is fought over even today, and implies O'Casey's criticism of the
fact that the politicians do not turn instead to the problems of our
time. For the present-day observer the details of the past are
becoming so confused that even O'Casey falls into an error:

according to his stage directions, the Binningtons' drawing-room is to be decorated with a portrait of Michael Collins (p. 13). Collins, however, was one of the signatories of the 1921 Treaty and was killed in an ambush in 1922 as the commander-in-chief of the forces of the Free State; the Republican Binnington would consider him a traitor and would never tolerate his portrait in his drawing-room.

Whereas the Prelude effectively integrates the more recent past of Ireland into present-day events, the historical perspective is again enlarged through the play-within-the-play. While O'Casey had already utilized the form of the prelude in *Oak Leaves and Lavender*, this is a new technical device in his work. Its introduction is skilfully motivated and directly related to the political theme. The young people of the town rehearse a historical play for the Tostal, set at the time of the rising of the United Irishmen. It is linked to the later struggle for independence by a reference to the well-known revolutionary ballad utilized by Lady Gregory for her equally well-known play: 'Gather the men together, Pat, by the risin' of th' moon, and we shall march' (p. 36). Yet the reference to the present, where the Tostal has become a new fight for independence, is equally clear:

We have stood quiet in our fields, on our hills, in our valleys; we have sat quiet in our homes, trusting the power that held us down would show justice; but we have found neither security nor peace in submission; so we must strike for the liberty we all need, the liberty we must have to live (pp. 34-35).

The actuality of such programmatic utterances is underlined by the fact that the role of the volunteer officer who speaks them is taken by Michael Binnington, the contemporary spokesman of the young people in their struggle for intellectual freedom. McGilligan, on the other hand, represents the older generation in their lack of comprehension for the continuing forces of the past: 'You won't resuscitate us be bringin' back shaddas o' men who done an' said things in a tormented time of long ago that have no bearin' on th' life we live today' (p. 32).

A third extension of the historical perspective is suggested in the song 'Lillibulero', introduced by Skerighan, the representative of Ulster, that becomes the object of a quarrel between Northern and Southern Irish. 'Lillibulero' was, of course, the battle song of the Protestant troops under William of Orange who, in 1690, defeated the Catholic troops under James II, finalizing the British dominion over Ireland and creating the conditions for the colonization of the North. Since then it has become the militant song of Protestant Ulster. It is used as a *leitmotiv* in Lady Gregory's historical play *The White Cockade* which, with a certain degree of poetic licence, recreates the decisive struggle for an independent Catholic Ireland. It is quite possible that O'Casey, as in the reference to *The Rising of the Moon*, is consciously referring to Lady Gregory. He uses the song, however, to show the absurdity of the political quarrel between Ulster and Eire. Skerighan is just as much a caricature as Binnington and McGilligan. He embodies the *cliché* of the fanatically industrious, uneducated, materialistic Ulsterman. His derogatory attitude to the South is entirely based on its economic backwardness; in this context he repeats some arguments that had been used before by Poges in *Purple Dust*. He is therefore incapable of understanding the aims of the Tostal. His idea of culture is limited to playing 'Lillibulero' on the piano. The ensuing quarrel shows that the political conflicts between North and South have become largely meaningless. When the sensible Mrs. McGilligan asks the others to explain the meaning of the song, nobody has an answer, which gives her a chance to unite them all under the Tostal flag:

Here we all are now, undher the Green Flag with its Golden Harp; th' harp that can play an Orange tune in Belfast an' a National tune in Cork, an' yet remains a thrue Harp; an' th' green grass that fattens th' cattle of Ulsther as well as it fattens the cattle on the plains of Meath, still remainin' th' thrue grass of our Irish pastures (p. 74).

A little later they even rehearse the graceful movements of a ceremonious reception without realizing that they are doing so to the tune of the song they pretend to hate so much. In other words, in the field of politics the conflicts can easily be overcome and even Skerighan can finally shout: 'tae hull with purtition' (p. 85). O'Casey here projects an understanding that in reality seems as remote as ever, for the extremists of both sides continue to oppose it.

*

The differences between the North and the Republic, however, are not merely political but also religious. This rift is much less easy to overcome, and in the play occasions a new flare-up of the quarrel. Skerighan deplores 'th' inseedious dumination of your

Church, on' th' waefu' intherfurence of your clergy in what ye
thry tae do' (p. 87). McGilligan, on the other hand, defends the
Catholic Church, attacking the beginnings of Protestantism in
England: 'St. Pether, an' afther him St. Pathrick, is our man, th'
Rock on which our Church stands. What's yours piled up on? On
a disgraceful, indecent attachment of a despicable English king for
a loose woman!' (p. 89). Such a controversy, calling forth on both
sides the familiar prejudices, cannot be settled with a mere appeal
to goodwill. O'Casey here falls back upon a device he had used
before, the figure of a *raisonneur* who pronounces the author's
opinion. Michael presents the concept of a God who is above
narrow-minded religious dissent: 'If God be what He ought to
be, must be, if He be God, then He has no time to bother about
the Anglican Thirty-nine Articles, the Westminster Confession,
or the Creed from the Council of Thrent' (p. 91). And with an
effective theatrical device he impresses both the people of
Doonavale and the audience:

[*Michael pulls the curtains aside, as the scene gets dark, and reveals a
sky filled with vast stars, one red, one green, one golden, with smaller
stars between them, all aglow with gentle but amazing animation in a
purple sky.*
MICHAEL. Our real roof, ladies and gentlemen, th' royal roof over
   Doonavale, over th' world – the stars. God's great nightcap. There
   they are – half th' host of them (p. 91).

He thereby purges the scene of all superficially comic effects, and
he is now in a position to pronounce, with deep seriousness, that
God on the one hand is 'more than He is even claimed to be . . .'
and on the other hand (like Father Ned!) 'but a shout in th' street'
(p. 92). This quotation from *Ulysses* is illustrated in a number of
phrases that shed some light on O'Casey's unorthodox views of
the deity:

It might be a shout for freedom, like th' shout of men on Bunker Hill;
shout of th' people for bread in th' streets, as in th' French Revolution;
or for th' world's ownership by th' people, as in th' Soviet Revolution;
or it might just be a drunken man, unsteadily meandhering his way
home, shouting out Verdi's [*he lilts the words*] 'Oh, Le-on-or-a' (p. 92).

In the play, this discussion cannot lead to any result, because
O'Casey's *dramatis personae* have not been designed as capable
of complete change of conviction. The scene is therefore cut short
with the appearance of Father Fillifogue who, characteristically,

is concerned with much more profane problems than the development of a new attitude to the deity. The audience, however, has been confronted with a religious vision that is taken up and concretized in many parts of the play.

The religious theme of *The Drums of Father Ned* has thus been outlined. A difference from the preceding play is that O'Casey is here less concerned with criticism of the existing religious order. Father Fillifogue, who is not even obeyed by his own organist, deserves nothing but pity. The bankruptcy of Catholicism is evident throughout, and Skerighan's militant Protestantism, in its impotence, is equally ridiculous. Instead, O'Casey develops a view of God which may appear naive to the academic theologian but certainly embodies more of the hopes of many people than the concept of a God controversially interpreted and squabbled over by hostile denominations. In Act I he suggests the idea of Christian socialism, just as he, to the end of his life, defended the idea that Christ had been 'a great communist'.[6] 'Our Blessed Lord often held the hammer an' He knew well the use of the sickle, but He also heard the rose of Sharon singin' her song, an' He saw the lilies of the field dancin' to the tune of a whistlin' wind, or doin' a floral minuet to a whisperin' one' (pp. 32-33). O'Casey's Christ is distinguished by two characteristics: he knows the work and the troubles of ordinary people, and he is devoted to joy and beauty as represented in song and dance. It is obvious that the accusation of atheism that was often directed at O'Casey can only derive from a narrow-minded religious parochialism. It would be much more appropriate to call him 'an intensely religious infidel',[7] who develops in *The Drums of Father Ned* his 'private theology' because 'none of our established ideologies or theologies have proved adequate to O'Casey's visionary and human concern.'[8]

The religious theme in this play is most clearly concretized in the figure of Father Ned. Critics have violently disagreed as to what Father Ned is supposed to mean: the scale ranges from the suggestion that he was a self-portrait of the ageing O'Casey to the claim that he was 'meant to be a portrait of the Deity Himself . . .'[9] Between these extremes, there lies a variety of further interpretations. Father Ned is seen as O'Casey's 'symbol of a good life . . .', as 'ein Anti-Bischof, ein Christus dessen Königreich von dieser Welt ist', as 'a kind of clerical Pan' or 'a cross between the cock in "Cock-a-doodle Dandy" and one or two good priests O'Casey has heard of but never met.'[10] On the one hand it is maintained that Father Ned 'must . . . be regarded as covering the best of Catholicism and Protestantism, the traditional authority of the one and the critical impetus of the other', on the other hand he appears as 'more an Irish demigod of joy, wisdom and mischief than a clergyman'.[11] The same critic probably came closest to the truth when he later maintained that Father Ned was 'the symbolic figure who unites what is best in Irish myth and history with what is best in Christianity.'[12]

O'Casey's models for this figure were more concrete than could be gathered from these quotations. In a letter[13] O'Casey names as the starting-point of *The Drums of Father Ned* two of those five priests to whom the play is dedicated. These five clergymen have in common that they opposed the authority of their bishops and had to endure personal disadvantages for this resistance. Among them is Dr. McDonald, lecturer in Maynooth, to whom O'Casey had dedicated *Inishfallen, Fare Thee Well* and whom he immortalized in the chapter 'Silence' of that volume. McDonald is one of those strange private saints of O'Casey's, the list headed by Shaw and George Jean Nathan, for whom his devotion never flagged. If O'Casey linked Father Ned to such a man, it is to be supposed that he was trying to create an ideal character who was to embody, like Father Boheroe, his vision of a 'good' priest. However, Father Ned is important beyond such concrete references.

O'Casey secures the symbolic ambiguity of his title character by a simple device: he does not appear on stage. Several contradictory descriptions indicate to the audience that Father Ned is a being with supernatural powers. Skerighan's account, in particular, is highly revealing, even though it is additionally confused as an indication of the fact that the Ulsterman has been involved in the excitements of the Tostal, i.e. the process of spiritual revival:

. . . fierce green eyes shinin' lak umeralds on fire in a white face thot was careerin' aboot though stayin' stull as an evenin' star, starin' up tae me frum doon in th' valley below . . . Aw'y, on' a wild flop of ruddy hair, flamin' lak a burnin' bush; one long white hond pointin' up, th' ither one pointin' doon, forbye th' sound of a clear voice sayin' naethin' on' meanin' all, all surrounded by a michty clerical collar round a neck I couldna see; all th' time, th' green eyes starin' doon at me frae th' top o' th' hill, on' up at me frae th' valley below that werena there (p. 64).

The religious associations ('burnin' bush'!) are especially noteworthy. This description is supplemented by a remark of the Man of the Musket, 'Father Ned's everywhere; he may be anywhere; he may be nowhere to a seeker who gets in his way' (pp. 67-68). This characterizes him as the embodiment of values that can be realized everywhere but are tangible only for those who willingly accept them. Father Fillifogue, for instance, attempts in vain throughout the play to meet Father Ned.

Whereas Father Ned is not visible to the audience, his presence is indicated by the sound of his drums. A '*very faint distant roll of drums*' can be heard at the end of the 'Prerumble' (p. 12); it indicates that the War of Independence has created the external conditions of existence for Father Ned, the chance of a spiritual liberation. Finally, his drums (and not Skerighan's martial drums from the North) conclude the events, indicating the victory of youth and liberation over reaction and convention. But Father Ned's existence is also discernible in his influence on the *dramatis personae* proper. While he has become a nightmare for Binnington, McGilligan and Father Fillifogue, the other inhabitants of the town concede him an unlimited authority. 'Father Ned says . . .' has become a recurrent figure of speech. Their actions, therefore, reflect the views of Father Ned. When they decorate the town, rehearse choral music or hoist the Tostal flag over the presbytery, they are acting under his orders. The Tostal as a whole is an expression of his views, and it is therefore equally symbolic.

Father Ned is characterized in particular by three important traits. Firstly, he is a *religious* figure, as indicated by his title and Skerighan's description. It has been stated correctly: 'Father Ned constitutes an obvious admission that the aim of O'Casey's dramatic world cannot be defined in social terms.'[14] O'Casey's vision of an ideal, life-determining authority is not complete without a transcendental dimension. Secondly, Father Ned supports the objects of the young people in their endeavours to establish a world filled with beauty and joy. Thirdly, he is associated with O'Casey's ideal figures from Irish mythology and history, especially with Angus the Young, the Celtic God of love and youth. The face of Angus, '*caught among the golden strings of his harp, a thin, poetic face, long black hair flowing behind his head . . .*' (p. 77) is represented on a shield painted for the Tostal, and he is accompanied by a bird coloured in green, red, black and gold, obviously symbolizing Ireland, Communism, the clergy and (gold) a synthesis of these elements.[15] Father Ned, in other words, is the most comprehensive ideal figure in O'Casey's works, embodying a combination (highly subjective no doubt) of what is best in Christianity, the pre-Christian Celtic tradition and youth's optimism for the future. The Tostal, inspired by him, represents in greater detail the values that O'Casey wishes to emphasize.

The Tostal is significant in several respects. On the one hand, it serves as a means of coming to terms with a past that until now has been largely ignored. As Nora explains: 'The things said be Ireland's old leaders are livin' still, and are needed as much today as when they were first spoken' (p. 32). Such a continuation of a living tradition is demonstrated when the young people rehearse the historical pageant. But the Tostal goes back even beyond this: as a festival of spring, youth triumphing over old age, it refers to Christian and pagan rites of resurrection. It is significant that these mythological references are most apparent in a play that presents O'Casey's vision of the *future*. The Tostal also symbolizes a new social order by abolishing prejudices of social caste. The preparations for the festival strengthen people's awareness of their common interests and weaken the social distinctions derived from the mere accident of birth and family. To the horror of the older people, the servant girl Bernadette can ask the 'Lady' Nora to help her bring in the coffee without insulting her at all (p. 84), and McGunty demonstrates to his employer McGilligan that in his free time he is no longer his subordinate (p. 70). Similarly, the young people liberate themselves from their dependence on the older generation. Michael and Nora will no longer permit their parents to select their spouses for them. Not only have they studied at the same college, but they have also lived in the same flat (p. 99). O'Casey, however, makes it clear that such an attitude requires a high degree of responsibility. Consequently, the two lovers are well aware of the transitoriness of the moment, and they hope: 'May our love pass quietly into companionship, for that is the one consummation of united life' (p. 83).

The Tostal further contributes to a reduction of political prejudices. When it is discovered that the shipload of timber that has arrived in the town's harbour is from Siberia, this is enough to rouse a mob headed by Father Fillifogue with the explicit purpose of burning the 'atheistical timber' (p. 95). But Michael, Nora and Tom, with Father Ned's authority, oppose such a senseless action: 'To burn it would be to burn th' homes of the people' (p. 96). Their demand for tolerance is based on their (and O'Casey's) religious views: 'Th' things of th' earth that God helps us to grow can't be bad, let them come from Catholic Italy, Protestant Sweden, or Communist Russia' (p. 97). This tendency is directly linked, too, to the abolition of literary censorship. Father Fillifogue orders a number of books of which he disapproves to

be removed from the municipal library and wants to see them
burned, but the library committee elected in the meantime (with
Father Ned as chairman) takes care that they are put back again.
In a larger sense, the Tostal liberates Doonavale from its dependence on the Catholic Church:

> You see . . . we're fed up bein' afraid our shaddas 'll tell what we're
> thinkin'. One fool, or a few, rules th' family life; rules th' school, rules the
> dance hall, rules th' library, rules th' ways of a man with a maid, rules th'
> mode of a girl's dhress, rules th' worker in fields and factory, rules th'
> choice of our politicians, rules th' very words we try to speak, so that
> everything said cheats th' truth; an Doonavale has become th' town of
> th' shut mouth (p. 98).

The Tostal also contributes to a cultural revival of the country.
The older generation is responsible for the fact that on the one
hand the Celtic cultural tradition has almost been forgotten,
while on the other hand foreign influences are warded off
because they allegedly endanger the native culture. The Celtic
cross of the Prelude stands '*a little crookedly, its symbol silent
now, and near forgotten*' (p. 1). Binnington and McGilligan are
not prepared to preserve the round tower of their town from
destruction although they would have had to do no more than
shake hands. Later, Binnington refers to the existence of the
native Irish tradition in language, music, dance and games
because this excuses him from facing up to foreign ideas. His
own contribution to Gaelic culture is limited to an occasional
reluctant donation (p. 20). Father Ned, on the other hand, confirms
'that through music, good books, an' good pictures, we may get
to know more about th' mysthery of life' (p. 19) and insists on
inviting an internationally famous string quartet. This conflict is
highlighted in the quarrel between Father Fillifogue and Mr.
Murray about the music of Mozart. The priest avers, 'There's
nothing apostolic or evangelical in the riddle-me-randy music of
Mozart', while the organist insists, 'When we worship Mozart,
we worship God . . .' (p. 43). In the optimistic context of *The
Drums of Father Ned* there is never any doubt that the latter view
will prevail. Another example of the Tostal's contribution to a
spiritual revival is the moment when McGunty, after long and
tedious attempts, succeeds in playing a tune on the cornet. When
Murray calls this 'A miracle, gentlemen!' (p. 80), he is totally
justified in the context of this play, because such a 'miracle' reveals
the God of Father Ned whose manifestations are beauty and joy.
The numerous literary quotations, too, indicate that culture and

everyday life have become mutually interdependent again. Such quotations, for instance from Tennyson's 'Locksley Hall' (p. 82), *Twelfth Night* (p. 89), *Ulysses* (p. 92), Yeats's 'The Lake Isle of Innisfree' (p. 104) or Blake's preface to *Milton* (p. 101), are remarkably frequent. The oblique reference to Eliot's 'The Hollow Men', on the other hand, 'Here's the whole town carrying a question to be answered, not with a whimper, but with a bang!' (p. 95) is ironical because this play's belief in the future contrasts sharply with the pessimism of Eliot's poem.

The greatest achievement of the Tostal is that it reinstates the joy of existence as the basic attitude for the people of Doonavale. The chorus of the Tostal song runs:

> Hurrah for the Tostal O,
> That tempts us from our sleeping O,
> When Erin sings and laughs and shouts,
> Instead of always weeping O! (p. 38).

And the Tostal poster, significantly placed '*Half over the picture of the Pope*', claims: 'WE *were* DEAD and *are* ALIVE AGAIN!' (p. 47). The town is decorated with flags and flowers, the young people, in contrast to the Binningtons and McGilligans, gracefully master the movements and gestures of courteousness (p. 75) and dare to admit their love in public. Under such conditions, the possibility of exile becomes finally irrelevant, and O'Casey's standard formula for the motif of exile is available to a different meaning: 'Lasses an' lads, it's time to go, for more life, more laughter; a sturdier spirit and a stronger heart. Father Ned is on the march!' (p. 102).

In *The Drums of Father Ned* O'Casey develops an image of Ireland and of human society in general that is at present bound to remain utopian. It is, however, a moving document of his faith in life, coming as it does almost at the end of his career after an existence as full of crises, problems and catastrophes as any. His attitude is reflected in the words he wrote in 1956, at the time when he must also have been working on *The Drums of Father Ned*: 'I am not waiting for Godot to bring me life; I am out after life myself, even at the age I've reached.'[16]

# PART V

# Bitterness and Reconciliation

Ireland is my true and only love.
(O'Casey in his last interview)

# 24. PREFATORY

When O'Casey published his last three plays,[1] he was eighty-one years old. It is remarkable that his creative vitality had remained undiminished until *The Drums of Father Ned*; it is not surprising that after this play it lost some of its strength. During the last years of his life, as can be seen from *Sunset and Evening Star*[2] as well as from his later letters and interviews, he became more and more obsessed with the situation of present-day Ireland. *Behind the Green Curtains*, *Figuro in the Night* and *The Moon Shines on Kylenamoe* present the dramatist's confrontation with his native country in dramatic terms. The personal element in these plays is much more explicit than in his previous phase; it replaces the high degree of universality that can be found in most of his works up to *The Drums of Father Ned*. It is, for instance, impossible to evaluate Chatastray's timidity in *Behind the Green Curtains* unless it is seen against the background of the dramatist's own attitude, his decision for an insecure but independent life in exile. In these plays it is essential, in other words, to be constantly aware of the author's own position which, by implication, is present throughout.

*Behind the Green Curtains* paints with great bitterness the picture of an Ireland dominated by the Catholic Church, characterized by psychological terror and the lack of any degree of intellectual independence, where people have only the choice between the lie as the principle of their existence and the flight into exile. *Figuro in the Night* adds derision to this pessimistic picture, contrasting the situation of Ireland with a utopian vision of brimming life. Finally, in *The Moon Shines on Kylenamoe* the motif of reconciliation reaches across the differences between the English and the Irish which at first had seemed utter and absolute, and suggests a higher degree of understanding for his native land on the part of the dramatist.

These plays have received little attention either from critics[3] or from the theatre. As the final phase of a remarkable dramatic output, however, they deserve the same careful analysis as

O'Casey's earlier plays. Detailed individual interpretations will form a more solid basis for an evaluation of their dramatic quality.

# 25.  BEHIND THE GREEN CURTAINS

*Behind the Green Curtains* was the first play since *Red Roses for Me* and *Hall of Healing* in which O'Casey used a Dublin setting; this time, however, it was not the city which had formed the scenario for the first half of his own life but the present-day Dublin as it presented itself to O'Casey in his remote Devonshire observation post. (The imaginary town Ballybeedhust where Chatastray lives is a prototype of the more fashionable suburbs of Dublin and is so closely connected with the city that one can even observe the demonstration from there). The time of the play immediately precedes the time when it was written, as can be gathered from the protest march against the trial of Cardinal Mindszenty (1956) and from the funeral of Lionel Robartes, obviously a reference to Lennox Robinson who had died in 1958. Additional references to the Dublin of the fifties are so explicit, too, that, in contrast to *The Plough and the Stars*, *Red Roses for Me* or *Hall of Healing*, it would be difficult indeed to transfer this play into another time or region. It is not the object of the present analysis to decipher those numerous allusions to persons and events of local interest which seem to make the play into a *pièce à clef*. Nor is it intended to weigh O'Casey's accusations against the Catholic Church (although some of them may appear less absurd when it is remembered that at this time it was still officially considered a mortal sin for a Catholic to study at Trinity College). The present analysis will concentrate on the author's theme, on the technique employed to shape his material into a drama and on the extent of his success in overcoming the limits of a quickly faded topicality.

The theme of the play is the timidity of the Dublin intellectuals when confronted with the Catholic Church's authority and abuse of power. This attitude finds its symbolic expression in the skilfully chosen title. Behind the closed curtains in Senator Chatastray's house the dramatist McGeera, the poet Horawn, the journalist McGeelish and the Abbey actor Coneen dare to speak their minds. Here they have decided to oppose the Catholic hierarchy's explicit command and to attend the burial service for Robartes which is to take place in a Protestant church. Here they also resolve not to let themselves be forced to join in the Mindszenty demonstration which is being turned into a forum for anti-communist propaganda. In the open daylight, however, and under the ever-present eyes of self-righteous informers, they soon forget their resolutions. In Act I[1] they hesitate long enough before entering the church until the Archbishop's final ban arrives, and then do not even dare to follow the hearse to the grave, although Robartes was a universally respected man. In Act II they are tracked down even behind the protecting green curtains and are finally too timid to oppose the open terror of a Catholic lay organisation when Chatastray's servant maid, and then the Senator himself, are kidnapped because of their allegedly immoral relationship. In Act III they then appear in sack-cloth to attend the demonstration.

With a harshness reminiscent of *Cock-a-doodle Dandy* and *The Bishop's Bonfire*, O'Casey here criticizes the psychological terror which, according to his views, was exerted by the Catholic Church, sometimes (as in Father Domineer's attack on the Foreman and the stoning of Loreleen) developing into straightforward physical terror.[2] He exceeds the bitterness of his earlier plays, for it is hardly mitigated here by comic scenes. The only section to carry any comic elements is the introductory scene with the two women who cannot keep their teetotaling pledge and mistake a portrait of Parnell – of all people – for a saint's picture. For the rest of the play, the squabbling of the intellectuals, however comical in itself, in no way alleviates the painful limitations of their situation in life, and even their potentially comic fear of the hierarchy is soon shown to have a very realistic foundation indeed. The only comic effect O'Casey occasionally achieves is by inter-weaving his dialogue with quotations and literary allusions, most of them quite irrelevant and merely designed to provide the educated reader with the satisfaction of recognizing familiar phrases. The heading of Act I, 'The Jittering Gate', for instance, refers to Lord Dunsany's play *The Glittering Gate* (Abbey Theatre, 1909), Coneen prepares for his role as 'Barney O Hay' (p. 28) in O'Casey's own *Time to Go*, Beoman calls Chatastray, echoing Robert Burns, a 'Wee, sleekit, cow'rin, tim'rous beastie' and ridicules the 'boys of the cold brigade' (p. 81).

As in many of his plays, the characters in *Behind the Green Curtains* embody several possible reactions to a given situation, here the menace to intellectual independence by the Catholic Church. This device makes for clearly distinguishable grades of moral quality, and the play as a whole presents an equally clear system of values. The most objectionable among the characters is Kornavaun, journalist for the *Catholic Buzzer*, a tale-bearer and informer for the higher clergy, who has become the terror of the intellectuals. As soon as they prepare for a 'daring' action, they mention his name ('I bet Kornavaun has an eye on us from some corner or other' [p. 19], 'I hope Kornavaun hasn't got wind of us bein' here together' [p. 35]), thus reducing their willingness to act. It is he who is responsible when Chatastray is beaten up and Noneen tied for a night to a lamp-post; he occasions the strike in Chatastray's factory when a Protestant engineer plans to marry a Catholic worker, and he sees to it that the authors of censored books are isolated socially too (p. 36). His actions do not proceed only from religious fanaticism: he also satisfies his personal desire for revenge towards Noneen who had previously sent him from the house when he had suggested that she had an immoral relationship with Chatastray. This personal motive serves to confirm one's disparagement of the attitude of religious intolerance he embodies. His behaviour shows the very real threat that emanates from this intolerance. Social isolation, financial boycott and even physical force can be the consequence when 'Everything a man, anyway prominent, says if he dares to have a thought of his own, is given a slant by this *Catholic Buzzer* to make it appear to be sympathetic to th' Reds or giving hope and courage to anti-clerical feeling' (p. 36). If this cannot be taken as an excuse for the intellectuals' timidity, it can at least serve to explain it. The character who comes closest to Kornavaun is McGeelish, who during Chatastray's absence sniffs through his papers. All the others, with their bickerings and their personal vanity, are equally unsympathetic, but their chief characteristic is their decision to take the path of least resistance and their refusal to defend what they recognise as morally right. Their behaviour is so reprehensible only because they are considered as the 'leaders of Ireland's thought' (p. 45) and utterly fail in this role.

The opposite position to Kornavaun is taken up by Beoman, Chatastray's chief engineer. As a dedicated 'red' he is a successor to Red Jim, Ayamonn, O'Killigain and Drishogue. Like these, he speaks his mind without reservation and behaves accordingly; he is the only one to oppose the semi-fascistical terror-squad. His interest in 'higher values' manifests itself in the fact that his boss presents him with post-card reproductions of famous paintings – a trait almost pathetic in its naivety which, in an earlier O'Casey play, would have made him the object of ridicule rather than sympathy. Beoman, in his entirely incredible idealism, is not a fit opponent for Kornavaun. When even he, towards the end, sees no other way except emigration to England, he confirms the author's deep pessimism with regard to the situation in his native country.

The character most closely to approach Beoman's attitude is Noneen, who refuses to ask the Bishop's pardon for having worked in the house of an unmarried man, and who prefers to go into exile. Reena finds it much harder to take this decision. She tries to reconcile her love of truth with her Catholic faith. When she has taken part in the banned funeral, she accepts the fact that she will no longer be allowed to publish her short stories, and sets about earning her living as a nurse. She even permits herself to have low organisational duties imposed on her by the Legion of Mary as a compensation for her 'offence'. Even after the kidnapping of Noneen, against which she, with Beoman, is the only protester, she still hopes to find a compromise between the demands of the Church and the determinants of her own existence. She attempts to win over Chatastray for a life in intellectual independence in Ireland itself, by symbolically trying to open his curtains. Only when he fails her, does she join Beoman on his way into emigration. She thus follows those numerous O'Caseyan women who overcome the petty scruples of men and show them, if often without success, a path into the future. Her credibility as a living character is, however, undermined by the fact that she becomes the mouth-piece of O'Casey's 'message'. She speaks in O'Caseyan epigrams like 'It isn't good to live an' move be candle-light when th' sun is out' (p. 62), '. . . when you shut out th' people, you are shutting out God' (p. 63) and 'As long as you're alive, you'll have to bear being touched by th' world you live in' (p. 60). And she also voices his criticism of contemporary Ireland, which is the theme of the play anyway and would be explicit enough without such additional emphasis:

We're all frightened – those in th' North as well as us in th' South; th' men who took Noneen an' you away with them were frightened of faith, and of anyone setting himself apart from th' others an' themselves; an' you an' your friends frightened of fighting for yourselves, or for anything disliked by th' clergy and th' foggy explosion of townsfolk talk . . . We are a huddled nation frightened undher th' hood of fear. (p. 59).

The central figure of the play is Chatastray to whom these words are addressed. He takes up a middle position between Beoman, Noneen and Reena on the one hand, Kornavaun, McGeelish and the intellectuals on the other, and he vacillates between the attitudes embodied in these two groups. When he finally copies the submission of the other intellectuals, this becomes the ultimate expression of the author's pessimism. Chatastray's character can be gathered, as often in O'Casey, from the stage setting; his study, which is described quite carefully, reflects his character-traits. It is *'safely furnished'* and contains some typical attributes of a conformist intellectual in Ireland: Paul Henry paintings of the West of Ireland, a picture of a Saint, an Abbey-poster and books in Gaelic (which incidentally he has never read). His own photograph decorating his desk points to his self-love; next to this is a vase from which the O'Caseyan symbol of life, the flowers are missing. The two coloured glass-windows are interpreted in the play itself: 'A clock an' a cross . . . servin' God an' man . . . His lookin'll wear away th' clock before it'll wear away th' cross' (p. 32). Even more important are the green curtains behind which he retires to read Ernest Renan's 'heretical' *Vie de Jésus*, which he hides in a drawer, or to exchange ideas with the other intellectuals – ideas for which he refuses to stand up outside this room.

For all this, Chatastray is not a despicable character. Not only has he manifold interests transcending his sphere as an industrialist, but he also encourages and supports several artists. He endeavours to foster his maid's understanding for music, and he contributes to his engineer's interest in painting. Moreover, he looks after Noneen and even protects her from her own drunken father. What he lacks is summarized by Reena in one word: 'Guts!' (p. 66). He does not dare to oppose an authority that he despises. The kidnapping of Noneen and himself, both 'punishments' for an offence that they have not committed, shocks him deeply, as can again be deduced from the appearance of his study: '. . . *it has lost its tidiness and sense of order*' (p. 55). But even so clear a demonstration of injustice cannot relieve him of his careful conformism: '*Although it is early daytime, the Green Curtains are still drawn* . . .' (p. 55). Here is the first suggestion of his final decision when, despite Reena's persuasions, he chooses intellectual bondage and takes part in the demonstration. The moment when Reena believes herself to have won him over to her side and is triumphantly watching the demonstration from the window, is the dramatic climax and the most convincing point in the whole play:

There they go, th' lot o' them, marching! Go on, go on; you go [*gesturing to the right*] that way to th' right; we go this way [*gesturing with her hand*] to th' left. [*Chatastray has slid the sash around his shoulder, and slides slowly towards the door, picking up the yellow and white rosette from the table. He opens the door softly, and goes out, leaving the door open behind him. She stretches an arm backward with a hand extended.*] Here, come here, Dennis, an' let's both stand hand in hand silently defying them as they all go marching by! [*After a pause.*] Come on, Dennis; look at them, and have the laugh of your life! [*She stays looking out for a moment, then sensing something wrong, wheels around, and sees that Dennis has gone. She notices that the sash and rosette are gone too. She runs to the door and calls out. At the door.*] Dennis, Dennis! [*There is no answer. She hurries to the window, and looks out on to the street below.*] Oh, there he goes, sash an' all on him, rushing along to overtake his frightened friends. [*She leaves the window and comes into the room.*] My Dennis is gone from me; poor frightened fool! (pp. 79-80)

This scene, in its effect, is not unlike Pegeen Mike's concluding words in the *Playboy of the Western World*: 'Oh, my grief, I've lost him surely. I've lost the only Playboy of the Western World'.[3] The difference is that the roles have been exchanged, Reena having gained an independence that Chatastray, like Pegeen, fails to attain.

Despite such incidental parallels, *Behind the Green Curtains* is, however, entirely different from Synge's masterpiece. The difference lies in the contrast between town and country, complexity and simplicity, civilization and naturalness, but it is even more a question of dramatic quality. In *Behind the Green Curtains*, Chatastray is the only character to achieve something of the dramatic vitality that is typical of even the minor figures in Synge. But even if the purpose of the play is seen primarily as a portrayal of Chatastray, this remains O'Casey's weakest play, and it has been accused not unjustly of 'aesthetic and imaginative falsity'.[4] Critical objections to the play can be summarized in the following four points.

First, the dramatic concentration on Chatastray as the only convincing character is only possible if one disregards the whole of Act I. The larger part of this Act consists of the tiresome rather than funny chatter of Angela and Lizzie, plus a shorter comic scene between Beoman and Basawn (who, like Angela and Lizzie, disappears for the rest of the play). Except for a few references to the funeral of Robartes and the demonstration, these scenes have no expository function (consequently Act II has to begin with a typical exposition-scene). They look like the remnants of another play that O'Casey did not complete. Even the latter part of the Act does not underline Chatastray's central position, and fails to emphasize the fact that he, too, accepts the Archbishop's verdict. In reality, *Behind the Green Curtains* is a two-act play and should be produced as such.

Secondly, the play contains a number of non-sequiturs which impair its credibility. It is hardly to be believed that Reena, as a punishment for her disobedience, should be given the important task of persuading the intellectuals to take part in the demonstration, just as it is less than credible that Chatastray, at thirty-five and unreliable as he is, should be a Senator. If minor offences such as those of Chatastray and Noneen lead to acts of physical terror, it is difficult to accept that Beoman should be permitted with impunity to confess himself a Communist. If anti-Communism is as rampant as it is depicted to be in this play, it would have been impossible for Chatastray to employ Beoman as a managing engineer. The discovery of 'naughty' photographs in Chatastray's desk remains a blind motif; the Senator is not depicted as a character who would own such pictures, and even less as someone who would fail to keep them under lock and key. Reena's entrance at the beginning of Act III and her immediate attempt to tidy up Chatastray's room are as unmotivated as is her precipitate decision for Beoman; and her love-scene with the latter is hardly compatible with her character, following as it does immediately on her wooing of Chatastray. In general, the play suffers from an inadequate handling of the characters' entrances and exits. This is one of the instances that permit one to gauge O'Casey's diminished powers of creation. In his previous plays such technical points had always been handled with exceptional skill.

It might be argued that *Behind the Green Curtains* is not a realistic work and that therefore the criteria of credibility do not apply. But this is precisely the basis for the third objection to the play. *Behind the Green Curtains* is, indeed, closer to stage realism than most of O'Casey's plays since *The Silver Tassie*. There are, it is true, certain moments where O'Casey deviates from the depiction of reality, as in the stage direction: '*A peal of thunder is heard, a slow rumble, with a sullen threat in it. They suddenly become stiff and still; the rumble gradually developing into, or changing into, the doorbell ringing clear and loud and demanding*' (p. 38). In general, however, O'Casey starts off with the premises of stage realism, striving for a logical explanation of events, modelling his dialogue on every-day speech and developing his symbols from a realistic basis. The play's non-sequiturs, therefore, are to be seen as the result of a lack of coordination rather than as a conscious deviation from the depiction of reality. It is difficult, too, to reconcile the satirical elements with the intention to portray reality. The figures of Kornavaun, McGeelish, McGeera, Horawn and Conneen have been reduced to a few negative traits which expose them to the spectator's criticism. On the one hand, O'Casey strives for realistic presentation to point up the (in his view) intolerable situation in Ireland, on the other hand he departs from such a representation to render his criticism more effective. Such a lack of unity in his stylistic devices is a far remove from his successful counterpointing of various moods and modes in his previous phase.

The fourth objection concerns the theme of the play. Even if one does not intend to reject O'Casey's attacks on the Catholic Church or to criticize his preference for Communism, it must be pointed out that this play does not depict any real confrontation of ideas. At the centre of the action is the question whether the intellectuals should join the demonstration or not. No reasons are given why they secretly rebel against it. None of them has any sympathies for Communism, they all see themselves as faithful members of their Church. The only argument against their participation is voiced by Horawn:

Th' writer's place is th' cool contentment of quiet, in a corner where no voice comes; no car drives by; no child's laugh disturbs; no touch from a woman to ruffle th' stillness of thought; only birdsong and th' gentle ripple of a rose on its own bush (p. 42).

As the stylistic exaggerations show, this is clearly intended ironically (O'Casey always opposed any attempts to separate 'art' and 'life'). Therefore it cannot explain why, according to the values of this play, participation in the march should be so objectionable. Perhaps the funeral of Robartes, hinted at in Act I, would have been a more suitable instance to point up the confrontation between the intellectual élite and the Church establishment. A similar criticism has to be voiced against the more personal conflict of Chatastray. Again, his tortuous decision to stay in Ireland and to subject himself to the authority of the Church is not developed through a confrontation of intellectual values. All the arguments he can marshal for his decision are summarized in the one sentence: '. . . this place is all I ever knew, an' it will be hard to break away from it' (p. 78). This may be quite sufficient for the average Irishman, but it is not enough for a play as a focal point of opposing ideas. *Behind the Green Curtains* lacks the natural conviction of O'Casey's early plays which derived a universal concern from the depiction of private life histories; but it equally lacks the universality of the later plays which use arbitrarily chosen examples to depict problems of general relevance.

# 26. FIGURO IN THE NIGHT

After the thematic diversity of the preceding plays, which was still apparent even in *Behind the Green Curtains*, O'Casey's deliberate limitation of *Figuro in the Night* to a single individual theme is surprising. The play deals satirically with the overwhelming prudishness with respect to perfectly natural instincts which, according to O'Casey, was characteristic of the Ireland of his time. The passages preceding the actual play in the printed edition (pp. 85-88) serve as a preparation for the play's limitations. The laboured subtitle (*In Two Scenes eloquently and humorously related, but vilely and maliciously inspired and created by dangerous and unseemly influences emanating from, and begotten in, the pernicious confines of atheistic and communistic lands*) and the double dedication (rather painfully named a 'Deadication') show that the author was not any longer capable of subordinating his tendency for comic variation and repetition to the requirements of the dramatic form. His subsequent quotations from the *Irish Press* make it clear that his criticism is aimed specifically at Ireland; however they do not explain why he transfers the situation in remote parishes to the capital. Finally, the lack of a list of *dramatis personae* confirms the fact that O'Casey was not interested in his figures as characters but only as representatives of certain opinions. *Figuro in the Night* has less dramatic qualities than any other play of O'Casey's; its lack of actuality and dramatic conflict is not compensated for by effective comedy or by the intensity of its ideas. This negative view of the play stands in contrast to a number of more favourable evaluations[1] and will have to be justified in some detail.

*Figuro in the Night* consists of two parts of approximately equal length. Both are set in a suburban street in Dublin, where the recent Irish past is visually present: A Celtic cross commemorates the dead of the War of Independence, an obelisk the victims of World War I. In Part I, the street is dark and empty. Behind the only window that is lit, a Girl waits for the return of the young man who promised her 'a bunch of blue ribbons' (p. 91), the popular symbol of fidelity. The street is also the scene of the meeting of an Old Woman, her face '*like a face that has been*

300

*fondled by the hand of death'* (p. 91), and a man who is also approaching death. They are a clear prefiguration of the Young Girl's future life. Many years ago, the Old Man gave the Woman those 'blue ribbons', but soon changed his mind, and both are now at the end of a useless life spent in loneliness and sterility. They have conformed to those conventions that designate any sexual relationship as sinful and praise continence as an attitude pleasing to God. Now, when it is too late, the Old Woman for a moment rebels against such an attitude and even welcomes the Fall as the moment when humanity was liberated from the passivity of Paradise into a life of autonomous responsibility:

The fruit from the tree of knowledge of good and evil set us free from coddling, and gave us the pain and the power to do our own thinking, walk on our own feet; clap our own hands at what ourselves had done. The lush laziness of the garden lovely was sappin' our life away (p. 100).

But she soon repents her straying from the prescribed path of virtue: 'My God, what was I sayin' a minute ago! Dhreamin' I was – a bad, bad dhream!' (p. 103).

Part I thus depicts the present-day situation in Ireland, as O'Casey saw it. Despite its comic elements, it gives a depressing image of human bondage that allows no room for the O'Caseyan values of life, joy, beauty, love, hope. In part, such criticism may have been justified. O'Casey, however, forgoes the effectiveness of his criticism when he abuses the satirist's freedom to simplify and exaggerate. Satire loses its thrust if it is no longer related to reality. His nonsense-dialogues, interpolated here as in previous works, have lost their function as justifiable comic relief and appear as the dramatist's attempt to extend his play to standard length.

The second part stands in sharp contrast to the first. A full moon illuminates the street, every window is lit, and the trees are now in full leaf and bear multi-coloured fruit. One can hear birds singing, cocks crowing and, in the distance, the lowing of contented cattle. *'Everything seems wonderful to eyes that see and ears that hear'* (p. 104). The ensuing dialogues disclose the reasons for the change into this O'Caseyan paradise which emanates joy, peace and the affirmation of life and is shot through with fertility symbols. Two Old Men, along with a Blind and a Deaf person as representatives of the Irish press, and eventually a Young Man, discuss the events that are happening in O'Connell Street. Inexplicably, a statue (the Figuro of the title), resembling the

*Manneken piss* in Brussels, has appeared there. It has become the cause of unheard-of scenes: full of wonder, the women are gathering in their thousands around the figure. O'Casey exhausts the comic potential of this situation. The girls tackle every man who happens to be near enough: 'Till I battled them down, getting rid of their tearing grips, I thought I'd lose me decent dangling accessory, so I did!' (p. 107). The police are powerless and have retired to the roofs, appealing to the women to form a queue. The Legion of Mary, on this as on all occasions, insist on their right to stand at the front. The women's guardian angels find themselves in extreme difficulty: '. . . thousands of Guardian Angels, beset with sudden anxiety, rushing woefully hitherwards and thither-wards searching for missing souls, chanting frantically, Where, oh where is me wandering child tonight!' (p. 111). This series of comic inventions, ultimately running into a complicated and fantastic story of the policeman who got mixed up with a girl, is the most successful part of *Figuro in the Night*.

O'Casey's ensuing attempt to render the significance of the events explicit once more is much less effective. It is obvious anyway that he was presenting the disastrous consequences of the repression of sexual instincts and that he was pleading for a liberation from such an unnatural situation. His criticism of Ireland is obvious enough too in his report of the women who congregate to admire the naked figure. Platitudinous remarks like 'Why did God make girls as they are and laddies as they are, if He didn't want them to get together – Answer me that!' (p. 116) add nothing new to this criticism. O'Casey here violates one of the principles of satire, namely that the interpretation be left to the reader. The appearance of the Birdlike Lad who, despite his green cap, resembles a crow, has a similar effect. It is to be supposed that O'Casey, who liked to see himself as a 'green crow' and published a book under this title, is here adding a fantastical self-portrait to the fantastical events. Twice before, the sound of crows had interrupted the dialogue. In Part I a crow had 'laughed' at the old people's submission to their parents' commands which prevented them from having contact with the other sex. In Part II the noise of a whole flock of crows, interpreted by the Old Man as 'evil things flitting about' (p. 111), accompanies the Young Man's rebellion against the identification of chastity with virtue and the will of God. The Birdlike Lad, as the author's representative, however, contributes little to the effectiveness of the play. His only function is to relate that the Figuro has also appeared in Cork, Limerick, Sligo and Galway and that even the North (now paradoxically the last bastion of Irish virtue) will not be spared. This extension to the whole of Ireland might also have been left to the imagination of the audience. On the other hand, the final scene in which the Young Man returns with his 'bunch of blue ribbons' to the waiting girl, in its combination of dancing, singing and visual fascination forms an effective conclusion to the events.

As was to be expected, O'Casey has been criticized for his attitude in this play: '. . . Ireland's difficulty has been Mr. O'Casey's opportunity, in the sense that it has afforded him still another outlet for an obsession with sex, every bit as inordinate in its own way as that "Ferocious Chastity" which it purports to condemn.'[2] Such reproaches have been countered by the observation that O'Casey was not propagating sexuality for its own sake but as part of his larger concept of love.[3] This statement is certainly true as far as O'Casey's personal attitude is concerned, and it can be confirmed by a glance at his earlier plays; yet in *Figuro in the Night* it is nowhere made clear that sexuality is only one aspect of the complex relationship of one human being with another. It is, therefore, difficult to disagree with those critics who see this play, in comparison with the complexity of his earlier works, as an all-too-narrow segment of his ideas.

# 27. THE MOON SHINES ON KYLENAMOE

We do not know exactly when *The Moon Shines on Kylenamoe* was written. It is little more than a speculation to regard this short play (as is suggested by its final position in the volume *Behind the Green Curtains*) as the last among O'Casey's later plays. Such a speculation is however all the more tempting because this small work takes up themes and motifs that had accompanied O'Casey throughout his life, and above all because it shows a more conciliatory attitude than do the preceding plays. As the conclusion of a life's work dominated by conflicts and controversies, it could thus take on a symbolic quality far transcending its dramatic merits.

The initial stage direction, resembling the opening of a novella, establishes the tone of harmony that prevails throughout the play:

*Just above the distant green mountains, the pale moon is shining, giving a quiet silence to the valley of Kylenamoe in the County of Melloe. It is just on midnight and here within the fifteen or so houses forming the village in the valley, all life is sleeping, the moon housing all the quiet homes there within a gentle lullaby light. Even the lover and his lass, if such there ever be on road, boreen, or field-path, in the village of Kylenamoe, had gone away from active service, and no further life would come to light till the sun of a new morning rose again – or, so it seemed* (p. 125).

Later, the same stage direction takes up a favourite idea of the younger O'Casey: to set a play in a railway milieu. Ever since he had worked on the tracks of the Great Northern Railway the surroundings had fascinated him, and even at the time of *Nannie's Night Out* and *The Plough and the Stars* he planned to use them in a play.[1] His suggested titles, *The Signal Light* or *The Red and the Green*, prefigure the use of the signal lantern as an important piece of scenery in *The Moon Shines on Kylenamoe*. In *Red Roses for Me* where, during the first two acts, one can see through the window '*the top of a railway signal, with transverse arms, showing green and red lights*', this idea was first put into practice. In *The Moon Shines on Kylenamoe* the almost naively affectionate description of the signal suggests that O'Casey was here giving rein to his personal reminiscences. Yet the setting of the play, a small Irish country railway-station, was not simply occasioned by the author's memories. It also serves as a meeting-place of two worlds which in O'Casey's works are juxtaposed again and again: *The Moon Shines on Kylenamoe* deals once more with the conflict between England and Ireland or, to be more explicit, the contrast between the English and the Irish mentality.

All the aspects of the play are subject to this theme. O'Casey, for instance, dispenses with a detailed characterization of his figures and, instead, presents them as 'the Englishman' and 'the Irishman', stressing their typial character-traits. *The Moon Shines on Kylenamoe* differs in three respects from O'Casey's other plays that deal with the same theme (especially *The Plough and the Stars*, *Purple Dust* and *Oak Leaves and Lavender*): first, O'Casey shows no preference for either of the two sides; secondly, he limits the conflicts strictly to the realm of the comic; thirdly, this enables him to conclude his play with a touch of reconciliation, if not of complete harmony.

The initial situation is simple. One evening, the British diplomat Lord Leslieson of Ottery St. Oswald arrives at the lonely station of Kylenamoe where a traveller hardly ever alights. He carries important dispatches for the British Prime Minister who is spending his holidays in the vicinity. Lord Leslieson, who has attempted to fortify his person against the hostile climate of this strange land with an array of various pieces of clothing, is from the beginning a comic figure, although he is unaware of this: '*He is sure of himself, utterly unconscious of his comic aspect; confident of his position and importance, and quite at his ease as the men of his place in society usually are*' (p. 129).

His ideas of Ireland consist of a few questionable clichés. He has heard of 'the Irish way of joking' (p. 130) and considers a ride in a creel-car with the tourist's superficial enthusiasm as 'Real Irish' (p. 156). Apart from this, Ireland appears to him as 'a dark and a lonesome land' (p. 150), where nothing is to be expected except 'Deceit and lies' (p. 149). Even his despair is shot through with a certain satisfaction as his prejudices are confirmed: 'Oh, what a stupid people, what a barbarous country' (p. 146); and his misconceptions are so deeply rooted that he finds proof of them wherever he goes. Ireland appears to him 'A country of desolation, of aimless chatter, dirt, and disease' (p. 154), and the image he invents himself appears to him as a happy inspiration: 'The Red

Light – it shines over all this country!' (p. 154). Such assumptions disqualify him for adapting himself to existing conditions. He expects the world to be like England: it is unthinkable that a railway-station should not be linked to a town where one can order a taxi, make telephone calls in the middle of the night or complain to the station-master; and it is equally impossible for him to imagine that courting couples going for a walk should not be considered a matter of course. He is so convinced of the importance of his mission that he brooks no other topic of conversation except his own troubles and difficulties. His arrogance towards the Irish is imprinted in every sentence that he speaks. The thin shell of civility in which he at first attempts to shelter himself from contact with the 'common people' is soon shattered when he does not achieve his end: the initial address 'gentlemen' (pp. 129-132) is soon exchanged for the condescending 'friends' (p. 133) or 'My good man' (p. 134) and eventually for the more explicit 'fool' (p. 135). His behaviour is occasioned, in part, by a basic insecurity and by his fear of being made a laughing-stock in the press. For that reason he counters every well-meant suggestion with distrust and even suspects an immoral suggestion when it is proposed that 'Jinnie' should take him to his goal, until he finds out that Jinnie is a donkey. He is incapable of adapting himself to an unexpected situation. When Kylenamoe, quite surprisingly, refuses to adapt itself to him, he is utterly confused, and his pride and stiffness finally turn into an almost touching helplessness.

This portrait of an English upper-class traveller, for all its overstatements probably not entirely incorrect, is reminiscent of the two pseudo-aristocrats in *Purple Dust*. In contrast to the earlier play, however, in *The Moon Shines on Kylenamoe* the ridiculous Englishman is confronted on the same comic level with equally ridiculous Irishmen. These, represented by the Guard, the railway-worker Sean Tomasheen, the engine driver Andy O'Hurrie and the old man Corny Conroy, are characterized by a similar array of weaknesses as Lord Leslieson. Sean's unreal hope that one day someone from the great world will visit Kylenamoe is an example of Irish wishful thinking, because this Kylenamoe, the 'wood of the cows', really has been forgotten by the world. It possesses no car, the telephone is inaccessible at night, fourteen of the thirty houses are empty and most of the people who still live here are over seventy years old. The appearance here of a stranger is bound to create a sensation that overshadows everything else. The train has arrived late anyway, and is left for half an

hour[2] until the passengers' revolt finally recalls the officials to
their duty. While their feeling of responsibility is underdeveloped,
their inclination to superstition is all the greater. They immediately
take Lord Leslieson for 'a sinisther figure' (p. 128) and try to
divert his attention, like the Cock's in *Cock-a-doodle Dandy*, by
attempting to ignore him.

The ensuing discussion displays, in comic exaggeration, a
number of Irish weaknesses as O'Casey saw them. With a rhetorical exuberance entirely unsuited to the issue, and leaving the
confines of logic far behind, the men attempt to solve the problem
of Lord Leslieson's destination. Every diversion is welcome
that will set the discussion on a new track. Minute incidents,
hardly noticeable to the outsider, result in violent revulsions
of mood; irritations lead to skilful sequences of invective,
climaxing in precise statements like 'All th' pharmaceutical
chemists of th' world couldn't mix a man into a bigger bastard
than you, Tomasheen!' (p. 137) and disintegrate almost in the
same breath. The penchant for exaggeration results in grotesque
visions: 'Go on, th' pair of yous, now, an' give your thrain a
chance of arrivin' where it's supposed to go, before th' poor
passengers dhribble away into old age!' (p. 152).

For all the instability of mood and opinion, however, two
views remain constant throughout: the Irish are equally narrow-
minded in questions of morals as they are suspicious towards
the English. The courting couple suggests terrible visions of 'evil
excitements within th' secret niches of th' night' (p. 134) and
leads to drastic admonitions: 'Take yourselves off, yeh fiddlers
with temptations! Home with the pair o' yous; an' hide yourselves
from decent people under th' clothes of your separate beds!' (p.
143). Lord Leslieson's unfortunate remark that the courting
couple was nothing to be surprised at, leads to the defamation of
England as the stronghold of immorality. Generally, the English
are credited with the inclination to do evil wherever they can; as
in *Purple Dust*, the old proverb: 'Hoof of a horse, horns of a bull,
smile of an Englishman . . .' (p. 133) is cited to express this distrust.[3]
Throughout the play, the Irish document their pathological fear
of not being taken seriously, or even of being pushed about, by
the neighbouring nation. In loud tones they insist on their
national independence: 'You'd do well, me lord, to remember
that the push of your hand or the back of your finger hasn't any
power or status in Ireland now' (p. 142).

The serious problems of post-revolutionary Ireland remain
untouched in *The Moon Shines on Kylenamoe* and therefore do

not detract from the audience's amusement. Thus the surprising turn that leads to a harmonious conclusion is quite credible. When the train finally departs, Lord Leslieson remains utterly destitute. His attempt to master the situation with his English education has failed. When Sean Tomasheen leaves him, it appears that he will have to spend the night, without carrying out his task, in the cold and lonely station square. But now he has to learn – and this is entirely new for Lord Leslieson – that humanity does not depend on the smooth functioning of the paraphernalia of civilization. Sean returns once more:

[*He comes back towards Leslieson. Anxious.*] I don't like leavin' you. [*A pause.*] I'll leave th' lanthern anyway; it'll warm your fingers anyhow. [*He leaves the lantern a little way from Lord Leslieson.*] It'll keep yeh company anyhow. [*A pause.*] Well, good night. You've the moon with you, anyway, thank God. [*He pauses again, but as Lord Leslieson is silent, he goes slowly out . . .*] (p. 155).

The lantern that at least will warm his hands is the first emblem of friendliness in apparently inimical surroundings. When Old Corny comes out of his cabin to offer him, with the understatements of genuine hospitality, the bed in front of the warming turf fire, he begins to understand the importance of this type of humanity: 'That is kind of you, but I couldn't . . .' (p. 156). But he has to learn even more: when he finally accepts the invitation and offers to pay for it, he is repudiated once again: 'You'll pay nothin' for it! A friend or enemy in disthress is welcome to share whatever we have. Payment would put a black spot on God's blessin'' (p. 156). Human solidarity is stronger than differences of class, nation or education; and in his newly-won modesty the diplomat answers, '[*surprised but a little awed*] Yes, yes, I see. I'm very grateful' (p. 156). The play ends emphasizing this friendliness which overshadows all previous differences:

[*Mrs. Conroy has appeared at the door, and stands a matronly figure in the centre of the warm, golden glow flooding the cosy, sheltering home.*]
MARTHA [*stretching out her two hands in welcome*]. Come on in, sir. You're welcome, an' God save you kindly.
L. LESLIESON [*very much moved*]. Thank you, thank you, an' God save you and your good man kindly, too! (p. 157).

This conclusion is not merely a once-off solution to an individual situation; it is symbolic. It is significant that O'Casey, when he contrasts the Irish and the English in *The Moon Shines on*

*Kylenamoe*, limits their conflicts to the realm of the comic, and that he finally suggests a possibility of overcoming their differences through an unpretentious humanity. This wistful ideal of reconciliation most certainly mirrors a deep desire on the part of the dramatist, who was always conscious of his position between the fronts and who had equally suffered from his estrangement from his Irish background as from his position as an outsider in his English 'exile'. Martha, the motherly figure who offers the shelter and warmth of a true home, embodies a hope that, for the dramatist himself, remained unfulfilled throughout his life.

The poignant immediacy to the dramatist's personal situation overshadows the artistic qualities of the play. It should, however, be pointed out that in this instance O'Casey is more successful with the form of the short play than in most of his earlier attempts. The play is consistent and unified; this effect is achieved by the playwright's skilful choice of scenery, by his observing one homogeneous stylistic level, by his adherence to one dominant theme as well as by his disregard of individual characterization and unrealistic episodes. The techniques of the comedy have been used both cautiously and skilfully; in addition to O'Casey's comic contrasting of characters it should be pointed out how cleverly he applies the expedient of surprise which interrupts all discussions precisely when they appear finally to be leading to a tangible result. The amateur stage, constantly in search of effective and actable short plays of some literary quality, ought to avail itself much more of *The Moon Shines on Kylenamoe* than it has done so far. For a survey of O'Casey's dramatic output it is more important, however, to note that in his final dramatic work, in an artistically satisfying form, the central conflicts of his life as a dramatist are overcome.

# PART VI

# Continuity and Originality

All O'Casey's plays are experiments in fusing the actual with
the symbolic.                                              (A. G. Stock)

Throughout O'Casey's dramatic work, there is a basic theme – a
conflict between life-forces and death-forces.
                                              (William A. Armstrong)

I am sorry, but I'm not Synge; not even, I'm afraid, a reincarnation.
                                              (Sean O'Casey)

As far as I'm concerned, all I can say is that O'Casey's like champagne,
one's wedding night, or the Aurora Borealis or whatever you call
them – all them lights.
                                              (Brendan Behan)

# 28. PREFATORY

The preceding interpretation of O'Casey's individual plays necessarily leads to a number of further, mutually overlapping questions which could not be discussed satisfactorily in the context of the individual works. These questions can be categorized under one of four headings, pinpointed by the four mottos quoted above: the forms of the drama that O'Casey utilizes, his recurrent themes and motifs, his literary models and anti-models, and his influence on other writers. A fifth and sixth subject, O'Casey's dramatic language, and the rich diversity of his characters, have been dealt with elsewhere in some detail.[1] The following chapters, therefore, are not to be seen as a summary of the preceding interpretations. Such an attempt would be not only futile but also absurd; it would lead to exactly the same faults that have marred previous criticism: the great variety of O'Casey's individual works would be reduced to convincing but simplified formulae, and would thereby be falsified. Instead, these chapters intend to do three things: they will summarize briefly the findings of previous scholarship, they will suggest some additional, and of necessity sketchy answers to general problems that lie beyond the scope of the individual work, and they will indicate some avenues for future research.

313

# 29. DRAMATIC FORMS

O'Casey uses a surprising variety of dramatic forms, alternating them not only from phase to phase, but also within the same phase and even within the same work. He calls on a large number of technical devices, tries them out, develops them further, rejects them and takes them up again. It is therefore impossible to include his work as a whole in any one category of modern drama, and it is even doubtful whether this is possible for individual plays. In this respect, few other experimental playwrights can be compared to him; O'Neill and Hauptmann come perhaps closest to O'Casey.

The individual interpretations in earlier chapters have already analyzed O'Casey's use of dramatic forms. The following remarks are intended to supplement these insights, emphasizing four points: (1) the interrelationship of realistic and unrealistic techniques; (2) exceptional devices in the field of dramatic structure; (3) O'Casey's adaptation, alteration and rejection of traditional dramatic types; (4) the special position of the short play. The few existing studies in these fields are often impressionistic and unsatisfactory.

*

The history of modern drama appears to the present-day critic as a constant interplay of realistic and unrealistic tendencies, combined in a variety of ways. One extreme of the scale is the attempt at an uncompromising depiction of reality on the stage, the other the complete rejection of empirical reality and the construction of an abstract and artificial world. Intermediate stages are, on the one hand, a consciously structured recreation of reality with symbolic overtones, on the other a new artistic reality structured from relics of the real world. It can be seen today that it is impossible to associate these tendencies with certain periods of the modern drama. Just as there were extremely unrealistic plays at the height of naturalist drama (Jarry's *Ubu roi* was produced as early as 1896), naturalism emerged again in the plays of the 'angry young men', and the 'documentary play'

314

stands side by side with the 'drama of the absurd'. There is little use in categorizing individual authors under certain stylistic tendencies, unless the whole of their dramatic output, as well as their dramatic tendencies, are in agreement with these.

O'Casey's dramatic works reflect these characteristics of modern drama. He utilizes almost all the combinations of realistic and unrealistic form, and his preference for one or the other is not limited to one period of his work. The one extreme, his closest approach to naturalist drama, can be seen in *Hall of Healing*, which stands between works like *The Star Turns Red* and *Cock-a-doodle Dandy* with their playful and confusing treatment of realistic elements. The other extreme, the allegorical *Kathleen Listens In*, stands side by side with the predominantly realistic *The Shadow of a Gunman*. It is therefore more fruitful to ask in what ways and with what success O'Casey combines realistic and unrealistic forms, than to determine to what degree O'Casey can be categorized under certain tendencies of modern drama.

At the time of his first successes, O'Casey was frequently seen as a 'photographic artist'[1] who, it was thought, faithfully reproduced events and dialogues which he had observed in his surroundings. Terms like 'skilful photography' and 'urban naturalism'[2] are occasionally employed by later critics, too; but there is some general agreement among most critics that even in his early plays his figures, events and dialogues have been critically selected and purposefully restructured into a new artistic reality. The early plays (with the exception of *Kathleen Listens In*) are different from the later plays (with the exception of *Hall of Healing*) *not* because they mirror reality, but because it is still possible for the audience to believe that they do so. Probability, not reproduction, is the key term for these early plays.

In his critical writings, O'Casey repeatedly discussed the current concept of realism, but as usual in his theoretical statements, it becomes clearer what he rejects than what he approves. His polemics are directed against those dramatists and critics who are content to reconstruct reality on stage or who see this as the supreme ideal of the drama:

Take people off the street or carry them out of a drawing-room, plonk them on the stage and make them speak as they speak in real, real life, and you will have the dullest thing imaginable . . . no real character can be put in a play unless some of the reality is taken out of him through the heightening, widening, and deeping of the character by the dramatist who creates him.[3]

For O'Casey the belief that genuine, unadulterated life can be transferred to the stage, is an illusion. Fake realism is the death of all artistic drama. Therefore he pleads for an unmitigated rejection of such representational tendencies and for the concept of an imaginative play:

This desire for real life on the stage has taken all the life out of the drama. The beauty, fire and poetry of drama have perished in a storm of fake realism. Let real birds fly through the air, real animals roam through the jungle, real fish swim in the sea, but let us have art in the theatre.[4]

Yet the outlines of this new, anti-realist drama remain rather vague:

The new form in drama will take qualities found in classical, romantic and expressionistic plays, will blend them together, breathe the breath of life into the new form and create a new drama . . . Gay, farcical, comic or tragical, it must be, not the commonplace portrayal of the trivial events in the life of this man or that woman, but a commentary of life itself.[5]

O'Casey takes a clear stand for the representative nature of drama. *Life*, a central but ill-defined term in his writings, is contrasted with the *reality* of the realist playwrights and is turned into a criterion for a play's quality and effectiveness. This does not necessarily imply a complete dismissal of the world. Even representative events can be bound by the limits of probability, as O'Casey shows in his Dublin plays. The obvious device to use in raising a reality-bound play above the individual and exceptional is the symbol. On the one hand, it is deeply rooted in the concrete world, on the other hand it points to a more general meaning. O'Casey employs a wide range of symbols: symbolic objects (e.g. the flag in *The Plough and the Stars*, the cup in *The Silver Tassie*, the rose, the statue and the flower-cross in *Red Roses for Me*), symbolic figures (e.g. Mrs. Tancred in *Juno and the Paycock* and Old Woman in *Hall of Healing* as symbols of suffering, Juno as the archetype of the mother), symbolic events (e.g. the flood in *Purple Dust*) or symbolic scenes (e.g. the 'occupation' of the room in *The Plough and the Stars* as a symbol of the occupation of the city). Such symbols may be central for the whole action, but they can also be limited to partial aspects of the play. The most complicated symbolic structure is undoubtedly to be found in *Red Roses for Me*, as has been shown above. Katharine J. Worth and Ronald G. Rollins have also analyzed some of the variations of O'Casey's symbolic techniques.[6] The concept of a predominantly 'realistic' play, consciously recreated, suffused with symbols but limited by the bounds of probability, can perhaps be seen as the basis of O'Casey's entire dramatic work. In many plays, however, he deviates from such a basis. In *Hall of Healing* he tends towards a programmatic naturalism that is bound much more closely to the immediacy of the world around us. In a few of his later short plays (*The End of the Beginning, A Pound on Demand, Bedtime Story, The Moon Shines on Kylenamoe*) he reiterates the realistic concept of his early works. In all the other plays he prefers to insert unrealistic elements or even to deviate completely from his realistic basis. It is interesting to note what devices he utilizes for this purpose (for more detailed analyses in the context of the individual play, see the interpretations above).

According to his own statement, O'Casey's break with the predominant form of drama and his rejection of *reality* in favour of *life* can be pinpointed quite precisely: '. . . I broke away from realism into the chant of the second act of *The Silver Tassie*'.[7] This Act will demonstrate even to an audience predisposed to accept an illusion of reality, that the stage does not simply mirror sections of everyday-life. The juxtaposition of an unrealistic act with events that are determined by the criteria of probability (repeated in *Red Roses for Me*) is a specifically O'Caseyan form of unrealistic writing. It serves the purpose of raising the play above its individual elements and of emphasizing the representative character of even the 'realistic' events portrayed. Such an act is characterized by its stylized setting, the appearance of anonymous characters in group or mass scenes, the abandoning of psychologically motivated behaviour, the introduction of a metaphorical dialogue that is largely divorced from the individual characters, the introduction of songs or chants as a substitute for dialogue, and the absence of a logically motivated plot. Here the individual and the exceptional is reduced or excluded in favour of the general and the universal. It was a special problem for the dramatist to integrate these acts into the individualized events of the rest of the plays, because the intended effect can be achieved only if, despite all the differences, the connecting links are clearly visible. This problem was discussed in some detail in the individual chapters. Act II of *The Plough and the Stars* had been a first step in this direction. It reaches the limits of what can still be accepted as 'probable'. Some of the figures' individual traits are reduced to emphasize their representativeness for certain groups, and in the three officers their representative function almost completely overshadows their individuality. The anonymous Speaker in the background who appears and disappears without psychological explanation, providing the key words for the future events, points forward to the function of the Croucher in *The Silver Tassie*; designing a setting in which his shadowy figure can still appear probable must be difficult indeed for any stage designer.

In two other of his plays O'Casey repeated the juxtaposition of more or less realistic events with clearly stylized scenes in a slightly different form. In *The Drums of Father Ned*, the prelude ('Prerumble') does not so much serve the purpose of underlining the universal aspects of the play as of establishing a historical perspective: '*The scene looks like a sudden vision of an experience long past conjured up within the mind of one who had gone through it*'. Yet the stylized presentation of a war situation, the anonymous figures ('. . . *they stand out vaguely as blacked-out humanity against the red glow of the burning town*') and the distant '*chant of misery and defiance*' (pp. 1-2) are immediately reminiscent of Act II of *The Silver Tassie*. *The Drums of Father Ned* is O'Casey's only play where he enlarges the historical perspective by introducing a third element, the 1798 Rising suggested in the play-within-the-play. Even more effective is the frame action in *Oak Leaves and Lavender* that combines both functions. The individual events of the present are not only, as in *The Drums of Father Ned*, connected with individual events in the past, but they are also integrated (by the dance of the shadows) into an historical process that encompasses centuries, thus underlining their universal significance. The transformation of the old manor house again emphasizes these representative traits. Even though O'Casey was not entirely successful in carrying out his design, one ought to appreciate his constant endeavour to lift his plays above mere reality by inserting unrealistic sections.

In four of his works he extended his unrealistic presentation to the whole of the play: *Kathleen Listens In*, *Within the Gates*, *The Star Turns Red* and *Figuro in the Night* do not claim any superficial probability; in these works, attempts at psychological motivation (as in *Within the Gates*) can even be disadvantageous. Despite their unrealistic nature, these plays show extreme differences, as has been demonstrated above. While *Kathleen Listens In* and *The Star Turns Red* represent O'Casey's closest approach to allegory, the more complex *Within the Gates* is O'Casey's most successful attempt at an unrealistic and nevertheless lively and effective dramatization.

The most complicated combination of realistic and unrealistic traits is to be found in *Cock-a-doodle Dandy* and *Time to Go*, where the author's imagination playfully manipulates the elements of reality, confusing his stage-characters as well as the audience. In the longer of the two plays he succeeds to such an extent that it has to be considered one of his best plays. Other works have only a limited number of individual unrealistic elements, e.g. the allegorical figure as an embodiment of the flood in *Purple Dust*, the statue of the strange Saint Tremolo in *The Bishop's Bonfire*, unmotivated noises in *Behind the Green Curtains* or traces of a mediating figure divorced from the plot in *Nannie's Night Out*. Only when all these attempts, entirely different in design and extent, are taken together, is it possible to appreciate how O'Casey wrestled with the problem of unrealistic drama.

If, as English and American critics tend to do, 'unrealistic drama' is equated with 'expressionism', O'Casey can indeed be termed an 'expressionist dramatist'.[8] Such a confusion of terms, however, serves little purpose. The true expressionist drama can be defined quite clearly both typologically and periodically; and it is distinguished from other works not only by certain formal features but also by the authors' programmatic attitude.[9] O'Casey, who did not even know what 'expressionism' meant,[10] remained untouched by the programme of the expressionists, even if (especially in *The Silver Tassie*) he took up a few suggestions in subject-matter and technique. Still more misleading is De Baun's assertion that *The Plough and the Stars* contains 'expressionist' elements.[11] Even if 'expressionist' is equated with 'unrealistic', his examples remain without conviction, because they do not transcend the bounds of probability, as does Act II of *The Silver Tassie*. It would be much more appropriate to keep the discussion of O'Casey's highly original work free from such misleading terms and to preserve it from false analogies that cannot be verified on closer inspection.[12]

*

O'Casey's originality manifests itself especially in his deviations from the traditional structure of the drama. Here, one has to distinguish between his short plays (discussed below) and his full-length plays. Significantly, in his earliest produced play the structure is determined by the *dramatis personae*, while in the longer plays following on *The Shadow of a Gunman*, the plot, usually composed of several lines of action, becomes dominant. In *Juno and the Paycock* O'Casey most closely approximates the traditional pattern of the drama as exemplified in the well-made play. The symmetrical action consists of three individual lines, each of them determined by a traditional motif: the unexpected inheritance, the seduction of the girl and the guilt that haunts the informer. Yet even this play, O'Casey's most 'conventional' one, deviates in several respects from the traditional pattern: one of the three lines of action is analytical rather than progressive, and the play is interspersed with static scenes that carry a special significance.

Quite different is the 'Chekhovian structure' of *The Plough and the Stars*. Nine individual lines of action are interwoven and represent different aspects of a common theme. Different again is *The Silver Tassie* where the two parallel actions of Harry Heegan and Teddy Foran are contrasted with that of Barney Bagnal, which runs in diametrical opposition to the first two. Even more important is that a whole act of this play remains outside the plot and that the other acts, too, show a number of static scenes that would be superfluous from the point of view of plot alone. This tendency is further developed in the following plays. The unrealistic *Within the Gates* has only rudiments of action, and in the following works the plot, again, does not dominate the structure. This is particularly noticeable in *Red Roses for Me*, where the main action and an insignificant sub-plot cannot guarantee the unity of the play, forcing the dramatist to utilize other devices. In *Oak Leaves and Lavender*, too, a minimal progression is suggested by three reduced lines of action. Not until *The Bishop's Bonfire* does O'Casey again create a structure of three fully-fledged plot lines, yet even here the number and extent of the additional static scenes is greater than in *Juno and the Paycock*.

If O'Casey tends to reduce action as the dominant structural device, it is important to note what he puts in its place. It is certain that the reduction in plot does not mean a loss of artistic unity. The structure simply becomes more complicated and can only be satisfactorily described in terms of each individual play. The underlying principle is that of contrast: O'Casey juxtaposes scenes that differ in their *dramatis personae*, in mood and in theme in such a way that they serve as commentaries on each other and increase their mutual effectiveness. Other structural devices vary from work to work. In *Within the Gates*, the unrealistic tendency of the whole play permits an allegorical presentation of human life by simultaneously presenting the times of the day and the seasons of the year. In addition to such a 'vertical' structure, it was shown above that the play has a 'horizontal' structure of 'world picture', 'satire' and 'religious quest'. The principle of the quest for a true belief regulates the sequence of the individual scenes. *Purple Dust* possesses a similar 'horizontal' structure of comedy, farce and satire which is responsible for the structuring of the scenes. Since the progression of events in this play is especially limited, O'Casey introduced towards the end an additional element in the form of the symbolic flood that enabled him to bring his action to a conclusion, as well as to deepen its meaning. The problem of dramatic structure in *Red Roses for Me* has been discussed above in some detail: the central character and a few central symbols here serve as structural elements that are responsible for the sequence of scenes. The plays of his fourth phase form the climax in O'Casey's creation of a unique dramatic structure. The grouping of the manifold scenes is here controlled by the central motif of a public celebration. O'Casey's introduction of fantastic and fairy-tale elements, however, enables him to dispense with a logical progression of events, and the most important device in controlling the variety of themes and stylistic levels is again the principle of contrast. In *Behind the Green Curtains* and *Figuro in the Night*, O'Casey's loss of artistic creativity makes itself felt in the lack of structural coherence.

So far, this brief survey of O'Casey's structural techniques has neglected one aspect which is possibly his most important achievement in the field of dramatic form. In a number of plays he projects the stage events, complicated as they may be, onto a general historical action that decisively influences the events on stage and raises them to a general, if not universal level. In *The Shadow of a Gunman* O'Casey utilizes the Irish struggle for independence, in *Juno and the Paycock* the Civil War, in *The Plough and the Stars* the Easter Rising of 1916, in *The Silver Tassie* the First World War, in *Red Roses for Me* an imaginary strike closely related to the Dublin Lockout of 1913, in *Oak Leaves and Lavender* the Second World War. In his later plays such a general background action (e.g. the visit of the President in *Cock-a-doodle Dandy*, of the Bishop in *The Bishop's Bonfire*) is of far smaller importance. In the six plays mentioned above, however, the background action decisively influences the dramatic impact. Nevertheless, O'Casey's technique is by no means the same in all. In *The Shadow of a Gunman, Juno and the Paycock* and *The*

*Silver Tassie,* for instance, he presents the image of an anonymous progression which the individual can scarcely influence, while *Red Roses for Me* shows a close correspondence between stage events and background action, suggesting a more optimistic view of history: human beings here are able to influence the course of historical events. The most successful integration of stage events and background action can be found in *The Plough and the Stars* which, not least because of this, may be seen as O'Casey's best play. As shown above, the stage events, without being in any way reduced in individuality, mirror the course of the Easter Rising. A reduction in reality and individuality, however, can be observed in *Kathleen Listens In* and *The Star Turns Red*, where the allegorical presentation suggests an isolated background action without any corresponding individual events.

*

These observations on O'Casey's dramatic structure confirm the impression of heterogeneity which his work presents. The same impression may be gained if one observes where O'Casey followed traditional types of drama and where he deviated from, or rejected these. A convenient starting-point is his choice of dramatic categories for his own plays, as evinced in their subtitles (although, of course, one should not expect these to conform to critical standards). In the course of his writing, O'Casey tended to abandon such categorization altogether. Four plays from his third, fourth and fifth phase (*The Star Turns Red, Cock-a-doodle Dandy, Behind the Green Curtains, The Moon Shines on Kylenamoe*) carry no subtitle at all; in three others (*Oak Leaves and Lavender, The Drums of Father Ned, Figuro in the Night*) the subtitle contains no reference to dramatic genre. In his first and second phases, on the other hand, he labelled all his plays clearly. The three full-length 'Dublin' plays are identified as 'tragedies', *Nannie's Night Out* and *The End of the Beginning* as 'comedies', *The Harvest Festival, Within the Gates* and *Red Roses for Me* as 'plays', *The Silver Tassie* as 'tragi-comedy' and *A Pound on Demand* as a 'sketch'. In six other cases the dramatic categories are qualified by additional terms: *Kathleen Listens In* is classified as *A Political Phantasy, Purple Dust* as *A Wayward Comedy, Hall of Healing* as *A Sincerious Farce, Bedtime Story* as *An Anatole Burlesque, Time to Go* as *A Morality Comedy* and *The Bishop's Bonfire* as *A Sad Play within the Tune of a Polka*. This survey may indicate O'Casey's insecurity in the application of a traditional dramatic nomenclature. He increasingly resorted to the use of characterizing attributes, or dispensed altogether with genre categories, thus underlining the individuality and originality of his work. Some of these modified terms, especially the subtitles of *Kathleen Listens In*, *Purple Dust* and *Time to Go*, are most fortunate, for they precisely characterize the particular play. On the other hand, it has already been shown that *Hall of Healing* is not a farce and *Bedtime Story* is unrelated to Schnitzler. Similarly, most of the early subtitles are inappropriate. The classification of *The Silver Tassie* as *Tragi-Comedy*, and of *A Pound on Demand* as *Sketch* are acceptable. In the other cases the traditional terms are unsuitable because O'Casey had turned away from the traditional forms of the drama.

Only two of his plays conform without qualification to traditional genres: *The End of the Beginning* and *A Pound on Demand* are typical farces. Most of the other plays tend to deviate from the traditional types to such a degree that they would be falsified by any dramatic category. Only one aspect of *Purple Dust*, for instance, is allowed for when critics characterize this complex work as 'comedy', 'satire' or 'farce'. For the majority of O'Casey's plays, a detailed critical description has to take the place of any mere categorization by genre or type.[13]

O'Casey's work lacks pure forms of tragedy as it lacks pure forms of comedy. Where it is possible to speak of 'tragic conflicts' and 'tragic deaths', the characters concerned are not at the centre of their plays. The most obvious tragic character in the whole of O'Casey's output is probably Foorawn Reiligan, but this does not turn *The Bishop's Bonfire* into a tragedy, because Foorawn's accidental death, and even more so the fate of the other characters, renders such an interpretation untenable. Other figures who are frequently called 'tragic' (e.g. Minnie Powell, Juno, Bessie Burgess, Nora Clitheroe, Jannice, Ayamonn, Drishogue) do not fulfil important prerequisites for such a role. They either lack the degree of human greatness that would raise a private fate above the level of individuality and thus excite compassion rather than pity (e.g. Nora), or they do not experience any inescapable conflict (e.g. Bessie), or they are unaware of their own situation (e.g. Minnie), or they do not 'fail' in life as a tragic character does (e.g. Juno, Ayamonn). The latter is the most important reason for the lack of tragic situations in O'Casey, because his basically optimistic view of humanity and history makes it impossible for him to present an unmitigated catastrophe. Juno's assertion of humanity in her decision for life and against death, or Ayamonn's death, which is seen as an important step towards a better future, or again the triumph of youth in *The Drums of Father Ned*, are all variations of a common attitude; they are O'Casey's attempt to show human beings as willing and capable of determining their own condition and of liberating themselves from the claws of a supposedly overpowering fate.

This, however, is not possible without sacrifice, pain, suffering, sorrow, even despair. O'Casey therefore is particularly close to the modern version of tragi-comedy. Until the eighteenth century the insertion of one of four elements into a tragedy – comic characters, comic events, colloquial dialogue or happy ending – was sufficient to define a tragi-comedy, but twentieth-century tragi-comedy can no longer be seen as a mere mixture of tragic and comic traits; the *simultaneity* of distressing and amusing effects now forms the decisive criterion. This fundamental feature (which of course existed long before it was discovered by critics) is characteristic of a number of O'Casey's plays, especially *The Shadow of a Gunman, Juno and the Paycock, The Plough and the Stars, Nannie's Night Out, The Silver Tassie, Red Roses for Me* and *Oak Leaves and Lavender*. A scene that has already been analyzed in some detail should again be pointed out as a model of the O'Caseyan version of tragi-comedy: at the end of *Juno and the Paycock*, the drunken Captain Boyle through his lack of discernment and self-criticism, evokes both amusement and deep distress. The standard works on tragi-comedy refer occasionally to O'Casey without pointing out his rank as one of the most significant representatives of this genre and without defining the special characteristics of his tragi-comedies,[14] while O'Casey critics tend to emphasize this particular aspect of his work without, however, describing in detail his adherence to, and deviation from, the general characteristics of modern tragi-comedy.[15]

Such an analysis would also have to consider the question to what degree and to what purpose O'Casey occasionally replaces the elements of tragedy and comedy with their popular counter-parts, melodrama and farce;[16] in other words it would have to inquire whether some of O'Casey's plays should not rather be termed 'melodrama-farce' than 'tragi-comedy'. It would also have to consider Metscher's thesis (here rejected for the early plays), 'Die Tragikomödie O'Caseys ist eine *satirische* Tragödie.'[17] It would become apparent that the concept of tragi-comedy is not acceptable for O'Casey's fourth phase. Several new terms have been suggested, for instance 'morality comedy' (O'Casey's definition of *Time to Go*), 'fantasy', or 'pastoral play'.[18]

What is more important than the actual term itself is that it would have to emphasize the element of independence from traditional forms; the term 'pastoral play' that suggests an affinity to a definite literary tradition is in this respect less than appropriate.

*

It has often gone unnoticed that O'Casey, like most twentieth-century English and Irish dramatists, has written a number of short plays in addition to his full-length plays. Yet the short play, often erroneously termed 'one-act play', is as independent of the longer drama as is the short story of the novel. It would be no help to point out that O'Casey wrote five plays in four acts, eight plays in three acts, two plays in two acts, and eight plays in one act.[19] What is important is the basic difference between fifteen full-length and eight short plays. The latter do not always conform to the structural principles characteristic of the best modern short plays whose decisive feature is their concentration. These are limited to one decisive crisis or final situation in the life of one or a few people; they tend to isolate a single character trait, a single emotion or event that stresses the universal significance of the play. A single moment often tends to illuminate a whole life, and the few compressed stage events mirror basic experiences of human existence.[20]

It appears that O'Casey was not fully conscious of the potential of the genre. No theoretical references of his to the short play are known, and his pejorative remarks on his own short plays suggests that he considered them of minor importance. If his early dramatic attempts (before *The Harvest Festival*) were written, as can be assumed, in the form of the short play, he probably had three external reasons for doing so: (1) the short play was the dominant dramatic form in the early years of the Abbey Theatre; (2) those amateur groups for whom O'Casey apparently intended some of his early plays preferred the short form; (3) the writing of short plays must have appeared to him as 'easier' than the composition of a longer work for which he then lacked the theoretical requirements. The earliest of his extant short plays betray no urgency to utilize this form to the exclusion of any other. *Kathleen Listens In* lacks the intensity as well as the unity of the best short plays, and in *Nannie's Night Out* the dramatist's impatience with the limitations of the form is palpable. In his later years, too, one feels that he did not devote the same intensity of labour to his short plays as to his longer works. *Bedtime Story*,

clearly divided into a satirical and a burlesque part, again lacks
unity, and in *Time to Go* his attempt to display the variety of
forms and themes of his later fantasies in the short form was
bound to fail. On the other hand, *A Pound on Demand, The End
of the Beginning, Hall of Healing* and *The Moon Shines on
Kylenamoe* are, in their various ways, highly successful short
plays. The two farces transfer the short play's typical preference
for crisis into the sphere of the comic. *Hall of Healing* is an
unusual experiment with the short form because it lacks both a
central character and a central critical event. The situation in this
play is characterized by its triviality and repetitiveness, and the
group of people is without a hero. It is one of O'Casey's great
successes as a dramatist that in this episodic play he achieved the
concentration of the best short plays and was able to transform
individual life histories into an image of general significance.
With *The Moon Shines on Kylenamoe*, O'Casey returned to the
level of untrammelled amusement, but achieved a similar artistic
unity as in *Hall of Healing*, and, confronting Lord Leslieson with
the value of sheer 'friendliness', he dramatized a basic human
experience. Although it would be inappropriate to place O'Casey
side by side with masters of the short play like Synge and Yeats,
he shows in these works that he has mastered this form as well,
and thus confirms the great variety and diversity of his dramatic
work.

# 30. THEMES AND MOTIFS

If one attempts to survey the central themes and motifs in O'Casey's plays, one is confronted with a similar variety as in the field of dramatic forms. It is impossible to identify any one basic theme of his work, unless one generalizes to such an extent that differences with respect to other dramatists are no longer visible. More pertinent than most such formulae is Armstrong's phrase: 'Throughout O'Casey's dramatic work, there is a basic theme – a conflict between life-forces and death-forces.'[1] And indeed all the phases of O'Casey's work testify to this conflict; it is present in Juno's struggle for her family against the destructive forces of the Civil War, in the songs of the Dreamer and the chants of the Down and Out, in Ayamonn's vision and the repressive forces of the police, in the life-giving dance of the Cock and the death-bringing violence of Father Domineer, in Reena's open world and the impenetrable green curtains of Chatastray's house. These examples show, however, that a general formula, even a good one, tends to obscure the individual traits of the plays. Just as misguided as the attempt to subsume all of O'Casey's plays under one thematic heading would be the opposite procedure of cataloguing all his themes and motifs. The present chapter endeavours to follow a middle course between these two extremes by discussing a number of prominent themes that O'Casey treated repeatedly and in various ways.

Previous studies have contributed little in this field, whether in surveying the full range of O'Casey's themes or in following a single theme through various works. The promising title 'Sean O'Casey's Development of a Basic Theme', for instance, hides a simple, chronological description of his major works, culminating in an entirely spurious 'theme', 'What is the meaning of the struggle for existence?',[2] a theme that could be discovered in almost any writer's work. In a similar way, Goldstone's definition is vague to the point where it can mean anything or nothing at all:

O'Casey's work . . . represents a whole achievement. It does so not merely because of a few recurring characteristics but because of a fundamental question or theme that underlines [*sic*] most of the plays and makes them part of an interesting vision . . . This underlying question or theme is that of commitment – the compelling need that many people have to try to find some central values that give meaning to their lives.

It is difficult to imagine a serious dramatist to whose work such a definition did not apply, especially when 'commitment' is later defined as synonymous with 'community'.[3] It would almost be equally to the point to argue that O'Casey's plays are 'about people'. Even those works that deal with O'Casey's social criticism and his socialist tendencies can hardly be said to achieve more than a general characterization of his œuvre.[4] More successful is Krause's discussion of the Ossianic theme, 'the conflict between the Christian mortification of the flesh and the pagan "joy of life" . . .'.[5] One of the best and most pertinent articles is certainly Armstrong's 'Sean O'Casey, W. B. Yeats and the Dance of Life', which shows in what ways O'Casey utilizes the motif of the dance as the expression of life-affirmation and joy. It is interesting to observe that methodological problems often seem to have prevented critics from analyzing the variations undergone by certain themes in various works. A great deal of O'Casey criticism illustrates the commonplace that the accidental stringing together of enthusiastic remarks is no substitute for clarity of object, method and presentation.

O'Casey's 'Mental Pilgrimage' is summarized by Rollins in the following passage:

The movement of O'Casey's mind from the Dublin war plays, through the five transitional dramas, to the final comic fantasies is erratic, wayward, and full of contradictions. He is alternately belligerent and pacifistic, confused and determined, as he scrutinizes the various political, economic, and religious problems that stand in the way of man's finding an energetic and useful life. He seems unable to decide fully upon one course of action as he condemns war in one play and approves of violent revolution in the next; exposes the gullibility of the English in one work and compliments them for their bravery in another; lashes a Catholic clergyman in one drama and sympathizes with a priest of the same faith in a later work; expresses contempt for vain Irish rebels in early dramas, and fills with pride at their courageous actions in England's defense in a later drama; admires the patience and compassion of women in early plays and criticizes their selfishness in another play; and, finally, expresses respect for Christianity at one moment and faith in Communism the next. O'Casey's mental pilgrimage has been a tortuous, winding one, terminating in a mood of anger, bafflement and near despair.[6]

Although some of these observations are scarcely tenable, it is correct to say that O'Casey not only returns to the same theme in various plays, but that he also treats it from different positions and arrives at varying results. This may, on the one hand, betray some uncertainty of judgement, but it also proves the dramatist's lack of bias and prejudice and his willingness to revise his own position when it appears no longer acceptable to him.

The best example of such a change in judgement is the theme of *war* that is present in at least seven of his plays. It is at the centre of the three great war plays *The Plough and the Stars*, *The Silver Tassie* and *Oak Leaves and Lavender*, in *The Shadow of a Gunman* and *Juno and the Paycock* it is equally indispensable, in *The Drums of Father Ned* it provides an additional perspective, while in *Purple Dust* it is merely episodic. If one adds to these plays *The Star Turns Red* and *Red Roses for Me*, which also depict a physical struggle for power, it is not entirely unjustifiable to call O'Casey 'in the main a war dramatist'.[7] It is, however, hardly possible to imagine greater differences in approach.

In the three full-length 'Dublin' plays, the situation of the Rising or the Civil War form the touchstone for the individual's failure or success. Even in *The Plough and the Stars*, where the Rising is mirrored in the stage events with great dramatic skill, the emphasis is predominantly on the personal factor. The presentation of the war itself is objective; the author leaves it to his characters to comment on it, but he does not single out any one of them to such an extent that their judgement could be credited with a higher authority. The situation in *The Silver Tassie* is diametrically opposed to this. The central theme here is the attack on war. Consequently the dramatic figures, although they are not devoid of individual character traits, serve predominantly as examples of a general fate; and Act II is entirely limited to the front-line experience of anonymous, suffering human beings, who are not given a single chance of personal success in life. By his method of presentation, therefore, the author himself takes up an unequivocal position, and he attempts to 'convert' the audience to his own opinion, although this opinion does not yet (as in some of the later plays) find direct expression in the text.

In the plays of the third phase the author's attitude again differs considerably from the objectivity of *The Plough and the Stars* and the personal engagement of *The Silver Tassie*:

The pacifism that we observed in *The Silver Tassie* has disappeared; the contention that even one life lost may be too high a price to pay in order to gain a political objective . . . is supplanted by the thesis that struggle must bring on sacrifice, sacrifice may result in death and the death of one or thousand and one is a necessary, though undesirable, step towards the realization of political goals.[8]

In *Purple Dust*, O'Killigain's participation in the Spanish Civil War receives the author's explicit approval, while Stoke and Poges' flight from the blitz in London is condemned. In *The Star Turns Red* and *Red Roses for Me*, the necessity of uncompromising dedication and the willingness to sacrifice one's life is never called in question. In *Oak Leaves and Lavender*, the most straight-forward war play of this phase, several conflicting intentions are simultaneously present: the realistic presentation of the war situation and its consequences for ordinary people (reminiscent of *The Plough and the Stars*), the explicit approval or disapproval of certain attitudes to the war, and finally the symbolic integration of the events into a historical process. While the dramatist in *The Silver Tassie* was convinced of the futility of *any* war, here he does not doubt the necessity of *this* war, and whoever fails to support it cannot expect lenient treatment. The conscientious objector Pobjoy, 'moving shamefacedly through the play like the reproachful ghost of an abandoned ideal',[9] is a case in point. The *dramatis personae* of earlier plays would take up completely different roles in *Oak Leaves and Lavender*: realists like Juno and Fluther, who place the welfare of the individual above the achievement of abstract political objectives, would here appear as traitors and would be denigrated, like Deeda Tutting, Constant and Pobjoy, through their external appearance and behaviour, while those who do not hesitate to fight, like Maguire, Johnny Boyle and Clitheroe, irrespective of their personal motivation, would become irreproachable heroes like Edgar and Drishogue.

Different again is the situation in *The Drums of Father Ned*. The war situation of the prelude serves, as in the early plays, as a touchstone of the individual's behaviour. An objective presentation is impossible not only because of the author's intruding voice but also because of the dream atmosphere that removes the war to a vaguely remembered past. The struggle for independence, and also the rising of 1798 in the play-within-the-play, serve to establish a historical perspective; what really matters is the present (as it has evolved from the struggles of the past) where the individual finds the author's approval when and to the extent that he shows himself worthy of earlier sacrifices.

The theme of war is a remarkable example of O'Casey's change of attitude as well as of his change in presentational method which, taken together, lead to entirely different plays. Similar conclusions can be drawn from the related theme of the *strike*. Ignoring, for a moment, the unproduced *The Harvest Festival*, the first real strike (apart from the allegorical worker's threat in *Kathleen Listens In*) is to be found in *Juno and the Paycock*. Mary's involvement in industrial action deprives the family of their last source of income. O'Casey does not, as some critics have thought, approve one-sidedly of Juno's critical remarks concerning Mary's attitude, but he is here far removed from his own position in the later plays, for he uses the strike, without taking up a definite standpoint himself, as one of the touchstones for the characters' humanity and view of life. The responsibility for the family's existence and the commitment to solidarity in a larger sphere are positions of equal value, and the choice of priority is left with the audience. In *The Plough and the Stars*, where the same theme is suggested in the figure of the Covey, O'Casey's approach is still the same.

Later, however, when the strike theme appears at the centre of two plays, the author's attitude has changed radically, returning to his early position in *The Harvest Festival*. Industrial action is now the only way to improve the material position of under-privileged people, and it is therefore the starting-point for an imperative alteration of the social structure, its necessity never being called in question. Whoever opposes the strike is a traitor and finds himself condemned to ridicule, like the comic cowards Foster and Dowzard in *Red Roses for Me*. There is no doubt whatsoever that the strike takes precedence over private ambitions; the request to break a strike can lead to the estrangement of individuals, and for the model hero Ayamonn this does not even call forth an inner conflict. In both plays, Juno's attitude to the strike would turn her into a traitor to the common cause. In *Cock-a-doodle Dandy*, this theme is taken up once more in the strike of the lorry drivers, and here, too, the comic presentation of the opponents to the strike makes it quite clear where the author's sympathies lie.

The strike theme is a special aspect of O'Casey's criticism of the existing social order and is thus related to his concept of a 'new' society which dominates several of his plays. A first attempt to criticize society is to be found, as has been shown above, in *The Harvest Festival* and *Nannie's Night Out*. The best example, later on, is *Hall of Healing*, an 'objective propaganda play' that rouses the audience's awareness of the necessity of change precisely through its objective presentation of the situation of the poor. In *Within the Gates*, too, and even in the plays of the fourth phase, the urgency of social change is still implied. The later plays, however, do not so much insist on material improvements as on the abolishing of class barriers which are an obstacle to natural human relations. Usually O'Casey shows how such attempts *fail*, most impressively in *The Bishop's Bonfire* where Daniel submits all too soon to the unwarranted authority of Keelin's father. In a few of the plays, he adds the utopian element of a new, better order to his criticism of existing society. It is one of the basic premises of *The Star Turns Red* and *Red Roses for Me* that the demonstrations in these plays will lead to such a change. The theme is present, too, in *Purple Dust* where the rise of the common man is one aspect of the symbolic conclusion, and in *Oak Leaves and Lavender* where the fate of the manor house implies a change of social structure. A particularly optimistic example of such a social utopia is *The Drums of Father Ned*, where the older generation is made to shoulder the responsibility for all the defects of the social order and where, therefore, the victory of the younger generation is bound to lead to happier conditions.

In a few plays only, particularly in the frame action of *Oak Leaves and Lavender*, and also in the decline of the Big House in *Purple Dust*, does O'Casey suggest that the substitution of the new for the old always means both gain *and* loss. More frequent is the situation where ideal characters, who stand in remarkable contrast to O'Casey's early socialists (Jerry Devine and the Covey), are responsible for the change and embody the author's belief in a more just world. Despite such characters of the Red Jim type, Jordan, however, is correct when he says: 'O'Casey, as an artist, is most pre-occupied with the sadness of defeat, and the partial victory of individuals, rather than with the triumph of a class. He is the most un-Marxist of professed subscribers to dialectical materialism.'[10]

Both the war and the strike are examples of themes that were suggested by the author's immediate personal experience (the Irish struggle for independence and the Civil War, the two World Wars, the Dublin General Strike and Lockout of 1913). Another theme that can be traced throughout O'Casey's work is also based on his personal impressions: the contrast between England and Ireland. It is true, of course, that this is a (perhaps *the*) basic theme of the whole of Anglo-Irish literature, yet it is particularly conspicuous in O'Casey who treats it as the central issue in some of his plays and deals with it even in works where this is not required by his subject matter (e.g. *Juno and the Paycock, Nannie's Night Out* and *Red Roses for Me*). Again, considerable differences in his presentation of the theme can be observed, although the author's change of position is perhaps not quite as extreme as in the examples discussed above. *The Shadow of a Gunman* and *The Plough and the Stars* deal with the *military* conflict between the English and the Irish. In the final act, this conflict advances onto the stage in the figures of the Auxiliary and the British soldiers. It is surprising to note that O'Casey delineates these representatives of British dominion without any tendentious distortion. They appear as tools of an anonymous power rather than as active agents, and they do not take advantage of their military superiority for private brutalities. It is even possible to discern a certain degree of good nature under the cloak of heavy-handed humour that they have adapted to cope with the unusual situation. Corporal Stoddard speaks '*impatiently, but kindly*' to Mrs. Gogan and reminds the men to 'bring a little snack' when they are led off into captivity (pp. 251, 254). Also, the death of Minnie Powell and Bessie Burgess is explicitly presented as a mistake, not as the result of intentional terror. The author shows here a remarkably objective attitude, certainly exceptional in the years when these plays were written, an attitude that is also mirrored in the *political* treatment of this conflict in *Kathleen Listens In*.

Later, in *Purple Dust*, he does not resume the military or political conflict and its bearing on the life of the individual, but dramatizes the more basic contrast between two peoples, a contrast that cannot be abolished by military victory or political negotiation. Even if O'Casey, in the symbolic conclusion, hints at the dis-establishment of British dominion in Ireland, his central issue in this play is the confrontation of Irish and English character-traits. His satire is directed with great bitterness at the two Englishmen whose weaknesses are condemned while those of the Irish are at best merely ridiculed. This presentation of the Englishman in Ireland (prefigured in the contrast between Bentham and the Boyles in *Juno and the Paycock*), is supplemented by the presentation of the Irishman in England in *Oak Leaves and Lavender* (one of the examples where this theme encroaches upon the moral central issues of the play). As in *Purple Dust*, O'Casey here sides primarily with the three Irishmen (Feelim, Drishogue, Foreman); their conviction of the importance of

Ireland in world history is not countered by any arguments of equal weight, even if it is presented with an excessive degree of naive national pride. O'Casey strengthens their position by turning them into the three decisive props of the war effort on the home front, the battle front and the armament front.

*Oak Leaves and Lavender* suggests that the differences between the English and the Irish can be overcome by a common engagement for a higher objective. In *The Drums of Father Ned* even the problem of the North, the most immediate conflict of all, seems to approach a possible solution. This optimistic play shows that empty reproaches can be replaced by the awareness of common interests, and O'Casey creates the impression that the coming into power of a less biased generation will suffice to abolish the hostilities of the past. He must have realized himself that such ideas, at present, are utopian at best. In his last play, *The Moon Shines on Kylenamoe*, the conflict between the English and the Irish is reduced to the sphere of the comic, applied impartially to both sides; simple humanity here forms the basis for a reconciliation that seems to reflect the author's deepest desire.

A related theme is O'Casey's criticism of present-day Ireland. This becomes more and more poignant with the progression of his work. In the early plays it is limited to individual figures (e.g. Seumas Shields), but it develops into something much more central and later receives the author's explicit support through his method of presentation. The first of these plays is *Red Roses for Me*, where the ideal character Ayamonn criticizes the nationalist Roory for his derogatory attitude to the proletariat and his intended restrictions on intellectual freedom. In the fourth and fifth periods, with a climax in *Behind the Green Curtains*, this criticism is expressed not only verbally but scenically as well, in the presentation of an Ireland dominated by intellectual terror, social injustice, moral dishonesty and clerical abuse of power. The problem of dramatic quality is particularly acute in this context; O'Casey's plays can be considered as universal only if the Irish situation can be seen as examples of conditions as they exist everywhere, and not if they reflect the author's private feud with his native country alone.

O'Casey's criticism of Ireland is always linked to his attacks on the Catholic Church. This theme, however, can also be seen in a different context, which O'Casey treats in many of his plays: the search for religious truth. As early as *Juno and the Paycock* he depicts a variety of attitudes to the numinous. The two extremes, embodied in Bentham and Devine, are characterized by Boyle in comic simplification: 'One that says all is God an' no man; an' th' other that says all is man an' no God!' (p. 39). Between these two extremes stand the materialistic Boyle who changes his attitude to the Church according to the expediences of the moment, the sceptical Mary, influenced by Devine, the superstitious Johnny, and Juno whose central prayer expresses not a simple belief but the insecurity of someone searching for the justice of God. If in *Juno and the Paycock* it is more important to prove oneself in this world than to search for the truth of the next, in *Within the Gates* the latter theme has become the central issue. The analysis above has shown that O'Casey here juxtaposes a great variety of religious attitudes, the validity of each of which is tested and rejected by Jannice, a human being in search of her God, until she arrives at O'Casey's own attitude embodied in the Dreamer. *Within the Gates* has justly been called 'a culmination of O'Casey's search for the meaning of existence.'[11] It is important to note that the principle of the quest has here also determined the structure of the play.

In his later plays, a religious belief is only one of several attitudes which a character can choose from, or it may be rejected altogether. This is particularly noticeable in *Red Roses for Me*, where trust in the deity is seen as insufficient and, in the action of the statue, is even revealed as superstitious: the allegedly divine miracle has in reality been performed by a human being whose character is by no means unproblematical. Catholicism and Protestantism are thus presented here as possible but questionable attitudes among others; at best they can take a share in Ayamonn's socialist synthesis of such attitudes. It is significant to note that O'Casey presents Ayamonn as a character who is absolutely sure which way he has to go. He is no longer a searcher like Jannice, because he has arrived at the goal of the quest, or at least the goal that O'Casey took for his ideal at this time of his life. In the other plays of this and the next period, the 'religious' theme has been reduced to the presentation of the comic or repellent priest or, at most, to the confrontation between the utopian 'good' and the absurd 'evil' priest.[12] Only in *The Bishop's Bonfire*, the most complex among the later plays, does the question of true belief resume its central position; here the author does not attempt to solve it precipitately himself but to dramatise it in the inner conflict of various characters, and for the first time since Jannice, a positive character (Foorawn) suffers from the apparent hopelessness of her quest.

Opposed to Foorawn's despair is the theme that takes up more and more room in the course of O'Casey's work: the liberation from the barriers of religious, moral, social, political and national prejudices and the confirmation of a joyful attitude to life, an attitude that is devoid of superficial optimism because it has been arrived at despite a series of depressing experiences. This theme, 'the joyous dance of life, the liberation of mind and body, the joyous *élan vital* which O'Casey celebrates in opposition to the anarchic and negative forces of modern life',[13] is touched upon for the first time in *Nannie's Night Out*, where the title character, an outcast from society, gains the courage which belongs to life from the very adversity of her circumstances and gives it expression in her symbolic dance. *Within the Gates*, in this respect, is an almost linear continuation of *Nannie's Night Out*. The Dreamer to whom Jannice turns at the end of her quest, embodies the O'Caseyan values of life: joy, love and beauty which find expression in poetry, song and dance. As frequently in O'Casey, however, Jannice's difficult path to this goal has found more convincing presentation than the goal, the Dreamer's view of life, itself.

The dramatic realization of the theme of life affirmation is most convincing wherever the characters have to struggle against restrictive and life-denying forces. Souhaun and Avril in *Purple Dust* undergo such a process of liberation when they free themselves from the materially secure but loveless relationship to Poges and Stoke; and Angela's independence in *Bedtime Story* can only be attained because she has rejected the moral prejudices of society. In the plays of the fourth period the theme of liberation and life affirmation moves to the centre of the plays and finds expression even in the grouping of the *dramatis personae*. The dancing cock in *Cock-a-doodle Dandy* is the most successful symbol for such an attitude, but *The Bishop's Bonfire* on the whole is the most moving dramatization of this theme, precisely because here O'Casey's ideal attitude is *not* successful. The necessity of liberation never appears quite as convincing as it does in the failure of Father Boheroe, who pleads for a life-affirming attitude to God, and in the fourfold defeat of Foorawn, Keelin, Daniel and Manus. O'Casey here succeeds in showing that the process of emancipation is not so much a struggle against external obstacles as an inner conversion.

There are several other plays where O'Casey delineates the failure of an attempt at self-liberation (e.g. in Sheila's adherence to morality and social conventions in *Red Roses for Me*, Chatastray's frightened conformism in *Behind the Green Curtains* or the Old Woman's outbreak in *Figuro in the Night*, repented almost immediately), but in these cases the failure to achieve liberation is limited to individual characters and does not, as in *The Bishop's Bonfire*, dominate the whole play. Paradoxically, *The Drums of Father Ned*, the play most whole-heartedly devoted to the theme of life-affirmation and liberation, is less effective than the examples of failure mentioned above. The opponents to the Tostal and the victory of youth are here far too weak, and one wonders why these people need a Father Ned at all, if the life-denying generation is as harmless, despicable and easy to overcome as it is in this play. For the present survey, however, it is more important to note that in this play the theme of liberation is presented in its greatest detail, if not with the highest intensity. The Tostal poster with the slogan 'WE *were* DEAD *and are* ALIVE AGAIN!' (p. 47) can serve as a motto for the play as well as for this element in O'Casey's work in general. With it, O'Casey takes up an exceptional position in modern literature: 'At a time when so much of modern literature has been obsessed with Original Sin, O'Casey expressed his faith in what might be called Original Joy.'[14]

O'Casey's thematic variety and flexibility cannot be adequately appreciated unless one realizes that, in addition to the 'dramatic ideas' discussed above, he dramatizes a number of recurrent motifs, basic situations of human life, applied in various ways to individual characters. Four of them, the motifs of exile, self-deception, betrayal and proof under trial, are of particular interest.

The motif of exile is usually linked to O'Casey's criticism of contemporary Ireland. Numerous characters in his later plays – like the author himself – leave the country in search of greater independence elsewhere. There are occasional examples in the earlier plays, too: for instance Bentham's flight (*Juno and the Paycock*) and Feelim's sudden appearance at Hatherleigh (*Oak Leaves and Lavender*); but only with his growing criticism of Ireland can emigration be seen as a decision against Ireland and for a voluntary exile. In *Cock-a-doodle Dandy*, the four 'positive' followers of the symbolic Cock leave the country, as do Kelly, Widda Machree and the tradition-conscious tourists in *Time to Go*; in *The Bishop's Bonfire* all the relations of the old Codger have gone this way, and Manus in his desperation departs for a second time; in *Behind the Green Curtains* Beoman, Noneen and Reena take the same decision. In the last-mentioned plays it is even seen as a major weakness in some of the central characters

(Daniel, Foorawn; Chatastray) that they cannot master the strength to go abroad where alone they might find fulfilment in life. The only play among those that deal with present-day Ireland where the alternative of exile remains unconsidered is the optimistically utopian *The Drums of Father Ned*; here Ireland itself offers the chances of self-realization which in the other plays is open to the exile alone.

Self-deception is, as has been shown above, the central motif in *The Shadow of a Gunman*. With the single exception of Maguire, all the *dramatis personae* are caught in a network of delusion, and O'Casey uses the principle of authorial irony to discover the discrepancies between aims and actions, between pretensions and actual behaviour. The motif is varied by showing that in some cases the deception reduces a character's willingness to assist others, while in other cases it does not. Davoren's is the only case where there is a suggestion that his self-deception might be overcome and a higher level of awareness and humanity attained. As in *The Shadow of a Gunman*, each of the figures in *The Plough and the Stars* is characterized by their self-deception, but they are more differentiated as to the importance of these illusions for their total behaviour. Risking a certain degree of simplification, one might say that the *dramatis personae* in *The Plough and the Stars* fall into three groups: those who are not prevented by their self-deception from looking after their personal interests (for instance Peter), those who uncompromisingly follow their illusions to the very end, even if they lead into danger or death (for instance Clitheroe), and those who show pity and humanity despite their self-deception (for instance Bessie).

In other plays O'Casey utilizes this motif predominantly for comic effect. The best example is 'Captain' Boyle who is inextricably caught in a whole web of illusions about himself (one of them suggested by his name) and who could never escape from them even if he wanted to. Other cases in point, where the audience gains an insight into the discrepancy between a character's self-assessment and reality, are the three suitors in *Nannie's Night Out*, Darry in *The End of the Beginning*, Poges in *Purple Dust* and Prodical in *The Bishop's Bonfire*. All of them undergo comic disillusionments, but nowhere does this lead them to a deeper insight into their own characters.

The motif of betrayal, like the motif of self-deception, pervades the whole body of O'Casey's writing. It is not the purpose of the present study to discuss the biographical reasons that may have led to such a preoccupation. The most obvious example is Johnny

in *Juno and the Paycock* where the interest is directed entirely
to the consequences, not to the causes of the betrayal. But the
motif had been suggested even before this play, when Minnie
in *The Shadow of a Gunman* is deserted by Davoren who later
acknowledges his own responsibility for her death. In *The
Plough and the Stars* the motif finds a different realization: when
Brennan and Clitheroe carry in the wounded Langon, betrayal
appears as an alluring temptation to escape the horrors of the
fight; yet despite Nora's entreaties the two officers return to the
barricades after they have carried their comrade to safety. Here,
again, the reasons for this decision are less important than its
consequences.

Particularly despicable roles are played by the four trade-union
officials, perfect opportunists, who desert Red Jim at the decisive
moment and are ready without the slightest scruple to sacrifice
him to their own advantage. They resemble the scabs in *Red
Roses for Me* and, more remotely, Constant and Pobjoy in *Oak
Leaves and Lavender* who are prepared to betray the common
cause of the war effort. In these cases, the traitors are far more
clearly condemned by O'Casey's method of presentation than
in the early plays, where the audience is made to experience
compassion rather than contempt for Davoren and Johnny.
Different again is the realization of the motif in *The Bishop's
Bonfire*. The failure of the four central characters is to be seen as
a kind of betrayal, but this is not so much a betrayal of individuals
than a betrayal of the ideals to which they had adhered for a
while, and which fear or weakness leads them to desert. Chatastray
in *Behind the Green Curtains* is also one of those who do what is
wrong (submission under unjustified authority) although they
have the critical insight to recognise what is right (i.e. to defend
the O'Caseyan ideals of freedom and life-affirmation).

O'Casey's dramatic work would be predominantly pessimistic
if such characters formed the majority of his *dramatis personae*.
Yet side by side with the motif of betrayal stands the motif of
proof under trial, and O'Casey repeatedly shows a number of
characters who do not evade the demands that life makes on
them. They are more important than those others for whom failure
in life is altogether impossible because they are presented from
the start as ideal characters, and it is these figures who are
responsible for the element of hope that is suggested again and
again in O'Casey's writings. The motif of proof in adversity
dominates in O'Casey's first phase, because here he leads his
characters into situations where failure and success seem equally

possible. Juno is the central character in this respect. Her superiority in the decisive scenes is so impressive precisely because those who surround her are submitted to similar situations. It has been shown above that this motif has a central function in *Juno and the Paycock*. Repeatedly various characters have to undergo the same test of endurance; the occasions for the test develop from banalities to the confrontation with fate which Juno alone can endure. In *The Shadow of a Gunman*, Davoren experienced a similar trial in which he failed miserably. In *The Plough and the Stars*, again, several characters are thrown into this situation, and Bessie and Fluther are thereby able to prove their superior humanity.

Among the later plays, *The Bishop's Bonfire* gives a number of characters the chance to prove themselves; where they fail, this motif is closely related to that of betrayal. Daniel in particular fails when he does not stand by Keelin. His situation is reminiscent of that of Mahan in *Cock-a-doodle Dandy* who does not protect Loreleen from the stone-throwing mob, and of Chatastray in *Behind the Green Curtains* who repents and joins the demonstration. If one disregards those plays which, because of their different themes, offer no room for this motif (e.g. *Within the Gates*), it is remarkable that, after *The Plough and the Stars*, O'Casey creates very few characters who are given the chance of a genuine decision. Although there are situations that resemble the character test, persons like Drishogue or Ayamonn are committed to such an extent to O'Casey's ideals that their behaviour is constantly predictable. Quite differently from Juno's great crisis, it is never doubtful that Ayamonn will resist the temptation to egoistic behaviour and will do so without any recognizable effort. Where failure and success would be equally possible, it is clear from the outset that these figures will remain impervious to temptation.

As in the survey of O'Casey's dramatic forms, the discussion of his most important themes and motifs cannot fail to demonstrate the variety, and occasionally also the inconsistency, of his writings. Each of the themes and motifs mentioned above would merit a special study.

# 31. MODELS AND ANTI-MODELS

In *Inishfallen, Fare Thee Well* O'Casey related how he was invited by Lennox Robinson, at the time of his early fame (probably in 1924), to the ceremonial dinner of a club of Dublin intellectuals presided over by Yeats. It is not surprising that O'Casey was not happy in these surroundings:

> So he did what he could to ingratiate himself with his hosts, eating what he thought was a badly-cooked meal as delightfully as he could; answering the questions put to him as wisely as possible; but discovering that he knew nothing about writers that were common names in the mouths of those who sat beside him. No, he had never seen or read *The Life of Man*, by Andreiev, or *Falling Leaves*, by Giacosa, or *Monna Vanna* and *Joyzelle*, by Maeterlinck; no, nor Benavente's *Passion Flower*, or Pirandello's *Right You Are (If You Think So)*; while Sean whispered the names of Shaw and Strindberg, which they didn't seem to catch, though he instinctively kept firm silence about Dion Boucicault, whose works he knew as well as Shakespeare's; afterwards provoking an agonised My Gawd! from Mr. Robinson, when he stammered the names of Webster, Ford, and Massinger.[1]

More than thirty years later O'Casey drew up a programme for a subsidised theatre that would be independent of the material restrictions of the usual repertory theatre, as had been the unrealized dream of almost every English man of the theatre since Henry Arthur Jones. The programme of the first season was to contain the following plays: Shaw's *Heartbreak House*, Chekhov's *The Cherry Orchard*, O'Neill's *Mourning Becomes Electra*, Strindberg's *Dream Play*, Saroyan's *My Heart's in the Highlands*, Gorki's *Yegor Bulychov*, Wedekind's *Spring's Awakening*, Shakespeare's *Midsummer Night's Dream*, Wilder's *Our Town*, Pirandello's *Six Characters in Search of an Author* and Giraudoux' *Enchanted*.[2]

If these two statements are representative of O'Casey's views at different stages of his development, the comparison may permit certain conclusions. It is remarkable how his literary horizon had been enlarged. At over forty, his knowledge of the

341

drama was still restricted to a few areas. He was familiar with the great English renaissance dramatists, with nineteenth-century melodrama represented by Boucicault and, in his own time, with Shaw and Strindberg, the only foreigner in his list. In 1958, on the other hand, he surveyed the whole range of Continental European as well as English and American drama. His programme (explained in detail in each case) contains a balanced selection of recognized masterpieces which would not have elicited an 'agonised My Gawd!' even from the well-read Lennox Robinson. On the other hand one will note a remarkable continuity in O'Casey's preferences. Of the names referred to in 1924, he mentions again in 1958 Shaw, Strindberg and Shakespeare, and his continuing interest in the melodrama's sentimentality, exaltation of feeling and selection of sensational events is documented by his reference to Wilder, Saroyan and Wedekind. New are the names of Chekhov, O'Neill, Gorki, Giraudoux and Pirandello (whom he had not known in 1924). The following brief survey will discuss whether this selection is characteristic of O'Casey's reading in general and what influences by these authors, or by any others, can be detected in his works. To do so, it will be necessary to summarize briefly the findings of previous O'Casey scholarship in this field. In some cases it will not be possible to do more than point out unsolved problems of influence. Nor will any attempt be made to go beyond the limited field of drama. A survey of all the influences from intellectual history that become relevant for O'Casey would have to range from the Bible to Karl Marx; it would be the subject for a separate book.

A possible approach to the literary influences on O'Casey, the discovery of quotations from and references to other literary works, has been suggested repeatedly in the preceding chapters. An extremely useful survey of such O'Caseyan quotations has recently been provided by John Jordan.[3] This survey, however, also reveals why such an approach will not lead to reliable clues as to literary influences: frequently these quotations simply reflect O'Casey's reading at any one time, and more often than not they are what one might call oblique references, introduced for parodistic purposes or simply for the sake of a pun. Possibly a survey of those other writers whom O'Casey actually names in his non-dramatic works will be more profitable – always bearing in mind, however, Hogan's appropriate warning that 'the best qualities of his style [and of his work in general] were his inventions and not his borrowings.'[4]

A detailed analysis of O'Casey's literary and theatrical criticism (collected predominantly in the volumes *The Flying Wasp, The Green Crow, Under a Colored Cap* and *Blasts and Benedictions*) as well as the six volumes of his autobiography, reveals that the names of twelve writers, predominantly dramatists, are referred to again and again: Shakespeare, Boucicault, Strindberg, Synge, Yeats, Lady Gregory, AE (George William Russell), Shaw, Joyce, O'Neill, Chekhov and Gorki, with Yeats and Shaw far ahead of the others in point of frequency. Not all of these references suggest literary influences; indeed many of them refer to O'Casey's private relationship with these writers. If there were models for O'Casey's drama, however, they will have to be looked for here. O'Casey critics have contributed only one more name to the list of possible influences: that of Toller. It is, of course, not impossible that future studies may lengthen the list; it has already been suggested above that James Stephens and Gerhart Hauptmann may have been additional influences. One always has to bear in mind that O'Casey, because of his unusual life-history and his largely autodidactic education, was bound to have missed certain tendencies in modern drama, while others reached him at a much later period. At different times of his writing, therefore, one has to expect different influences; one cannot simply discuss 'O'Casey's literary models'; rather, one has to consider the models for certain periods or individual works. The only exceptions to this rule are the names of Shaw, Shakespeare and Boucicault which represent dominant influences throughout his life.

*

O'Casey's description of his introduction to the works of the 'second Saint Bernard', as he called him later, has already been quoted.[5] It can be dated approximately to the year 1910; it happened definitely before his earliest dramatic attempts which, as Joseph Holloway states, were decisively influenced by Shaw: ' "He told me that when he started to write plays he thought he was a second Shaw sent to express his views thro' his characters and was conceited enough to think that his opinions were the only ones that mattered." '[6] And as late as 1964, a few weeks before his death, O'Casey quite naturally quoted Shaw in support of his own views.[7] His prose writings are interspersed with a chain of references to this author whose opinions are treated as a sacrosanct authority on a variety of problems; and O'Casey's more detailed descriptions of his relationship with Shaw, three articles in *The Green Crow*, two articles in *Blasts and Benedictions*, his important letter to Ronald Ayling, and the chapters 'Green Fire on the Hearth' in *Drums under the Windows* and 'Shaw's Corner' in *Sunset and Evening Star*,[8] contain enthusiastic homage rather than critical discussion. In his hero-worship he even saw Shaw as 'our genuine St. Patrick' whose 'mitre will show, to the right, the silver star of Bethlehem, to the left, the red star of Communism: both blazing'.[9] It is not surprising that his attitude to Shaw influenced the writing of his own plays. As has been shown above, this is most conspicuous in *Purple Dust* where, despite O'Casey's own denial,[10] *John Bull's Other Island* emerges clearly as a model. In *The Shadow of a Gunman* O'Casey quotes, as has been noted before, from Dubedat's confession of faith in *The Doctor's Dilemma*, and it has also been shown that the death of Jannice in *Within the Gates* is equally closely related to Dubedat's death-bed speech. One can further see a relationship between O'Casey's Father Boheroe (*The Bishop's Bonfire*) and Shaw's Father Keegan (*John Bull's Other Island*). But Shaw's influence goes beyond the provision of models for individual figures, passages or motifs. It is probably due to this influence more than any that O'Casey, after the writing of *The Plough and the Stars*, turned again to an intellectual drama with a satirical and didactic tendency.

Several detailed studies have been devoted to the importance of Shaw for O'Casey. Cowasjee and Rollins describe the parallels as well as the differences between *John Bull's Other Island* and *Purple Dust*.[11] Metscher deals with Shaw's considerable influence on the development of O'Casey's satirical-didactic passages of dialogue.[12] The personal relationship between the two writers is studied by Weintraub who sees O'Casey as 'Shaw's Other Keegan'.[13] Parker provides a more comprehensive analysis, discussing the biographical relationship of the two dramatists, their political opinions, the importance of Shaw's concept of Creative Evolution and of the Life-Force for O'Casey, and their attitude to Ireland and finally even tackles the most difficult problem of all, Shaw's influence on the development of O'Casey's dramatic technique. Although he has gathered a wealth of observations, Parker has to admit their incompleteness: 'There is enough material for a book.'[14] Some suggestions for such a book about the influence of Shaw on O'Casey (there is little trace of an influence in the opposite direction) are provided by Habart,[15] who, however, in the main does not go beyond a parallel description of Shaw's and O'Casey's development and their attitudes to certain problems, tracing few comparisons and omitting the question of influence. These studies are more of a stock-taking than an evaluation of O'Casey's relationship to Shaw. The influence of such an important dramatist has, in general, been seen as unquestionably favourable and positive. Therefore it may be interesting to quote Denis Johnston, who never disguised his critical attitude to O'Casey. In this case he speaks of the 'damage done by the honeyed poison of G.B.S.' and calls Shaw 'O'Casey's worst friend'.[16] Whoever, like Johnston, sees the three great Dublin plays as the climax of O'Casey's writing, is bound to deplore his growing attachment to the model of Shaw.

The detailed attention that critics have devoted to the importance of Shaw for O'Casey is an exception. Even O'Casey's relationship to Shakespeare has found less consideration. It is true that Shakespeare is occasionally referred to as a model for O'Casey's plays, but there is only one brief study that supports such an assertion with proper evidence.[17] The Shakespearian influence is generally ascribed to three fields. First, the interaction of tragedy and comedy, of moving pathos and exuberant laughter has been seen as a Shakespearian heritage.[18] One ought to add, however, that O'Casey in this respect goes far beyond Shakespeare, admitting neither social nor dramaturgical barriers for the separation of serious and comic scenes. The alternation between the field of the serious and the comic can happen in a flash, in the same scene and for the same characters, and his burlesque passages are usually not only comic relief but serve (as has repeatedly been shown above) as ironic commentaries in scenic form on the serious action. Secondly, the 'Elizabethan' character of O'Casey's language is frequently stressed. Especially Trewin, who published a study under the title 'O'Casey the Elizabethan' and calls O'Casey 'an Elizabethan re-born',[19] has emphasized this factor, but his essay ends in an uncritical accumulation of metaphors without being able to show more than certain parallels between O'Casey and the Elizabethan dramatists. Thirdly, Falstaff has been seen as a model for O'Casey's comic 'heroes', especially 'Captain' Boyle, 'the closest approximation to Falstaff in contemporary literature'.[20] Here, one is on safer ground, especially if one adds Sir Toby Belch as an additional source. O'Casey himself called Falstaff 'probably the greatest character ever thrust upon a stage',[21] and this pre-eminent model has certainly helped to transform his acquaintances from the Dublin slums into the almost lovable good-for-nothings and braggarts of his plays.

A more detailed analysis of the Shakespearean influence would have to start with the personal experience of young O'Casey. As early as about 1892 (the autobiography provides no exact dates) he rehearsed a number of Shakespearean scenes which he was to produce with his stage-struck brother Archie. A year later he went on stage in a number of Shakespearean roles in a converted stable that Archie's amateur company used for its performances.[22] At the time of his early plays he was therefore well acquainted with Shakespeare whose attitude to life he praised: 'Now Shakespeare never ignored Life. His plays were full of it; that was why he was such a great playwright.'[23] Later, when he himself was a highly respected playwright, he pleaded for more frequent Shakespearean productions and regretted that the English stage neglected its greatest dramatist.[24] In 1964 he showed himself happy about Shakespeare's growing popularity and described Shakespeare's life and opinions, using criteria which he derived (perhaps unconsciously) from his own past.[25] These parallels between his own life history and that of the Elizabethan dramatist are the clearest expression of his admiration and his desire to be seen as a successor. Even on his death-bed he asked his wife to read to him from Shakespeare's works and from a biography of Shakespeare.[26]

Another important starting-point for a study of these influences are the Shakespearean quotations that O'Casey inserts in his works. They seem to be most frequent in *Red Roses for Me* (where a scene from *Henry VI* is also rehearsed) and in *Oak Leaves and Lavender*; but many more such disguised quotations might well be discovered. Such a study would have to discuss their function as well as O'Casey's references to whole Shakespearean scenes, for instance the use of a scene from *Romeo and Juliet* in *Oak Leaves and Lavender* or the associations of Ophelia in the scene of the deranged Nora in *The Plough and the Stars*. One would also have to ask whether the ubiquitous juxtaposition of comic and serious scenes can be traced back to Shakespeare only, or whether O'Casey's reading did not also contain other possible models. The most obvious candidate would be Dion Boucicault.

Mrs. O'Casey said shortly after his death: 'Of course, Shakespeare was his god . . .,' but she added in the same sentence: '. . . and so was Boucicault.'[27] The young O'Casey was introduced to the world of drama and the theatre through an acquaintance with Shakespeare *and* Boucicault, and there is no doubt whom he preferred at the start: 'What a pity they hadn't chosen a bit outa *Conn the Shaughraun* insteada pouncin' on Shakespeare's

stiff stuff. If they only knew, Boucicault was the boyo to choose.'[28]
In *Pictures in the Hallway* O'Casey describes in some detail
how he was permitted one evening to take the role of Father
Dolan in *The Shaughraun* in place of an indisposed actor,
because he possessed a free pass to the Mechanics' Theatre and
knew many Boucicault parts by heart. The same play was the
first that O'Casey saw in a professional theatre (the Queen's).
Later, when his own plays were performed on the stage of the
Mechanics' Theatre, that had by then been turned into the Abbey
Theatre, his memories of the Boucicault plays he had once seen
there were revived [29] O'Casey, however, was clever enough to
keep these memories to himself, Boucicault being considered as
a representative of that form of show business that every serious
dramatist was expected to despise. Only when he was an accepted
author did he refer to his early interest in Boucicault and give the
'sentimental, but brightly-coloured melodramas of Dion
Boucicault' an important place in his survey of Irish drama.[30] His
memories of the Boucicault productions of his youth lasted until
old age. In *The Drums of Father Ned* the duel of the play-within-
the-play is rehearsed '*in the method of the old melodrama*' (p.
36). Probably O'Casey was thinking of Boucicault's *Arrah-na
Pogue or The Wicklow Wedding* which, like the theatre scene in
*The Drums of Father Ned*, is set during the rebellion of 1798.

Critics have repeatedly taken up O'Casey's references to
Boucicault. They have suggested a Boucicault influence on the
alternation of comic and tragic scenes in O'Casey, on O'Casey's
humour, on his use of Hiberno-English, on passages of 'shoddy
rhetoric'[31] in O'Casey or on individual scenes and figures, for
instance the death scene of Foorawn in *The Bishop's Bonfire*, the
entrance of Mrs. Tancred in *Juno and the Paycock* or the minor
figures in *Cock-a-doodle Dandy*.[32] Such conjectures, however,
lose some of their value inasmuch as most critics know a good
deal less about Boucicault than O'Casey did. They frequently see
Boucicault as a typical representative of the whole of nineteenth-
century drama and consider any contact with him as pernicious.
It is true that melodrama, like the Gothic Novel, the detective
novel and other fields of popular literature, contains a staple of
recurrent figures, motifs, structural, thematic and emotional
elements that are frequently passed on from one writer to the
next. Boucicault, however, was not only the unrivalled master of
this form, but in his best works he also goes beyond its limits.
The most popular and lovable figure in his Irish plays, for
instance, the talkative, vainglorious, law-breaking but helpful

Irishman who always comes to the rescue in an emergency
without expecting any reward (Conn the Shaughraun, Myles-na-
Coppaleen, Shaun the Post etc.) does not fit into the hero-villain
pattern of the conventional melodrama. This should not be
overlooked, for O'Casey, although in his youth he possessed
'literally hundreds of Dick's [sic] STANDARD PLAYS, mostly
melodramas',[33] usually refers quite explicitly to Boucicault.
Krause who, as an editor of some Boucicault plays, is aware of his
special position, emphasizes that O'Casey did not imitate any
elements from Boucicault for the sake of their sensational or
sentimental effect, but subordinated them to the new purposes
of his own plays. With the exception of the Shaun type, however,
he does not state in detail to what elements he is referring.[34]
Ritchie has more stereotyped ideas of the melodrama but suggests
a Boucicault influence on O'Casey in three respects, 'the use of
music and song, the alternation of comedy and tragedy, and the
use of the tableau'.[35] He also refers to some of the changes that
these elements underwent in O'Casey's works, for instance the
transition from unmotivated background music and spontaneous
songs in Boucicault to the realistically motivated use of song and
music in *Juno and the Paycock*. Similar results are stated by Colum,
who, in his analysis of the autobiographies, sees Boucicault as 'a
major influence on Sean O'Casey'.[36] A more detailed study of the
influence of Boucicault and the alterations that these influences
underwent is not yet available. Such a study would also have to
touch upon the question whether O'Casey was influenced by
other forms of the popular Victorian theatre, especially the farce
and the music-hall sketch.

*

At first sight O'Casey's famous Dublin contemporaries seem
more likely models for his writings than the authors mentioned
above. There is little, however, to substantiate such a conjecture.
Joyce can only be considered a possible model for O'Casey's *prose*
writings. In his autobiography, critics have indeed discovered a
Joycean influence – Orwell in his famous, but unjustifiably
malignant dictum called O'Casey's style in *Drums under the
Windows* 'basic Joyce'.[37] Benstock has discussed the role and the
function of the priest figures in Joyce and O'Casey, but has
restricted himself to a parallel description without attempting to
discover literary influences.[38] — While O'Casey always admired
Joyce, whom he called 'the bravest and finest soul in literature

Ireland has had for many years',[39] he ridiculed AE in *Inishfallen, Fare thee Well* as 'Dublin's Glittering Guy'.[40] This makes an influence on O'Casey just as improbable as an influence of Lennox Robinson, for whom O'Casey had little time either as a person or as a dramatist. The only effect of Lady Gregory, whose energy, selflessness and motherly care he always admired and whom, while being sceptical of her plays, he attempted to celebrate in Dame Hatherleigh (*Oak Leaves and Lavender*),[41] can be detected in her famous advice to O'Casey, '. . . your strong point is characterisation'.[42]

O'Casey was initially seen as a tireless visitor to the Abbey Theatre from whose repertory he was supposed to have derived numerous suggestions. This conjecture had to be dropped when O'Casey stated quite clearly that before the production of *The Shadow of a Gunman* he had seen only two Abbey productions. He was not even acquainted with the plays of Synge, the most important Irish dramatist of the day, until after he had written *The Shadow of a Gunman;*[43] Synge, therefore, cannot have influenced O'Casey's early conception of the drama. With the exception of *Purple Dust*, where one can find certain stylistic and thematic references to Synge, and *Cock-a-doodle Dandy* where these are possibly taken up again, O'Casey's work has probably remained quite free of influences from this source.

Nevertheless, the two dramatists have frequently been compared, and O'Casey has been called 'a city Synge', 'that great Irish successor of Synge', or 'der großstädtische Erbe Synges',[44] statements that tend to incorporate O'Casey into a Synge tradition. More detailed comparisons (which, however, do not suggest any literary influence) are to be found in Fox and Wittig and, in a stylistic context, in Krause.[45] Rollins compares *The Shadow of a Gunman* to *The Playboy of the Western World* in the context of a common theme, 'the Irishman's extreme fondness for heroes and heroic speech and action . . .'[46] Ayling, on the other hand, declares emphatically: '. . . no useful critical purpose is served by making false analogies between dissimilar plays.'[47] This is even more true for those studies where Synge and O'Casey are contrasted in order to prove Synge's superiority, for instance by Krutch ('. . . the shocking blather of O'Casey's characters is Synge's "Irish poetry" gone rancid'), Williams and Fréchet.[48] For a study of O'Casey's models, these comparisons are virtually useless. O'Casey's own references to Synge, especially his balanced understanding appreciation of the earlier dramatist,[49] and his occasional parodistic uses of Synge quotations,[50] do not indicate any influence. As early as 1926, in a letter to Lennox Robinson, he emphasized his literary independence: 'I am sorry, but I'm not Synge; not even, I'm afraid, a reincarnation.'[51] O'Casey's relationship to Synge, Lady Gregory, AE, Joyce and other Irish contemporaries leave little room for future studies. Even where critics are clearly in disagreement (for instance on the question which of Synge's plays was the special model for the 'Synge scenes' in *Purple Dust*) future studies are unlikely to achieve any more satisfactory results.

*

O'Casey's attitude to a number of Continental dramatists and to O'Neill, on the other hand, deserves more attention than it has found so far. Hogan has shown quite convincingly that *The Plough and the Stars* betrays surprising structural parallels to the plays of Chekhov, especially *The Three Sisters*.[52] Less successful is his attempt to detect this Chekhovian structure in other O'Casey plays. Nevertheless it is possible that O'Casey was acquainted with the plays of Chekhov at the time of writing *The Plough and the Stars*; in his article 'One of the World's Dramatists', written in 1943 and published in the Soviet Union, O'Casey speaks of a thirty years' acquaintance with the works of Chekhov.[53] It would be a difficult but profitable task to follow up Hogan's suggestion, '. . . in his early plays . . . he proved that Chekhovian structure was both copyable and capable of the greatest results'.[54]

Even more difficult to define is O'Casey's relationship to Gorki. The present study has suggested certain parallels between *Hall of Healing* and *The Lower Depths* without insisting on a concrete influence. In an article written in 1946, where Gorki is placed besides Strindberg, Ibsen, Hauptmann and Chekhov as one of the most significant modern dramatists, O'Casey describes his first introduction to his work. This makes it clear that certain similarities between Gorki's plays and the 'Dublin' phase of his own career ('. . . le premier O'Casey fait penser à un Gorki plus ironique et plus tendre à la fois . . .'[55]) do not derive from a concrete literary influence. The first Gorki play with which O'Casey became acquainted (after he had gone to London) was significantly *The Lower Depths*, and his revealing sentence, 'Then I realised that the streets of St. Petersburg and those of Moscow were, in all essentials, the very same as those of Dublin', shows that he was aware of the parallels between Gorki's and his own life history.[56]

It required only one further step to dramatize again the situation of the Dublin poor, now under the premises developed by Gorki. If *Hall of Healing* was the result of such a consideration, it is an open question, however, how one is to understand the parallels between *Hall of Healing* and Hauptmann's *Die Weber*. Unless more biographical material comes to light, it will remain uncertain whether O'Casey was at all acquainted with the works of Hauptmann, whom he mentions only in his article on Gorki and in a single letter.

O'Casey's attitude to O'Neill has received more attention. Especially Rollins has attempted to prove that the American dramatist influenced O'Casey.[57] Surprisingly, the starting point for these studies is not O'Casey's meeting and immediate friendship with the normally so reticent O'Neill in New York, and not even O'Casey's later 'Tribute to O'Neill'[58] or his own reference to the setting of *Mourning Becomes Electra* on which he modelled the setting of *Within the Gates*, but the alleged influence of *The Hairy Ape* on *The Silver Tassie* and *Within the Gates*. There is nothing on which to found such a conjecture; there are dozens of plays that are as much like the works of O'Casey's second phase as is *The Hairy Ape*. Another critic's more modest conclusion from the comparison between O'Neill and O'Casey, that both of them share the basic tendency to escape the fetters of realism, is still the only indisputable insight.[59]

Rollins suspects that O'Neill's plays, but especially *The Hairy Ape*, were the starting point for O'Casey's introduction to the world of expressionism. It is an indubitable fact that O'Casey was influenced by certain representatives of this movement. O'Neill, however, is not among them. The most important authors in this context were Toller and – if the term 'expressionism' is used as comprehensively as is normally the case in O'Casey criticism – Strindberg.

In this context, Fallon's reminiscences of the Dublin Drama League are crucially important.[60] It was one of those theatre clubs that guaranteed its members a certain number of productions per year. Founded by Lennox Robinson, it flourished between 1919 and 1929 when its function was taken over by the newly founded Gate Theatre. During this time, which, significantly, covers the period of O'Casey's 'Dublin' plays, the Drama League provided approximately five productions per season, all of them works that did not fit into the predominantly Irish repertoire of the Abbey ensemble, and most of them taken from the contemporary

Continental European theatre. Although the standard of these productions cannot have been very high, because there were rarely more than two performances, the Dublin Drama League played an important part in the cultural life of the city and offered one of the few chances of escaping the provincial isolation of Ireland which was favoured by the political nationalists. According to Fallon, O'Casey saw most of these productions and thus, for the first time, received some insights into the various tendencies of the Continental drama. For an autodidact well-read in Boucicault and the classics of the English theatre, it must have been an overwhelming experience to see on stage works by Claudel, Pirandello, Andreyev, Schnitzler, Molnar, Strindberg, Toller and others, especially since most of them were not available in published translations in English. Critics ought to pay more attention to the ideas that O'Casey must have derived from these plays. There is no doubt that they contributed to his change of style in *The Silver Tassie*. It would be a most rewarding task to analyze in detail the programme of the Dublin Drama League and its consequences on *The Silver Tassie* and *Within the Gates*.

According to Fallon, O'Casey showed himself particularly impressed by one play: Toller's *Masse – Mensch*:

But the play in the Drama League's repertoire which had a lasting (and some say a blasting) effect on Sean O'Casey's career as a dramatist was undoubtedly Toller's *Masse Mensch* which was presented at the Abbey Theatre under the title *Masses and Man*; and it was the form even more than the content of the play that appealed to him.[61]

The parallels and differences between this play and *The Silver Tassie* have been discussed above; they have been confirmed by various critics.[62] Other critics add the possible influence of Toller's *Hinkemann* or *Die Wandlung*.[63] This must suffice to refute Krajewska's statement that O'Casey did not have any direct contact with German expressionism, as well as McHugh's assertion that such contact did not take place until O'Casey had settled in London.[64] Quite another question is the extent of this influence and its evaluation; St. John Ervine, for instance, declared: 'The resemblance between Mr. O'Casey's play [*Within the Gates*] and the work of the German Expressionists is entirely superficial, for he retains the humanity of people, while they reject it.'[65] While it is at least clear that O'Casey derived certain suggestions from Toller, his attitude to Strindberg is still highly doubtful, although he mentioned his name at the 1924 dinner and called him in 1945 'one of the greatest playwrights of his time and ours.'[66] As with the term expressionism itself, critics have also been extremely careless with the literary influences that led to O'Casey's so-called 'expressionist' works.

★

Influences discussed so far have been connected with writers and works to which O'Casey must have felt some affinity and from which he therefore – consciously or subconsciously – accepted certain suggestions for his own writings. There is, however, also the case of 'negative influence' and the anti-model. O'Casey, a fighter by nature, was always willing to take sides, to be enthusiastically for or unreservedly against other writers. In his case particularly it is to be supposed that he did not only follow certain models but that he also tried to dissociate his own works from those authors whom he rejected. This kind of negative influence has so far found little attention.

The sources of influences of this kind are to be expected in two areas. One can be defined by the names Pinero – Barrie – Lonsdale – Coward – Sherriff. These were the dramatists who at the time of O'Casey's arrival in England dominated the London theatres, or at least those that were at all open to the serious drama. Most critics considered them as the protagonists of a renaissance in English drama. O'Casey, on the other hand, although not generally critical of successful dramatists (he spoke most approvingly of Granville Barker and Giraudoux,[67] and, of course, Shaw was also a successful dramatist!) always treated these writers with great disdain. Even in Dublin he criticized Coward's *The Vortex* and *Hay Fever*: '. . . the characters in these two plays were not people, had neither flesh nor blood in their make-up.'[68] When, in London, he saw more plays of this kind, his contempt grew: 'Sean had seen them all, and had sighed, and was silent. There wasn't a human heartbeat, no, nor even a human foot-step in one of them; not a knock at the door; not a sob in the silence; not a stone flung through any amiable window of thought.'[69] As a reaction he wrote the three articles called 'Coward Codology' in *The Flying Wasp*[70] and the satire 'Dramatis Personae Ibsenisensi'[71] in which he describes how Ibsen sets out from Norway to give birth to all the modern dramatists: whereas before the birth of Shaw and O'Neill he suffers terrible labour-pains, he gives birth to authors like Pinero almost without noticing it, while drinking a glass of port in a restaurant, and Barrie is set down on the banks of Loch Lomond, with a stick of sugar rock in his hand, Ibsen himself retiring from the scene hastily and in great shame.

It is hardly to be doubted that O'Casey's plays of the second and third phase are his reaction to the type of drama that dominated the stage of his time. It is true that he probably began writing *The Silver Tassie* before he could have seen Sherriff's *Journey's End* on stage (which otherwise might have triggered off his own dramatization of the war), but in general O'Casey attempted to dissociate himself with his 'London' plays from the prevailing fashions. He especially rejected the superficial stage realism, far removed from the events of true life, to which Coward and his colleagues clung, and he thoroughly disagreed with their self-imposed limitations in the choice of characters, actions and themes all of which were closely associated with the English upper classes. The fact that O'Casey turned to experiments with unrealistic forms of the drama, that he continued to draw his characters from the working classes, derived his problems from their sphere of life and strictly avoided drawing-room settings, the most popular scenario of contemporary English drama, must also be seen as a reaction to those colleagues of his whom he so despised.

The second anti-model for O'Casey as a dramatist was William Butler Yeats, a figure with whom his prose writings are engaged in perennial, if intermittent, controversy. In his autobiography, from *Drums under the Windows* onwards, Yeats is the person referred to most frequently, and O'Casey uses quotations from his works with various intentions in a variety of places. The contrast between the two authors is based, no doubt, on the differences in their personal background. At the time of his first successes Yeats, the man of the world, idealized and theatrical, treating him with a fatherly condescension, must have appeared to O'Casey like the inhabitant of another world, to be avoided or evaded wherever possible. In contrast to Lady Gregory, who soon won the confidence of the awkward, outspoken worker, Yeats kept his distance from him, and it was bound to appear at the time that he did so from sheer arrogance, while it is known today that Yeats hid a considerable degree of shyness under his theatrical cloak of superciliousness. The quarrel over the rejection of *The Silver Tassie* naturally deepened the conflict between these two radically different persons, a conflict that was never to be completely overcome.[72]

A harmless off-shoot of these personal differences can be seen in *Purple Dust* where O'Casey includes an ironic reference to

Yeats. O'Casey, who had no use for Yeats's exalted traditionalism, appears to allude to Yeats's restoration of, and residence each summer in, Thoor Ballylee when in the second version he gives the decaying mansion the name Ormond Manor and has its new proprietors refer repeatedly and with comic exaggeration to the Ormond flag and coat-of-arms. It is well-known that Yeats was particularly proud of his descent from the Butlers, Earls of Ormond, one of the most respected medieval Anglo-Irish families. When one tries to summarize the personal relationship between Yeats and O'Casey, it is to be remembered that for Yeats it was not more than one episode among many, while for O'Casey it belonged to the basic experiences of his life. Hone's biography deals with Yeats's relationship to O'Casey on less than two out of five hundred pages,[73] while for every biographer of O'Casey it is a central issue.

Despite the contrast in their lives and the resulting opposition in their attitudes, O'Casey always treated Yeats the poet with admiration: 'He is the great poet of the period, and so far possibly (to me, certainly), the greatest poet writing in the English language.'[74] This dictum from the time of the poet's death is no isolated statement; it is echoed in frequent variation throughout the autobiographical writings and critical articles, where O'Casey often defends Yeats against the hostility of other Irish writers. On the other hand, O'Casey treats Yeats the dramatist with conspicuous reserve, which he breaks only once when he speaks of his visit to one of the drawing-room productions (in this case, *At the Hawk's Well*) which had become the ideal ambience of the ageing poet. Here O'Casey ridicules the audience's ceremonious behaviour, imagines what would happen if Fluther Good were to enter and provoke a free-for-all, and denies all authenticity to Yeats's adaptation of Noh-play conventions. Indeed, the highly stylized, de-individualized forms of the Noh-play on the one hand, and the vulgar, vigorous, highly individual Fluther on the other characterize the two extremes of Yeats's and O'Casey's conceptions of the drama. There is no doubt that O'Casey's dramatic intentions were influenced by his attempt to avoid any proximity to Yeats's type of play: 'A play poetical to be worthy of the theatre must be able to withstand the terror of Ta-Ra-Ra-Boom-Dee-Ay, as a blue sky, or an apple tree in bloom, withstands any ugliness around or beneath them.'[75] The flight into the drawing-room and into the conventions of a distant theatre world appeared to O'Casey as a flight from life itself. He put up with vulgarity and coarse effects because their presence was part of the fullness of life. Confronted with a choice between the conventions of the Noh-play and Victorian melodrama, O'Casey would not have hesitated to choose the latter.

The contrast between these two writers, deepened by their mutual indignation at the other's behaviour, found its clearest theoretical expression in the controversy in letters that followed on the rejection of *The Silver Tassie*. As this has been discussed repeatedly in preceding studies, it need only be added here that it was not the first difference of opinion between Yeats and O'Casey on the function of the drama. As early as 1922, after *The Crimson in the Tri-Colour* had been rejected, O'Casey defended his attitude against Yeats's criticism, which Robinson had passed on to him.[76] Much more important is the question what consequences O'Casey drew from the conflict for his own writings. It has been shown above that *Oak Leaves and Lavender* can be seen as a continuation of *The Silver Tassie* controversy with the weapons of the dramatist. O'Casey tries to show (not entirely successfully) the superiority of his own dramatic concept: a play with a general historical event at its centre, without a dominant character and a conspicuous plot, with a juxtaposition of comic and tragic elements and with a clearly recognizable opinion as its foundation. That, in *Oak Leaves and Lavender*, he entered into an undisguised competition with Yeats, can also be seen from the fact that he utilized Yeatsian stylistic devices that normally were quite foreign to him, for instance the ghostly dancers, the framework of the prelude and the after-play. There is little doubt that in other plays, too, O'Casey saw himself in straightforward opposition to Yeats, especially when he defended his right to display his own opinions on the stage. This question deserves a more detailed study than it has found so far. The following paragraphs present no more than a few suggestions for such a study.

O'Casey repeatedly puts himself into clear opposition to Yeats's *Cathleen ni Houlihan*. He contrasts Yeats's image of Ireland with his own less romantic and more realistic vision of the country. This is quite explicit in *Kathleen Listens In* and *Red Roses for Me*, but several other women who figure in his Irish plays, for instance Minnie Powell, Juno, Irish Nannie and even Bessie Burgess and Rosie Redmond have to be seen in this context, too, as counter-images to the view of Ireland stamped by Yeats's play. This matter has been considered in an excellent article by Armstrong,[77] the only study that refers in detail to O'Casey's reactions to the plays of Yeats. Armstrong finds such reactions

especially in *Nannie's Night Out* and *Red Roses for Me*, calling
the latter play 'a spirited rejoinder to Yeats's despairing portrayal
of contemporary Ireland and Irish youth in his last two plays,
*Purgatory* and *The Death of Cuchulain*, both completed in 1939.'[78]

A continuation of this controversy must be seen in *The Drums
of Father Ned* where O'Casey, at about the age of Yeats when he
wrote *Purgatory*, presents once more an optimistic image of an
Ireland that is full of vitality and hope for the future. Armstrong
is certainly right when he speaks of 'O'Casey's own plays for
dancers whose full meaning is sometimes to be sought in
O'Casey's reactions to Yeatsian ideals.'[79] In this context, one
should also note O'Casey's ironic adaptation of a quotation from
*The Dreaming of the Bones* in *Cock-a-doodle Dandy*. Quite
possibly the concept of the Cock as a symbol of life affirmation
first suggested itself to O'Casey as an attempt to distinguish
himself from Yeats. Another reference is offered by Lindsay who
sees a general relationship between the use of Irish mythology in
Yeats and O'Casey:

O'Casey . . . draws on Irish mythology for imagery of heroic liberation
and renewal, and, in so doing, brings it vigorously to life; he, whom
Yeats rejected, here [in *Purple Dust*] achieves the very things Yeats long
wanted to do – to vivify the mythic images by linking them effectively
with modern life and its issues. O'Casey has found the method which he
triumphantly carried forward into *Cock-a-doodle Dandy*, *The Bishop's
Bonfire*, and *The Drums of Father Ned*.[80]

Less convincing is Bromage's comparison between *The Silver
Tassie* and Yeats's *Where There Is Nothing*.[81]

★

This brief survey of O'Casey's models and anti-models is no
doubt incomplete. Previous studies, if they exist at all, are sketchy
and frequently based on mere conjectures. There is ample room
for further studies in this field, especially for detailed analyses of
O'Casey's relationship to Shakespeare, Boucicault, the Continental
dramatists produced by the Dublin Drama League, and Yeats.
O'Casey himself was well aware of such interdependences, to
the extent that he perhaps even underestimated the originality of
his own work: 'However hard and long we think; however bold
we be; however fine we write, it's hard to say more than a bare
amen to all that's said afore.'[82]

# 32. INFLUENCES AND REACTIONS

The importance of a dramatist depends at least in part on the degree of his influence on other contemporary authors as well as on later generations. It is most significant to note to what extent a writer has experimented with new forms of the drama, discovered new themes and established new standards that have been recognized as binding by others. Twentieth-century drama has been influenced most decisively by writers like Strindberg, Ibsen, Chekhov and Brecht; looking back, it is hard to imagine its development without their contribution. The question to what degree O'Casey, too, has exerted an influence on younger dramatists has rarely been asked and never been answered in detail. Critics are usually content to maintain: 'Manch einer der jüngsten britischen Dramatiker – z.B. Wesker, Delaney, Behan, John Arden, Willis Hall, Errol John – knüpft sprachlich und thematisch unmittelbar an O'Casey an.'[1] Nor does the characterization of John Arden as 'a writer whose theatrical genius is strangely similar to that of O'Casey'[2] help pin down possible influences. Even vaguer is the following passage which leaves the question of influence itself entirely open:

... O'Casey extended his experiment by mixing realistic and non-realistic techniques in his plays – a mingled form which he was to use in all his later plays, and which has subsequently been used by most modern dramatists, to mention some representative examples, Obey's *Noah* (1931), Wilder's *Our Town* (1938), Giraudoux's *Madwoman of Chaillot* (1945), Williams' *The Glass Menagerie* (1944), Miller's *Death of a Salesman* (1949).[3]

The following study of O'Caseyan influences and of reactions to his work can therefore do no more than demarcate an almost unknown territory, establishing a few bases for more detailed exploration. It should also be stressed at the outset that it is highly dangerous to set down every superficial parallel as a possible influence; serious research into literary influences has been discredited by source-hunting of this kind.

Although the available material is as yet scarce, it can already be stated that O'Casey's influence is not comparable to that of dramatists like Ibsen and Brecht. There are several reasons for this fact: (1) At no time in his life did O'Casey have access to a larger circle of writers. Initially his descent and his fragmentary, autodidactic education prevented him from being accepted by other authors. When he settled down in Devon (1938) he isolated himself in another sense from the literary scene either in London or Dublin. Only during his stay of slightly more than ten years in or near London did he have a chance to make closer contact with other writers, but even then he seems not to have availed himself more than occasionally of this opportunity. Therefore he had little personal influence on younger writers who simply did not know him well enough. (2) After 1926, O'Casey also lacked direct contact with a particular theatre that could have staged model productions of his plays. An influence like the one exerted by Brecht through the Theater am Schiffbauerdamm, was impossible for him after 1926. (3) Moreover, with the exception of *Juno and the Paycock* and *The Plough and the Stars*, O'Casey's works did not exert any great influence through the theatre simply because they were not acted frequently enough. Most of his plays after *The Plough and the Stars* received during his lifetime only one or two productions in the English-speaking world. Younger dramatists did not have a chance of seeing more than an accidental selection of his complete work on stage. (4) O'Casey did not develop any coherent dramatic theory. His various statements on literary theory are highly relevant to an understanding of his own works, but they do not constitute any organic system of critical insights. (5) Because he lacked any basic dramatic theory, his plays are markedly divergent. Few of them are based in any way on experiences derived from the preceding work; especially in the second and third phases, each play constitutes a new departure and tries to solve new problems. This variety makes of O'Casey a truly experimental playwright, but it has certainly reduced his influence on other authors, and it is a difficult task indeed to recognize any influence derived from the whole body of his work. As will be shown below, one cannot normally discover more than the influence of a single play or small groups of plays.

*

A basic approach to the question of influence is to survey what other writers have said about a particular author. If such statements, as in the following examples, take on the form of enthusiastic appreciation, it is more than probable that the speakers were also willing to learn, possibly to imitate. Perhaps this cannot be said of Hugh MacDiarmid who, at the end of an article on O'Casey, confesses: 'There has not been in the over seventy years of my life any writer in Great Britain I am prouder to have known, and stood alongside in all essential matters than Sean O'Casey . . .'[4] O'Casey's and MacDiarmid's literary works diverge too sharply for any influence beyond the field of personal admiration to be suggested. An entirely different case is Brendan Behan who called O'Casey 'the greatest playwright living in my opinion' and added on another occasion:

I come from the same area as Sean O'Casey about whom I don't intend to say anything for the simple reason that it would be like praising the Lakes of Killarney – a piece of impertinence. As far as I'm concerned, all I can say is that O'Casey's like champagne, one's wedding night, or the Aurora Borealis or whatever you call them – all them lights.[5]

Behan read *Juno and the Paycock* and *The Plough and the Stars* in the British Borstal and felt they were 'like a visit from home. I knew Juno, and I knew Fluther Good in the *Plough*.'[6] Later, in his characteristically unconventional way, he put the Irish critics of O'Casey in their place:

O'Casey – a benignant colossus bestriding the theatre of the great world from Moscow to New York – is as great an Irishman, and as Catholic as Colmchille. Like Colmchille, he is able to take his own part in Irish, and I've often wished he could answer his clerical detractors in that language – to leave them speechless. However, being Catholic, he is universal, and must work for the great audiences of the world.
    In the United States, O'Casey is studied and praised in schools and universities all over the country. In the U.S.S.R. he is a highly respected artist. O'Casey is one of the few remaining unifying influences in a divided world. Why the hell should he care about a few crawthumpers in Ireland.[7]

O'Casey was equally interested in Behan's fate. In an interview he declared: 'I have used the Muse to the best of my ability, and I am mad at Brendan Behan in that respect. He has a wonderful talent, but he is killing himself, and by doing so destroying his genius.' When Behan died, 'O'Casey was very moved. He spoke about the tragedy of Behan drinking and the great talent that had been killed.'[8]
    In the case of John Arden, too, the admiration seems to have been mutual. O'Casey always exempted Arden when he criticized

the younger English dramatists, and he especially praised *Serjeant Musgrave's Dance*:

Arden . . . isn't one of the *avant-garde* and doesn't deal only with nonsense and savagery. Indeed it seems to me that Arden's *Serjeant Musgrave's Dance* is far and away the finest play of the present day, full of power, protest, and frantic compassion, notwithstanding that on its first presentation, it was scowled and scooted from the theatre by most of our intelligent and unintelligent drama critics.[9]

Arden, on his part, pleads at length for O'Casey: '. . . I have been continuously inspired and excited by his plays – from all periods of his work . . .'[10] In a similar way, Arnold Wesker named O'Casey as a significant influence on his work.[11] More surprising is the voice of Arthur Adamov:

J'ai souvent dit et répété mon attachement à l'oeuvre de Sean O'Casey, où l'ambiguité des situations et des personnages n'entrainent presque jamais confusions et équivoques, et où la sévérité, non plus, ne devient pas hargneuse. La tendresse d'O'Casey pour ses personnages me frappe à chaque nouvelle représentation, et c'est peut-être là que se trouve son plus exceptionnel mérite.[12]

Adamov even places O'Casey on the same level as Brecht:

. . . obwohl Brechts Werk für mich das wichtigste des zwanzigsten Jahrhunderts bleibt . . . so glaube ich doch, daß es bei O'Casey einiges gibt, das ich vorziehen würde. Wenn Sie wollen: ich träume von einem Theater, das Brecht und O'Casey zugleich ist. Das heißt: einem Theater, wo die Vorgänge bloßgelegt werden wie bei Brecht und wo dennoch die Personen, die Individuen inmitten der bloßgelegten Vorgänge ihr individuelles Leben weiterleben.[13]

More complicated is Denis Johnston's attitude to O'Casey, a life-long mingling of admiration and criticism. Johnston published a number of articles on his famous fellow countryman (the first as early as 1926, the last in 1964), in which he praised *Juno and the Paycock* and especially *The Plough and the Stars* as masterpieces: 'The consummate craftsman who could create the second act of *The Plough and the Stars* clearly knows as much as need be known about the English language, and any way he chooses to write after that is obviously intentional.'[14] Yet he denigrates the later plays as the slightly naive products of a 'dyed-in-the-wool Romantic'.[15] In the introductions to his own plays, too, he repeatedly discusses O'Casey.[16] The title of his play on the Easter

Rising, *The Scythe and the Sunset*, is, of course, a persiflage on *The Plough and the Stars*, and Johnston saw his own play as a *pendant* to O'Casey's work which he considered as pacifist: despite his irony he concentrates on the heroism of the insurgents, not the suffering of the ordinary people. In *The Old Lady Says 'No!'*, Johnston introduces a Mr. O'Cooney who is announced as a great dramatist and must be considered a parody on O'Casey at the time of his early fame. O'Cooney attends a reception by the Minister for Arts and Crafts in his working clothes and delights the other guests by his coarse language: 'And why the bloody hell shouldn't I wear my cap in the drawing- room?' In the second part of this play, Johnston inserts snatches of dialogue in the style of O'Casey's early plays, and some of these contain genuine O'Casey quotations: 'Who's a twister? I'm a twister? You're a twister? He's taken a header into the Land of Youth. Anyway, he was a damn sight better than someone I could name, and there's no blottin' it out.'[17] (The phrase 'a header into the Land of Youth' is taken from O'Casey's reply to Yeats after the rejection of *The Silver Tassie*). In the first version of Johnston's play, he even quoted Boyle's *chassis* speech from *Juno and the Paycock*.[18] Johnston, next to Shaw one of the great intellectual dramatists in the English language, has been strangely neglected by the stage. In many ways he represents the opposite extreme to O'Casey, and it would be rewarding to analyse in detail to what degree this is the result of a conscious confrontation with O'Casey's plays.[19]

Distinctly negative statements on O'Casey by well-known authors are rarer. They usually belong to Irish colleagues of O'Casey's, for instance Liam O'Flaherty and F. R. Higgins, who found that public interest in their works was diminishing through O'Casey's sudden fame. Brinsley MacNamara (John Weldon), too, dismissed O'Casey's works and criticized the Abbey audiences because of their 'wholly uncritical, and I might say, almost insane admiration for the vulgar and worthless plays of Mr. O'Casey.'[20] This is to be seen in direct contrast to Brian Friel's statement about recent Irish drama: 'We all came out from under his overcoat.'[21]

Critics have usually seen O'Casey's influence as limited to one field, that of English drama since *Look Back in Anger*. In 1952 it was still possible to say: 'O'Casey's influence on the contemporary stage has . . . to date been negligible.'[22] Twelve years later the situation is entirely different: now 'proclameert de jonge generatie van Britse toneelschrijvers hem tot een erflater.

A. Wesker, S. Delaney, B. Behan, J. Arden, W. Hall bekennen, zowel wat taal als wat motieven betreft, bij hem in de schuld te staan.'[23] Others suspect an influence on the *language* of the younger dramatists; in this field 'hat O'Casey bahnbrechend gewirkt, wie die kürzlich aufgetretene Flut der Dialekt- und Cockney-, Arbeiter- und Zigeunerdramen von Wesker, Delaney, Behan, Errol John, Willis Hall, John Arden, Bernard Kops u.a. zeigt.'[24] It should be added that the introduction of farcical elements, one of the characteristics of the 'new wave' of English drama, finds a parallel and possibly a source in O'Casey. Such statements, however, are not more than conjectures; detailed studies will have to show whether they are at all capable of proof. The only attempt so far at a general, if brief, survey of O'Casey's influences is a recent article by Hogan, and it is highly advisable to follow his warning against indiscriminate influence-hunting: 'O'Casey had more impact than influence . . .'[25]

*

Less difficult to pin down than the general influence of writers on one another is the relationship between individual works. Several such possible influences have been pointed out above. Louis D'Alton's *This Other Eden* (1953), one of the most impressive mid-century Irish plays, which again takes up the theme of the contrast between Irishmen and Englishmen, is difficult to envisage without the influence of *Purple Dust*, although *John Bull's Other Island* with its particular constellation of *dramatis personae* and its frequently epigrammatic wealth of ideas is another likely model. Another such influence is that of Susie in *The Silver Tassie* on Lennox Robinson's Marian in *The Far-Off Hills*. *The Silver Tassie* is furthermore said to have influenced the change from 'naturalism' in Act I to 'expressionism' in Act II of Patrick White's *A Cheery Soul*.[26] It is also possible that the choric technique of O'Casey's *Within the Gates* served as a model for Eliot's *The Family Reunion*. Eliot had seen the London production of *Within the Gates* in 1934 and showed himself impressed by O'Casey's use of chants in this play; he later thought that he might have been unconsciously influenced by O'Casey.[27]

These isolated and exceptional influences are, however, entirely insignificant in comparison to the unmistakable function of *Juno and the Paycock* as a model for a number of other plays. It is O'Casey's only work to initiate a new and still living literary tradition, the tradition of the family play set in the slums.

Conspicuous parallels between *Juno and the Paycock* and a number of other plays cannot be explained merely by their common descent from the tradition of the bourgeois tragedy, because it is precisely those traits which O'Casey added to the tradition that were copied repeatedly, especially the transfer of the events into the squalid quarters of big-city slums. *Juno and the Paycock*, of course, was not the first play to be set in the slums, but in the English-speaking world such plays remained rare and without great influence (even the authors of the realistic 'Manchester school of drama' preferred a lower-middle-class milieu), and foreign plays set in slums had little influence on the English stage. *Juno and the Paycock* was the first such play to have an undoubted success. Moreover its specific combination of dramatic motifs reappeared in a number of plays, rendering a concrete influence more than probable.

One of the best-known English plays between the two world wars, justly appreciated by audiences throughout Britain, was *Love on the Dole* by Ronald Gow and Walter Greenwood, a play set in the world of the unemployed (the première took place in Manchester in 1934). Like several other twentieth-century plays (from Harold Brighouse's *Hobson's Choice* to Shelagh Delaney's *A Taste of Honey*) it is set in a working-class quarter of Salford, Lancashire. Its constellation of *dramatis personae*, however, is that of *Juno and the Paycock*: the unemployed father, the indefatigable mother who alone keeps the family together, the daughter striving for 'higher' values. As in *Juno and the Paycock* the action is determined by the dual motifs of seduction and of unexpected wealth that disappears as soon as it has been won, and it is interspersed with comic elements. As in O'Casey's play, the necessity of strikes and demonstrations is discussed. Although none of these elements alone would suffice to constitute an influence, their combination points quite clearly to O'Casey.

Clifford Odets' *Awake and Sing!* (1935) belongs to the same period as *Love on the Dole*. Of this play it has been said: '*Awake and Sing!*, though not so great a play, is *Juno and the Paycock* transposed from the Dublin slums to the Jewish Bronx of New York. It has the same pattern of coarseness and sensibility, the quality that can send poetry, like a shaft of sunlight, through the squalor of a tenement.'[28] The specific Dublin milieu, unique in language and characters, has here been replaced by another, equally specific milieu. It is true that in O'Casey's Dublin the Berger family's standard of living would hardly qualify them as the inhabitants of a slum, but the higher material demands of the

American way of life classify them as members of the lowest social class whose existence is constantly threatened by unemployment. It is significant that the descriptions of the *dramatis personae* with which Odets prefaces his play, could be transferred, with very slight modifications, to the characters in *Juno and the Paycock*. The relationship of Bessie to Juno, for instance, can hardly be overlooked:

BESSIE BERGER, as she herself states, is not only the mother in this home but also the father. She is constantly arranging and taking care of her family. She loves life, likes to laugh, has great resourcefulness, and enjoys living from day to day. A high degree of energy accounts for her quick exasperation at ineptitude. She is a shrewd judge of realistic qualities in people in the sense of being able to gauge quickly their effectiveness. In her eyes all of the people in the house are equal. She is naive and quick in emotional response. She is afraid of utter poverty. She is proper according to her own standards, which are fairly close to those of most middle-class families. She knows that when one lives in the jungle one must look out for the wild life.[29]

She tyrannizes her family because she is deeply concerned about their happiness. She asserts herself against her husband who has been defeated by life and lives in fruitless memories of the past, as well as against her son who rebels against a purely materialistic attitude, and she cares for her self-confident daughter who would like to dissociate herself from the family, when she expects an illegitimate child and finds that no other refuge is left to her. Like the motif of seduction, the motif of unexpected wealth (Jacob's insurance money when he kills himself), points to the model of O'Casey's play. Even more reminiscent of O'Casey is the fact that this family in the process of disintegration, shaken by various catastrophes, entirely cut off from the world outside and thrown upon itself, is nevertheless not presented as an image of hopelessness and despair. Small gestures of affection are still capable of fending off the apparently all-powerful fate of poverty, and the final victory of Juno's humanity is here paralleled in Ralph's defeat of resignation and material dependence, even though Odets' solution seems to be less organic than O'Casey's.

Arnold Wesker's early play *Chicken Soup with Barley* (1958) is set in a similar and equally well-defined social context as *Awake and Sing!*, the world of East European Jewish emigrants in London. Although it appeared more than twenty years later, it has its starting point in the same historical situation, the thirties, a period overshadowed by economic crisis and mass unemployment that

seemed to predict an imminent end to the capitalist bourgeois
way of life. In *Chicken Soup with Barley* the now familiar constellation of *dramatis personae* from *Juno and the Paycock* is
again clearly recognizable (in the other two plays of the *Chicken
Soup Trilogy* it is still present, though less obvious). The resolute
and optimistic mother who fights for the material wealth of her
family, the resigned, passive, egocentric father, the son who is
engaged in political activities and his elder sister, initially
equally active but later disillusioned, all owe their existence as
much to the model of the Boyle family as to Wesker's personal
experience. The relationship is sometimes underlined in conspicuous details. Ada, for instance, turns one of 'Captain' Boyle's
favourite terms against her father who is so closely related to
Boyle: 'Daddy – you are the world's biggest procrastinator.' And
Sarah's indefatigable care for her family's welfare is symbolized
in the same action as Juno's motherliness: her never-tiring
readiness to make tea as a spontaneous cure-all for problems,
sorrows and disease:

SARAH. Sit down, both of you; I'll get the kettle on. [*Goes off to
    kitchen.*]
MONTY [*to Bessie*]. Always put the kettle on – that was the first thing
    Sarah always did. Am I right, Harry? I'm right, aren't I? [*shouting to
    Sarah*] Remember, Sarah? It was always a cup of tea first.[30]

Juno reacts in an identical way:

MRS. BOYLE. There, now; go back an' lie down again, an' Ill bring you
    in a nice cup o' tay.
JOHNNY. Tay, tay, tay! You're always thinkin' o' tay. If a man was dyin',
    you'd thry to make him swally a cup o' tay! (p. 7)

Even more important is the fact that *Chicken Soup with Barley*,
like *Juno and the Paycock*, is projected onto a historical
background action which intensifies the stage events and raises
them to a univeral plane. The changing role of Socialism in the
England of the thirties, forties and fifties that dominates the
discussions of the stage characters and is occasionally projected
on stage when they take part in demonstrations and, like Johnny,
are wounded, is depicted with the same sceptical objectivity as
the Civil War in *Juno and the Paycock*, the author refraining from
restricting his characters' individuality by imposing an opinion
of his own. *Chicken Soup with Barley* is the most remarkable
example of the far-reaching influence that O'Casey exerted,

without, however, in any way constraining his successors' originality of creation.

Another, not quite so conspicuous example is Errol John's *Moon on a Rainbow Shawl* of which Doris Lessing has said with some exaggeration: '. . . it is nearer to O'Casey than anything else in our language.'[31] O'Casey's Dublin tenement milieu has here undergone a more unusual transformation, and yet the ugly slums of Port of Spain, Trinidad, show surprising parallels to the world of 'Captain' Boyle, underlining the universality of O'Casey's play. The precise representation of a world of poverty characterized by its dialect, habits and types of persons is equally reminiscent of O'Casey as is the unsentimental poetisation of this world. As in *Juno and the Paycock*, brutal egoism exists side by side with a most admirable altruism, and one finds the resigned adaptation to apparently unavoidable necessities as well as the attempt at revolt. The situation of Mary has been shared between two characters, Rosa who will be alone to care for her child, and Esther, who has not (yet?) given up the struggle against the repressive forces of her surroundings. The clearest O'Casey influence is, however, again to be found in the parents: Sophia has been made ruthless and angry by the responsibilities that have been forced upon her, but she takes her role as the protectress of the family as seriously as Juno, while Charlie in his resignation flees from his duties into drunkenness and the reminiscences of his past as a cricket star.

*

This list of international plays influenced by *Juno and the Paycock* could probably be enlarged. Even more conspicuous, however, is O'Casey's influence in one particular field, English-language drama in Ireland. Here, the opposition to O'Casey and the desire not to be seen as a follower may have been as important as any direct imitation. O'Casey's importance as a model *and* an anti-model for the whole of Anglo-Irish drama since the twenties can be appreciated when one observes that the only literary history in this field, Hogan's *After the Irish Renaissance*, cites him on almost every page as a standard of evaluation for all other authors. The influence of O'Casey's *early* plays, especially *Juno and the Paycock*, is predominant. For a while it had looked as if the O'Caseyan influence would produce a flood of melodramatic plays about the Irish War of Independence and Civil War. This is underlined by an amusing review of a long-forgotten play

(Gerald Brosnan's *Before Midnight*) from 1928, when O'Casey
had already turned away from this material:

I do not suppose that the spiritual father of the Abbey gunmen, C.I.D.
men and prostitutes who has recently forsaken his offspring will claim
the literary paternity of Mr. Gerald Brosnan, or that Mr. Brosnan will
acknowledge any relationship with him. I do not suppose, either, that
the Abbey audience will accept *Before Midnight* even as a drop of
O'Casey war-substitute. But I do plead for a Kellogg pact of dramatic
disarmament and the blowing-up of dumps. In art there is no such thing
as a successful school. O'Casey, as a man of genius, closed the door he
opened. It makes a strong man blench to think of an O'Casey school, to
think of the myriad of Mr. Brosnan's unproduced colleagues who are
raiding Dublin tenement houses, stuffing their plays in vain with
revolvers and prostitutes and C.I.D. men.[32]

Fortunately the reviewer's misgivings did not come true. A few
works only of this particular tradition have been preserved. The
most remarkable among them is undoubtedly Brendan Behan's
*The Hostage*, 'a gaily subversive play in the O'Casey tradition',
which had the greatest success of all Irish works in that mould.[33]

Behan's indebtedness to O'Casey can fully be gauged only
when one considers the original Gaelic version, *An Giall*, in
addition to Joan Littlewood's English adaptation. Here the
action has not yet been broken up into 'alienating' music-hall
acts, and the parallels to O'Casey are much more obvious. It is
not, however, sufficient to speak simply of an influence on the
part of O'Casey, for Behan in many respects went beyond his
model, developing and sometimes exaggerating O'Caseyan
motifs. As in *The Shadow of a Gunman*, *Juno and the Paycock*
and parts of *The Plough and the Stars*, the scenery of *The Hostage*
is a room in a tenement house; like O'Casey, Behan was thinking
of a definite house in Dublin. Several of his characters are
immediately reminiscent of O'Casey's figures; the humorous,
sceptical, quarrelsome and nevertheless helpful Pat cannot be
imagined without the model of Fluther Good, and Teresa, in
her strange mixture of fairy-tale naiveté, shyness, healthy self-
confidence, practical altruism, courage and affection is closely
related to Minnie Powell. It is also tempting to see Monsewer,
who in his ridiculous kilt haunts the play as a symbol of the dead
past and is treated by everybody with mock respect, as a relation
of the Man in the Kilts in *Kathleen Listens In*; yet it is unlikely
that Behan knew O'Casey's early play, for it was not published
until 1961. It is more certain, however, that he refers to Rosie

Redmond, the first and most famous prostitute on the Irish stage, when, in characteristic exaggeration of his model, he depicts a whole brothel whose inmates, prostitutes, pimps, homosexuals, are treated with the same humour, understanding and compassion as Rosie.

The stage events in *The Hostage* are projected onto a politico-military background action that repeatedly erupts on stage, immediately affecting the stage characters. Behan, however, is much more critical of the historical process than his predecessor. The I.R.A. activities of the fifties, as an anachronistic continuation of the struggle for independence, are not only, as in O'Casey, criticized by some of the stage-figures, but are disparaged by the action itself: the senseless and accidental death of young Leslie condemns those who are responsible for his kidnapping. In addition, the guerilla fighters are, in contrast to O'Casey, shown here in a decidedly negative light. On the other hand, the real struggle for independence which is constantly present in the conversation of the stage figures, is treated with a similar objectivity to that found in O'Casey. In both cases, however, it is not the politico-military action but its effects on individual, well-defined characters that is at the centre of the play. In his juxtaposition of serious and comic elements, Behan goes beyond O'Casey, although at the time of *Juno and the Paycock* this must have appeared hardly possible. O'Casey has a number of scenes (for instance the entrance of the wounded officers in *The Plough and the Stars* or the arrest of Johnny in *Juno and the Paycock*) that are exempted from subversion by comic elements; only subsequently are they set off by farcical passages. In *The Hostage*, Behan has achieved a perfect simultaneity in both elements, making high demands on the audience's emotional adaptability. At the end, for instance, Teresa's lament for the senseless killing of Leslie, 'He died in a strange land, and at home he has no one. I will never forget you, Leslie. Never till the end of time,' stands side by side with the corpse's music-hall song:

> The bells of hell
> Go ting-a-ling-a-ling,
> for you but not for me . . . [34]

There is no doubt that Behan could achieve this extreme blending of styles only after the path had been prepared for him by O'Casey.

*The Hostage*, as a late reaction to O'Casey's plays of the Revolution and the Civil War, takes up an exceptional position.

In the meantime, O'Casey's early plays had been much more influential in another field of Irish drama. O'Casey was the first to introduce the world of the Dublin slums to world literature, and in Ireland, as abroad, the specific tradition he created is that of the family play set in the slums. Once the tradition had been established, dozens of plays were set in the tenements around Mountjoy Square. Only few of them have appeared in print; Seamus de Burca's *The Howards*, Robert Collis's *Marrowbone Lane* (1939) and Brendan Behan's short-play *Moving Out* (one of two plays from an unfinished series) may be cited as examples. All three deal with family histories from the Dublin slums and belong to the O'Casey tradition in a wider sense, although they do not show any specific indebtedness to O'Casey.

However, several plays written under the influence of O'Casey's works may be seen to derive more directly from *Juno and the Paycock*. Louis D'Alton's *The Mousetrap* (1938), for instance, is set in a family strongly reminiscent of *Juno and the Paycock*, with a sneering and domineering but unsuccessful father, a long-suffering mother, a son who through one rash action mars his whole future life and is finally arrested for murder, and a daughter who is left pregnant by the intruder from the outside world. Like O'Casey's seminal play, *The Mousetrap* is realistic in intention, with roughly sketched characters and nicely observed dialogue, but the plot is far too contrived, the disasters succeeding each other with improbable rapidity because, unlike O'Casey, the author tries to confine his action within the classically acceptable 24 hours limit. It is interesting to note that at the time of its publication the author's obvious sympathy for the 'fallen' girl, and his understanding for the seducer, together with his contempt for the upholders of conventional morality, apparently made the play unacceptable for the Irish stage, while its model has become a staple of the Irish theatrical repertoire.

Walter Macken's *Mungo's Mansion* (1946) transfers O'Casey's characters from the Dublin tenements to the slums of Galway.[35] The unemployed Mungo is another 'Captain' Boyle, seen slightly less critically, whose excitability is motivated at least in part by a previous accident. His love-hate relationship to the ragged Mowleogs is immediately reminiscent of Boyle and Joxer, a similarity underlined by the unexpected win in the sweep-stake. As in O'Casey, this play, under the rather repulsive surface of quarrels and egoism, hides a great deal of attachment, helpfulness and uncomplicated humanity. The chief differences are the absence of a character comparable to Juno and the absence of a politico-military background action.[36]

A Juno-like character is present, however, in a play that transfers the atmosphere of O'Casey's drama to yet another town, a poor area of Waterford: this is James Cheasty's *Francey* (1961). Again, as in *Mungo's Mansion*, the conflict between the care-worn, protective mother and her spendthrift husband is intensified by the presence of a parasitic character, a direct successor of Joxer, revealingly named Jock, who exploits the title character, a direct successor of 'Captain' Boyle, and turns against him when the source has fallen dry. There is also a hare-brained neighbour addicted to the lowest type of gossip whose words could have come directly from O'Casey's Mrs. Madigan, without, however, taking on her thematic function in the play. Francey himself is another braggart who lives in a world of fantasy and cares nothing for his wife, senselessly spending the compensation money he has received after a road accident until his married life, as well as his children, are ruined. Unlike O'Casey's play the motif of unexpected, destructive wealth has become central, triggering off a melodramatic action that leads to an unmitigated catastrophe. The protective forces embodied in Juno are here not strong enough to counteract the destructive forces of 'Captain' Boyle. Obviously the author has taken over the individual ingredients of O'Casey's play without grasping their contextual, supra-individual meaning. It is, perhaps, the absence of a more general background action, more than anything else, that leads Cheasty into the double abyss of sentimentalism and sensationalism.

Both the Juno-character and the general background action are present in a work that more than any other resembles the O'Casey play: Joseph Tomelty's *The End House* (1944). In this case it is sufficient to characterize Tomelty's work, without any explicit comparison, in order to draw attention to the obvious parallels with *Juno and the Paycock*. *The End House* is set in a poor, Catholic quarter of Belfast; the historical background consists of the Troubles of 1938. The central characters are the unemployed braggart and show-off MacAstocker, his wife Sar Alice, who throughout her life has been struggling for the survival of her family and does not expect any more from life than to provide enough to eat for her relations, her daughter Monica, who hopes to achieve a higher station in life and wants to leave the influence of the slums behind her, and her son Seamus, who has just been released from a prison sentence for his membership in the illegal I.R.A. The initial situation of the play is the death of a neighbour who has been shot by I.R.A. men because he had betrayed one of them to the police. The audience learn about his death when the play is opened by the reading of a newspaper article. This event is succeeded by a series of catastrophes: Sar Alice loses her insurance money, MacAstocker is injured in an accident, Monica falls in love with an English soldier who deserts with the money borrowed from her and leaves her helpless, possibly pregnant, Seamus is probably involved in the killing of the neighbour and is himself shot during a raid. Sar Alice and Monica remain as the victims, who are not even able to repay the money they borrowed from their neighbours and thus lose their good name. In view of all these parallels, which are supported by many minor details, it is necessary to emphasize the differences between the two plays in order to protect Tomelty from the accusation of plagiarism. The characters in *The End House* are seen less critically. MacAstocker is less depreciated by his actions than Boyle, and there is no character comparable to Joxer. In his place, Tomelty introduces two 'positive' helpful neighbours, and the cornet player Stewartie is his most interesting innovation. Due to the absence of a Joxer-like character, *The End House* lacks a great deal of the humour of *Juno and the Paycock*; its emotional tone, therefore, is more homogeneous. It is stamped by the author's compassion for the victims of the political situation. Although there is no attempt to make the theme explicit as O'Casey had done in Juno's prayer, the author's purpose in the play is more obvious and more unified. If all the stage characters are seen with sympathy, and are presented as innocent victims, the responsibility for such a situation must fall entirely on the existing political system which here is additionally criticized in the brutality and despotism of the police.

A direct continuation of *The End House* may be seen in John Boyd's *The Flats* (1971), set in the Belfast of 1969. The 'end house' has here been replaced by the 'end flat', situated in a strategic position in a block of flats. It is commandeered both by the British Army and the Civil Defence Committee, at a time when a Protestant mob threatens to attack the flats inhabited pre-dominantly by Catholics. This situation gives rise to extended discussions of various political viewpoints: militant repub-licanism, moderate nationalism, pacifism, socialism, the self-styled neutrality of the British Army, and a wholly understandable individualism concerned only with personal survival. Whereas the political background events have thus been up-dated, the mechanism for projecting them onto the stage is still that provided by O'Casey in *Juno and the Paycock*. The list of *dramatis personae* again reads like a description of O'Casey's play. There is the same constellation of the unemployed father who neglects his family, the care-worn mother untiring in her efforts to keep the family together, the outsider son who engages in subversive activities, and the disillusioned daughter who hopes for an escape from the slums through her fiancé who comes over from England. It is true that Boyd has omitted the time-worn motifs of seduction and unexpected riches, but the whole atmosphere of slum life under the pressure of a military conflict is closely reminiscent of *Juno and the Paycock*, and so is his use of test situations to distinguish between various attitudes to life, even to the point where a British soldier is to be given a cup of tea, and the characters react in various ways to this challenge, just as Johnny's demand for a glass of water had helped to distinguish between Juno and Mary. Even if Joe Donellan is not such a despicable good-for-nothing as 'Captain' Boyle, numerous details (including Kathleen's concluding prayer) point to the immense influence of O'Casey's work. It is a measure of O'Casey's success that his play is so much more convincing, unified, life-like, moving and universal than its successors and will be remembered when all the others are forgotten.

*

At the beginning of this chapter it was emphasized that the importance of a dramatist can in part be gauged from his influence on later authors. This statement deserves to be supplemented by another: the quality of a literary work may also be documented by its uniqueness, making all imitation or borrowing impossible. Moreover an author may be so far ahead of all his successors that they will not catch up with him for decades. In any case, wide-ranging influence is not, on its own, an unmistakable indication of the importance of a writer's work. When O'Casey is the writer in question, both these considerations are valid. His early work, and especially *Juno and the Paycock*, has exerted a considerable influence on younger dramatists. His later works, especially his great plays from the third and fourth phases, whose importance was emphasized in the present study, have, on the other hand, remained almost without tangible influence. It would be wise to consider this not as a criterion of their transitoriness but as an indication of the great variety of his work and his exceptional position in the spectrum of modern drama.

# NOTES

PART 1

1. PREFATORY
1  Sean O'Casey, *Autobiographies II* (London, 1963), pp. 95-98. All references to O'Casey's autobiography are to the two-volume edition.
2  See Herbert Coston, 'Sean O'Casey: Prelude to Playwriting', *Tulane Drama Review*, V, i (Sept. 1960), pp. 102-112; and Robert Hogan, 'O'Casey's Dramatic Apprenticeship', *Modern Drama*, IV (1961/62), pp. 243-253. There are also a few references in *The Letters of Sean O'Casey*, vol. II (New York, 1980), pp. 21, 33, 43, 149, 987.
3  Cf. Sean O Meadhra, 'Theatre: Poet and Peasant', *Ireland To-day*, I, ii (1936), pp. 62-65.
4  John J. Fitzgerald, 'Sean O'Casey's Dramatic Slums', *Descant*, X, i (1965), p. 26.
5  All stylistic aspects of O'Casey's plays are aptly analyzed by Thomas Metscher, *Sean O'Caseys dramatischer Stil* (Braunschweig, 1968).
6  Harold Clurman, *Lies Like Truth: Theatre Reviews and Essays* (New York, 1958), p. 122.
7  Andrew E. Malone, 'The Shadow of Sean O'Casey', *Bookman*, LXX (1926), pp. 104, 106.
8  E.g. Vincent C. De Baun, 'Sean O'Casey and the Road to Expressionism', *Modern Drama*, IV (1961/62), pp. 254-259.

2. THE HARVEST FESTIVAL
1  Sean O'Casey, *The Harvest Festival: A Play in Three Acts* (New York and Gerrards Cross, 1980). A German translation had been published in 1978: *Das Erntefest*, transl. Konrad Zschiedrich, in: Sean O'Casey, *Stücke 1: 1920-1940* (Berlin, 1978), pp. 15-62.
2  *Autobiographies II*, p. 96. This phrase is not contained in the official letter of the Abbey directors reprinted in *Letters* I, pp. 91-92.
3  John O'Riordan, 'Introduction', *The Harvest Festival*, p. xii.
4  A few of these parallels are indicated by O'Riordan, *ibid.*, p. xiii.
5  *Letters* II, pp. 21, 43.
6  Printed as an Appendix to the published edition of *The Harvest Festival*.
7  For a more detailed analysis, and a balanced evaluation, of *The Harvest Festival* see Ronald Ayling, 'Seeds for Future Harvest: Propaganda and Art in O'Casey's Earliest Play', *Irish University Review*, X (Spring, 1980), pp. 25-40.

3. THE SHADOW OF A GUNMAN
1  See Gabriel Fallon, *Sean O'Casey: The Man I Knew* (London, 1965), pp. 3-7, for a description of the first production. Cf. O'Casey's own report in *Inishfallen, Fare Thee Well, Autobiographies II*, pp. 103, 143.
2  Michael J. Lennon even claimed, with some exaggeration: 'Davoren in *The Shadow of a Gunman*, is O'Casey of these days.' 'Seán O'Casey and His Plays', *Catholic World*, CXXX (1929/30), p. 301.

375

3   William A. Armstrong, 'History, Autobiography, and *The Shadow of a Gunman'*, *Modern Drama*, II (1959/60), pp. 417-424; Saros Cowasjee, *Sean O'Casey: The Man Behind the Plays* (Edinburgh & London, 1963), pp. 32-34; R. M. Fox, 'Civil War and Peace', in: Sean McCann (ed.), *The World of Sean O'Casey* (London, 1966), pp. 43-49.

4   This holds also true for the acoustic dimension of the stage-directions. See, e.g., the interesting discussion of 'The Knocking Motif in Sean O'Casey's *The Shadow of a Gunman*' by Paul Foley Casey, *Literatur in Wissenschaft und Unterricht*, XIII (1980), pp. 170-175.

5   David Krause, *Sean O'Casey: The Man and His Work* (London, 1960), p. 75. Krause also (p. 90) supports a favourable view of Maguire, but contradicts it by presenting Shields' pacifist views as the thematic centre of the play.

6   Kenneth Tynan, *Curtains: Selections from the Drama Criticism and Related Writings* (London, 1962), p. 286.

7   Cowasjee, *Sean O'Casey*, p. 37.

8   Martin Dolch, '*The Shadow of a Gunman*', in: John V. Hagopian and Martin Dolch (eds.), *Insight II: Analyses of Modern British Literature* (Frankfurt, 1964), p. 268.

9   Walter Starkie, 'The Plays of Sean O'Casey: The Drama of the City Worker', *Nineteenth Century and After*, CIV (1928), p. 228.

10  Krause, *Sean O'Casey*, p. 67.

11  Dietrich Peinert, 'Sean O'Casey, *The Shadow of a Gunman*', *Praxis des neusprachlichen Unterrichts*, XV (1968), p. 42. Davoren as a poet is also criticised by Dolch, '*The Shadow of a Gunman*', p. 267; Fitzgerald, 'Sean O'Casey's Dramatic Slums', p. 27; Krause, *Sean O'Casey*, p. 67.

12  'I believe in . . . the might of design, the mystery of color, the redemption of all things by Beauty everlasting . . .' *The Complete Plays of Bernard Shaw* (London, 1965), p. 540. The central terms of this passage are taken up by Davoren in his speech on the role of the poet in the world, p. 127.

13  Krause, *Sean O'Casey*, p. 66.

14  *Ibid.*

15  Bernice Schrank, 'Poets, Poltroons and Platitudes: A Study of Sean O'Casey's *The Shadow of a Gunman*', *Mosaic*, XI (1977), pp. 56, 59.

16  Malone, 'The Shadow of Sean O'Casey', p. 104.

17  William A. Armstrong, *Sean O'Casey*, Writers and Their Work no. 198 (London, 1967), p. 11.

4. KATHLEEN LISTENS IN

1   Critics disagree as to the details. According to O'Casey himself, *Kathleen Listens In* was 'performed after a major play had ended' (*Autobiographies II*, p. 144). Robert Hethmon, 'Great Hatred, Little Room', *Tulane Drama Review*, V, iv (1961), pp. 51-55, claims that this was a revival of Shaw's *Arms and the Man*. Fallon, who himself took part in the production, remembers a triple bill consisting of *The Man of Destiny*, *The Rising of the Moon* and *Kathleen Listens In* (*Sean O'Casey*, p. 14). Robert G. Lowery cites a triple bill of *Kathleen Listens In*, *The Man of Destiny* and Synge's *Riders to the Sea* ('Sean O'Casey at the Abbey Theatre', in: David Krause and Robert G. Lowery, eds., *Sean O'Casey: Centenary Essays*, Gerrards Cross, 1980, p. 229).

2   *Autobiographies II*, p. 144. Cf. also Ronald Ayling (ed.), *Blasts and Benedictions: Articles and Stories* (London, 1967), pp. 96-97.

3   Quoted by Robert Hogan (ed.), *Feathers from the Green Crow: Sean O'Casey, 1905-1925* (London, 1963), pp. 273-276.

4 *Ibid.*, p. 274.
5 Fallon, *Sean O'Casey*, p. 14. Fallon took the role of the Man in the Kilts. For the reception of the play see also Donal Dorcey, 'The Great Occasions', in: McCann (ed.), *The World of Sean O'Casey*, pp. 53-54.
6 Cowasjee, *Sean O'Casey*, p. 40. According to Fallon, it was never acted after 1923 (*Sean O'Casey*, p. 14).
7 *Tulane Drama Review*, V, iv (1961), pp. 36-50, ed. by Robert Hethmon.
8 Hogan (ed.), *Feathers from the Green Crow*, pp. 277-299. All references in the text are to this edition.
9 Reconstructed from the actors' parts by Robert Caswell and Saros Cowasjee (personal information from Robert Caswell; cf. Cowasjee, *Sean O'Casey*, p. 40n.).
10 A useful brief analysis of the political allegory in *Kathleen Listens In* is provided by C. Desmond Greaves, *Sean O'Casey: Politics and Art* (London, 1979), pp. 110-112.
11 See also O'Casey's critical remarks in *Drums under the Windows*, especially the chapters 'Lost Leader' and 'Gaelstroem', *Autobiographies I*, pp. 520-547.
12 O'Casey had dealt with this conflict as early as 1919 in *The Story of the Irish Citizen Army*.
13 Cowasjee, *Sean O'Casey*, p. 41.
14 'The Man and the Echo', *The Collected Poems of W. B. Yeats* (London, 1965), p. 393.
15 Cowasjee, *Sean O'Casey*, p. 42.
16 Quoted by Hethmon, 'Great Hatred, Little Room', p. 51.
17 Collected by Hogan in *Feathers from the Green Crow*.
18 *Ibid.*, pp. 244-247; first published in *Poblacht na h'Eireann*, March 29, 1922.
19 Cf. David Krause, *A Self-Portrait of the Artist as a Man: Sean O'Casey's Letters* (Dublin, 1968), pp. 11-13.
20 Cf. *Inishfallen, Fare Thee Well, Autobiographies II*, p. 95. It is not clear from this description whether *The Robe of Rosheen* was perhaps identical with *The Seamless Coat of Cathleen*.
21 Cf. Saros Cowasjee, 'O'Casey Seen through Holloway's Diary', *Review of English Literature*, VI, iii (1965), pp. 58-69. According to Cowasjee, O'Casey saw *Cock-a-doodle Dandy* as a return to his 'first principle of fantasy' (p. 66).

5. JUNO AND THE PAYCOCK
1 For an eyewitness account see Fallon, *Sean O'Casey*, pp. 19-23.
2 Cowasjee, *Sean O'Casey*, pp. 43-47.
3 Cf. Andrew E. Malone, 'From the Stalls: The Triumph of Juno', *Dublin Magazine*, II (1924/25), pp. 535-538.
4 See, for instance, James Lansdale Hodson, 'Some Dramatists: Sean O'Casey', *No Phantoms Here* (London, 1932), p. 154.
5 Cowasjee, *Sean O'Casey*, p. 48, referring to a remark by Milton Waldman.
6 Fallon, *Sean O'Casey*, p. 17.
7 *Ibid.*, p. 25.
8 *Ibid.*, p. 17. For the biographical background see *Inishfallen, Fare Thee Well, Autobiographies II*, p. 100.
9 Cowasjee considers Johnny as 'stupidly idealistic', *Sean O'Casey*, p. 51; cf. Krause, *Sean O'Casey*, pp. 68-69.
10 It is not true to say, as Cowasjee maintains (*Sean O'Casey*, p. 53), that O'Casey ridicules Mary's attempts at emancipation.
11 The parallels are discussed in detail by Alice Fox Blitch, 'O'Casey's

Shakespeare', *Modern Drama*, XV (1972), pp. 283-290.

12  See Roger McHugh, 'The Legacy of Sean O'Casey', *Texas Quarterly*, VIII, i (1965), p. 129; and Cowasjee, *Sean O'Casey*, pp. 55-56. Cowasjee also quotes O'Casey's own views who reacted sharply when in the Columbia recording the final scene was cut. According to O'Casey, this scene is 'the comic highlight (and tragic highlight too) of the play.'

13  Katharine J. Worth, 'O'Casey's Dramatic Symbolism', *Modern Drama*, IV (1961/62), p. 260.

14  Cf. Raymond Brugère, 'Sean O'Casey et le théâtre irlandais', *Revue Anglo-Américaine*, III (1925/26), pp. 215-216.

15  Christopher Fry, *The Dark is Light Enough: A Winter Comedy* (London, 1955³), pp. 29-30.

16  McHugh, 'The Legacy of Sean O'Casey', p. 129.

17  Robert Fricker, 'Sean O'Casey, *Juno and the Paycock*', in: Horst Oppel (ed.), *Das moderne englische Drama* (Berlin, 1976³), pp. 197, 205.

18  E.g. Starkie, 'The Plays of Sean O'Casey', p. 231.

19  Brugère, 'Sean O'Casey et le théâtre irlandais', p. 219; cf. Jules Koslow, *The Green and the Red: Sean O'Casey, the Man and His Plays* (New York, 1950), p. 31.

20  Kaspar Spinner, *Die alte Dame sagt: Nein! Drei irische Dramatiker: Lennox Robinson — Sean O'Casey — Denis Johnston* (Bern, 1961), p. 64.

21  Where wert thou, mighty Mother, when he lay,
    When thy son lay, pierced by the shaft which flies
    In darkness?
    *The Complete Poetical Works of Percy Bysshe Shelley*, ed. by Thomas Hutchinson (London, 1907), p. 427. The reference was first noticed by Kurt Wittig, *Sean O'Casey als Dramatiker* (Diss. Halle, 1937), p. 32.

22  Gabriel Fallon, for instance, considers this sentence as the central 'message' of the play, 'The Man in the Plays', in: McCann (ed.), *The World of Sean O'Casey*, p. 207.

23  Errol Durbach, almost alone among O'Casey's critics, has recognized 'the steadily attenuating grace of the Mother of God' who becomes a *'dea abscondita'*, leaving Juno to fight against the realities of life ('Peacocks and Mothers: Theme and Dramatic Metaphor in O'Casey's *Juno and the Paycock*', *Modern Drama*, XV, 1972, p. 20).

24  It is not entirely true to say, as Joseph Wood Krutch does, that O'Casey 'offers no solution; he proposes no remedy; he suggests no hope. Artistically as well as intellectually there is only the clash between the preposterous and the terrible. Like Captain Boyle, he finds nothing to say except that "everything is in a state of chassis".' *'Modernism' in Modern Drama: A Definition and an Estimate* (New York, 1962), p. 99. While O'Casey indeed offers no 'solution', the hope embodied in Juno remains as a bulwark against chaos.

25  J. M. Synge, *Collected Works*, Volume III, Plays, Book I, edited by Ann Saddlemyer (London, 1968, Gerrards Cross and Washington D.C., 1982), p. 23.

26  On this comparison, see also René Fréchet, 'Sean O'Casey: Un épisode de la vie du théâtre irlandais', in: *Le Théâtre Moderne: Hommes et Tendances*, ed. by Jean Jacquot (Paris, 1958), pp. 330-331. Fréchet thinks that 'Evidemment la supériorité de Synge est ici incontestable.'

27  According to Cowasjee, *Sean O'Casey*, p. 45, the 'Shawn' in this play is O'Casey himself. This view is refuted by Ronald Ayling, 'Introduction', *Sean O'Casey: Modern Judgements* (London, 1969), p. 15.

28  Robert de Smet, 'Sean O'Casey et la tragédie des "tenements" ', *Revue des Vivants*, VIII (1934), p. 420.

29  Ever since Malone called *Juno and the Paycock* 'tragedy at its best and greatest' ('From the Stalls', p. 536), this term has been used widely but with little critical reflection. Cf., for instance, William Armstrong, 'The Integrity of *Juno and the Paycock*', *Modern Drama*, XVII (1974), pp. 1-9.

30  It is not correct to describe Juno as 'une sorte de Mère Courage qui ignore le marxisme et qui ne comprend pas ce qui lui arrive'; Robert Abirached, 'Deux Pièces de Sean O'Casey', *Etudes*, XCIV (June 1961), p. 385.

31  *Hebbels Werke in drei Bänden* (Berlin & Weimar, 1966), I, p. 153.

32  See Chapter 32 'Influences and Reactions' in Part VI.

## 6. NANNIE'S NIGHT OUT

1  *Autobiographies II*, p. 146. Cf. Fallon, *Sean O'Casey*, p. 41; and Hogan, *Feathers from the Green Crow*, p. 301.

2  See in particular Ronald Ayling, '*Nannie's Night Out*', *Modern Drama*, V (1962/63), pp. 154-163. The most negative review was by A. E. Malone, 'From the Stalls: A Night Out', *Dublin Magazine*, II (1924/25), pp. 221-222.

3  *Feathers from the Green Crow*, pp. 303-335. All page references are to this edition.

4  *Autobiographies I*, pp. 462-473. For a comparison see William A. Armstrong, 'Sean O'Casey, W. B. Yeats and the Dance of Life', in: Ayling (ed.), *Sean O'Casey*, pp. 131-142.

5  Brugère, 'Sean O'Casey et le théâtre irlandais', p. 216.

6  On O'Casey's use of the farce see the chapter on *The End of the Beginning* and *A Pound on Demand*, below.

7  Reprinted in *Feathers from the Green Crow*, pp. 331-334.

8  Cf. *ibid.*, p. 302.

9  According to Fallon, who took the part of Oul Joe in the first production, the play ended with the death of Nannie (*Sean O'Casey*, p. 40). This would imply that O'Casey's first version had ended with the arrest of Nannie and that the death scene had been suggested by the Abbey directors. This view is supported by Hogan who speaks of 'O'Casey's preferred ending, in which Nannie is dragged off to the police station . . .' ('O'Casey's Dramatic Apprenticeship', *Modern Drama*, IV, 1961/62, p. 252). On the other hand, Ayling concludes from his correspondence with O'Casey that the author preferred the death scene while one of the other two was acted ('*Nannie's Night Out*', p. 160). This is confirmed by Brugère who seems to have known the acting version: '. . . à la fin de l'acte elle est de nouveau traînée au poste, après une lutte forcenée avec un agent' ('Sean O'Casey et le théâtre irlandais', p. 217). Dorcey, too, emphasizes that it was the Abbey directors who insisted on such a change: 'She was arrested for drunkenness by the police and carried off screaming. This drastic change made the play quite meaningless but O'Casey didn't seem to mind' ('The Great Occasions', p. 56). The same conclusion can be drawn from a letter from Lady Gregory: 'L. Robinson says he saved Nannies life – and I applaud him – I should not easily have forgiven her death . . .' (*Letters*, I, p. 116).

10  Brugère, 'Sean O'Casey et le théâtre irlandais', pp. 216, 217.

11  Armstrong, 'Sean O'Casey, W. B. Yeats and the Dance of Life', pp. 134-135.

12  *New York Times* (Dec. 27, 1925); *Letters*, I, p. 160.

## 7. THE PLOUGH AND THE STARS

1  Cf. *Autobiographies II*, pp. 146-157; also Hugh Hunt, *The Abbey: Ireland's National Theatre* (Dublin, 1979), pp. 124-130; Fallon, *Sean O'Casey*, pp. 90-99;

William Rocke, 'May Craig recalls that Abbey uproar', *Irish Digest*, LXXX, i (March, 1964), pp. 71-73.

2   *Autobiographies II*, pp. 146-148, 156-157, 241-244; and Fallon, *Sean O'Casey*, pp. 71-81, 86-90.

3   There are six noteworthy differences between the two versions: (1) The second version has reduced the Cockney dialect of the two English soldiers to render the text less difficult to read. (2) The quarrel between Nora and Jack over the burning of the letter has been intensified by the following significant stage direction: '*While this dialogue is proceeding, and while Clitheroe prepares himself, Brennan softly whistles "The Soldiers' Song"* '. (3) Peter's ridiculous attitude is underlined by the repetition: 'I was burnin' to dhraw me sword, an' wave *an' wave* it over me —' (p. 48/p. 195). (4) The second version omits the Covey's remark: 'Fluther's well able to take care of himself' (p. 79/p. 218). (5) In the second version, the stage direction demands only one window for Bessie's room, underlining its narrowness, darkness and poverty. (6) In the description of Bessie's death, '*Bessie . . . stands stiffly upright for a moment . . .*', the second version omits the word *upright* (p. 132/p. 258).

4   Anonymous review of the book edition of *The Plough and the Stars*, *Dublin Magazine*, n.s. I, iii (1926), pp. 64-65. Cf. the anonymous review in *Contemporary Review*, CXXX (1926), pp. 123-125; and S. R. Littlewood, 'Isles of Drama', *Bookman*, LXX (1926), pp. 128, 130.

5   See Cowasjee, *Sean O'Casey*, pp. 62-63; and Colm Cronin, 'The O'Casey I Knew', in: McCann (ed.), *The World of Sean O'Casey*, pp. 165-167.

6   See especially the last five chapters in *Drums under the Windows*, *Autobiographies I*, pp. 607-666.

7   *Ibid.*, pp. 612-613.

8   Hogan, *The Experiments of Sean O'Casey*, pp. 16-54.

9   *Ibid.*, e.g. p. 29.

10  'One of the World's Dramatists', *Blasts and Benedictions*, pp. 42-45.

11  According to Harry Bergholz, *The Plough and the Stars* is 'in erster Linie . . . die Tragödie einer liebenden Frau' ('Sean O'Casey', *Englische Studien*, LXV, 1930/31, p. 61). Starkie sees Fluther as O'Casey's 'ironical mouthpiece character' ('The Plays of Sean O'Casey', p. 231). Cowasjee considers Rosie as 'the only one with whom the dramatist aligns himself' (*Sean O'Casey*, p. 67). To Renée Saurel, it is the Covey 'qui reflète le mieux la croyance d'O'Casey en l'avenir d'un socialisme libérateur . . .' ('Un dramaturge inconfortable', *Temps Modernes*, XVII, 1961/62, no. 193, p. 1943); cf. Maureen Malone, *The Plays of Sean O'Casey* (Carbondale, Ill., 1969), p. 6.

12  Hogan, *The Experiments of Sean O'Casey*, cites eight central characters; he overlooks the importance of Brennan.

13  William Irwin Thompson, *The Imagination of an Insurrection: Dublin, Easter 1916: A Study of an Ideological Movement* (New York, 1967), p. 209.

14  See, for instance, Krause, *Sean O'Casey*, p. 73.

15  The flag is now in the National Museum, Dublin.

16  See *Autobiographies II*, p. 103, and '*The Plough and the Stars* in Retrospect', *Blasts and Benedictions*, pp. 95-98. According to Fallon, parts of *The Crimson and the Tri-Colour* that was equally rejected by the Abbey, have also been used for *The Plough and the Stars*. This surmise is rejected by Ronald Ayling, 'Sean O'Casey: Fact and Fancy', *Massachusetts Review*, VII (1966), p. 605.

17  W. A. Armstrong, 'The Sources and Themes of *The Plough and the Stars*', *Modern Drama*, IV (1961/62), pp. 235-236.

18  Cf. O'Casey's positive remarks on Pearse, quoted by Ronald G. Rollins, 'Form and Content in Sean O'Casey's Dublin Trilogy', *Modern Drama*, VIII (1965/66), p. 424; also *Autobiographies I*, pp. 617-618, 623-624.

19  At a later stage, O'Casey criticised this scene quite sharply: '. . . the Woman [was] as unnatural where she was as a bishop would be were he found as a lodger in a Dublin tenement.' *The Green Crow* (London, 1957), p. 24.

20  Anthony Butler, 'The Early Background', in: McCann (ed.), *The World of Sean O'Casey*, p. 29.

21  Ronald G. Rollins, 'Dramatic Symbolism in Sean O'Casey's Dublin Trilogy', *West Virginia University Philological Papers*, XV (1966), p. 52.

22  'Nationalism and *The Plough and the Stars*', *Blasts and Benedictions*, p. 93.

23  *Autobiographies I*, p. 647.

24  Thompson, *The Imagination of an Insurrection*, p. 209.

25  Desmond MacCarthy, '*The Plough and the Stars*', *New Statesman*, XXVII (1926), p. 170.

26  'If they knew no fear, then the fight of Easter Week was an easy thing, and those who participated deserve to be forgotten in a day, rather than to be remembered for ever.' *Irish Independent* (Feb. 20, 1926); *Letters*, I, p. 169.

27  E.g. Cowasjee, *Sean O'Casey*, p. 73. The sharply contrasting views of critics are epitomized by the following phrases, both reprinted in the same volume: ' "The Plough" is the work of a pacifist; this fact is crystal clear' (Gabriel Fallon, 'The Man in the Plays') – 'There is no evidence in his writings that he believed in pacifism and, indeed, plenty to show that he did not' (R. M. Fox, 'Civil War and Peace'), both in McCann (ed.), *The World of Sean O'Casey*, pp. 208, 47.

28  See his story 'A Fall in a Gentle Wind', *Windfalls: Stories, Poems, and Plays* (London, 1934), pp. 119-132, and *The Green Crow*, pp. 272-278.

29  Joseph Wood Krutch, 'Poet Laureate', *Nation*, CXXV (1927), p. 718.

PART II

8. PREFATORY

1  *Letters*, I, pp. 207, 211, 215-216, 218, 224. An additional useful source for this period is Fallon, *Sean O'Casey*, chap. VIII.

2  *Letters*, I, p. 230.

3  Cowasjee, *Sean O'Casey*, pp. 113-114.

9. THE SILVER TASSIE

1  *Autobiographies II*, pp. 271-280, 335-338.

2  See Heinz Kosok, 'The Revision of *The Silver Tassie*', *Seán O'Casey Review*, V, i (1978), pp. 15-18.

3  A number of details in Act III are based on O'Casey's own experiences. Cf. the chapter 'St. Vincent Provides a Bed' in *Drums under the Windows*, *Autobiographies I*, pp. 626-639, and Fallon, *Sean O'Casey*, pp. 69-70.

4  Allardyce Nicoll calls *The Silver Tassie* 'perhaps the most powerful tragic drama of our time', *British Drama: An Historical Survey from the Beginnings to the Present Time* (London, 1958⁴), p. 484. Cf. Cowasjee, *Sean O'Casey*, *passim*, and Krause, *Sean O'Casey*, *passim*.

5  Starkie, 'The Plays of Sean O'Casey', p. 236.

6  'The Plays of Sean O'Casey: A Reply', *Nineteenth Century and After*, CIV (1928), p. 400.

7  On the changes in Susie's language see Metscher, *Sean O'Caseys dramatischer Stil*, pp. 89-90.

382                                          Notes to pages 99-111

8    The figure of Susie has a parallel in Marian from Lennox Robinson's *The Far-Off Hills* who undergoes a surprising change from a fanatically religious person obsessed by her duties to a life-affirming girl who is free from illusions. *The Far-Off Hills* was premièred by the Abbey in October 1928, half a year after Robinson, as an Abbey director, had read the manuscript of *The Silver Tassie*; it is likely, therefore, that he was influenced by O'Casey.

9    This view is supported by G. Wilson Knight: 'O'Casey's uncompromising belief in the right to happiness for those who can find it resists even his sense of suffering in those who cannot. This is high dramatic thinking.' *The Golden Labyrinth: A Study of British Drama* (London, 1962), p. 376.

10   Cf. Winifred Smith, 'The Dying God in the Modern Theatre', *Review of Religion*, V (1940/41), pp. 264-275; and Jacqueline Doyle, 'Liturgical Imagery in Sean O'Casey's *The Silver Tassie*', *Modern Drama*, XXI (1978), pp. 29-38.

11   These medals, which indicate his physical superiority, are sharply contrasted with his war decorations of Act IV which have turned him into a tiresome and helpless outsider.

12   Smith, 'The Dying God in the Modern Theatre', p. 270.

13   *Ibid.*, p. 269.

14   O'Casey apparently did not understand this type of interpretation, as can be gathered from a letter to Ronald G. Rollins, although Rollins cites this letter in support of the 'sacrificial theme' of the play. 'O'Casey's *The Silver Tassie*', *Explicator*, XX (1961/62), item 62.

15   'Blasphemy and *The Silver Tassie*', *Blasts and Benedictions*, p. 109.

16   *Ibid.*

17   J. L. Styan, *The Dark Comedy: The Development of Modern Comic Tragedy* (Cambridge, 1962), p. 150.

18   Denis Johnston, *Dramatic Works*, II (Gerrards Cross, 1979), p. 5.

19   Quoted by Heinz Zaslawski, 'Die Werke Sean O'Caseys, unter besonderer Berücksichtigung seiner zweiten Periode', unpubl. diss. (Vienna, 1949), p. 81.

20   For a photograph see *Sean O'Casey Review*, V, i (1978), p. 7.

21   E.g. Richard Findlater, *The Unholy Trade* (London, 1952), p. 174; Hogan, *The Experiments of Sean O'Casey*, p. 64-65; Charles Morgan, 'On Sean O'Casey's *The Silver Tassie*', in: James Agate (ed.), *The English Dramatic Critics: An Anthology 1660-1932* (New York, 1958), p. 348.

22   E.g. Morgan, 'On Sean O'Casey's *The Silver Tassie*', p. 348.

23   Cf. T. R. Henn, 'The Bible in relation to the study of English literature today', *Hermathena*, no. 100 (Summer, 1965), pp. 29-43. This passage may have been suggested by Shakespeare's *King Henry V*, IV, i; cf. Fallon, *Sean O'Casey*, pp. 51-52.

24   Quoted by Cowasjee, *Sean O'Casey*, p. 120.

25   Fallon, *Sean O'Casey*, pp. 46-48.

26   *Ibid.*, p. 47. Contrary to a generally held belief, this shows that O'Casey came into contact with expressionist drama *before* he left Ireland.

27   Ronald G. Rollins, 'O'Casey, O'Neill and Expressionism in *The Silver Tassie*', *Bucknell Review*, X (1962), p. 365.

28   Cf. Ernst Toller, *Seven Plays* (London, 1935), p. vi. O'Casey reviewed this volume in 1935 for the *New Statesman and Nation* (Feb. 9).

29   Cowasjee, *Sean O'Casey*, pp. 126-127.

30   A. Brulé, 'Sean O'Casey et le Théâtre Moderne', *Revue Anglo-Américaine*, VI, (1928/29), p. 57.

31   Cowasjee, *Sean O'Casey*, p. 122.

32   *Ibid.*

33 Krause, *Sean O'Casey*, p. 121.

34 Spinner, *Die alte Dame sagt: Nein!*, p. 76.

35 Additional parallels between Act II and the rest of the play in the fields of theme, imagery and verbal patterns have been documented by Naomi S. Pasachoff, 'Unity of Theme, Image and Diction in *The Silver Tassie*', *Modern Drama*, XXIII (1980), pp. 58-64.

36 Nevertheless, not all critics seem to have realized this meaning: Cowasjee, for instance, explains erroneously: the tassie 'also signifies the consecrated chalice of the Mass. His [Harry's] drinking from it in lust is a sacrilege for which he atones later by being injured in the war.' *Sean O'Casey*, p. 119.

37 Cf. *Rose and Crown, Autobiographies II*, pp. 268-270.

38 *Poetical Works of Robert Burns*, ed. by William Wallace (Edinburgh, London, 1958), p. 282.

39 John Jordan, 'A World in Chassis', *University Review* (Spring, 1955), p. 24.

40 Leslie Rees, 'Remembrance of Things Past: On Meeting Sean O'Casey', *Meanjin*, XXIII (1964), p. 417; Gerard A. Larson, 'An Interview with Mrs. Sean O'Casey', *Educational Theatre Journal*, XVII (1965), p. 238. Occasionally O'Casey preferred *Cock-a-doodle Dandy*; cf. Krause, *A Self-Portrait of the Artist as a Man*, p. 34, and O'Casey, 'Cockadoodle Doo', *Blasts and Benedictions*, p. 143.

## 10. THE END OF THE BEGINNING and A POUND ON DEMAND

1 Spinner, *Die alte Dame sagt: Nein!*, p. 141.

2 'The two One-Act Sketches were written when funds were low, to bring in a little money, but no attempt was made to market them, and so they shiver among the unemployed.' O'Casey, *Windfalls*, p. vii.

3 *Sunset and Evening Star, Autobiographies II*, p. 652. In his article, 'Bonfire under a Black Sun', he even maintains that it is 'born out of a folk-tale, known to children all over the world' (*The Green Crow*, p. 131).

4 Fallon, *Sean O'Casey*, pp. 45-46, 142.

5 Armstrong, *Sean O'Casey*, p. 32.

6 e.w., 'Realistische Spässe', *Theater heute*, VI, xii (Dec. 1965), pp. 44-45.

## 11. WITHIN THE GATES

1 See O'Casey, 'No Flower for Films', *The Green Crow*, pp. 172-176, and *Autobiographies II*, pp. 351-353.

2 Cf., for instance, Derek Verschoyle, 'The Theatre', *Spectator* (16 Feb, 1934), p. 235. See also J. C. Trewin, *The Turbulent Thirties: A Further Decade of the Theatre* (London, 1960), p. 72. James Agate in his devastating review ('Beyond the Agates', *First Nights*, London, 1934, pp. 271-276) seems to confuse the shortcomings of the production with those of the play.

3 *Autobiographies II*, p. 359. See also p. 340: '. . . *Within the Gates*, hearsed within an atrocious production, had appeared on the London stage; had run home to hide in a corner of a silent room.'

4 For a detailed, albeit highly critical review of the New York production see John Mason Brown, 'Without Mr. O'Casey's Gates', *Two on the Aisle: Ten Years of the American Theatre in Performance* (New York, 1938), pp. 126-130.

5 O'Casey, 'The Church Tries to Close the Gates', *Blasts and Benedictions*, pp. 124-131; *Autobiographies II*, pp. 421-425.

6 For a detailed comparison see R. Mary Todd, 'The Two Published Versions of Sean O'Casey's *Within the Gates*', *Modern Drama*, X (1967/68), pp. 346-355.

7   In *Within the Gates* O'Casey uses the term 'scene' instead of 'act' (*A Play of Four Scenes in a London Park*), but to avoid confusion the four larger units of the play are here designated 'acts' while the smaller units, distinguished by theme, mood and groups of *dramatis personae*, are termed 'scenes'.

8   O'Casey, *Within the Gates* (London, 1934), pp. 11-12.

9   *Ibid.*, p. 169.

10  Herbert Goldstone, 'The Unevenness of O'Casey: A Study of *Within the Gates*', *Forum*, IV, vi (1965), p. 38.

11  O'Casey himself emphasized his objectivity in the play; see 'Within the Gates and Without', *Blasts and Benedictions*, p. 119.

12  Findlater, *The Unholy Trade*, p. 176; also L. Cazamian in his review in *Revue Anglo-Américaine*, XII (1935), pp. 451-453.

13  Krause, *Sean O'Casey*, p. 144.

14  'From Within the Gates', *Blasts and Benedictions*, p. 115. In this article, O'Casey gives 'explanations' (not always wholly applicable) of all the major *dramatis personae*. According to Cowasjee (*O'Casey*, p. 61) this article was originally used as a programme note for the New York production.

15  'From Within the Gates', p. 115.

16  *The Complete Plays of Bernard Shaw*, p. 540. The phrase is taken from the same context as the quotation used in *The Shadow of a Gunman*.

17  *Ibid.*, p. 530.

18  This view is opposed to that of Goldstone who sees Jannice as a psychologically credible, complex character ('The Unevenness of O'Casey', pp. 41-42). On the other hand it is just as misleading to associate Jannice with the Roman deities Janus and Diana, with a 'fertility figure' and with a 'Christian knight struggling for salvation' (Bill Jack Harman and Ronald G. Rollins, 'Mythical Dimensions in O'Casey's *Within the Gates*', *West Virginia University Philological Papers*, XVI (Nov. 1967), pp. 72-78).

19  Knight, *The Golden Labyrinth*, p. 378.

20  Patricia Baggett, 'Sean O'Casey's Development of a Basic Theme', *Dublin Magazine*, XXXI, iv (1956), p. 29.

21  *Autobiographies II*, p. 367. Cf. his article 'The Church Tries to Close the Gates', *Blasts and Benedictions*, p. 128.

22  Agate, 'Beyond the Agates', p. 271. Krause (*Sean O'Casey*, pp. 138-144) summarizes the controversies that led to, and resulted from, this judgement.

23  Findlater, *The Unholy Trade*, p. 176.

24  Goldstone, 'The Unevenness of O'Casey', p. 42.

25  Cowasjee, *Sean O'Casey*, p. 146.

26  Krause, *Sean O'Casey*, p. 145.

27  Homer E. Woodbridge, 'Sean O'Casey', *South Atlantic Quarterly*, XL (1941), p. 57; cf. Goldstone, 'The Unevenness of O'Casey', p. 39.

28  Koslow, *The Green and the Red*, p. 62.

29  Ronald G. Rollins, 'O'Casey, O'Neill, and Expressionism in *Within the Gates*', *West Virginia University Philological Papers*, XIII (1961, publ. 1962), pp. 76-81.

30  Quoted by O. Cargill, N. B. Fagin and W. J. Fisher (eds.), *Eugene O'Neill and his Plays: A Survey of His Life and Works* (London, 1962), p. 115.

PART III

12. PREFATORY

1   See Cowasjee, *Sean O'Casey*, p. 167.

2   O'Casey's Socialist views are briefly summarized by Cowasjee, *Sean O'Casey*, pp. 167-170, and *O'Casey*, pp. 67-70. A detailed survey is provided

by Robert G. Lowery, 'Sean O'Casey: Art and Politics', in: David Krause and Robert G. Lowery (eds.), *Sean O'Casey: Centenary Essays* (Gerrards Cross, 1980), pp. 121-164. This is in part a rejoinder to Greaves' controversial study *Sean O'Casey: Politics and Art.*

3   As evidenced in Fallon's book *Sean O'Casey.*
4   Quoted by Arthur and Barbara Gelb, *O'Neill* (London, 1962²), p. 830.
5   On these figures see also John Jordan, 'Illusion and Actuality in the Later O'Casey', in: Ayling (ed.), *Sean O'Casey*, p. 145.
6   Michel Habart, 'Introduction à Sean O'Casey,' *Théâtre populaire*, no. 34 (2me trimestre 1959), p. 32.

13. THE STAR TURNS RED
1   On the details of the two Unity Theatre productions of *The Star Turns Red* and their consequences, including O'Casey's revisions of the text, see Heinz Kosok, 'Unity Theatre and *The Star Turns Red*', *Sean O'Casey Review*, VI (1980), pp. 68-74.
2   See also his letter to Gabriel Fallon, *Letters*, I, pp. 881-882, and his criticism of the propaganda play in 'The Theatre and the Politician', *Blasts and Benedictions*, pp. 20-23.
3   Quoted by Krause, *A Self-Portrait of the Artist as a Man*, p. 15.
4   According to Cowasjee, the Lord Mayor of Dublin, Alfie Byrne, served as a model for the Lord Mayor, and the trade-union leaders have been patterned on the opponents of Jim Larkin in the Irish trade-union movement (*Sean O'Casey*, pp. 171, 178). Pat M. Esslinger mentions a model for Brannigan ('Sean O'Casey and the Lockout of 1913: *Materia Poetica* of the Two Red Plays', *Modern Drama*, VI, 1963/64, p. 60).
5   Findlater, *The Unholy Trade*, p. 177.
6   Cf. Cowasjee, *Sean O'Casey*, pp. 170-177; Malone, *The Plays of Sean O'Casey*, pp. 67-72; and Spinner, *Die alte Dame sagt: Nein!*, pp. 103-104.
7   Letter quoted by Esslinger, 'Sean O'Casey and the Lockout of 1913', p. 58; cf. Ronald G. Rollins, 'Sean O'Casey's *The Star Turns Red*: A Political Prophesy', *Mississippi Quarterly*, XVI (1963), p. 75.
8   Cowasjee, *Sean O'Casey*, p. 169.
9   Cowasjee, *O'Casey*, p. 70.
10  Quoted by Cowasjee, *Sean O'Casey*, p. 171.
11  Letter quoted by Rollins, 'Sean O'Casey's *The Star Turns Red*', p. 69.

14. PURPLE DUST
1   Cf. *Autobiographies II*, pp. 556-557, and Cowasjee, *Sean O'Casey*, pp. 155-156.
2   Original version (London, 1940), p. 7 / *Collected Plays* text, p. 7.
3   P. 154/103.
4   Pp. 34-40/25-28; p. 133/90; p. 57/39; p. 59/41; p. 62/42.
5   Pp. 63-65/43-44; pp. 82-84/56-57; p. 113/76; pp. 121-122/81-82; p. 141/95.
6   Pp. 159-161/106-110.
7   In: Sylvan Barnet, Morton Berman and William Burto (eds.), *The Genius of the Irish Theatre* (New York, 1960), pp. 265-343 ('third version').
8   *Collected Plays* text, pp. 7-8/third version pp. 268-269.
9   P. 10/271.
10  P. 16/275; on p. 332 of the third version 'the young thorntree' has been retained by mistake.
11  P. 21/278.
12  P. 54/299.

13   Pp. 59-61/302-303; pp. 64-66/305-306; p. 82/316.
14   Pp. 74-76/311-312.
15   Pp. 105-110/331-334.
16   P. 119/340.
17   According to Ronald Ayling; letter dated 3 August 1969.
18   *Collected Plays* text, pp. 74-76/ *Three More Plays* (London, 1965), pp. 180-181.
19   There is, however, little point in seeing *Purple Dust* as a combination of traits of the 'Old Comedy' and the 'New Comedy' – whatever these may be. See Walter C. Daniel, 'Patterns of Greek Comedy in O'Casey's *Purple Dust*', *Bulletin of the New York Public Library*, LXVI (1962), pp. 603-612.
20   Findlater, *The Unholy Trade*, p. 179; J. C. Trewin, *The Theatre since 1900* (London, 1951), p. 289; Ronald G. Rollins, 'Sean O'Casey's Mental Pilgrimage', *Arizona Quarterly*, XVII (1961), p. 298; Hogan, *The Experiments of Sean O'Casey*, p. 102.
21   Vivian Mercier, 'The Riddle of Sean O'Casey', *Commonweal*, LXIV (1956), p. 368; Zaslawski, 'Die Werke Sean O'Caseys', p. 111.
22   On the farcical elements in *Purple Dust*, cf. Hogan, *The Experiments of Sean O'Casey*, pp. 99-106. Hogan emphasizes the importance of these elements for the structural unity of the play.
23   Cf. Metscher, *Sean O'Caseys dramatischer Stil*, pp. 90-93.
24   Stanza VI: '. . . Annihilating all that's made/To a green Thought in a green Shade.' *The Poems & Letters of Andrew Marvell*, ed. by H. M. Margoliouth, vol. I (Oxford, 1952²), p. 49. Cf. Krause, *Sean O'Casey*, p. 179.
25   There is no justification in the text for Krause's view that O'Casey here uses 'references to genuine pastoral experiences' as a 'contrast to the above burlesque of pastoral affectations' (*Sean O'Casey*, p. 179).
26   'Oh, to be in England/Now that April's there . . .' *The Poems and Plays of Robert Browning* (New York, 1934), p. 45.
27   *Autobiographies II*, pp. 312-321.
28   See especially B. L. Smith, *O'Casey's Satiric Vision* (Kent State U.P., 1978), pp. 88-97.
29   *Autobiographies I*, p. 558.
30   *Autobiographies II*, p. 484; 'Purple Dust in Their Eyes', in: *Under a Colored Cap: Articles Merry and Mournful with Comments and a Song* (London, 1963), p. 263. Cf. the chapter 'Shaw's Corner' in *Sunset and Evening Star* and three articles on Shaw in *The Green Crow*, pp. 177-189 and 222-229.
31   The topicality of the problems treated in these two plays can be gathered from the fact that Louis D'Alton in *This Other Eden* (1953), one of the best Irish plays of the 'fifties, takes up the same basic situation as Shaw and O'Casey.
32   For detailed comparisons between the two plays see Ronald G. Rollins, 'Shaw and O'Casey: John Bull and His Other Island', *Shaw Review*, X (1967), pp. 60-69, and Cowasjee, *Sean O'Casey*, pp. 156-165. See also Hogan, *The Experiments of Sean O'Casey*, pp. 101-102, and R. B. Parker, 'Bernard Shaw and Sean O'Casey', *Queen's Quarterly*, LXXIII (1966), pp. 13-34.
33   Worth, 'O'Casey's Dramatic Symbolism', p. 267; Ernst Wendt, 'O'Casey's Narrenspiele: Über Aufführungen in Wuppertal, Ostberlin und Stuttgart', *Theater heute*, IV, viii (August 1963), p. 26; Malone, *The Plays of Sean O'Casey*, p. 95.
34   Bernard Benstock, 'A Covey of Clerics in Joyce and O'Casey', *James Joyce Quarterly*, II, i (1964), pp. 27-28; Spinner, *Die alte Dame sagt: Nein!*, p. 109.
35   *Ibid.*, p. 110; Cowasjee, *Sean O'Casey*, p. 166.

36  Benstock, 'A Covey of Clerics in Joyce and O'Casey', p. 28.
37  'Purple Dust in Their Eyes', p. 262.
38  O'Casey's letter quoted by Daniel, 'Patterns of Greek Comedy in O'Casey's *Purple Dust*', p. 612.
39  'Purple Dust in Their Eyes', p. 265.
40  *Ibid.*, p. 264. Cf. *Letters* I, p. 133, on the destruction of Irish mansions.
41  David Krause, ' "The Rageous Ossean": Patron-Hero of Synge and O'Casey', *Modern Drama*, IV (1961/62), pp. 268-291.
42  This relationship is discussed by Krause, *Sean O'Casey*, pp. 185-186; cf. Krause, ' "The Rageous Ossean" ', p. 287. Spinner analyzes the linguistic differences between *Purple Dust* and *The Shadow of the Glen* (*Die alte Dame sagt: Nein!*, pp. 111-113) which do not, however, disprove the parallels between the two plays. Metscher rejects a comparison with *The Shadow of the Glen* and cites passages from *The Well of the Saints* and *Deirdre of the Sorrows* instead (*Sean O'Caseys dramatischer Stil*, pp. 153-157). Cowasjee thinks an influence from *The Playboy of the Western World* more likely (*Sean O'Casey*, p. 164).
43  J. M. Synge, *Collected Works*, Volume III, *Plays*, Book I, edited by Ann Saddlemyer, p. 49.
44  Hogan, *The Experiments of Sean O'Casey*, p. 103; Krause, *Sean O'Casey*, p. 187.

## 15. RED ROSES FOR ME

1  For a discussion of the textual variants of the play, see Heinz Kosok, 'The Three Versions of *Red Roses for Me*', *O'Casey Annual*, I (1982), pp. 141-147.
2  See Cowasjee, *Sean O'Casey*, pp. 180-184; Esslinger, 'Sean O'Casey and the Lockout of 1913'; Maureen Malone, '*Red Roses for Me*: Fact and Symbol', *Modern Drama*, IX (1966/67), pp. 147-152; Malone, *The Plays of Sean O'Casey*, pp. 102-106.
3  Sean McCann, 'The Girl He Left Behind Him', in: McCann (ed.), *The World of Sean O'Casey*, pp. 30-42.
4  Mrs. O'Casey's letter to Cowasjee, *Sean O'Casey*, p. vii.
5  Hogan, *The Experiments of Sean O'Casey*, p. 94. Hogan provides a detailed analysis of the structure of *Red Roses for Me*.
6  The rose is a frequent symbol both in Gaelic and Anglo-Irish literature. Whereas its connotations in the poetry of Yeats are highly complex, in earlier Irish poetry it often symbolizes Ireland. The various meanings of this symbol are discussed by Barbara Seward, *The Symbolic Rose* (New York, 1960).
7  *Autobiographies I*, p. 309.
8  My italics.
9  My italics.
10  Worth, 'O'Casey's Dramatic Symbolism', p. 262.
11  Raymond Williams, *Drama: From Ibsen to Eliot* (London, 1954), p. 173.
12  O'Casey's description, *Autobiographies I*, pp. 379-384, corresponds quite closely to the stage directions of Act III.
13  Spinner, *Die alte Dame sagt: Nein!*, p. 117. Nor is it correct to say that 'The shift to expressionism in the third act is not integrated schematically . . .' (Allan Lewis, 'Irish Romantic Realism – Sean O'Casey: *Red Roses for Me*', *The Contemporary Theatre: The Significant Playwrights of Our Time*, New York, 1962, p. 187).
14  See Daniel O'Keeffe (ed.), *The First Book of Irish Ballads* (Cork, 1965[4]), pp. 25-26.
15  Benstock, 'A Covey of Clerics in Joyce and O'Casey', p. 29.
16  Cf. Renée Saurel: 'L'idée qui se dégage de la pièce est bien celle d'O'Casey:

la religion, quelle qu'elle soit, freine la libération de l'homme et les honnêtes de ses représentants, comme le Révérend Clinton, sont impuissants. Il ne leur reste que la prière et les bonnes paroles, qui ne donnent pas de pain et ne ressuscitent pas les morts.' 'Vilar sur la brèche', *Les Temps Modernes*, XVI (1960/61), no. 179, pp. 1241-1242.

17  Hogan, *The Experiments of Sean O'Casey*, p. 93.
18  Clurman, *Lies Like Truth*, pp. 122-123.
19  See especially Williams, *Drama*, pp. 173-174.
20  Cowasjee, *Sean O'Casey*, p. 194.
21  Review in *The Times* (Feb. 27, 1946), quoted *ibid.*, p. 194.
22  Krause, *Sean O'Casey*, p. 164.
23  Hogan, *The Experiments of Sean O'Casey*, p. 91.
24  According to Esslinger, Ayamonn 'does not have the greatness or the immensity of a flaw that would elevate his death and the cause for which he dies. His faults are those of petulance, not tragedy' ('Sean O'Casey and the Lockout of 1913', p. 61). O'Casey, on the other hand, saw Ayamonn as 'one of his "noblest" figures' (Rollins, 'Sean O'Casey's Mental Pilgrimage', p. 298n.).
25  Werner Mittenzwei, on the other hand, maintains that Ayamonn becomes a credible individual character because of his anti-capitalist stance (*Gestaltung und Gestalten im modernen Drama*, Berlin and Weimar, 1965, pp. 95-97).
26  *Letters*, I, p. 272.
27  Lewis, 'Irish Romantic Realism', p. 191.
28  Baggett, 'Sean O'Casey's Development of a Basic Theme', p. 32.

16. OAK LEAVES AND LAVENDER
 1  The only exception is Knight who (surprisingly) calls *Oak Leaves and Lavender* 'a work of exact and impersonal integration showing the impact of the numinous on a realistic and historically significant action' (*The Golden Labyrinth*, p. 379).
 2  Trewin, *Dramatists of Today*, p. 64.
 3  *Autobiographies II*, p. 655.
 4  *Letters*, I, p. 268.
 5  Spinner, *Die alte Dame sagt: Nein!*, p. 122.
 6  Hogan, *The Experiments of Sean O'Casey*, p. 107.
 7  *Ibid.*, p. 110.
 8  Cowasjee, *Sean O'Casey*, p. 197.
 9  The village of Hatherleigh north of Okehampton (in *Devon*) merely provided the name of the family. The dialect of the country people in *Oak Leaves and Lavender* is specifically Cornish, and Monica, a native girl, calls herself 'a thoroughbred Cornish lass' (p. 62).
10  Malone in *The Plays of Sean O'Casey*, pp. 73-90, deciphers many of the allusions to the contemporary historical scene.
11  Trewin (a Cornishman himself) in *Dramatists of Today*, p. 65. Other natives of Cornwall have, however, testified to the authenticity of the Cornish dialect in this play.
12  The figure of Constant is justified by the contemporary historical situation, even if it is not successfully integrated into the context of the play. Approximately 11,000 women and children from wealthy families fled in 1940 from Britain, see A. J. P. Taylor, *English History: 1914 to 1945*, The Oxford History of England, XV (Oxford, 1965), p. 493.
13  Hogan, *The Experiments of Sean O'Casey*, p. 113.

14  J. B. Priestley, 'O'Casey's Predicament: How Can One Dramatise the English?', *Our Time*, V (1945/46), p. 238.
15                    Here with a Loaf of Bread beneath the Bough,
                     A Flask of Wine, a Book of Verse – and Thou
                        Beside me singing in the Wilderness –
                     And Wilderness were Paradise enow.
    Edward FitzGerald, *The Rubaiyat of Omar Khayyam* (London, 1859), quatrain 11.
16  Knight, *The Golden Labyrinth*, p. 380.
17  Zaslawski, 'Die Werke Sean O'Caseys', p. 125.
18  Spinner, *Die alte Dame sagt: Nein!*, p. 124n.
19  Another autobiographical trait endangers the homogeneity of this character. Dame Hatherleigh confesses: 'I cabled forty dollars over to Saskatoon's bishop for a symbol guaranteeing instant admission to heaven to the bearer, should he fall in the fight; and a subsidiary guarantee bringing the bearer safely home' (pp. 71-72). This primitive superstition, not in keeping with her courageous attitude, was suggested by O'Casey's rage over similar frauds he describes in *Inishfallen, Fare Thee Well* (*Autobiographies II*, p. 208).
20  Worth, 'O'Casey's Dramatic Symbolism', p. 266.
21  Knight, *The Golden Labyrinth*, p. 380.
22  *Autobiographies II*, pp. 534-538.
23  George Meredith, *Diana of the Crossways* (London, 1922), p. 20.
24  Cf. his article 'There Go the Irish', *Blasts and Benedictions*, pp. 245-261.
25  *Autobiographies II*, p. 10.
26  Jordan, 'A World in Chassis', p. 27.
27  Hogan, *The Experiments of Sean O'Casey*, p. 108.
28  Mercier, 'The Riddle of Sean O'Casey', p. 368.

17. HALL OF HEALING
1  John O'Donovan suggests that *Hall of Healing* belonged to those early unpublished plays written before *The Shadow of a Gunman* ('The Big Three', in: McCann, ed., *The World of Sean O'Casey*, p. 187), but there is no evidence whatsoever to support his thesis.
2  Cowasjee, *Sean O'Casey*, pp. 242, 243.
3  Spinner, *Die alte Dame sagt: Nein!*, p. 144.
4  *Lady Gregory's Journals: 1916-1930*, ed. by Lennox Robinson (London, 1946), p. 320.
5  See the chapter 'The Hill of Healing' in *I Knock at the Door* (*Autobiographies I*, pp. 21-25) and *Sunset and Evening Star*, *Autobiographies II*, pp. 651-653.
6  Starkie had called him in 1928 'essentially a photographic dramatist' ('The Plays of Sean O'Casey', p. 235).
7  *Letters*, I, p. 208.
8  'Great Man, Gorki!', *Blasts and Benedictions*, pp. 230-233. There are several approving references to Gorki in O'Casey's letters.
9  O'Casey's only reference to Hauptmann in his *Letters* (I, p. 907) suggests that he may have known *The Weavers*.
10  *Autobiographies II*, pp. 651-652.

18. BEDTIME STORY
1  Bobby L. Smith, 'The Hat, The Whore, and The Hypocrite in O'Casey's *Bedtime Story*', *The Serif*, IV, ii (1967), p. 4n.
2  Jean Selz, 'Sean O'Casey', *Lettres Nouvelles*, VII (1959), no. 31, p. 17.

3   'Under a Colored Cap, Part Two', *Under a Colored Cap*, p. 54.
4   For an attempt at emphasizing the homogeneity of *Bedtime Story*, see Jack
     Mitchell, 'In Defence of Sean O'Casey's One-Acters', *Gulliver*, no. 7 (1980),
     pp. 36-45.
5   'Badtime Story', *Blasts and Benedictions*, pp. 132-134.

PART IV
19.  PREFATORY
 1   For Armstrong, O'Casey's later phase begins with *Red Roses for Me*, which
     disregards completely the new development beginning with *Cock-a-doodle
     Dandy* (*Sean O'Casey*, pp. 23-30). Malone sees the criticism of contemporary
     Ireland as the unifying element in these plays, overlooking all additional
     thematic and structural correspondences (*The Plays of Sean O'Casey*, pp.
     118-149). Herbert Goldstone groups all of O'Casey's plays from 1949 together
     under the misleading heading 'Ireland Revisited' (*In Search of Community:
     The Achievement of Sean O'Casey*, Cork and Dublin, 1972).
 2   Frederick Lumley, *New Trends in 20th Century Drama: A Survey since Ibsen
     and Shaw* (London, 1967), p. 295.
 3   'Cockadoodle Doo', *Blasts and Benedictions*, p. 145, my italics.
 4   Discussed in detail by Malone, *The Plays of Sean O'Casey*, pp. 118-149.
 5   See, for instance, Alec Reid, 'The Legend of the Green Crow: Observations on
     Recent Work by and about Sean O'Casey', *Drama Survey*, III (1963), pp. 155-164.
 6   Metscher, *Sean O'Caseys dramatischer Stil*, p. 139.
 7   O'Casey had met Stephens in Lady Londonderry's house during his early
     London years; see Eileen O'Casey, *Eileen* (London and New York, 1976), pp.
     73-74).
 8   James Stephens, *The Crock of Gold* (London, 1953), p. 16.
 9   'Tender Tears for Poor O'Casey', *The Green Crow*, pp. 164-165.
10   Hogan, *The Experiments of Sean O'Casey*, p. 7.
11   John Jordan, 'The Irish Theatre: Retrospect and Premonition', in: John
     Russell Brown and Bernard Harris (eds.), *Contemporary Theatre*, Stratford-
     upon-Avon Studies 4 (London, 1962), p. 178.

20.  COCK-A-DOODLE DANDY
 1   'Cockadoodle Doo', *Blasts and Benedictions*, pp. 142-145. The carelessness of
     much of O'Casey criticism is documented by Walter C. Daniel when he
     maintains 'it was not one of his favorite plays' ('The False Paradise Pattern in
     Sean O'Casey's *Cock-a-doodle Dandy* ', *College Language Association Journal*,
     XIII, 1969, p. 137).
 2   Christopher Murray has successfully shown that the play has a very personal
     dimension as well ('Two More Allusions in *Cock-a-doodle Dandy*', *Sean
     O'Casey Review*, IV, 1977, pp. 6-18), but it is not necessary for a general under-
     standing to realize these allusions.
 3   Ronald G. Rollins, 'O'Casey's *Cock-a-doodle Dandy*', *Explicator*, XXIII (1964/
     65), item 8.
 4   Krause, *Sean O'Casey*, p. 188.
 5   It is simply naive to disregard all but the surface events of the play and then
     to regret that 'O'Casey insists on flogging certain horses that in this mid-
     century of ours are dead or dying, even in rural Ireland' (Robert Greacen's
     review, *Irish Writing*, no. 9, October 1949, pp. 69-70).
 6   As in *Within the Gates*, O'Casey employs the term 'scene' for the three larger
     units of the play, but to avoid confusion they are here treated as 'acts'.

7   To O'Casey, the existence of Lourdes was one of the weightiest arguments against the Catholic Church. In *Inishfallen, Fare Thee Well* (written at about the same time as *Cock-a-doodle Dandy*) he vents his indignation about this 'Coney Island of misery, agony, and woe' with an acerbity that is exceptional even for O'Casey (*Autobiographies II*, p. 239; cf. pp. 205, 238-241).

8   Cowasjee, *Sean O'Casey*, p. 206. However, Cowasjee's criticism that it would be impossible for Julia to travel to Lourdes in the morning and to return on the same day is inappropriate, because it disregards the unrealistic quality of the play. Hogan attempts to justify the existence of the two scenes (*The Experiments of Sean O'Casey*, p. 121).

9   *The Collected Plays of W. B. Yeats* (London, 1960), pp. 437, 438, 445.

10   'Cockadoodle Doo', p. 145.

11   Cowasjee, *Sean O'Casey*, p. 208.

12   Cf. O'Casey's characterization of *The Shadow of the Glen* that suggests a comparison with Synge: in this play 'is the call of a brave heart for the fullness of life; a character ready, at last, to go through life with a steady step, and add its vigour to the energetic and everlasting song of nature' ('John Millington Synge', *Blasts and Benedictions*, p. 37).

13   Charles Villiers Stanford (ed.), *The National Song Book* (London, 1906), p. 88. The song is here attributed to Burns, but was probably written by one Lady Caroline Keppel (*The Oxford Dictionary of Quotations*, London, 1949[6], p. 224).

14   For such an attempt see Cowasjee, *Sean O'Casey*, p. 214, and Philip Burton, 'Something to Crow About: An Approach to *Cock-a-doodle Dandy*', *Theatre Arts*, XLII, xi (November 1958), pp. 22-24.

15   It is more than far-fetched, however, to regard Marthraun as 'an ingenious character creation in his ironic contrast to Archangel Michael in *Paradise Lost*,' (Daniel, 'The False Paradise Pattern', p. 138).

16   Krause, *Sean O'Casey*, p. 192.

## 21. TIME TO GO

1   Cf. B. Roland Lewis's introduction to his *Contemporary One-Act Plays: With Outline Study of the One-Act Play and Bibliographies* (New York, 1922), still one of the best analyses of the form of the short play.

2   *Autobiographies II*, p. 653.

3   For an interesting attempt at stressing the formal and thematic coherence of the play see Manfred Pauli, *Sean O'Casey: Drama – Poesie – Wirklichkeit* (Berlin, 1977), pp. 178-184.

4   O'Casey's own description of the form of the play, 'realism touched with fancy' (*Letters*, II, p. 684), is less than satisfactory, because it suggests a closer relationship between the worlds of reality and the fairy-tale than is to be found in the play.

5   *Autobiographies II*, e.g. pp. 231, 235, 236.

6   *Ibid.*, p. 244.

## 22. THE BISHOP'S BONFIRE

1   Cf. Cowasjee, *Sean O'Casey*, pp. 224-228, and Tyrone Guthrie's reminiscences in his autobiography, *A Life in the Theatre* (London, 1960), pp. 267-269.

2   O'Casey has explained these references in 'O'Casey's Drama-Bonfire', *Blasts and Benedictions*, pp. 138-141.

3   All page references are to *The Bishop's Bonfire: A Sad Play within the Tune of a Polka* (London, 1961).

4   Lumley, *New Trends in 20th Century Drama*, pp. 295-296.

5   John Jordan's admirable review of the play (an exception among Irish critics) in *Irish Writing*, No. 31 (Summer, 1951), pp. 59-60.
6   Tony Gray, *The Irish Answer: An anatomy of modern Ireland* (London, 1966), p. 278.
7   Krause, *Sean O'Casey*, p. 212.
8   Under the title 'Jeep be Jeepers' in *New Statesman and Nation* (July 18, 1953); also in *Sunset and Evening Star, Autobiographies II*, pp. 643-647, cf. *ibid.* pp. 659, 662, 663.
9   Reid, 'The Legend of the Green Crow', p. 160.
10  Quoted by Cowasjee, *Sean O'Casey*, p. 220.
11  Rollins, 'Sean O'Casey's Mental Pilgrimage', p. 301; Audrey Williamson, *Contemporary Theatre: 1953-1956* (London, 1956), p. 77.
12  Krause, ' "The Rageous Ossean" ', p. 290.

23. THE DRUMS OF FATHER NED
1   Cf. Ron Ayling, 'Rowdelum Randy: A Postscript on O'Casey and his Critics', *Enquiry*, I, ii (June, 1958), p. 36; see also O'Casey's own statement, *ibid.*, pp. 37-39. The affair is also discussed in most full-length studies of O'Casey. For an opposite view see Reid, 'The Legend of the Green Crow', pp. 160-162.
2   *Autobiographies II*, pp. 96-97.
3   'Bonfire Under a Black Sun', *The Green Crow*, p. 144.
4   All page references are to: *The Drums of Father Ned: A Mickrocosm of Ireland* (London and New York, 1960).
5   Hogan, *The Experiments of Sean O'Casey*, p. 136.
6   Quoted in: David Krause, 'Sean O'Casey: 1880-1964', *Massachusetts Review*, VI (1965), pp. 233-251.
7   Richard Findlater, 'Hurrah for Hornchurch', *Time and Tide*, XLI (1960), p. 1438.
8   G. Wilson Knight, 'Ever a Fighter: On Sean O'Casey's *The Drums of Father Ned'*, *The Christian Renaissance* (New York, 1962[2]), p. 342.
9   Krause, *Sean O'Casey*, p. 224; Phillip L. Marcus, 'Addendum on Joyce and O'Casey', *James Joyce Quarterly*, III (1965), pp. 62-63.
10  Hogan, *The Experiments of Sean O'Casey*, p. 138; Spinner, *Die alte Dame sagt: Nein!*, p. 140; Findlater, 'Hurrah for Hornchurch'; Henry Hewes, 'The Green Crow Flies Again', *Saturday Review* (May 9, 1959), p. 22.
11  Knight, 'Ever a Fighter', p. 345; Armstrong, 'The Irish Point of View', p. 93.
12  Armstrong, *Sean O'Casey*, p. 29.
13  Quoted in Hogan, *The Experiments of Sean O'Casey*, p. 134.
14  Knight, 'Ever a Fighter', p. 345.
15  *Ibid.*, p. 347. Knight also provides a detailed, if somewhat exaggerated analysis of the figure of Angus.
16  'Not Waiting for Godot', *Blasts and Benedictions*, pp. 51-52.

PART V
24. PREFATORY
1   *Behind the Green Curtains – Figuro in the Night – The Moon Shines on Kylenamoe: Three Plays* (London and New York, 1961). All page references are to this edition.
2   Cf. the chapter 'Outside an Irish Window', *Autobiographies II*, pp. 637-648.
3   Cf. Gabriel Fallon, 'How Green Are Our Curtains?', *Kilkenny Magazine*, no. 5 (Autumn/Winter, 1961), pp. 34-41, Robert Hogan's reply 'How Green Are Our Critics?', no. 6 (Spring, 1962), pp. 37-39, and Fallon's rejoinder 'Not Quite So Green!', *ibid.*, pp. 40-41.

## 25. BEHIND THE GREEN CURTAINS

1 Like *Within the Gates* and *Cock-a-doodle Dandy*, *Behind the Green Curtains* is divided into 'scenes' instead of acts, but to avoid confusion, the larger units of the play are here termed 'acts' and the smaller sections 'scenes'.

2 It is, however, an exaggeration to see *Behind the Green Curtains* and *Cock-a-doodle Dandy* as 'companion pieces in that both show Irish youth successfully defying repressive forces' (William A. Armstrong, 'The Irish Point of View: The Plays of Sean O'Casey, Brendan Behan, and Thomas Murphy', in: Armstrong, ed., *Experimental Drama*, London, 1963, p. 88). Neither are there enough similarities between the two plays to justify such a term, nor is Irish youth in these plays very successful in defying repressive forces.

3 J. M. Synge, *Collected Works*, vol. IV, *Plays*, Book II, ed. by Ann Saddlemyer, p. 173.

4 Jordan, 'The Irish Theatre', p. 178.

## 26. FIGURO IN THE NIGHT

1 For instance Metscher, *Sean O'Caseys dramatischer Stil*, p. 30, and Robert Hogan, *After the Irish Renaissance: A Critical History of the Irish Drama since 'The Plough and the Stars'* (Minneapolis, 1967), pp. 250-251.

2 Fallon, 'How Green Are Our Curtains?', p. 37.

3 Hogan, *After the Irish Renaissance*, p. 251.

## 27. THE MOON SHINES ON KYLENAMOE

1 Fallon, *Sean O'Casey*, pp. 44-45.

2 This is the only trait that *The Moon Shines on Kylenamoe* has in common with Martin J. McHugh's *A Minute's Wait* (Dublin, 1918). It is therefore untenable to maintain (insinuating plagiarism) that O'Casey's play 'inevitably suggests in many respects Martin J. McHugh's *A Minute's Wait* – one of the Abbey's pre-O'Casey presentations' (Fallon, 'How Green Are Our Curtains?', p. 37). There are simply no parallels between the plays – O'Casey did not require a literary source to invent the delayed departure of an Irish train. And it is even more misleading to say that McHugh's silly farce 'is by far the better of the two' (*ibid.*).

3 Cf. *Purple Dust, Collected Plays*, III, p. 71.

## PART VI

## 28. PREFATORY

1 Metscher, *Sean O'Caseys dramatischer Stil*; Bernard Benstock, *Paycocks and Others: Sean O'Casey's World* (Dublin and New York, 1976).

## 29. DRAMATIC FORMS

1 Malone, 'The Shadow of Sean O'Casey', p. 104.

2 Gilbert Norwood, 'The New Writers: IV. Sean O'Casey', *Canadian Forum*, X (1929/30), pp. 250-251; Cowasjee, *Sean O'Casey*, p. 87. James R. Scrimgeour even speaks of 'the more naturalistic Irish-Elizabethan early plays' – whatever that may be! (*Sean O'Casey*, TEAS 245, Boston, 1978, p. 167). J. A. Snowden's rejection of such views is unfortunately marred by his limited view of naturalism as exclusively determined by the plays of Ibsen ('Sean O'Casey and Naturalism', *Essays and Studies*, XXIV, 1971, pp. 56-68).

3 'Green Goddess of Realism', *The Green Crow*, p. 80.

4 'From Within the Gates', *Blasts and Benedictions*, p. 113.

5 *Ibid.*, p. 116.

6  Worth, 'O'Casey's Dramatic Symbolism'; Ronald G. Rollins, 'Dramatic Symbolism in Sean O'Casey's Dublin Trilogy', *West Virginia University Philological Papers*, XV (1966), pp. 49-56.

7  'Cockadoodle Doo', *Blasts and Benedictions*, p. 143. For a well-argued, highly specialized study of this transition see Jochen Achilles, *Drama als problematische Form: Der Wandel zu nichtrealistischer Gestaltungsweise im Werk Sean O'Caseys* (Frankfurt and Bern, 1979).

8  See especially Hogan, *The Experiments of Sean O'Casey*, pp. 55-79; Metscher, *Sean O'Caseys dramatischer Stil*, pp. 173-187; Rollins, 'O'Casey, O'Neill, and Expressionism in *The Silver Tassie*'; Rollins, 'O'Casey, O'Neill, and Expressionism in *Within the Gates*'. A balanced view of this question is presented by Wanda Krajewska, 'Sean O'Casey i Ekspresjonizm', *Kwartalnik Neofilologiczny*, XII (1965), pp. 363-379.

9  The first study that attempts to relate O'Casey's plays to Strindberg and the works of German Expressionism is: Joan Templeton, 'Sean O'Casey and Expressionism', *Modern Drama*, XIV (1971), pp. 47-62.

10  Cf. Cowasjee, *Sean O'Casey*, p. 120; De Baun, 'Sean O'Casey and the Road to Expressionism', p. 254n.

11  De Baun, 'Sean O'Casey and the Road to Expressionism'.

12  The most balanced discussion of O'Casey's relationship to expressionism is Carol Kleiman's article 'O'Casey's "Debt" to Toller: Expressionism in *The Silver Tassie* and *Red Roses for Me*', *Canadian Journal of Irish Studies*, V, i (1979), pp. 69-86.

13  A case in point is Smith's study *O'Casey's Satiric Vision* which, setting out with a highly diffuse concept of satire, attempts to subsume the whole of O'Casey's work under this term.

14  Karl S. Guthke, *Modern Tragicomedy: An Investigation into the Nature of the Genre* (New York, 1966), pp. 79, 89, 141, 180; Styan, *The Dark Comedy*, pp. 149-153.

15  Especially Krause, *Sean O'Casey*, ch. II: 'The Tragi-Comic Muse', pp. 47-93; Metscher, *Sean O'Caseys dramatischer Stil*, pp. 192-214. Unfortunately, a study by Donald Douglas Wilson with the promising title *Sean O'Casey's Tragi-Comic Vision* (Brooklyn, N.Y., 1976) is next to useless as criticism.

16  For a detailed analysis of O'Casey's use of popular dramatic forms and their calculated effect on the audience see Burchard Winkler, *Wirkstrategische Verwendung populärliterarischer Elemente in Sean O'Caseys dramatischem Werk unter besonderer Berücksichtigung des Melodramas* (Göppingen, 1977).

17  Metscher, *Sean O'Caseys dramatischer Stil*, p. 211; my italics.

18  *Ibid.*, pp. 137, 139; Hogan, *After the Irish Renaissance*, pp. 235-252.

19  In a few plays (*Within the Gates*, *Cock-a-doodle Dandy*, *Behind the Green Curtains*, *Figuro in the Night*) O'Casey uses the term 'scene' instead of 'act', but there is no difference in meaning.

20  Cf. Lewis (ed.), *Contemporary One-Act Plays*, and Diemut Schnetz, *Der moderne Einakter: Eine poetologische Untersuchung* (Bern and München, 1967).

30. THEMES AND MOTIFS
1  Armstrong, 'The Irish Point of View', p. 83.
2  Baggett, 'Sean O'Casey's Development of a Basic Theme', p. 25.
3  Goldstone, *In Search of Community*, pp. 4-5.
4  For instance Koslow, *The Green and the Red*; Jack Lindsay, 'Sean O'Casey as a Socialist Artist', in: Ayling (ed.), *Sean O'Casey*, pp. 192-203; Zaslawski, 'Die Werke Sean O'Caseys'.

5   Krause, ' "The Rageous Ossean" ', p. 287.
6   Rollins, 'Sean O'Casey's Mental Pilgrimage', p. 301.
7   Knight, *The Golden Labyrinth*, p. 373.
8   Koslow, *The Green and the Red*, p. 88; cf. Fréchet, 'Sean O'Casey', p. 334.
9   Malone, *The Plays of Sean O'Casey*, p. 90.
10  Jordan, 'Illusion and Actuality in the Later O'Casey', p. 150. On O'Casey's personal attitude towards Socialism see, for instance, Cowasjee, *Sean O'Casey*, ch. VI: 'O'Casey and Communism', especially pp. 167-170; and Krause, 'Sean O'Casey: 1880-1964'. The most detailed study of O'Casey's political development is Greaves' highly controversial *Sean O'Casey: Politics and Art.*
11  Baggett, 'Sean O'Casey's Development of a Basic Theme', p. 29.
12  Cf. Benstock, 'A Covey of Clerics in Joyce and O'Casey'.
13  Krause, *Sean O'Casey*, p. 136.
14  *Ibid.*, p. 188.

31. MODELS AND ANTI-MODELS
1   *Autobiographies II*, p. 105. Cf. Fallon, *Sean O'Casey*, pp. 48-49.
2   'Melpomene an' Thalia Beggin' for Bread', *Blasts and Benedictions*, pp. 27-29.
3   John Jordan, 'The Passionate Autodidact: The Importance of *Litera Scripta* for O'Casey', *Irish University Review*, X (1980), pp. 59-76.
4   Robert Hogan, 'O'Casey, Influence and Impact', *Irish University Review*, X (1980), p. 152.
5   *Autobiographies I*, p. 558.
6   Cowasjee, 'O'Casey Seen through Holloway's Diary', p. 62.
7   Krause, 'Sean O'Casey: 1880-1964', p. 146.
8   'A Whisper about Bernard Shaw', *The Green Crow*, pp. 177-183; 'Bernard Shaw: An Appreciation of a Fighting Idealist', *ibid.*, pp. 184-189; 'Shaw – Lord of a Century', *ibid.*, pp. 222-229; 'G.B.S. Speaks out of the Whirlwind', *Blasts and Benedictions*, pp. 195-200; 'Shaw's Primrose Path', *ibid.*, pp. 201-204; letter to Ayling, quoted by Cowasjee, *Sean O'Casey*, pp. 253-254; 'Green Fire on the Hearth', *Autobiographies I*, pp. 557-572; 'Shaw's Corner', *Autobiographies II*, pp. 596-623.
9   'Tribute to Bernard Shaw', *Icarus* (January 1956), p. 80.
10  Quoted by Rollins, 'Shaw and O'Casey', p. 69.
11  Cowasjee, *Sean O'Casey*, pp. 156-166; Rollins, 'Shaw and O'Casey'.
12  Metscher, *Sean O'Caseys dramatischer Stil*, pp. 131-136.
13  Stanley Weintraub, 'Shaw's Other Keegan: O'Casey and G.B.S.', in: David Krause and Robert G. Lowery (eds.), *Sean O'Casey: Centenary Essays* (Gerrards Cross, 1980), pp. 212-227.
14  Parker, 'Bernard Shaw and Sean O'Casey', p. 14.
15  Michel Habart, 'Une mère et deux fils', *Cahiers de la Compagnie Madeleine Renaud – Jean-Louis Barrault*, Nr. 37 (February 1962), pp. 17-31.
16  Denis Johnston, 'Sean O'Casey: A Biography and an Appraisal', *Modern Drama*, IV (1961/62), p. 327.
17  Blitch, 'O'Casey's Shakespeare'.
18  Kurt Wittig, *Sean O'Casey als Dramatiker: Ein Beitrag zum Nachkriegsdrama Irlands* (Diss. Halle, 1937), p. 57. Cf. Metscher, *Sean O'Caseys dramatischer Stil*, pp. 194-196.
19  J. C. Trewin, 'O'Casey the Elizabethan', *New Theatre*, III, i (June 1946), pp. 2-3; *The Theatre since 1900*, p. 187; 'Lord of Language', *Drama: The Quarterly Review*, no. 35 (Winter, 1954), pp. 34-38.

20  Vivian Mercier, *The Irish Comic Tradition*, p. 240; Cf. Krause, *Sean O'Casey*, pp. 76-77.
21  'The Play of Ideas', *Blasts and Benedictions*, pp. 24-26; cf. 'The Power of Laughter: Weapon against Evil', *The Green Crow*, p. 206.
22  Cf. the chapters 'Shakespeare Taps at the Window' and 'Touched by the Theatre' in *Pictures in the Hallway, Autobiographies I*, pp. 191-197, 297-309.
23  Quoted by Fallon, *Sean O'Casey*, p. 31.
24  Cf. 'The Public Death of Shakespeare' and 'Shakespeare Lives in London Lads', *The Flying Wasp*, pp. 1-9, 163-167.
25  'Shakespeare among the Flags', *Blasts and Benedictions*, pp. 30-34.
26  Larson, 'An Interview with Mrs. Sean O'Casey', p. 237.
27  *Ibid.*, p. 235.
28  *Autobiographies I*, p. 195.
29  *Autobiographies I*, pp. 297-309; *Autobiographies II*, pp. 246, 142-143, 157.
30  'Melpomene in Ireland', *Blasts and Benedictions*, pp. 188-194.
31  McHugh, 'The Legacy of Sean O'Casey', p. 124; Krause, *Sean O'Casey*, pp. 248-249; Metscher, *Sean O'Caseys dramatischer Stil*, p. 117; Mercier, 'The Riddle of Sean O'Casey', p. 368.
32  Cowasjee, *Sean O'Casey*, p. 52; Krause, *Sean O'Casey*, p. 200.
33  O'Casey's letter, quoted by Harry M. Ritchie, 'The Influence of Melodrama on the Early Plays of Sean O'Casey', *Modern Drama*, V (1962/63), p. 166.
34  Krause, *Sean O'Casey*, pp. 56-62; 'The Theatre of Dion Boucicault', *The Dolmen Boucicault* (Dublin, 1964), pp. 9-47. Cf. Robert Hogan, *Dion Boucicault*, TUSAS 163 (New York, 1969), pp. 109-111.
35  Ritchie, 'The Influence of Melodrama on the Early Plays of Sean O'Casey', p. 169.
36  Padraic Colum, 'The Narrative Writings of Sean O'Casey', *Irish Writing*, no. 6 (November 1948), pp. 65-66.
37  Cf. *Autobiographies II*, p. 546.
38  Benstock, 'A Covey of Clerics in Joyce and O'Casey'.
39  'Censorship', *Blasts and Benedictions*, p. 167. Cf. Joseph Prescott (ed.), 'Sean O'Casey Concerning James Joyce', *Massachusetts Review*, V (1964), pp. 335-336.
40  *Autobiographies II*, pp. 167-186.
41  Cf. the chapters 'Blessed Bridget O'Coole' and 'Where Wild Swans Nest' in *Inishfallen, Fare Thee Well, Autobiographies II*, pp. 102-125; and 'A Protestant Bridget', *Blasts and Benedictions*, pp. 205-212. For a detailed account of O'Casey's personal relationship with Lady Gregory, see Mary FitzGerald, 'Sean O'Casey and Lady Gregory: The Record of a Friendship', in: David Krause and Robert G. Lowery (eds.), *Sean O'Casey: Centenary Essays* (Gerrards Cross, 1980), pp. 67-99.
42  *Lady Gregory's Journals*, p. 73.
43  Cf. *Autobiographies II*, p. 96; Cowasjee, *Sean O'Casey*, p. 95; and O'Casey's letter, quoted by Krause, *Sean O'Casey*, p. 36.
44  Metscher, *Sean O'Caseys dramatischer Stil*, p. 116.
45  R. M. Fox, 'Realism in Irish Drama', *Irish Statesman*, X (1928), pp. 310-312; Wittig, *Sean O'Casey als Dramatiker*, pp. 73-76; Krause, *Sean O'Casey*, pp. 227, 232-235.
46  Rollins, 'O'Casey and Synge', p. 218; cf. Fréchet, 'Sean O'Casey', pp. 328-329, and Katharine Worth, 'O'Casey, Synge and Yeats', *Irish University Review*, X (1980), pp. 105-109.
47  Ayling, 'Introduction', *Sean O'Casey*, p. 21; cf. Denis Johnston, 'Sean O'Casey', *Nation*, CIC (1964), p. 198.

48 Krutch, *'Modernism' in Modern Drama*, pp. 97-101; Williams, *Drama*, p. 171; Fréchet, 'Sean O'Casey', p. 330-331.
49 'John Millington Synge', *Blasts and Benedictions*, pp. 35-41.
50 For instance *Autobiographies II*, p. 58.
51 Quoted by Krause, *A Self-Portrait of the Artist as a Man*, p. 22.
52 Hogan, *The Experiments of Sean O'Casey*, pp. 16-54.
53 *Blasts and Benedictions*, pp. 42-45.
54 Hogan, *The Experiments of Sean O'Casey*, p. 180.
55 Abirached, 'Deux Pièces de Sean O'Casey', p. 383. Cf. R. M. Fox, 'Sean O'Casey: A Worker Dramatist', *New Statesman*, XXVI (1926), pp. 805-806; Laurence Kitchin, *Drama in the Sixties: Form and Interpretation* (London, 1966), p. 103.
56 'Great Man, Gorki!', *Blasts and Benedictions*, pp. 230-233.
57 Rollins, 'O'Casey, O'Neill and Expressionism in *The Silver Tassie*' and 'O'Casey, O'Neill and Expressionism in *Within the Gates*'.
58 See *Autobiographies II*, p. 454; Gelb, *O'Neill*, pp. 787-790; and O'Casey, 'Tribute to O'Neill', in: O. Cargill, N. B. Fagin and W. J. Fisher (eds.), *Eugene O'Neill and His Plays: A Survey of His Life and Works* (London, 1961), p. 96.
59 Wittig, *Sean O'Casey als Dramatiker*, p. 78.
60 Gabriel Fallon, 'Thanks to the Dublin Drama League', *Irish Monthly*, LXVIII (1940), pp. 444-449; and *Sean O'Casey*, pp. 46-49. See also the short history by Brenna Katz Clarke and Harold Ferrar, *The Dublin Drama League 1919-1941* (Dublin, 1979).
61 Fallon, *Sean O'Casey*, p. 47. O'Casey knew the play as early as 1924; cf. Krause, *A Self-Portrait of the Artist as a Man*, p. 19.
62 Cf. the chapter on *The Silver Tassie*, above; and Wittig, *Sean O'Casey als Dramatiker*, pp. 64-65; Habart, 'Introduction à Sean O'Casey', p. 31; Walter Starkie, 'Sean O'Casey', in: Lennox Robinson (ed.), *The Irish Theatre* (London, 1939), p. 167.
63 Bergholz, 'Sean O'Casey', p. 63; Cowasjee, *Sean O'Casey*, pp. 126-127; Habart, 'Introduction à Sean O'Casey', p. 31; Metscher, *Sean O'Caseys dramatischer Stil*, pp. 174, 182.
64 Krajewska, 'Sean O'Casey i Ekspresjonizm'; McHugh, 'The Legacy of Sean O'Casey', p. 131.
65 St. John Ervine, 'Mr. O'Casey's Apocalypse', *Observer* (7 January 1934).
66 'Censorship', *Blasts and Benedictions*, p. 167. Cf. Spinner, *Die alte Dame sagt: Nein!*, pp. 152-153; and Eric Bentley, *The Playwright as Thinker: A Study of Drama in Modern Times* (New York, 1946), p. 220. The question of a possible influence of Strindberg on O'Casey is dealt with at some length by Templeton, 'Sean O'Casey and Expressionism'. Rollins remains vague on this as on many other issues. See Ronald Gene Rollins, *Sean O'Casey's Drama: Verisimilitude and Vision* (Alabama U.P., 1979), pp. 47, 93.
67 See Hodson, *No Phantoms Here*, p. 155; and *The Green Crow*, p. 127.
68 Fallon, *Sean O'Casey*, p. 50.
69 *Autobiographies II*, p. 261; cf. pp. 260-266, 305-306, 335; and 'Shakespeare among the Flags', *Blasts and Benedictions*, p. 31; Hodson, *No Phantoms Here*, p. 149; Rees, 'Remembrance of Things Past', pp. 417-418.
70 *The Flying Wasp*, pp. 129-161.
71 *Blasts and Benedictions*, pp. 46-50.
72 Cf. the chapters 'The Friggin Frogs' and 'Black Oxen Passing By' in *Rose and Crown, Autobiographies II*, pp. 281-291, 334-347.
73 Joseph Hone, *W. B. Yeats: 1865-1939* (London, 1962²), pp. 387-389.

74  'Literature in Ireland', *Blasts and Benedictions*, pp. 170-181, p. 176; cf.
    O'Casey's article on Yeats, 'Ireland's Silvery Shadow', *Blasts and Benedictions*,
    pp. 182-187; and Krause, 'Sean O'Casey: 1880-1964', pp. 153, 155-156.
75  *Autobiographies II*, pp. 232-234.
76  See Krause, *A Self-Portrait of the Artist as a Man*, pp. 14-16.
77  Armstrong, 'Sean O'Casey, W. B. Yeats and the Dance of Life'. For a more
    positive view of possible Yeatsian influence, especially on *Within the Gates*,
    see Worth, 'O'Casey, Synge and Yeats', pp. 109-117.
78  *Ibid.*, p. 139; cf. Armstrong, 'The Irish Point of View', pp. 85-86.
79  Armstrong, 'Sean O'Casey, W. B. Yeats and the Dance of Life', p. 131.
80  Lindsay, 'Sean O'Casey as a Socialist Artist', p. 200.
81  Mary C. Bromage, 'The Yeats-O'Casey Quarrel', *Michigan Alumnus Quarterly
    Review*, LXIV (1957/58), p. 140. For an unusual comparison between Yeats
    and O'Casey – without reference to the question of influence – see two
    articles by Seamus Deane, 'Irish Politics and O'Casey's Theatre', *Threshold*,
    XXIV (1973), pp. 5-16, and 'Exemplary Dramatists: Yeats and O'Casey',
    *Threshold*, XXX (1979), pp. 21-28.
82  *Autobiographies II*, p. 529.

## 32.  INFLUENCES AND REACTIONS

 1  Fricker, 'Sean O'Casey: *Juno and the Paycock*', pp. 181-182.
 2  Kevin Casey, 'The Excitements and the Disappointments', in: McCann (ed.),
    *The World of Sean O'Casey*, p. 218. Ronald Ayling, too, refers in passing to
    Arden's 'clearly and consciously following in O'Casey's footsteps', 'Patterns
    of Language and Ritual in Sean O'Casey's Drama', in: Alison Feder and
    Bernice Schrank (eds.), *Literature and Folk Culture: Ireland and Newfoundland*
    (St. John's, Newfoundland, 1977), p. 35; similarly in *Anglo-Irish Studies*, II
    (1976), p. 26.
 3  Krause, *Sean O'Casey*, p. 99.
 4  Hugh MacDiarmid, 'Slàinte Chùramach, Seán', in: Ayling (ed.), *Sean
    O'Casey*, p. 259; cf. MacDiarmid, *The Company I've Kept* (Berkeley and Los
    Angeles, 1967), pp. 161-169.
 5  Brendan Behan, *Confessions of an Irish Rebel* (London, 1965), p. 30; *Brendan
    Behan's Island: An Irish Sketch-book* (n.p., 1962), pp. 12-14.
 6  *Borstal Boy* (London, 1960[2]), p. 234, cf. p. 249.
 7  Letters to the *Irish Times* (29 August 1961), quoted by John O'Riordan,
    'O'Casey's Dublin Critics', *Library Review*, XXI, ii (1967), p. 63. Cf. *Confessions
    of an Irish Rebel*, pp. 184, 201, 243.
 8  Sean Maxwell, 'Conversation with O'Casey', *Irish Digest*, LXXX, iv (June
    1964), p. 39; Aidan Hennigan, quoted by Cronin, 'The O'Casey I Knew', p. 180.
 9  'The Bald Primaqueera', *Blasts and Benedictions*, pp. 73-74; cf. 'Mr. Wesker's
    March Past', *ibid.*, p. 60; and Krause, 'Sean O'Casey: 1880-1964', p. 152.
10  Letter to the *Observer* (27 September 1964), quoted by O'Riordan, 'O'Casey's
    Dublin Critics', p. 63.
11  Laurence Kitchin, *Mid-Century Drama* (London, 1960), pp. 114, 216; and
    *Drama in the Sixties: Form and Interpretation* (London, 1966), p. 101.
12  Adamov, ' "La femme avenir de l'homme" dans l'œuvre de Sean O'Casey'.
13  Arthur Adamov, Roger Planchon, René Allio, 'Wie stehen wir zu Brecht?',
    *Sinn und Form*, XIII (1961), pp. 938-939, cf. pp. 940, 942.
14  'Sean O'Casey: An Appreciation', *Daily Telegraph* (11 March 1926); 'Sean
    O'Casey', in: *Living Writers: Being Critical Studies Broadcast in the B.B.C.
    Third Programme*, ed. by Gilbert Phelps (London, 1947), pp. 28-38; 'Joxer in

Totnes: A study in Sean O'Casey', *Irish Writing*, no. 13 (December 1950), pp. 50-53; 'Sean O'Casey: A Biography and an Appraisal', *Modern Drama*, IV (1961/62), pp. 324-328; 'Sean O'Casey', *Nation*, CIC (1964), p. 198. The quotation is from 'Joxer in Totnes', p. 52.

15 In Phelps (ed.), *Living Writers*, p. 34.
16 Denis Johnston, *Dramatic Works* II (Gerrards Cross, 1979), p. 5, and I (Gerrards Cross, 1977), p. 86.
17 *Dramatic Works* I, pp. 53, 70.
18 Bonamy Dobrée, 'Sean O'Casey and the Irish Drama', in: Ayling (ed.), *Sean O'Casey*, p. 104.
19 For a comparison of the two playwrights, see also Ronald Rollins, 'O'Casey and Johnston: Different Reactions to the 1916 Easter Rising', *Sean O'Casey Review*, IV (Fall, 1977), pp. 19-29; Bernice Schrank, 'The Low and the Lofty: A Comparison of Sean O'Casey's *The Plough and the Stars* and Denis Johnston's *The Scythe and the Sunset*', *Modern Language Studies*, XI (1980), pp. 12-16; and Jochen Achilles, 'Sean O'Casey's and Denis Johnston's National Plays: Two Dramatic Approaches to Irish Society', in: Heinz Kosok (ed.), *Studies in Anglo-Irish Literature* (Bonn, 1982), pp. 269-277.
20 Cowasjee, *Sean O'Casey*, p. 84; Krause, *Sean O'Casey*, p. 41; Hogan, *After the Irish Renaissance*, p. 32.
21 Brian Friel, *Sean O'Casey Review*, IV (1978), p. 87.
22 Findlater, *The Unholy Trade*, p. 184.
23 C. Tindemans, 'Requiem voor Sean O'Casey', *Streven*, XVIII (November 1964), pp. 171-177, p. 171.
24 Fricker, 'Sean O'Casey: *Juno and the Paycock*', p. 196.
25 Hogan, 'O'Casey, Influence and Impact', p. 155.
26 Thelma Herring, 'Maenads and Goat-Song: The Plays of Patrick White', *Southerly*, XXV (1965), pp. 220-221.
27 Ronald Ayling, 'The Poetic Drama of T. S. Eliot', *English Studies in Africa*, II (1959), pp. 247-250.
28 Audrey Williamson, *Theatre of Two Decades* (London, 1951), p. 165. Critical studies of the works of Odets frequently refer to Odets' indebtedness to O'Casey.
29 Clifford Odets, *Golden Boy, Awake and Sing!, The Big Knife* (Harmondsworth, 1963), p. 117.
30 Arnold Wesker, *The Wesker Trilogy* (Harmondsworth, 1976[12]), pp. 40, 58.
31 Quoted in the blurb of Errol John, *Moon on a Rainbow Shawl* (London, 1963[2]).
32 C.P.C., 'Before Midnight', *Irish Statesman* (21 July 1928), p. 392.
33 Kitchin, *Drama in the Sixties*, p. 98. The similarities between Behan's *The Quare Fellow* and the plays of O'Casey (emphasized by Armstrong, 'The Irish Point of View', pp. 94, 97) are much less pronounced. On the language of Behan and O'Casey, see also Hogan, *The Experiments of Sean O'Casey*, pp. 151-152.
34 Brendan Behan, *The Hostage* (London, 1959[2]), p. 92.
35 Cf. Hogan, *After the Irish Renaissance*, pp. 66-68; Cowasjee, *Sean O'Casey*, p. 22n; and A. J. Leventhal, 'Dramatic Commentary', *Dublin Magazine*, XXII, ii (1947), pp. 44-46.
36 On the relationship between Macken and O'Casey, see Heinz Kosok, 'O'Casey and An Taibhdhearc', *O'Casey Annual*, III (1984), pp. 115-123.

# INDEX